# DICKENS

CHARLES DICKENS (*c.* 1850)

# DICKENS

*His Character, Comedy, and Career*

*by*

HESKETH PEARSON

WITH FIFTEEN PLATES

METHUEN & CO., LTD. LONDON
*36 Essex Street, Strand,* W.C.2

*First published in 1949*

CATALOGUE NO. 5149/U

PRINTED IN GREAT BRITAIN

TO MY LOVE
(WHO IS RESPONSIBLE)

# ACKNOWLEDGMENTS

MY grateful thanks are due to my wife for her work of many months in the British Museum reading room; to Mr. Frank Allen, Mrs. Alan Grant, Mr. Hugh Kingsmill, and Miss Eleanor O'Connell, for sending me material I would otherwise have missed; to Mr. J. Herbert Bolton, Hon. Curator of Eastgate House Museum, Rochester, for the frontispiece to my book; to Mr. Leslie C. Staples, Hon. Editor of *The Dickensian*, for his help in the choice of illustrations; and to Mr. William Kent for reading my proofs.

Permission to quote from the letters of Dickens to his wife has been granted me by the owner of the copyright, Mr. H. C. Dickens; and Messrs. John Murray Ltd. have allowed me to print part of a letter written by Jane Carlyle.

I have further to acknowledge the courtesy of the following owners of Dickens's correspondence, passages from which are quoted in my text; the Comte de Suzannet, the Executors of Walter Dexter, the Executors of Wilfred Meynell, the Trustees of the Henry E. Huntingdon Library, San Marino, the Harvard College Library, the Pierpoint Morgan Library, the Wm. M. Elkins Collection in the Free Library of Philadelphia.

# ACKNOWLEDGMENTS

My grateful thanks are due to my ... for her work of many months in the British Museum reading room; to Mr. Frank Allen, Mrs. Alan Crane, Mr. Hugh Kingsmill, and Miss Eleanor O'Connell for sending me material I would otherwise have missed; to Mr. J. Herbert Bolton, Hon. Curator of Eastgate House Museum, Rochester, for the frontispiece to my book; to Mr. Leslie C. Staples, Hon. Editor of The Dickensian, for his help in the choice of illustrations; and to Mr. William Kent for reading my proofs.

Permission to quote from the letters of Dickens to his wife has been granted me by the owner of the copyright, Mr. H. C. Dickens; and Messrs. John Murray Ltd. have allowed me to print part of a letter written by Jane Carlyle.

I have further to acknowledge the courtesy of the following owners of Dickens's correspondence, passages from which are quoted in my text: the Comte de Suzannet, the Executors of Walter Dexter, the Executors of Wilfred Meynell, the Trustees of the Henry E. Huntingdon Library, San Marino, the Harvard College Library, the Pierpont Morgan Library, the Wm. M. Elkins Collection in the Free Library of Philadelphia.

# CONTENTS

# CONTENTS

# ILLUSTRATIONS

* *From photographs supplied by The Dickens House, 48 Doughty Street, London, W.C.1.*

# ILLUSTRATIONS

# I

## TAKING NOTICE

AN amiable clerk in the Navy Pay Office at Portsmouth took his wife to a dance one evening early in 1812. Their second child, Charles Dickens, was born the following day, February 7th, and though we cannot prove cause and effect, it is difficult to resist the feeling that the excitement of the dance and its unexpected result had some influence on one who was at his happiest in a whirl of activity and whose behaviour was so frequently surprising.

In character and disposition he owed practically nothing to his parents. His father, John Dickens, son of a footman and housemaid who became a butler and housekeeper, was a genial if slightly pompous fellow, friendly, agreeable, easy-going, light-hearted, open-handed, partial to funny stories, and much too partial to wine and spirits. His mother, socially rather above his father, some of her relations being civil servants, was a gentle, kindly, upright soul, rather feather-headed, and quite incapable of influencing her husband or of grappling with the realities of life as they developed under his benign but wholly disastrous management of affairs.

When Charles was nearly five months old the family moved from his birthplace in Mile End Terrace to Hawke Street, Portsea, where they remained until 1814, when they went to London. Towards the close of his life Dickens gave a public reading from his works in Portsmouth, and was strolling with his agent through the streets when he noticed the name of a terrace. 'By Jove!' he exclaimed: 'here is the place where I was born.' But he could not locate the number. They walked up and down, Dickens pointing to one house and saying that he must have lived there because it looked so much like his father; then he favoured another because it looked like the birthplace of a man who had deserted it; then he picked on a third because it had obviously been the home of a puny weak child such as he had been; and so on, until it appeared that he had been born at every house in the terrace. Since his time more careful investigators have discovered the exact spot, which is now No. 387 Commercial Road, Mile

End, Landport. But his extraordinary powers of observation began to function before the age of two, for in after life he remembered the garden of his second home in Hawke Street, where he toddled about with his elder sister, watched by their nurse through a kitchen-window; he had a vivid recollection of being taken to see the soldiers drilling; and he recalled that when they left Portsmouth the ground was covered with snow.

From 1814 till 1817 the family remained in London, after which they moved to Chatham, where John Dickens held a responsible post in the dockyard, his salary in the Navy Pay Office gradually rising from £110 to £350 a year. They lived at No. 2 (now 11) Ordnance Terrace for four years, and at 18 St. Mary's Place, The Brook, for two more, these six years being the happiest period in the life of young Charles. Certainly the most fruitful and tranquil moments of his manhood were spent in recreating and reliving in memory those early years at Chatham. For him childhood was 'a time to be remembered like a happy dream through all our after life', and so intense was his own awareness of it that he could recall 'every little incident, and even slight words and looks of those old days.' He watched everyone, he noticed everything, he enjoyed the peace of contemplation and the thrill of revelation. He was a sickly child, suffering from spasmodic attacks, and took no part in the games of other boys, though he liked to see them playing as he looked up from whatever book he happened to be reading. He made friends with an older boy next door, whom he eventually idealised as Steerforth; he observed the habits and oddities of those who lived in the same terrace, and stored up his knowledge for use in *Sketches by Boz*; he was taken by his father to the Mitre Inn, where he and his sister Fanny, nearly two years older than himself, sang to the company; he exhibited a keen interest in amateur theatricals, and went to see Shakespeare's *Richard III* and *Macbeth* at the Theatre Royal, Rochester; there were singing and acting and recitations and magic lantern shows at home; there were trips up and down the river with his father, and walks in the country, on several of which they passed the house at the top of Gadshill, the boy saying how much he loved it, the father replying that if he worked very hard he might some day live in it; and either alone or with his sister he explored the castle, the cathedral, the streets and byways of Rochester, the docks of Chatham, the park at Cobham, the Kentish fields and downlands.

Charles learnt how to read and write from his mother, who also gave him a grounding in Latin, but her frequent pregnancies interrupted his studies, and the fact that she was compelled at regular intervals to transfer her interest from him to the latest baby checked his affection for her, making him feel that her love was unstable. His ill-health cut him off from the society of other boys and made him more than usually self-centred; which explains his failure to appreciate his mother and the relative warmth of his feeling for his father, who was his chief companion up to the age of eleven. Yet while his mother was bearing one child after another, running the house, and educating the family, his father was spending more money than he earned, enjoying a life of comparative ease among jovial companions, borrowing sums which he could not repay, sacrificing his family's future comfort, and buoyantly, jauntily, stepping down the path which led them all in due course to a debtors' prison.

Between 1810 and 1822 Mrs. Dickens had seven children, two of whom died in infancy. An eighth was born in 1827. By the time Charles was nine years old his father's financial position called for retrenchment, and they left the pleasant house in Ordnance Terrace for a much cheaper residence in St. Mary's Place. Suddenly life became more earnest. The recitations and songs and magic lantern shows were abandoned. Charles went to a school where a capable young Baptist minister encouraged him to read the English classics and won his gratitude with sympathy. But although there was less money to spend, the home life of the family was still a happy one. Their nurse, Mary Weller, described Mrs. John Dickens as 'a dear good mother and a fine woman', and Charles as 'a lively boy of a good, genial, open disposition, and not quarrelsome as most children are at times.' She also said that he was 'a terrible boy to read.' He sat with a book in his left hand, the wrist of which he clasped with his right, swaying his body to and fro while sucking sounds proceeded from his mouth. He discovered a number of books which his father had put in a little unused room upstairs next to his bedroom, and every minute of his spare time was devoted to *Roderick Random, Peregrine Pickle, Humphrey Clinker, Tom Jones, The Vicar of Wakefield, Don Quixote, Gil Blas, Robinson*

*Crusoe* and *The Arabian Nights*. This was his chief education at that time, and the main solace of his life. He put himself into the leading characters of these novels, and fancied himself in their situations. 'I have been Tom Jones . . . for a week together. I have sustained my own idea of Roderick Random for a month at a stretch . . . When I think of it, the picture always rises in my mind of a summer evening, the boys at play in the churchyard, and I sitting on my bed, reading as if for life. Every barn in the neighbourhood, every stone in the church, and every foot of the churchyard, had some association of its own, in my mind, connected with these books, and stood for some locality made famous in them. I have seen Tom Pipes go climbing up the church-steeple; I have watched Strap, with the knapsack on his back, stopping to rest himself upon the wicket-gate; and I *know* that Commodore Trunnion held that club with Mr. Pickle in the parlor of our little village alehouse.' From which we also know that the church and its graveyard which David Copper-field saw from his bedroom window at Blunderstone near Yarmouth were seen by Charles Dickens from his bedroom in St. Mary's Place, Chatham.

Early in 1823 the family left for London without Charles, who may have been in the middle of a school term, but he followed them later in the year. John Dickens had been recalled for duty at Somerset House, and he was probably glad to leave his Chatham creditors. But Charles was deeply grieved by the move. Having to leave school at the age of eleven was a dreadful blow to him, and No. 16 Bayham Street, Camden Town, was to a sensitive boy an appalling social declension from the naval officer atmosphere of Chatham. True, there was the Mother Red Cap tea-garden at the top of the street, there were country lanes and more tea gardens at Chalk Farm less than a mile away, and he had only to walk out of the front-door to see the wooded hill of Hampstead; but against such rustic charms had to be placed the meanness of their house, the low social tone of their neighbours, and the fact that, as they could only afford to keep a little house-hold drudge, an orphan girl from Chatham Workhouse, Charles had to clean the family boots, look after his younger brothers and sisters, do housework and run errands. He felt completely isolated and absolutely neglected; he had no friends of his own age; he could no longer enjoy the feeling of progress and enlightenment which his lessons at school had given him; and even the companion of his youth was denied him, for his sister Fanny became a pupil at the Royal Academy of Music, and many years later he told a friend 'what a stab to his heart it was, thinking of his own disregarded condition, to see her go away to begin her education amid the tearful good wishes of everybody in the house.'

Though he did not perceive it at the time, his real education was being given him in the slums of London, just as his true vocation had been determined by the stories of Smollett, Fielding and Cervantes. Already he had written a tragedy and begun to invent tales for domestic consumption; now he was to obtain the raw material for creating characters by wandering through the city and its 'obscured purlieus.' At first he contented himself with the neighbourhood of Hampstead Road. Then he became more adventurous. His mother's elder brother, a civil servant named Thomas Barrow, had a lodging in Gerrard Street, Soho, where he often went, and which was the next district to be explored. His godfather, Christopher Huffam, an oar, mast and rigging maker, lived in Church Row, Limehouse, and the boy was fascinated by the nautical activities down there, not to mention the life of the East End as he went and came. Covent Garden and the Strand were favourite resorts, and he spent hours standing and staring at street corners and peeping down dark courts and noting the dwellers in dismal smelly alleys. But the most marvellous place of all was Seven Dials. 'What wild visions of prodigies of wickedness, want and beggary, arose in my mind out of that place!' he once exclaimed. It was terrifying, but it was thrilling beyond words to a lad who was still weak, subject to spasms, under-sized and over-sensitive. Unconsciously he hoarded his observations and emotions in these places, all of which and some of their inhabitants were to give him the background and characters for several of his stories.

While Charles was increasing his stock of knowledge, his father's stock of credit was dwindling. John Dickens had obtained his job through the influence of his mother's employers, and had kept it, presumably, because nothing short of malversation could deprive him of it. There is no doubt that he was a very pleasant and popular fellow, but his son's tribute to him gains emphasis from the lad's coolness towards his mother: 'I know my father to be as kind-hearted

and generous a man as ever lived in the world. Everything
that I can remember of his conduct to his wife, or children,
or friends, in sickness or affliction, is beyond all praise. By
me, as a sick child, he has watched night and day, unweariedly
and patiently, many nights and days. He never undertook
any business, charge or trust, that he did not zealously, con-
scientiously, punctually, honourably discharge. His industry
has always been untiring.' As the main charge and trust
undertaken by John Dickens was a wife and family, this
tribute needs toning down. His easy temper, gregarious
disposition, and tendency to lavish hospitality on all and
sundry, produced want and misery for his family, alienated
his wife's relations, who refused to go on making gifts of
cash which it pleased him to describe as loans, and deprived
his eldest son of education and the companions of his class.
No doubt one of the reasons why Charles always spoke so
well of his father, and portrayed him as Micawber and Old
Dorrit with affection, was that John Dickens greatly admired
the boy's comic singing, and was thus his first wholly
appreciative audience. So deep was the son's gratitude for
his father's care in sickness, friendship in health, and pride
in his performances, that when the real test came, and the
consequences of the older man's incapacity reduced the
youngster to despair, Charles never forgave the behaviour of
his mother, who deserved nothing but praise for her hopeless
struggle to keep things going when, thanks to her husband,
everything had gone.

Poor Mrs. Dickens did her best when the crisis came,
though her best amounted to nothing. She decided to open
a school, took a house in Gower Street north, had a brass
plate with the words 'Mrs. Dickens's Establishment' fixed to
the front door, and sent Charles round the neighbourhood
distributing circulars. She made no preparations whatever to
receive scholars, which was sensible of her, because no one
paid the smallest attention to her establishment. Meanwhile
there was trouble with the butcher and baker, who had the
curious notion that their bills ought to be paid, and the family
had very little to eat. At last John Dickens was arrested for
debt, and taken to a sponging-house. Charles ran backwards
and forwards between his father and his distracted family, his
eyes streaming with tears, trying to choke back his sobs,
wretched beyond expression; and his father's last remark

before being sent to Marshalsea prison—that the sun had set on him forever—made the lad feel that his heart was broken. Very soon he paid a visit to the Marshalsea: 'My father was waiting for me in the lodge, and we went up to his room . . . and cried very much. And he told me, I remember, to take warning by the Marshalsea, and to observe that if a man had twenty pounds a year, and spent nineteen pounds nineteen shillings and sixpence, he would be happy; but that a shilling spent the other way would make him wretched.' Charles stayed for dinner, and was sent upstairs to borrow a knife and fork from another prisoner named Captain Porter. 'I looked at nothing that I know of, but I saw everything', says David Copperfield, and though Charles was only a minute or so on the threshold of Captain Porter's room he left with a photographic memory of everything in it, and a knowledge of the exact relationship between the Captain and his fellow-lodgers, a dirty woman and two wan girls. Even in his misery nothing escaped that quick though apparently abstracted eye of his.

But his father's situation was not as horrible as his own. The home in Gower Street was gradually emptied of its furniture, and Charles was compelled to pay many visits to pawn shops. The first things to go were his sacred books, which were followed by chairs, pictures, fire-irons, tables, crockery, and so on, until the family had to camp in two uncarpeted rooms. Seeing the condition to which they were reduced, the manager of a blacking business named James Lamert, who had lodged with them in Chatham and Camden Town and was a connection of Mrs. Dickens by marriage, suggested that Charles should be employed at his warehouse with a salary of six shillings a week. The arrangement satisfied the boy's parents, who, Charles thought, could hardly have shown more satisfaction if he had been going to College after distinguishing himself at a public school. The blacking business was situated at Hungerford Stairs, in a part of London that was demolished some years later to make way for Charing Cross Station and Hungerford Bridge. The warehouse, which overlooked the river and swarmed with rats, was dirty and decayed and stank of rotting wood. 'My work', wrote Charles, 'was to cover the pots of paste-blacking; first with a piece of oil-paper, and then with a piece of blue paper; to tie them round with a string; and then to clip the paper close and neat, all round, until it looked as smart as a pot of ointment from an apothecary's shop. When a certain number of grosses of pots had attained this pitch of perfection, I was to paste on each a printed label; and then go on again with more pots. Two or three other boys were kept at similar duty downstairs on smaller wages. One of them came up, in a ragged apron and a paper cap, on the first Monday morning, to show me the trick of using the string and tying the knot. His name was Bob Fagin; and I took the liberty of using his name, long afterwards, in *Oliver Twist*.'

Bob Fagin was the only bright spot in that blacking warehouse; he protected Charles from the other boys, treated him as 'a young gentleman', occasionally played with him, and nursed him through a bad attack of the internal pains which had troubled him from infancy. 'I suffered such excruciating pain that time, that they made a temporary bed of straw in my old recess in the counting-house, and I rolled about on the floor, and Bob filled empty blacking-bottles with hot water, and applied relays of them to my side, half the day. I got better, and quite easy towards evening; but Bob (who was much bigger and older than I) did not like the idea of my going home alone, and took me under his protection. I was too proud to let him know about the prison; and after making several efforts to get rid of him, to all of which Bob Fagin in his goodness was deaf, shook hands with him on the steps of a house near Southwark bridge on the Surrey side, making believe that I lived there. As a finishing piece of reality in case of his looking back, I knocked at the door, I recollect, and asked, when the woman opened it, if that was Mr. Robert Fagin's house.'

When this happened the Marshalsea prison was the lad's home. No one having shown the least inclination to inquire as to the desirability of Mrs. Dickens's educational establishment, she left Gower Street in March, 1825, after a six months' residence there, and transferred herself and her family to the Marshalsea. Her husband was still drawing his salary of £6 odd a week from the Navy Pay Office, and as they could not be worried by creditors in prison their existence was far more comfortable than it had been for some years. It practically amounted to a fresh start in life, and the head of the family made no attempt to pay the debt for which he had been arrested. Charles and Fanny did not accompany them, but Charles called for Fanny every Sunday at the Royal Academy of Music and they spent their free day in prison with the rest. At first the boy lodged in Camden Town with 'a reduced old lady' who was one day to be known to the world as Mrs. Pipchin in *Dombey and Son*; but he was half-starved and so unhappy there that he appealed to his father, and a back attic near the prison was found for him in Lant Street, Southwark, where the population was migratory, 'usually disappearing on the verge of quarter-day and generally by night', and where the landlord, his wife and son, were very kind to him, tending him during one of his periodical illnesses and earning a place in *The Old Curiosity Shop* as the Garland family. Another character of these days provided some hints for the Marchioness in that book: the Chatham orphan, who continued to work for the Dickens family. Every morning Charles met her by London Bridge; and while waiting for the prison gates to open, he told her extraordinary stories, which he almost believed himself, about the Tower and the wharves and the other objects within sight. He always had breakfast and supper with his family in prison, but there was not sufficient time to join them for the midday meal, which usually consisted of a roll or a slice of pudding or some bread and cheese, and on rare occasions a glass of beer. Once he walked into a beef-house in Clare Court, Drury Lane, with a loaf of bread under his arm, and demanded a small plate of beef to eat with it. The waiter who served him, together with a companion equally hungry for novelties, stared at him while he ate his meal. Another time he entered a public house in Parliament Street, Westminster, and asked the landlord 'What is your very best—the *very best*—ale, a glass?' On being told it was twopence, he said 'Then just draw me a glass of that, if you please, with a good head to it.' The landlord called his wife, and together they gazed upon him. After they had asked him many questions, and he had invented the answers, the landlord gave him a glass of ale and the landlady gave him a kiss. But there was seldom enough money for such luxuries.

The six months he spent in the blacking warehouse was a period of sorrow and shame. He felt humiliated, abandoned, utterly cut off from everything that had made life endurable, helpless and hopeless. 'That I suffered in secret, and that I suffered exquisitely, no one ever knew but I', he wrote in a private statement many years after. So deeply was he affected by the experience that, although he recurred to it a dozen times in his books, he never spoke about it to his own children, who were first made aware of it in the pages of his biography by Forster; and until the whole district was altered out of recognition he never went near the scene of his servitude. 'My old way home by the borough', he was later to confess, 'made me cry after my eldest child could speak.'[1]

But though he was lonely and miserable as he wandered through the Adelphi streets and arches, his interest in the human scene never slackened, his curiosity was incessant. 'When I went to the Marshalsea of a night, I was always delighted to hear from my mother what she knew about the histories of the different debtors in the prison.' One scene he recalled in the years ahead with a vividness peculiar to him. The forthcoming birthday of the King had inspired John Dickens to draw up a petition that the prisoners should be granted a sum wherewith to drink their monarch's health. Charles got a day's leave from business to witness the event. The prisoners filed up outside and entered the room, one at a time, to sign the petition: 'To everybody in succession Captain Porter said "Would you like to hear it read?" If he weakly showed the least disposition to hear it, Captain Porter, in a loud sonorous voice, gave him every word of it. I remember a certain luscious roll he gave to such words as "Majesty", "Gracious Majesty", "Your Gracious Majesty's unfortunate subjects", "Your Majesty's well-known munificence", as if the words were something real in his mouth, and delicious to taste: my poor father meanwhile listening with a little of an author's vanity, and contemplating (not severely) the spikes on the opposite wall.'

While the rest of the family were passing their time in the Marshalsea, Fanny Dickens was doing well at the Royal Academy of Music, and one day several of them went to see her receive a prize. It was a painful moment for Charles: 'I could not bear to think of myself—beyond the reach of all such honourable emulation and success. The tears ran down my face. I felt as if my heart were rent. I prayed, when I went to bed that night, to be lifted out of the humiliation and

---

[1] He was not the only one to feel ashamed of his connection with the blacking business. His mother's relations were respectable enough never to refer to it except vaguely. Some years later, when Charles was trying to get a job on a newspaper, his uncle John Barrow, on being asked how he had been employed, replied evasively that 'at one time he had assisted Warren the blacking man in the conduct of his extensive business, and among other things had written puff verses for him. In this way as well as others he had shown ability.'

neglect in which I was. I never had suffered so much before. There was no envy in this.' His prayer was soon answered. In April, 1824, John Dickens's mother died; John inherited about £250; and his brother obtained his release by paying his debt. The family returned to Camden Town, where they lodged for a while with the 'reduced old lady' we know as Mrs. Pipchin, and then took a house of their own in Johnson Street, which they occupied for three years. Meanwhile the blacking business had been transferred to a spot close to where Chandos Street joins Bedford Street, and for the sake of the light Charles and the other boys worked near the window, where they were exposed to the observation of the passers-by. One day his father entered the place, and may have been annoyed by the fact that Charles was being exhibited to the public view. Whatever the cause, John Dickens wrote an insulting letter to Lamert, who promptly sacked Charles. 'I cried very much, partly because it was so sudden, and partly because in his anger he was violent about my father, though gentle to me . . . With a relief so strange that it was like oppression, I went home. My mother set herself to accommodate the quarrel, and did so next day. She brought home a request for me to return next morning, and a high character of me, which I am very sure I deserved. My father said I should go back no more, and should go to school. I do not write resentfully or angrily: for I know how all these things have worked together to make me what I am: but I never afterwards forgot, I never shall forget, I never can forget, that my mother was warm for my being sent back.' We must make allowances for both mother and son. She, as a desperate housekeeper who had slaved away to rear her family, was naturally concerned over the loss of six shillings a week, and anxious to maintain friendly relations with such members or connections of her own family as were still on speaking terms with them. Charles, just as naturally, could not appreciate her situation, and a return to the blacking warehouse was for him simply a return to misery without end and the death of hope. Our sympathies go to Charles, not because he was right and his mother wrong, but because he was twelve and she was old enough to be his mother.

At the end of 1824 John Dickens was pensioned off by the Navy Pay Office, receiving £145 a year, and almost immediately, through the influence of a brother-in-law, was appointed parliamentary reporter to a newspaper, in which job he was no doubt able to polish up the eloquence of His Majesty's ministers of state. Some months previously his son Charles had become a day-boy at Wellington House Academy in Hampstead Road, where he remained for more than two years. They were certainly happy years, if only because of the social contrast between his new companions and those of the immediate past, and the cultural difference between parsing Latin and pasting labels. The headmaster, or Chief as the boys called him, was ignorant of everything except the use of the cane, and his assistants seemed relatively omniscient. He was always very polite to the French master, wrote Dickens, 'because (as we believed) if the Chief offended him, he would instantly address the Chief in French, and for ever confound him before the boys with his inability to understand or reply.' In spite of his insufficiency, or because of it, the Chief was to have a more abundant life than most headmasters, for he became Creakle in *David Copperfield*.

Dickens did well at school, where he was taught English, dancing, Latin, mathematics, and above all a profound respect for money. He won several prizes and ended up as first boy. He was by now a handsome, curly-headed, high-spirited youth, amiable, irreverent, smart and popular. With another boy he issued a weekly newspaper, written on copybook scraps, which was lent to anyone willing to pay in marbles or pieces of slate pencil. The principal currency in the school was slate pencil, a hoard of which constituted wealth. He wrote and produced plays, one of which dealt in blank verse with the purely imaginary atrocities committed by the father of a pampered pupil, and got him into trouble. He gave his attention to the training of white mice, a favourite pastime among the boys, and became expert in the use of an outlandish language totally incomprehensible to grown-ups. In short, he enjoyed himself.

# 2

# FIRST LOVE

IN the spring of 1827, at the age of fifteen, Dickens left school and faced a world of which he had already experienced the harshness. The scenes of his childhood now seemed to have taken place in another state of existence: 'Magic scenes indeed', he called them, 'for the fancies of childhood dressed them in colours brighter than the rainbow, and almost as fleeting!' At first, and for a few weeks, he was office-boy to a solicitor in Symonds Inn, where it seems he made the acquaintance of Thomas Mitton, a clerk in the same office, who became a lifelong friend; but a relation of his mother's was again helpful, and in May 1827 we find him with Ellis and Blackmore, a firm of solicitors at 1 Raymond Buildings, Grays Inn, where he remained as a clerk or rather office-boy for eighteen months, during which his salary rose from 13/6 to 15/- a week. It was a useful job for a future novelist, and quite a few of the queer folk who called on business were admitted to the pages of *Pickwick* and other works. Private conferences with the solicitor were retailed to the outer office by whichever clerk was on duty at the keyhole. One visitor, perhaps, had failed to keep his employer's accounts 'with that dull accuracy which custom has rendered necessary.' Another, possibly, had claimed the protection of the law against someone who had addressed him in these terms: 'I shall alter the expression of your countenance so completely that the next time you look in the glass you'll ask vether you're gone out of town, and ven you're likely to come back again.' The rooms in Grays Inn were bug-infested and dust-coated, and Dickens remembered how one set of chambers was so dirty that 'I could take off the distinctest impression of my figure on any article of furniture by merely lounging upon it for a few moments; and it used to be a private amusement of mine to print myself off—if I may use the expression—all over the rooms. It was the first large circulation I had.'

With a lad of his own age he roamed the streets of London, went to as many theatres and drank as much beer as they could afford, joked a great deal when they were not putting on airs, and found everything very entertaining and themselves extremely interesting. Seven Dials was no longer a place of terror, but a scene of humour, as Dickens was shortly to explain: 'Now anybody who passed through the Dials on a hot summer's evening, and saw the different women of the house gossiping on the steps, would be apt to think that all was harmony among them, and that a more primitive set of people than the native Diallers could not be imagined. Alas! the man in the shop ill-treats his family; the carpet-beater extends his professional pursuits to his wife; the one-pair front has an undying feud with the two-pair front, in consequence of the two-pair front persisting in dancing over his (the one-pair front's) head, when he and his family have retired for the night; the two-pair back *will* interfere with the front kitchen's children; the Irishman comes home drunk every other night, and attacks everybody; and the one-pair back screams at everything. Animosities spring up between floor and floor; the very cellar asserts his equality. Mrs. A "smacks" Mrs. B's child, for "making faces". Mrs. B forthwith throws cold water over Mrs. A's child for "calling names". The husbands are embroiled—the quarrel becomes general—an assault is the consequence, and a police-officer the result.' Though mention is here made of hot summer evenings, apparently the weather was just as capricious in the eighteen-twenties as in the nineteen-forties: 'Four successive fine days in London! Hackney-coachmen became revolutionary, and crossing-sweepers began to doubt the existence of a First Cause.'

He was still living with his family, now in Somers Town, and his father's knowledge of shorthand may have encouraged him to master it, for he wished to enter journalism by way of parliament. With the assistance of Gurney's book on the subject, he threw himself into the business of making English look more difficult than Chinese. It did not come naturally to him, and his dreams were troubled by dots and circles and curves and things that reminded him of cobwebs or rockets or the legs of flies; but he went through with it, and in a year and a half was sufficiently advanced to leave the firm of solicitors and to perfect himself with practice in Doctors Commons while waiting for employment.

In those days Doctors Commons did the work that was later undertaken by the Probate Court. It was 'the place where they grant marriage-licenses to love-sick couples, and divorces to unfaithful ones; register the wills of people who have any property to leave, and punish hasty gentlemen who call ladies by unpleasant names.' The same judges dealt with naval and religious matters, and Dickens could never understand why experts in ecclesiastical law should be considered competent to deal with nautical affairs. For the first time his eyes were opened to the anomalies and absurdities of the law, and he never afterwards shut them. The law and its ministers became a major part of his stock-in-trade, and no profession ever had so keen a pair of eyes upon it. In addition to the entertainment he derived from the antics of judges and barristers, he made the interesting discovery that human nature on oath in the witness-box is displayed in its vainest, most variable, and therefore funniest moods; and he rightly concluded that the most useful period of his life was spent as an observer in Doctors Commons. For a while he had to content himself with observation. He was a free-lance reporter and relied on his efficiency to get jobs from the attorneys, or proctors as they were called in the spiritual courts. After a time one firm employed him to take notes of cases, and he worked away with great diligence, somehow supporting himself on the money he earned and greatly improving his dexterity at shorthand.

Though regular in his attendance at Doctors Commons for some three years, he improved his education throughout that period by reading assiduously in the British Museum; and, feeling a strong inclination to go on the stage, he took lessons in elocution and deportment from a professional actor, learnt a large number of parts, and spent hours before a mirror practising how to sit down on a chair, how to get up from it, how to enter and leave a room, how to bow and shake hands, how to express scorn, charm, love, hate, hope, despair, and all the other emotions. At length he applied for and was granted an audition at Covent Garden Theatre; but when the day came he was too ill to turn up, and by the next season he had become a successful parliamentary reporter, so the stage as a career was abandoned. But something of far greater moment to him than learning how to kiss a hand before a looking-glass was happening during these years: he had fallen in love.

The Dickens family were in fairly comfortable circumstances in the year 1829. The father had his pension and a newspaper job, Charles was earning enough to help, and Fanny was able to invite her musical friends to evening parties, when everyone who had a voice lifted it in song. Among the warblers was a young fellow named Henry Kolle, who was engaged to the daughter of a bank manager named Beadnell. Kolle took a fancy to Charles Dickens and invited him to the Beadnell home in Lombard Street. There were three daughters in the family, all of them musical, and Charles was instantly attracted to the youngest, Maria, who played a harp. The attraction quickly grew to passion, but it was not reciprocated  Maria enjoyed the amusement of flirtation and drove Charles to distraction with her sudden caprices. Now she was warm and tender, now cool and abrupt; sometimes she was sweet to another lover in order to enrage him, sometimes she petted him in order to irritate the other. She had not the least intention of marrying a struggling stenographer with apparently no future, though his songs were amusing, his good looks pleasing, his adoration flattering. She had an eye to business, and in her world this could only mean good prospects in the city. But it was very pleasant to play at love, and for a long time Charles was permitted to believe that she cared for him. He worked as he had never worked before, his sole object in life being to improve his position to the point where he could offer her a home and an assured income. When they were both over forty, he wrote to her: 'It is a matter of perfect certainty to me that I began to fight my way out of poverty and obscurity, with one perpetual idea of you.'

He never forgot the incidents of those days. She asked him to match a pair of blue gloves for her, and he recalled the precise shade twenty-five years later. One day he met her, with her mother and a male friend, in Cornhill on their way to buy clothes. He accompanied them to the dress-maker's door in St. Mary Axe, where Mrs. Beadnell, not wishing him to enter with them, said most emphatically 'And now, Mr. Dickin, we'll wish *you* good morning.' That, too, was a permanent memory. At last he got a job on a paper to report the parliamentary debates, and many a time he walked from the House of Commons to Lombard Street between two and three in the morning merely to look at the house where she lay asleep. All sorts of strange ideas concerning her floated through his head, and he described one aspect of his behaviour at a period when he could see the humour of it:

'She was older than I, and had pervaded every chink and crevice of my mind for three or four years. I had held volumes of Imaginary Conversations with her mother on the subject of our union, and I had written letters more in number than Horace Walpole's to that discreet woman, soliciting her daughter's hand in marriage. I had never had the remotest intention of sending any of those letters; but to write them, and after a few days tear them up, had been a sublime occupation. Sometimes, I had begun "Honoured Madam. I think that a lady gifted with those powers of observation which I know you to possess, and endowed with those womanly sympathies with the young and ardent which it were more than heresy to doubt, can scarcely have failed to discover that I love your adorable daughter, deeply, devotedly." In less buoyant states of mind I had begun, "Bear with me, Dear Madam, bear with a daring wretch who is about to make a surprising confession to you, wholly unanticipated by yourself, and which he beseeches you to commit to the flames as soon as you have become aware to what a towering height his mad ambition soars." At other times—periods of profound mental depression, when She had gone out to balls where I was not—the draft took the affecting form of a paper to be left on my table after my departure to the confines of the globe. As thus: "For Mrs. Onowenever, these lines when the hand that traces them shall be far away. I could not bear the daily torture of hopelessly loving the dear one whom I will not name. Broiling on the coast of Africa, or congealing on the shores of Greenland, I am far far better there than here." (In this sentiment my cooler judgment perceives that the family of the beloved object would have most completely concurred.) "If I ever emerge from obscurity, and my name is ever heralded by Fame, it will be for her dear sake. If I ever amass Gold, it will be to pour it at her feet. Should I on the other hand become the prey of Ravens——" I doubt if I ever quite made up my mind what was to be done in that affecting case; I tried "then it is better so"; but not feeling convinced that it would be better so, I vacillated between leaving all else blank, which looked expressive and bleak, or winding up with "Farewell!"'

All his life he was to remember every little trick of Maria's, so that her name, her harp-playing, the way her eyebrows drew together, anything he heard or saw that reminded him of her gave him a shock and brought it all back. 'I have always believed since, and always shall to the last, that there never was such a faithful and devoted poor fellow as I', he told her long afterwards. 'Whatever of fancy, romance, energy, passion, aspiration and determination belong to me, I never have separated and never shall separate from the hard-hearted little woman—you—whom it is nothing to say I would have died for, with the greatest alacrity!' He believed that she had been the cause, not only of his early success in life, but of a radical alteration in his character: 'My entire devotion to you, and the wasted tenderness of those hard years which I have ever since half loved, half dreaded to recall, made so deep an impression on me that I refer to it a habit of suppression which now belongs to me, which I know is no part of my original nature, but which makes me chary of showing my affections, even to my children, except when they are very young.'

He lived in an agony of uncertainty, one day enraptured by her seeming fondness for him, the next utterly downcast by her heartlessness. He wrote to ask her sister Anne what his chances were. 'My dear Charles', she replied, 'I really cannot understand Maria, or venture to take the responsibility of saying what the state of her affection is.' His exaltations and dejections, hopes and despairs, were brought to an issue at the celebration of his twenty-first birthday. The family were then living at 18 Bentinck Street, Cavendish Square, whither they had migrated from Somers Town by way of 70 Margaret Street and 13 Fitzroy Street, each move suggesting a slight improvement in their circumstances due to the rise of Charles in his profession as a parliamentary reporter. The hero of the occasion managed to get someone to take his place in the House of Commons gallery that night, and 'it was a beautiful party. There was not a single animate or inanimate object connected with it (except the company and myself) that I had ever seen before. Everything was hired, and the mercenaries in attendance were profound strangers to me. Behind a door, in the crumby part of the night when wine-glasses were to be found in unexpected spots, I spoke to Her—spoke out to Her . . . She was all angelical gentleness, but a word was mentioned . . . which, as I remarked at the moment, "scorched my brain". She went away soon afterwards, and when the hollow throng (though to be sure it was no fault of theirs) dispersed, I issued forth, with a dissipated scorner, and, as I mentioned expressly to him, "sought oblivion". It was found, with a headache in it, but it didn't last; for, in the shaming light of next day's noon, I raised my heavy head in bed, looking back to the birthdays behind me, and tracking the circle by which I had got round, after all, to the bitter powder and the wretchedness again.'

After a painful internal struggle, he tied her letters up with blue ribbon and returned them to her. 'Our meetings of late', he wrote, 'have been little more than so many displays of heartless indifference on the one hand, while on the other they have never failed to prove a fertile source of wretchedness and misery . . . I have felt too long the feeling of utter desolation and wretchedness which has succeeded our former acquaintance. Thank God I can claim for myself and *feel* that I deserve the merit of having ever throughout our intercourse acted fairly, intelligibly and honourably; under kindness and encouragement one day and a total change of conduct the next, I have ever been the same . . . Believe that nothing will ever afford me more real delight than to hear that you, the object of my first and my last love are happy.'

But Maria managed to extract a little more fun out of the situation. A friend of hers named Mary Anne Leigh confided in Fanny Dickens that Maria had told her everything that had passed between herself and Charles. A little later Miss Leigh went to a performance got up by Charles in Bentinck Street and took the opportunity of flirting with him, afterwards telling Maria Beadnell that Charles had not only flirted with her but had told her everything that had passed between himself and Maria. The knowledge of all this came to the ear of Charles, who wrote to Maria contradicting what Miss Leigh had said about himself. Maria, wanting to prolong the entertainment, pretended to believe Miss Leigh, and got another communication from Charles: 'I have borne more from you than I do believe any creature breathing ever bore from a woman before', he complained. 'The slightest hint however even now of change or transfer of feeling I cannot bear and do not deserve.' Having written a letter of scornful reproof to Miss Leigh, he then sought the solace of wine, announcing to his friend Kolle, who was about to be married to Maria's sister, that 'yesterday I felt like a maniac, today my interior resembles a lime basket.' On the same day, May 19th, 1833, while still suffering from a hangover, he made a last appeal to Maria, promising her that 'all that anyone can do to raise himself by his own exertions and unceasing assiduity I have done, and will do', and once again assuring her that 'I never have loved and I can never love any human creature breathing but yourself.' Maria, however, was now tiring of the game. She answered him coldly and reproachfully; and so he went his way, and she hers, the one to immortalise the other in the most endearing and the most devastating portraits of a living woman in English fiction.

The intense reality of love must have made Dickens extremely susceptible to the absurd unreality of politics. He became a press reporter in the House of Commons in the spring of 1832, when the Reform Bill was going through parliament, and the mass of Englishmen believed that the country was shortly to be transformed into paradise. Having listened to the nation's representatives, and noted the effect of their deliberations, Dickens came to the conclusion that the average politician was a windbag, a time-server, a flunkey, and a self-seeker, and that the triumph of any party merely benefited a class. He described the antics of M.P.s while still in his early twenties, and as he never saw reason to change his opinion of the game at Westminster, we may read this as his first and last view of the subject:

'We take it that the commencement of a session of parliament is neither more nor less than the drawing up of the curtain for a grand comic pantomime; and that his Majesty's most gracious speech, on the opening thereof, may be not inaptly compared to the clown's opening speech of "Here we are!" "My lords and gentlemen, here we are!" appears, to our mind at least, to be a very good abstract of the point and meaning of the propitiatory address of the ministry . . .

'Perhaps the cast of our political pantomime never was richer than at this day. We are particularly strong in clowns. At no former time, we should say, have we had such astonishing tumblers, or performers so ready to go through the whole of their feats for the amusement of an admiring throng. Their extreme readiness to exhibit, indeed, has given rise to some ill-natured reflections; it having been objected that by exhibiting gratuitously through the country when the theatre is closed, they reduce themselves to the level of mountebanks, and thereby tend to degrade the respectability of the profession . . .

'But, laying aside this question, which after all is a mere matter of taste, we may reflect with pride and gratification of heart on the proficiency of our clowns as exhibited in the season. Night after night will they twist and tumble about, till two, three, and four o'clock in the morning; playing the strangest antics, and giving each other the funniest slaps on the face that can possibly be imagined, without evincing the smallest tokens of fatigue. The strange noises, the confusion, the shouting and roaring, amid which all this is done, too, would put to shame the most turbulent sixpenny gallery that ever yelled through a boxing-night.

'It is especially curious to behold one of these clowns compelled to go through the most surprising contortions by the irresistible influence of the wand of office, which his leader or harlequin holds above his head. Acted upon by this wonderful charm he will become perfectly motionless, moving neither hand, foot, nor finger, and will even lose the faculty of speech at an instant's notice; or, on the other hand, he will become all life and animation if required, pouring forth a torrent of words without sense or meaning, throwing himself into the wildest and most fantastic contortions, and even grovelling on the earth and licking up the dust . . .

'Strange tricks—very strange tricks—are also performed by the harlequin who holds for the time being the magic wand which we have just mentioned. The mere waving it before a man's eyes will dispossess his brains of all the notions previously stored there, and fill it with an entirely new set of ideas; one gentle tap on the back will alter the colour of a man's coat completely; and there are some expert performers, who, having this wand held first on one side and then on the other, will change from side to side, turning their coats at every evolution, with so much rapidity and dexterity, that the quickest eye can scarcely detect their motions. Occasionally, the genius who confers the wand, wrests it from the hand of the temporary possessor, and consigns it to some new performer; on which occasions all the characters change sides, and then the race and the hard knocks begin anew.'

After about six months of reporting for an evening paper, Dickens got a job on the *Mirror of Parliament*, a publication run by his maternal uncle J. H. Barrow. He soon became the fastest and most accurate reporter in the press gallery, and his uncle frequently asked him for week-ends to Norwood, where the attraction for Charles, following his separation from Maria Beadnell, was 'a very nice pair of black eyes.' Barrow was so much impressed by the young man's industry and efficiency that he arranged a meeting with the proprietor of *The Morning Chronicle*, as a result of which Charles was engaged by that paper at a weekly salary of five guineas, and was soon to be seen about in a new hat, a blue coat with black velvet facings, 'which he threw over his shoulders *à l'Espagnole*', and other striking habiliments. Life as a parliamentary reporter was not enjoyable, because in addition to the tedium of taking down the barren verbiage droned forth by politicians there were the crowding and discomfort of the strangers' gallery, at the back of which the pressmen sat; the bad lighting, the stuffiness, the jostling, the turmoil, the sweat and the stench; the pain of maintaining one position for protracted periods, and the greater pain of shifting it: 'I felt the gentle pressure of his foot on mine; our corns throbbed in unison.' The House of Commons was destroyed by fire in the autumn of 1834, and its members temporarily occupied the House of Lords. The only change for Dickens was that instead of sitting in extreme discomfort he had to stand in acute distress, neither condition deepening his love of his species; and we are not surprised to learn that his companions thought him reserved but polite, while the only friend he made was Thomas Beard, who remained a friend for life.

When the House was not in session, his work became more interesting. He went into the country for *The Morning Chronicle* to report speeches of ministers, to describe elections, conflagrations, and anything else that was supposed to interest an age which so much resembled every other age that his reference to its leading characteristic will be read now as an apt comment on the present generation: 'In these days of derangement of the nervous system and universal lassitude, people are content to pay handsomely for excitement.' He thoroughly enjoyed his sensational expeditions into the country. The coach journeys by day when every stopping place provided him with a crowd of comic characters, and by night when he experienced the added thrill of accidents; the dashes through the countryside in postchaises at the reckless speed of fifteen miles an hour, when breakages, dislocations, upsets, 'exhausted horses and drunken post-boys', were common occurrences; all this gave a zest to life and provided him with rich material for his work. To write his articles with such accompaniments, often when the only light was a wax candle or a dark lantern, and the swaying and pitching and shaking and shouting were almost continual, was a feat which exercised his utmost patience, fortitude and ingenuity; yet he revelled in the work, in the bustle and confusion of the elections, in the danger and discomfort of travelling, above all in the organisation of road transport, coach, carriage, post-chaise, horses, whereby he could get a fuller report at an earlier hour to his newspaper than the other reporters could to theirs. In September 1834 he went to Edinburgh to witness the presentation of the Freedom of the City to Earl Grey. A pavilion was erected for the occasion in the High School Yard on Calton Hill, and here dinner was to take place at five o'clock; but Grey and the other important people did not arrive till after six, and Dickens's description of what happened was less formal than the average reporter's on such imposing occasions:

'A gentleman . . . having sat with exemplary patience for some time in the immediate vicinity of cold fowls, roast beef, lobsters, and other tempting delicacies (for the dinner was a cold one), appeared to think that the best thing he could possibly do would be to eat his dinner, while there was any-thing to eat. He accordingly laid about him with right good-will, the example was contagious, and the clatter of knives and forks became general. Hereupon, several gentle-men, who were not hungry, cried out "Shame!" and looked very indignant; and several gentlemen who were hungry cried "Shame!" too, eating, nevertheless, all the while, as fast as they possibly could. In this dilemma, one of the stewards mounted a bench and feelingly represented to the delinquents the enormity of their conduct, imploring them for decency's sake to defer the process of mastication until the arrival of Earl Grey. This address was loudly cheered, but totally unheeded; and this is, perhaps, one of the few instances on record of a dinner having been virtually concluded before it began.'

On arrival of the distinguished guests, the chairman, Earl Rosebery, 'entreated the assembly to postpone the commence-ment of the dinner for a few moments. The Reverend Mr.

Henry Grey was in attendance for the purpose of saying grace; but he was outside the room, and the crowd was so great that he could not get in . . . As the major part of the company had already dined, they acceded to the request with the utmost good humour.'

November of the same year saw Dickens in Birmingham, 'the town of dirt, iron-works, radicals, and hardware.' In January 1835 he was present at elections held in Ipswich, Sudbury, and Chelmsford, driving himself in a gig from the latter place to Braintree and back. 'I actually did the four and twenty miles without upsetting it . . . Every time the horse heard a drum he bounced into the hedge on the left side of the road, and every time I got him out of that he bounded into the hedge on the right side.' He thought Chelmsford 'the dullest and most stupid spot on the face of the earth', and on a dismal Sunday he stood in a room of the Black Boy Hotel 'looking out of a damned large bow window at the rain as it falls into the puddles opposite, wondering when it will be dinner time, and cursing my folly in having put no books into my portmanteau. The only book I have seen here is one which lies upon the sofa. It is entitled "Field Exercises and Evolutions of the Army, by Sir Henry Torrens." I have read it through so often that I am sure I could drill a hundred recruits from memory.' In May he was off to Exeter to report a speech by Lord John Russell. The meeting was held under pelting rain in the castle yard, and 'two good-natured colleagues who chanced to be at leisure held a pocket-handkerchief over my note-book, after the manner of a state canopy in an ecclesiastical procession.' He returned home with a touch of rheumatism and *perfectly deaf*. A few months later he went down to Bristol for another of Russell's speeches, stopping for a moment at the George and Pelican, Newbury, to pen a private note: 'I am in such a chaotic spate of confusion just now, surrounded by maps, road-books, ostlers and post-boys, that I have not time to devote to anything but business.' By means of a chaise and four, saddle horses, and their own endeavours, he and Beard managed to beat all the other papers with their accounts of the Bristol meeting and a public dinner at Bath. That same year saw him at the Salisbury Arms, Hatfield, where he was writing a description of the fire at the great house. 'Here I am, waiting until the remains of the Marchiouness (*sic*) of Salisbury are dug from the ruins of her ancestor's castle . . . I am waiting for the Inquest which cannot be held until the bones (if the fire has left any) are discovered.'

In December he visited Kettering to 'watch' an election, putting up at the White Hart. He found the place, like Chelmsford, 'dreadfully stupid and dull', but he and his colleague discovered a bagatelle board, which they erected in his bedroom, 'a large apartment at the extreme end of a long gallery, with a couple of windows commanding an interesting view of the stable yard. There is a little passage leading to the room at the entrance of which is a door which we have fastened, and on the outside of which we have affixed a poker as a temporary knocker.' Secure from interruption, they played bagatelle when not engaged in reporting the unpleasant scenes outside, and one day they asked three acquaintances to the bed-and-bagatelle room for a Christmas dinner, which consisted of cod and oyster sauce, roast beef, a pair of ducks, plum pudding and mince pies. Dickens's description of an old-fashioned election is instructive. Never, he declares, had he set eyes on such a ruthless set of bloody-minded villains as the Tories: 'In their convivial moments yesterday, after the business of the day was over, they were perfect savages. If a foreigner were brought here on his first visit to an English town to form his estimate of the national character, I am quite satisfied he would return forthwith to France, and never set foot in England again . . . beastly as the electors usually are, these men are superlative blackguards. Would you believe that a large body of horsemen, mounted and armed, who galloped on a defenceless crowd yesterday, striking about them in all directions, and protecting a man who cocked a loaded pistol, were *led* by clergymen and magistrates? or that I saw one of these fellows with my own eyes unbuckle one of his stirrup-leathers and cut about him in the crowd with the iron part of it—communicating to the blows all the additional force that swinging it at the end of the leather could give them? Anything more sickening and disgusting, or anything that roused my indignation so much, I never beheld.' The noises on polling-day were, it seems, more discordant, if not so hellish, as those produced by modern loud-speakers. Bells rang, candidates raved, bands played, men fought, women screamed, 'and the voters themselves are drinking and guzzling and howling and roaring in every house of entertainment there is.' Dickens, his head 'actually splitting', retired into his bedroom and played bagatelle.

But something far more significant to the world and himself than the political turmoils of the time had occurred while he was risking life and limb as a press reporter. A number of Sketches by a writer named Boz were creating much interest in the newspaper world, and their author was engaged to be married.

## 3

# THE INIMITABLE BOZ

ONE autumn evening in 1833 Dickens, whose rejection by
Maria Beadnell had compelled him to occupy his mind by
writing sketches from real life and to risk the rejections of
publishers, disappeared down Johnson's Court in Fleet Street
and dropped the first, later to be known as 'Mr. Minns and
his Cousin', into the letter-box of the *Monthly Magazine*. It
appeared in the December number, and the young author
'walked down to Westminster Hall, and turned into it for
half an hour, because my eyes were so dimmed with joy and
pride, that they could not bear the street, and were not fit to
be seen there.' He announced the great news to Henry Kolle,
saying 'I am so dreadfully nervous that my hand shakes to
such an extent as to prevent my writing a word legibly.'
Though the editor made it clear that his contributors must be
content with fame instead of cash, Dickens went on sending
sketches, all of which were published anonymously until
August 1834, when for the first time the author's pseudonym
was given as 'Boz', 'the nickname of a pet child, a younger
brother, whom I had dubbed Moses, in honour of *The Vicar
of Wakefield*; which being facetiously pronounced through the
nose, became Boses, and being shortened, became Boz.'

People soon began to notice the sketches, and one of them
was calmly appropriated by an actor, who turned it into a
farce, which he produced at the Adelphi Theatre, without
troubling the author about it one way or another. In those
days the theatres were not affected by the laws of copyright,
so the managers were usually considerate enough not to
pester authors for their permission or advice and were
particularly careful not to insult them with royalties. Several
journals of the time also complimented Boz by reprinting his
sketches in full, and the honoured author began to feel that
he would rather have gold than glory. He allowed the paper
for which he was reporting, *The Morning Chronicle*, to publish
several sketches for nothing, but when the same firm started
*The Evening Chronicle* he wrote to the editor George Hogarth
asking that his salary should be increased in consideration of

the series of sketches he was about to write for the new publication, adding that he hoped they would consider his request 'fair and reasonable.' They did; and his salary was raised from five to seven guineas a week.

The first of his well-known contemporaries to seek his acquaintance as a result of these sketches was Harrison Ainsworth, seven years his senior, whose *Rookwood* made a hit in 1834. Dickens was asked to the Sunday parties given by Ainsworth at Kensal Lodge, where he was introduced to the publisher John Macrone, who admired the sketches and published the first series in two volumes, illustrated by Cruikshank, in 1836, another series in one volume following a year later. 'They comprise my first attempts at authorship', wrote Dickens, 'with the exception of certain tragedies achieved at the mature age of eight or ten, and represented with great applause to overflowing nurseries.'

Though only twenty-one when he started to write them, *Sketches by Boz* reveal him as a close observer of the human scene, already gifted with an expansive form of humour that was to make him famous, and especially conscious of the misery which people create for themselves. Here is an example of a Boz character who was to reappear, with variations, throughout his works: 'He was never happy but when he was miserable . . . The only real comfort of his existence was to make everybody about him wretched—then he might be truly said to enjoy life . . . he contributed largely towards the support of two itinerant methodist parsons, in the amiable hope that if circumstances rendered any people happy in this world, they might perchance be rendered miserable by fears for the next.' The coming of the great age of mechanical and scientific advance obviously made Dickens apprehensive: 'He is clearly on the eve of some great experiment. Pray heaven that it be not a dangerous one; but the interests of science must be promoted, and I am prepared for the worst.' We note also a trick of style which was to become a mannerism as he grew older, and which, though largely due to his natural love of emphasis, may have originated in the journalist's desire to fill up his space by saying the same thing twice over in different words. Thus he describes someone as 'more than half asleep and less than half awake.' As a writer Dickens was influenced by two men: Defoe and Smollett. He had learnt more from *Robinson Crusoe* and *Roderick Random* than from all the other books he had read, which simply means that they had appealed to something in his own nature more than all the rest. He knew Shakespeare well, as any reader who knows Shakespeare well can discover in his novels; he liked Fielding and admired Scott; but temperamentally he was not akin with any one of his three greatest predecessors; while, as for Richardson, he probably looked at Clarissa just long enough to know that he did not want to look at it any longer. But other men's influence counts for little in Dickens, who was an original if any man may be called so.

While writing the sketches which appealed so strongly to editors because they did not have to pay for them, Dickens was leading a nomadic sort of life. For a while he had rooms in Cecil Street, Strand, but the people there 'put too much water in their hashes, lost a nutmeg grater, attended on me most miserably, dirtied the table cloth, &c., &c.; and so (detesting petty miseries) I gave them warning', and left. He lived with his family in Margaret Street, Fitzroy Street, and Bentinck Street; and for the amusement of himself, his family and his friends, he got up several entertainments at the last-named residence. Kolle took part, and received a rehearsal call in these terms: 'The family are busy. The corps dramatic are all anxiety. The scenery is all completing rapidly, the machinery is finished, the curtain hemmed, the orchestra complete and the manager grimy.' Kolle was also asked to North End, where Dickens occasionally spent a day or two at Collins's Farm,[1] rising at seven in the morning and riding a horse of which he said: 'To look at the animal in question you would think (with the exception of dog's meat) there was no earthly purpose to which he could be applied.'

The spasms to which he had always been subject recurred at intervals, and lack of money was a constant anxiety. In 1834 his father was again arrested for a debt that he owed to a wine-firm. Somehow Dickens scraped the money together and set him at liberty. Then Mrs. Dickens fell ill and extra bills had to be met. Her husband did not make things easier by disappearing whenever he was wanted for debt, leaving his family in total ignorance of his whereabouts. Charles was constantly mortgaging his own salary to help them along and save his father from prison. In fact it may be said that from

[1] Collins's Farm was a favourite spot with Dickens. Now known as 'Wyldes', it stands on the western edge of Hampstead Heath, behind the Bull and Bush inn. William Blake was a constant visitor there when his friends, the Linnells, occupied it.

the moment Dickens began to earn money he kept all his family some of the time, most of his family most of the time, and some of his family all the time. No man was ever so relation-ridden as he. At length they left Bentinck Street, split up, and Dickens took his small brother Frederick with him to chambers at 13 Furnivals Inn, which he could not furnish properly because most of his salary went to maintain the family, and where he had to receive visitors in an uncarpeted room containing a deal table, two or three hard chairs, and a few books. In spite of all his worries he was high-spirited enough to write 'I open my letter to say that nothing whatever has occurred since I folded it up', and optimistic enough to face the prospect of marriage on seven guineas a week, with a wife and potential family of his own to support, in addition to his parents and an actual family of theirs.

His friendship with George Hogarth, a Scot who published a series of his sketches in *The Evening Chronicle*, led to his being invited to the Hogarth home, where he quickly became popular with Mrs. Hogarth and her daughters. He had everything to make him liked: good looks, vivacity, a growing reputation, a pleasing repertory of comic songs, a fund of entertaining stories, a fondness for parlour tricks, and an irresistibly droll way of behaving. For instance, one summer evening when the family were sitting in their drawing-room after dinner, Dickens, in the guise of a sailor, bounded through the french windows from the lawn, danced a hornpipe, whistled the accompaniment, and leapt out again. A few minutes later, in his ordinary clothes, he made a dignified entrance by the door, shook hands gravely all round, and solemnly seated himself. The family looked so stupified that he burst into laughter. His high spirits and engaging manners fascinated the Hogarths, and he became a daily visitor: he even took lodgings for a while in Selwood Place in order to be near their home at 18 York Place, Queens Elms, Brompton; and it was not long before he had asked the eldest daughter Kate to marry him.

The chief need of Dickens's nature was to be loved, and perhaps his tragedy was that he asked more than he could give. Having missed, as he thought, the love of his mother, he was always looking for it in other women, but never found the supply equal to the demand. He had loved Maria Beadnell with the intensity of one who longs for love, and when she failed him it was almost a dead certainty that the next woman who appealed to him and who seemed to return his affection would become his wife. Kate was the only Hogarth girl of marriageable age, and, having little individuality, was therefore fated to be Mrs. Charles Dickens. She was a gentle, pretty, sweet-natured, reserved, plump, easy-going girl, inclined to laziness, with a fresh-coloured complexion, heavy-lidded blue eyes, rather retroussé nose, fine forehead, small round red-lipped mouth, and weak chin. Her movements were slow and a little clumsy. She had a sleepy look, spoke in a pleasant tone of voice, and a charming smile lit up her face when she talked. People who knew her said that she reminded them of Agnes in *David Copperfield*, and we can well believe it; but Maclise's portraits of her add a sort of bashful sensuality to her attractions. That she had a sense of humour is proved by her husband's letters to her, but she mostly expressed it in puns. Such was the girl who benefited from the backwash of Dickens's surging emotion for Maria Beadnell; but neither of them was aware of that at the time. Dickens, for a reason that will appear when we analyse his character, was playing the part of a lover for all he was worth; Kate was carried off her feet by his impetuosity; and she was not intelligent enough to perceive that a man who is really in love with a woman does not come to a pre-nuptial agreement with her that, if either of them should ever fall in love with someone else, the fact should be disclosed to the other. This cancellation clause in a marriage contract is much as if a man, just before his reception into the Roman Catholic Church, were to inform the priest that nothing must be placed in his way should he wish later on to become a Mahomedan.

Trouble arose three weeks after their engagement, and from the letter he wrote to her in May 1835 it is clear enough that her love-making was not ardent enough for him. 'The sudden and uncalled-for coldness with which you treated me just before I left last night, both surprised and deeply hurt me —surprised, because I could not have believed that such sullen and inflexible obstinacy could exist in the breast of any girl in whose heart love had found a place; and hurt me, because I feel for you far more than I have ever professed.' He then advised her how to behave in future, and warned her not to trifle with him. 'What you do not take the trouble to conceal from a lover's eyes will be frequently acted before those of a husband . . . If you really love me I would have you do justice to yourself, and shew me that your love for me, like mine for you, is above the ordinary trickery and frivolous absurdity which debases the name and renders it ludicrous.' Against her capriciousness, he placed his own steadfastness: how he had forsaken his friends to be with her, how upset he had been when she was ill, how joyful when she recovered. He wrote in haste, he said, but not in anger: 'I am *not* angry, but I *am hurt*, for the second time.' He underlined 'hurt' twice, and implied that she could scarcely be expected to understand the sense in which he used the word. Such was not the tone of his correspondence with Maria Beadnell. He had been fooled by one girl, but he was not going to be fooled by another: which is what his letter amounted to.

Kate instantly came to heel. Her reply displayed 'all that amiable and excellent feeling which I know you possess, and for which I believe from my heart you are unrivalled. If you would only determine to *shew* the same affection and kindness to me, when you feel disposed to be ill-tempered, I declare unaffectedly I should have no one solitary fault to find with you. Your asking me to love you "once more" is quite unnecessary—*I have never ceased to love you for one moment since I knew you; nor shall I.*' A few days later he repeated his 'solemn assurances of entertaining for you a love which nothing can lessen—an affection which no alteration of time or circumstance can ever abate', and devoutly hoped that 'the dearest hopes I ever entertained may be realised (with your good leave) at an even earlier period than we anticipate.' As a rule Kate mistook the conventional phrases of love for the real thing, and Charles was sufficiently in need of her to give them the ring of conviction. Here are a few:

'I have not seen you, you know, dearest, since seven o'clock yesterday evening. It seems an age.'

'Were I to endeavour to embody the least of the feelings I entertain for you in words, it would be a useless and hopeless attempt.'

'Ever yours unchangeably.'

'God bless you, my more than life.'

'Take care of yourself for *my* sake, not for your own. I am very selfish.'

ELIZABETH  DICKENS

*Painting by*
JOHN W. GILBERT
*By courtesy of*
*Mr  Henry C. Dickens*

JOHN  DICKENS

*Painting by*
JOHN W. GILBERT
*By courtesy of*
*Mr  Henry C. Dickens*

MRS CHARLES DICKENS (1846)
(CATHERINE HOGARTH)

*Engraving after Painting by* DANIEL MACLISE, R.A.

He addressed her 'My own dearest love', 'My own darling', 'My own dearest Mouse', 'My own dearest darling Pig', and sent her thousands or millions or 'an unlimited number' of kisses. They indulged in baby-language, which shows that they were soon at ease with one another. 'Not "coss" I hope?' he added to a letter written from Kettering, while from Hatfield he assured her that his love was 'more than I can possibly 'press.'

Sometimes he was too busy to see her; often he was too much exhausted by his labours to do more than send a hurried scrawl; and she complained of his absences and pre-occupations. There are even sentences in his letters which suggest that she did not quite believe in his sincerity as a lover, e.g.: 'The pleasure you think I take in being away from you'; and 'I am very sorry my dear Girl that you should have thought my letter of the other day stiff and formal . . . it was quite unintentional'; and 'I perceive you have not yet subdued one part of your disposition—your distrustful feel-ings and want of confidence'; and 'Believe me (if you have any faith in your nature) Ever yours most sincerely and affectionately.'

Unable to visit her after the long day's work, he would beg her to come with her sister Mary and make breakfast for him in the morning. On all such occasions he would insist on punctuality. His brother Fred was his messenger between Furnivals Inn and Brompton, but was too small to act as a chaperon: 'I do not like your traversing the West End of London, of all other parts, accompanied only by Fred. If you knew how eagerly I long for your society this evening, or how much delight it would afford me to be able to turn round to you at our own fireside when my work is done, and seek in your kind looks and gentle manner the recreation and happiness which the moping solitude of chambers can never afford, you would believe me sincere in saying that necessity and necessity alone induces me to forego the pleasure of your companionship for one evening in the week even. You will never do me the justice of believing it however, and all I can do until my book is finished will be to reflect that I shall have (God willing) many opportunities of shewing you in years to come how unjust you used to be, and of convincing you then of what I would fain convince you now—that my pursuits and labours, such as they are, are not more selfish than my pleasures, and that your future advancement and happiness is the mainspring of them all.'

Occasionally he was prostrated by illness as a result of overwork. Once he took a strong calomel pill, which performed 'such singular evolutions in my interior that I am at present quite unable to leave home.' Headache, dizziness, physical lassitude, were constant, and after grinding away till three one morning he 'passed the whole night, if night it can be called after that hour, in a state of exquisite torture from the spasm in my side far exceeding anything I ever felt'; but he was 'so used to suffer from this cause that it never alarms me'. Kate and her mother caught scarlet fever in the autumn of 1835, and Charles spent many hours every day by Kate's bedside; but she was inclined to play for sympathy, and her lover did not always play up to her. 'It is very hard to preach consolation when one stands in no small need of it oneself', he wrote, ' . . . indeed my dearest girl, your situation is almost an enviable one, compared with mine.' As for her fever, 'I am in a fever myself to be with you.'

All through 1835 he was compelled to borrow small sums of money in order to keep his family and himself, but unlike his father he repaid every penny with scrupulous exactitude. Twice he asked Macrone to 'apply the spur' to Cruikshank, who was illustrating *Sketches by Boz*, so that he could benefit from the publication of the book. He even went up to call on the artist, found him out, and 'strolled about Pentonville thinking the air did my head good, and looked at one or two houses in the new streets. They are extremely dear, the cheapest I looked at being £55 a year with taxes. Their situation for business is undeniable certainly, and the houses themselves are very pretty, but this is too much.' As an added attraction to the volumes he decided to write an essay on Newgate prison, for which purpose he went over it, was 'intensely interested in everything I saw', and collected many anecdotes to tell Kate, some of them rather amusing. But his financial situation was desperate, and while he was wondering how to raise the rent for a house, how to keep his father out of gaol, how to supply his family with food and lodgings, how to furnish his chambers, and how to look presentable when he called on his publisher or his new acquaintances, the tradesmen were badgering him for settlement of their accounts: 'The Butcher wrote me last night to say that his boy was going to take out a warrant against me for an assault. I wrote word back that the sooner he did it the better, and that I had instructed my clerk to take in no more insolent attempts to extort money.' Apparently brother Fred had been promoted to the position of 'my clerk'.

But the year 1836 was to see a complete change in his fortunes. *Sketches by Boz* came out in the first week of February, and sold well. A few days later the recently established firm of Chapman and Hall offered him £14 a month to write the adventures of a Nimrod Club, 'the members of which were to go out shooting, fishing, and so forth, and getting themselves into difficulties through their want of dexterity.' The adventures were to be published in monthly parts, and the writer's contribution had to be subsidiary to the illustrations of a popular artist named Robert Seymour. 'The work will be no joke', Charles informed Kate, 'but the emolument is too tempting to resist.' As the publishers were anxious that the work should be a joke, a good joke, and nothing but a joke, they had to defer to the author's criticism: 'I objected, on consideration, that although born and partly bred in the country I was no great sportsman, except in regard of all kinds of locomotion; that the idea was not novel, and had been already much used; that it would be infinitely better for the plates to arise naturally out of the text; and that I should like to take my own way, with a freer range of English scenes and people, and was afraid I should ultimately do so in any case, whatever course I might prescribe to myself at starting . . . My friends told me it was a low, cheap form of publication, by which I should ruin all my rising hopes; and how right my friends turned out to be, everybody now knows.'

Having established the primary importance of the author in the undertaking, Dickens settled down to the first number of *Pickwick Papers*. It did not go easily at first. 'The sheets are a weary length', he grumbled, 'I had no idea there was so much in them.' But he was well into his stride by chapter 2: 'I have at this moment got Pickwick and his friends on the Rochester coach, and they are going on swimmingly, in company with a very different character from any I have yet described, who I flatter myself will make a decided hit.' Though Jingle did not make a decided hit at the time of his appearance, it is interesting to observe that the first of the typically Dickensian characters was an actor, whose sparkle was shared by his creator.

With his thoughts full of the subject, Jingle's creator moved to a better set of chambers in Furnivals Inn, and prepared them for the reception of his future wife. Some time in March they decided to get married on April 2nd, and he obtained a special licence. 'Here's another day off the fortnight. Hurrah!' he wrote in great excitement. They were married at St. Luke's, Chelsea, two days after the publication of the first number of *Pickwick*. It was a simple affair, and the best man, Tom Beard, was the only guest apart from the Dickens and Hogarth families. John Dickens was still unpopular with his wife's relations, and Charles, in writing to announce the marriage to his uncle Thomas Barrow, said how sorry he was that he could not introduce his wife, but 'If I could not as a single man, I cannot as a married one, visit at a relation's house from which my father is excluded; nor can I see any relations here who would not treat him as they would myself.' Barrow had, his nephew felt, failed in a proper estimation of John Dickens's character; and hoping no doubt to soften Uncle Thomas's attitude towards his own father, Charles described his wife's father, George Hogarth, as 'a gentleman who has recently distinguished himself by a celebrated work on music, who was the most intimate friend and companion of Sir Walter Scott, and one of the most eminent among the literati of Edinburgh.'

Charles and Kate spent their honeymoon at the village of Chalk in Kent. It lasted one week. Charles became restless and wanted to get back to London. The reason is obvious: he found his wife's undiluted society monotonous; which means that he had made the common mistake of confusing sexual desire with love. But, quicker and more determined than most people, he discovered his error within a week and resolved what to do. The last letter he wrote to her, before their marriage, began 'My dearest Wig'. The first letter he wrote to her, after their marriage, began 'My dear Kate'.

Back in Furnivals Inn, Dickens saw Seymour's design for an etching to accompany 'The Stroller's Tale' in the second number of *Pickwick*. It did not do justice to the characters in the story, and Dickens asked Seymour to call and talk it over. They had not previously met one another, and the situation was a ticklish one, not only because Seymour's original idea of the book had been superseded by Dickens's more promising conception, but because Seymour, twelve years older than Dickens, was a very well-known artist, of a nervous highly-strung disposition, who had already quarrelled with his literary collaborators, and who must have been extremely irritated by the fact that the usual positions of etcher and writer were in this case reversed. Dickens, knowing the value of Seymour's work, was therefore on his best behaviour, and his letter was extremely conciliatory: 'I had intended to write to you, to say how much gratified I feel by the pains you have bestowed on our mutual friend Mr. Pickwick, and how much the result of your labours has surpassed my expectations.' He went on to say that Seymour's design for 'The Stroller's Tale', though 'extremely good', was not quite his idea, and that 'I shall feel personally obliged to you if you will make another drawing. It will give me great pleasure to see you, as well as the drawing, when it is complete.' He then mentioned the alterations he wanted, and added: 'The furniture of the room, you have depicted *admirably*. I have ventured to make these suggestions, feeling assured that you will consider them in the spirit in which I submit them to your judgment.'

Seymour called. We can only imagine what happened. Knowing Dickens, we may feel certain that he was most cordial, solicitous and charming. He had still his way to make. *Pickwick* was not yet a success. Seymour was famous for his pictures of sporting scenes; the collaboration reflected credit on the author; and if the artist turned rusty it would be very difficult to find an adequate substitute. Dickens would therefore do all that engaging manners and earnest entreaties could effect. But he would not give way. He knew what he wanted, and was determined to get it. There must not be two Richards in the field; and if prayers failed, they would be followed by commands. Seymour, we may be sure, stood upon his dignity and was inclined to be sulky. He probably said very little. To be told by a young upstart, an opinionative journalist, as he doubtless regarded Dickens, that the characters in his design were unsympathetic, and that one of them was 'too repulsive', must have jarred upon him, hurt his self-esteem as a man and wounded his vanity as an artist. The meeting was certainly inharmonious, and closed abruptly. Seymour went home and started a fresh design the following day. But while working on it a sense of grievance, humiliation and frustration must have been welling up within him, for he abandoned his work suddenly, rushed into the garden, and shot himself. It was a tragedy that arose from the nature of things, and the responsibility must rest with the creator of all things.

The publishers were in a quandary. *Pickwick* had been Seymour's idea; they had hoped to sell it on Seymour's name; the sale of the first number had been poor; and now Seymour was dead. It was a bad outlook for a new firm. But the self-assurance and vitality of Dickens gave them courage, and they engaged another artist, Robert Buss, whose plates were not considered satisfactory. There were several applicants for the vacancy, among them two young men named John Leech and William Makepeace Thackeray. Six years later the former illustrated *A Christmas Carol*. Eleven years later the latter was illustrating his own *Vanity Fair*. But Dickens did not consider the work of either suitable for *Pickwick*, and managed to persuade Chapman and Hall that Hablot K. Browne, who as 'Phiz' had just done some plates for a pamphlet by Dickens called 'Sunday Under Three Heads', was the man for the job. He was given it, and no one had cause to regret the appointment. He entered into the very spirit of Dickens's creations, touched the right note of caricature, and to this day it is difficult to visualise a Dickens character except in the form presented by Phiz. When Dickens got rid of Phiz twenty-three years later, he was trying hard to get rid of himself, of the man he had been.

By the autumn of 1836 the name of Pickwick was better known throughout England than the Prime Minister's. The original notion of the book was derived from Pierce Egan's *Life in London* and *Finish*, and even the protagonist's surname was taken from the village where Egan's Fat Knight appears on the scene; but Dickens created a world of his own which owes nothing to any ideas he picked up from others, and it is curious that *Pickwick Papers*, published monthly from March 31st, 1836, to November '37, was a complete failure for the first four months of its existence. Only four hundred copies were printed of Part I, but with the appearance of Samuel Weller in the fifth number the sales began to soar, reaching forty thousand before the completion of the monthly parts. Sam was the making of the book, but most modern readers feel that he comes near to unmaking it. No famous comic character in fiction is less funny, except Touchstone, of whom there is mercifully nothing like so much. For us the greatest creation in the work is Sam's father, Tony Weller, whose description of his wife's death is almost worthy to stand beside Mistress Quickly's description of Falstaff's. But parts of *Pickwick* are unique, and, except for two or three of Walter Scott's novels, it contains the most richly humorous scenes in English fiction. The famous Trial is one of them, and it is interesting to note that where Dickens is most imaginative he is most factual. We have the evidence of Sir Chartres Biron that his understanding of court work was almost uncanny in a layman: 'No author has ever reproduced so surely the atmosphere and feeling of a trial. There is hardly an aspect of the law courts that is not caught and crystallised for ever in the *cause célèbre* of Bardell *v* Pickwick.' Dickens is usually at his best with a minor character who is dismissed in a page or two, and one of the most amusing passages in the book is the introduction of Dowler, whom the Pickwickians meet on their way to Bath and whose wife is to travel with them in the coach:

'She's a fine woman', said Mr. Dowler. 'I am proud of her. I have reason.'

'I hope I shall have the pleasure of judging', said Mr. Pickwick, with a smile.

'You shall', replied Dowler. 'She shall know you. She shall esteem you. I courted her under singular circumstances. I won her through a rash vow. Thus. I saw her; I loved her; I proposed; she refused me.—"You love another?"—"Spare my blushes."—"I know him."—"You do."—"Very good; if he remains here, I'll skin him."'

'Lord bless me!' exclaimed Mr. Pickwick, involuntarily.

'Did you skin the gentleman, sir?' inquired Mr. Winkle, with a very pale face.

'I wrote him a note. I said it was a painful thing. And so it was.'

'Certainly', interposed Mr. Winkle.

'I said I had pledged my word as a gentleman to skin him. My character was at stake. I had no alternative. As an officer in His Majesty's service, I was bound to skin him. I regretted the necessity, but it must be done. He was open to conviction. He saw that the rules of the service were imperative. He fled. I married her. Here's the coach. That's her head.'

Nothing like the furore caused by *Pickwick* had occurred in the history of literature. Those who did not altogether approve of it called the general excitement 'Bozomania'. There were 'Pickwick' hats, coats, canes, cigars. Dogs and cats were called 'Sam', 'Jingle', 'Bardell', 'Trotter'. People were nicknamed 'Tupman', 'Winkle', 'Snodgrass', 'Stiggins'. The 'Fat Boy' went into the language. The moment a monthly part was published, the cheap periodicals of the day printed long extracts from it. The work was pirated, plagiarised and dramatised, and the one person who did not benefit immediately from all this was the author, who wrote to his publishers: 'When you have quite done counting the sovereigns realised for Pickwick, I should be much obliged to you to send me up a few.' At the dinner which was held in November, 1837, to celebrate the completion of the book, it was revealed that there had been no written agreement between author and publishers, everything having been conducted by verbal agreements, but that all concerned had been completely satisfied with the result. As Chapman and Hall had made a net profit of some £20,000, while Dickens had received about £2500, it is doubtful whether the author was as satisfied as the publishers. At any rate Dickens made up his mind that henceforth the satisfaction of the author should be a major consideration, and that the sun of verbal agreements had definitely set.

# 4
## VERBAL DISAGREEMENTS

THE first fruits of Dickens's success were his resignation from
*The Morning Chronicle* and a cottage in the country, Elm Lodge,
Petersham, which he rented furnished for the late summer of
'36. The proprietors of the paper were furious when they
received a month's notice from him; he was indignant over
their failure to recognise the value of his services; and they
parted coldly, or warmly, as the case may be. But as publishers,
editors and theatre managers were falling over one another
in their anxiety to share the spoils of his triumph, he could
afford to take a high line with his old employers. The moment
it became apparent that whatever he wrote would be snapped
up by anyone who could publish it or serialise it or produce
it or do anything else with it, he turned at once to the theatre,
writing a farce in two acts, *The Strange Gentleman*, a comic
opera in two acts, *The Village Coquettes*, and a farce in one act,
*Is She His Wife?*, all of which were produced at the recently-
built St. James's Theatre, the first in September '36, the
second in December '36, the third in March '37. Although
they were quite successful, it is clear that Dickens quickly
tired of the business. If he had been producer and chief actor
as well as author, all would have been well. But to be subjected to the caprices of players, singers and stage-managers,
was more than he could bear. Two actresses did not like the
line 'Well warmed to bed they go', and Cramers, the publishers
of the comic opera, wanted several changes in the text. The
author remonstrated: 'If the young ladies are especially horrified at the bare notion of anybody's going to bed, I have no
objection to substitute for the objectionable line "Around old
stories go". But you may respectfully signify to Cramers that
I will see them damned before I make any further alteration.'
He never liked to hear of these pieces in later life. Only seven
years after their appearance on the stage he said that they had
been done 'without the least consideration or regard to
reputation. I wouldn't repeat them for a thousand pounds
apiece, and devoutly wish them to be forgotten.' And a year
before his death he remarked that if copies of the opera were

in his house, and he could get rid of them in no other way, he would burn the wing of the house that contained them.

His irritation with the actors found additional vent when he heard that Cruikshank had suggested some changes in the text of the second series of *Sketches by Boz*. This time he was on his own ground, and in a letter to John Macrone he let fly: 'I have long believed Cruikshank to be mad, and his letter therefore surprises me not a jot. If you have any further communication with him you will greatly oblige me by saying *from me* that I am very much amused at the notion of his altering my manuscript, and that had it fallen into his hands I should have preserved his emendations as "curiosities of literature". Most decidedly am I of opinion that he may just go to the Devil; and so far as I have any interest in the book, I positively object to his touching it.' If illustrations were needed, he said, Phiz would be the best man for the job.

The fact that Dickens's first choice after making a success was to write for the stage reveals the most important feature of his character, which must now receive our attention: he was a born actor. As on the stage, so in real life, there are two main types of actor: there is the 'straight' actor who is only happy when appearing as himself, and there is the 'character' actor who is only at ease when disguised as someone else. Of performers in real life who concentrated on themselves, building up their own personalities until everything they said or did seemed to be characteristic of them, there were two excellent specimens in the nineteenth century: Benjamin Disraeli and Oscar Wilde. The most perfect example of the other kind, always imagining himself as someone else and constantly projecting his personality into any quantity of seemingly different parts, was Charles Dickens, a David Garrick in real life who might have been another Garrick on the stage and did become a super-Garrick on the platform. It was the great ambition of his early life to be a professional actor, and the great regret of his after-life that he had not been one; but fortunately for us his histrionic genius went into the creation of fictional figures, most of which have a curiously theatrical flavour and are so vividly conceived that if their creator had impersonated half a dozen of them on the stage he would have been the greatest actor of his time. So entirely did he live the characters of his imagination that he never knew how much of his essential

self he put into them, and thus we find bits of him in widely
dissimilar parts which he went out of his way to make comically repulsive, not perceiving that their vitality was his, the
source of his histrionic nature.

The born actor is a man who has all the ordinary human
sensibilities in an exaggerated form and is tortured with the
desire to exhibit them; he laughs more heartily, weeps more
tearfully, reacts more quickly than other people to all forms
of stimuli. In this important respect Dickens was unlike every
other great novelist of the past. One thinks of Fielding or
Smollett or Scott or Thackeray or Hardy or Wells as an actor,
and one instantly dismisses the thought. But Dickens was an
actor through and through. His characters, his comedy, his
sentiment, are of the stage; he had the quick eye for human
oddity, the photographic power of reproducing it and the
love of repeating it, which is possessed by a Garrick or a
Kean; he pours out his emotions as only an actor can; he
describes a storm as a stage-manager would like to produce
it; his villains are melodramatic, his heroes and heroines are
stagey, his scenes are of the theatre; and far more than any
other novels, his have attracted both actors and dramatists.
If he were alive today he would be the king of film writers,
with Hollywood at his feet.

The man was like his work. He was restless, vivacious,
excitable, full of energy and enthusiasm, intensely aware of
everything about him, highly emotional, hilarious, constantly
changing in mood, now gregarious, now disposed to solitude;
he laughed with those who laughed and wept with those who
wept, outdoing both; and he flung himself wholeheartedly
into whatever he did, lost himself utterly in the thrill of
performance, abandoned himself to whatever rôle he was
called upon to play or for which he had cast himself. 'What
a face is his to meet in a drawing-room!' was Leigh Hunt's
first impression. 'It has the life and soul in it of fifty human
beings.' And Carlyle, who saw him at a dinner-party in the
early days of his success, gives us a striking snapshot: 'He is
a fine little fellow, Boz, I think; clear blue intelligent eyes that
he arches amazingly, large, protrusive, rather loose mouth, a
face of the most extreme *mobility*, which he shuttles about—
eyebrows, eyes, mouth and all—in a very singular manner
while speaking. Surmount them with a loose coil of common
coloured hair, and set it on a small compact figure, very small,

and dressed à la D'Orsay rather than well—this is Pickwick. For the rest, a quiet, shrewd-looking little fellow, who seems to guess pretty well what he is and what others are.' It is noteworthy that another contemporary, the famous actor Macready, a touchy and irascible man, found Dickens's society so congenial that he was the only friend with whom he never quarrelled; while the French actor Fechter became one of Dickens's favourite companions towards the close of his life.

Carlyle, a tallish person, exaggerates the littleness and smallness of Dickens; but observers invariably differ on the subject of height, judging it in relation to their own. Napoleon would have thought Wellington tall; John Nicholson would have described both as dwarfs. In *American Notes* Dickens puts his height at five feet nine inches, probably including the heels of his boots. As near as a tall biographer can judge, he was five feet eight inches in his socks, just the right size for a 'character' actor or a man of action. The colour of his eyes, according to one woman, was a very distinct and brilliant hazel, according to another dark blue: the evidence, including Carlyle's, favours blue. His hair was not 'common coloured', but a rich brown; it was luxuriant, wavy, and worn long in the style of the eighteen-thirties. The portrait by Maclise was considered a speaking likeness. His emotions, whether of anger, admiration, pity or pleasure, were instantly registered on his face, in which could be detected an unusual alertness, eagerness, candour and intelligence. In spite of his dandified clothes and an almost effeminately youthful complexion, the general impression he gave was not that of an artist but of a keen, practical man of affairs. There was energy in his movements; his carriage was spirited, his manner brisk and decisive; the firm nose and wide nostrils suggested power; and his features could sometimes look, in Jane Carlyle's phrase, 'as if made of steel.' The mixture of temperamental actor and tough salesman will shortly be apparent in his dealings with publishers.

At the end of 1836 Dickens met his future biographer, John Forster, at the house of Harrison Ainsworth. They took to one another at once, though Forster seems to have been equally surprised and delighted by the celerity with which the impulsive nature of Dickens converted their acquaintanceship into close friendship. To earn the gratitude or affection of some men, it is necessary to seek their advice or ask favours of them, and Dickens gained Forster's love and esteem by doing both frequently. It happened that, owing to Dickens's extraordinary success at the age of twenty-four and his eagerness to make the most of it, the help and advice of a prudent man were essential to him. The friendship of Forster was exactly what he needed, and his friendship was exactly what Forster needed. In the exuberance engendered by his rapidly growing fame and expanding powers Dickens was planning as many works as he was capable of conceiving, and making arrangements for their publication before a word of them was written. One has the impression that he would have liked to provide every publisher in London with a book and sign as many contracts blindfold as they cared to push under his nose. From the early days of their friendship Forster took his affairs in hand, beginning with Macrone.

In May 1836, with the fortune of *Pickwick* still in the balance, Dickens had entered into an agreement with John Macrone to write a novel called *Gabriel Vardon*, for the first edition of which he would receive £200 on delivery of the manuscript at the end of November. In August of the same year, when Sam Weller had turned the scales in favour of *Pickwick*, Dickens had arranged with another publisher named Richard Bentley to write two novels for £1000. On November 1st he wrote to his *Pickwick* publishers in a mood of thankfulness, friendliness and jocosity: 'I hereby nominate and appoint William Hall and Edward Chapman of No. 186 Strand, their heirs, executors, administrators, and assigns, my periodical publishers, until I am advertised in the daily papers as having been compressed into my last edition—one volume, boards, with brass plates.' Three days later he accepted an offer to edit Richard Bentley's magazine at £20 a month, starting the following January, and to supply a serial story for it. The story was *Oliver Twist*, which began in the February number of *Bentley's Miscellany* and continued until March, '39. Seated in his editorial chair, it occurred to him that so many agreements were bound to end in disagreements; so he took steps to cancel the first. For the sum of £100 he gave Macrone the full copyright of both series of *Sketches by Boz*, and the contract to write *Gabriel Vardon* was cancelled. But Macrone was not a publisher for nothing. With the *Pickwick* craze at its height, two old books by Boz in print were worth more than a new one in the author's brain, and he decided to reissue all the *Sketches* in monthly parts, got up to look as much like the monthly parts of *Pickwick* as possible.

The moment he heard of Macrone's intention Dickens dashed off a letter to Forster: 'I have a very natural and most decided objection to being supposed to presume upon the success of the Pickwick, and thus foist this old work upon the public in its new dress for the mere purpose of putting money in my own pocket.' Macrone had already made 'very great profits' out of the *Sketches*, and had never mentioned, when the copyright was made over to him, that he intended to reproduce them in this form. Two periodical publications by Dickens were then appearing, *Pickwick Papers* in monthly numbers and *Oliver Twist* in Bentley's paper, and a third publication of the same nature would prove seriously prejudicial to his reputation. Having worked himself up into a state of indignation, he then wrote a passage which the cautious Forster was careful to omit from his biography of Dickens: 'I feel it necessary to add—not as a hasty threat, but as my deliberate and well-considered determination—that if this new issue does appear, I shall advertise in all the newspapers that it does so, not only without my sanction, but in opposition to my express request; that it is of no advantage, whatsoever, to me; and that I most earnestly and emphatically entreat all my friends and supporters to abstain from purchasing it. Wherever he advertises the work, I will advertise this statement.' He ended by saying that in case Macrone's preparations had already involved him in great expense, Chapman and Hall were prepared to buy the copyrights.

Backed by these complaints and threats, and fortified by this proposal, Forster called on Macrone, who quite naturally took the view that he could do what he liked with his own property. To Forster's suggestion that the copyright of the *Sketches* might be repurchased in order to prevent their monthly issue, Macrone replied that the author could have them for a trifle over £2000. Forster retired, shocked by the avarice of publishers, and advised Dickens to do nothing. But doing nothing where his interests were involved was not a characteristic of Dickens, who placed the matter at once in the hands of Chapman and Hall. At the interview which followed between themselves and Macrone, they were compelled to agree that £2250 for the repurchase of the copyrights was not excessive: the bargain was struck, and it was arranged that the *Sketches* should be reissued by Chapman and Hall in monthly parts, such being the only way in which the cost of repurchase could be covered and a profit made. Thus Dickens's main objection to Macrone's action was forgotten in the excitement of the transaction. One sees his point, of course. If an old work is to be foisted on the public for the purpose of putting money into somebody's pocket, a certain amount of it should be allowed to trickle into the author's, even when he is opposed to the process on principle. But Dickens's attitude is largely explained by the liberties which were being taken with his work in every direction. *Pickwick* was being imitated, parodied and adapted, in books, in the press and on the stage, with a whole-hearted enthusiasm which may have flattered him but which certainly riled him. And though he had no reasonable case against Macrone, the universal piracy of which he was the victim induced in him a frame of mind which converted a perfectly rational action into a predatory plot. A man of strong and quickly generated emotions, his compassion was as easily aroused as his passion, and when Macrone died some two years later, leaving a widow and children in poverty, Dickens raised about £300 for them by editing and contributing to a collection of tales and essays, the sale of which was greatly helped by his title: *The Pic-Nic Papers*.

Sometimes his emotions were uncontrollable, never more so than over an event in his early married life which affected him more than anything that had gone before, except perhaps his frustrated adoration of Maria Beadnell. The result of this later experience was manifested in one of his books, which choked his age with sobs and was largely responsible for making him the most loved and popular author in the English language.

In the autumn of 1836 Kate Dickens's sister Mary, a girl of sixteen, went to live with them in Furnivals Inn. Dickens, flushed with success, was rapidly extending his circle of friends, which now included the well-known painters, Daniel Maclise and Clarkson Stanfield, the most famous actor of the day, William Macready, a leading barrister, T. N. Talfourd, two front-rank critics, William Jerdan and John Forster, and a notable editor, Leigh Hunt. He was dining out a lot, and sometimes rather too well: 'I arrived home at one o'clock this morning dead drunk, and was put to bed by my loving missis', he wrote to a friend. Their first child, a boy, was born on January 6th '37. Kate's health gave him some anxiety following this event, and they stayed for a while in the lodgings at Chalk where they had spent their honeymoon. Overwork and overworry brought on a violent pain in his head, when he was 'immediately ordered as much medicine as would confine an ordinary-sized horse to his stall for a week.' *Bentley's Miscellany* was an instant success, and he became a member of the Garrick Club on the proposal of his publisher. What with two serials, occasional articles, and a dozen other things to keep him busy, he was beginning to feel the strain. 'I cannot do more than one pair of hands and a solitary head can execute', he complained to Cruikshank. Yet he found time to go househunting with Mary, and at the beginning of April '37 Dickens, his wife, child, brother, and sister-in-law, moved into No. 48 Doughty Street, which was to be the home of Charles and Kate for nearly three years.

Always more inclined to love what was beyond his reach than what was within it, Dickens formed an attachment to Mary which, though he would not have admitted it at the time, went much deeper than the feeling he had for his wife. She was pretty, amusing, sympathetic and intelligent. Obviously she thought him the most wonderful person in the world, and his writings the most marvellous productions in existence. He was extremely susceptible to such hero-worship; and as the nature of their relationship set a curb on desire, he began to idealise her as a saint. This suited his disposition, for it was his idea of perfection to enjoy a completely harmonious affinity with a woman devoted exclusively to his interests. While his wife was preoccupied with domestic responsibilities he took Mary all over the place, to receptions, to the houses of friends, to picture exhibitions, to the theatre. It was the happiest period of his life: he revelled in the applause of the world and basked in the admiration of Mary. But the period was as brief as it was happy. On Saturday evening, May 6th, only five weeks after they had taken possession of their new home, Kate and Mary went with Dickens to a performance at the St. James's Theatre. After spending a happy evening, Mary retired to bed at one o'clock 'in perfect health and her usual delightful spirits.' But before she had undressed she was taken ill. A doctor was instantly

MARY HOGARTH

*Painting by*
' PHIZ '
(HABLOT K. BROWNE)

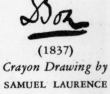

(1837)
*Crayon Drawing by*
SAMUEL LAURENCE

*By courtesy of*
*Lord Glenconner*

GEORGINA HOGARTH
(c. 1850)
*Painting by*
AUGUSTUS EGG, R.A.

GEORGINA HOGARTH
(c. 1912)
*Photograph by*
C. G. BERESFORD

sent for; his services were unavailing; and she died of heart-disease the following afternoon. 'Thank God she died in my arms', wrote Dickens, 'and the very last words she whispered were of me.'

The shock was terrible, and it was fortunate for him that his immediate responsibilities kept him from brooding. His mother-in-law, Mrs. Hogarth, fainted, remained insensible for the next twenty-four hours, and practically incapable of motion for a week, during which Kate had to console her, leaving Charles to write the letters and make the arrangements necessary on such occasions. 'You cannot conceive the misery in which this dreadful event has plunged us', he told a relation. 'Since our marriage she has been the peace and life of our home—the admired of all for her beauty and excellence—I could have better spared a much nearer relation or an older friend, for she has been to us what we can never replace, and has left a blank which no one who ever knew her can have the faintest hope of seeing supplied.' In letter after letter he spoke of her with the repetitiveness of one who is nearly numb with grief: she was 'the light and life of our happy circle', 'the grace and ornament of our home', 'the grace and life of our home', and he saw her then as the girl who would one day be known to the world as Little Nell in *The Old Curiosity Shop*: 'I solemnly believe that so perfect a creature never breathed. I knew her inmost heart, and her real worth and values. She had not a fault.'

Unable to concentrate on his work, he dropped *Pickwick* and *Oliver Twist*, neither of which appeared that month, and the readers of Bentley's paper were told that he was mourning the death 'of a very dear young relative to whom he was most affectionately attached and whose society has been for a long time the chief solace of his labours.' After the funeral they went to Collins's Farm, Hampstead, whence he wrote to Harrison Ainsworth: 'I have been so much unnerved and hurt by the loss of the dear girl whom I loved, after my wife, more deeply and fervently than anyone on earth, that I have been compelled for once to give up all idea of my monthly work and to try a fortnight's rest and quiet.' Ainsworth called one Sunday morning, but found that he had gone to church. Forster stayed with them, and Maclise went there to comfort him. All things considered, his wife must have been a very sweet-natured woman to have won these tributes from him

4

at such a time: 'She has borne up through her severe trial like what she is—a fine-hearted noble-minded girl.' 'She knows that if ever a mortal went to heaven, her sister is there. She has nothing to remember but a long course of affection and attachment, perhaps never exceeded. Not one cross word or angry look on either side even as children rests in judgment against her, and she is now so calm and cheerful that I wonder to see her.' The shock of her sister's death brought on a miscarriage, but that would have been the least of her troubles.

For a long time Dickens was haunted by the memory of Mary. When he visited the St. James's Theatre he would not sit on the same tier as that in which they had occupied a box on the evening before her death, nor would he sit in any part of the house where that particular box was visible. In describing Rose Maylie in *Oliver Twist* he could not help picturing Mary as his fancy liked to paint her: 'She was not past seventeen. Cast in so slight and exquisite a mould; so mild and gentle; so pure and beautiful; that earth seemed not to be her element, nor its rough creatures her fit companions. The very intelligence that shone in her deep blue eye, and was stamped upon her noble head, seemed scarcely of her age, or of the world; and yet the changing expression of sweetness and good humour, the thousand lights that played about the face, and left no shadow there; above all, the smile, the cheerful, happy smile, were made for Home, and fireside peace and happiness.' His own desire to join her in death is expressed in the same book: 'Gradually, he fell into that deep tranquil sleep which ease from recent suffering alone imparts; that calm and peaceful rest which it is pain to wake from. Who, if this were death, would be roused again to all the struggles and turmoils of life; to all its cares for the present; its anxieties for the future; more than all, its weary recollections of the past!'

Six months after the tragedy he wrote to her mother: 'I have never had her ring off my finger by day or night, except for an instant at a time, to wash my hands, since she died. I have never had her sweetness and excellence absent from my mind so long. I can solemnly say that, waking or sleeping, I have never lost the recollection of our hard trial and sorrow, and I feel that I never shall . . . I wish you could know how I weary now for the three rooms in Furnivals Inn, and how I miss that pleasant smile and those sweet words which, bestowed upon our evening's work, in our merry banterings round the fire, were more precious to me than the applause of a whole world would be. I can recall everything she said and did in those happy days, and could show you every passage and line we read together.' In his diary on January 1st, 1838 he noted: 'A sad New Year's day . . . if she were with us now, the same winning, happy, amiable companion, sympathising with all my thoughts and feelings more than anyone I knew ever did or will, I think I should have nothing to wish for but a continuance of such happiness.' And five days later: 'I shall never be so happy again as in those chambers three storeys high—never if I roll in wealth and fame. I would hire them to keep empty, if I could afford it.' She appeared continually in his dreams, and when he visited Yorkshire in February '38 he wrote to tell his wife 'I have dreamt of her ever since I left home, and no doubt shall till I return.' Even as late as October '41, though he had cleansed his bosom of Little Nell in the interval, he confided in Forster: 'The desire to be buried next her is as strong upon me now, as it was five years ago; and I *know* (for I don't think there ever was love like that I bear her) that it will never diminish.'

Most people tend to over-indulge their grief when losing those who are dear to them, and if Dickens's grief seems excessive we must recognise what it must have meant to one of his needful nature and histrionic temperament to lose the only person who had ever wholly sympathised with his joys, aspirations and moods. At the same time we cannot overlook the effect of his too articulate emotions on his wife, who was probably made to feel that Mary had meant much more to him than herself, an effect which neither time nor Dickens did much to mitigate.

After their fortnight's 'rest and quiet' at Collins's Farm, Dickens and his wife returned to Doughty Street, where he immediately plunged into work with his accustomed impetuosity, varying it with bursts of recreation which would have exhausted less dynamic constitutions. Either alone or with Forster or Maclise or Ainsworth he walked at a steady rate of four miles an hour over Hampstead Heath, often dining at Jack Straw's Castle. Sometimes they went on foot as far north as Finchley, as far west as Barnes, as far east as Greenwich. Or they took horses and rode to Richmond, Twickenham, Barnet, Hampton Court, Epping. There were

no pauses except for dinner. Once started, Dickens kep
them going with no lessening of the pace until their destina
tion was reached, and he always insisted on punctuality at the
outset. Early in July he took his wife for their first trip
abroad. Hablot K. Browne went with them, and they drove
about Belgium in a postchaise, seeing 'Ghent, Brussels
Antwerp, and a hundred other places, that I cannot recollec
now and couldn't spell if I did.' Home again he struggled
with *Pickwick* and *Oliver*, writing to Forster: 'If you know
anybody at St. Paul's, I wish you'd send round and ask then
not to ring the bell so. I can hardly hear my own ideas a
they come into my head, and say what they mean.' In Sep
tember the family went to Broadstairs, where they were often
to stay in the years to come and which became popular because
Dickens liked it.

We have a picture of the family on their first visit to the
place by Eleanor Christian, who was then a girl. Dickens'
parents and brother were staying with him, and Eleanor tell
us that Mrs. John Dickens was a sensible woman with a worn
deeply-lined face, while John Dickens was a plump, well
dressed person rather addicted to fine sentiments and elaborate
sentences. Mrs. John liked dancing; and though Charles dic
not care to see his mother indulging in so frolicsome a pastime
he occasionally danced with her. John Dickens confessed
himself an optimist: he was like a cork, he said; if pushed
under the water in one place, he always bobbed up cheerfully
in another, feeling none the worse for the dip. The family
did not seem quite at ease with Charles, whose moods were
variable, now genial and gay, now preoccupied and morose
He pretended to flirt with Eleanor, calling her 'Queen of my
heart', 'Fair enslaver', 'Beloved of my soul', and asking her
to dance with him in a style of humour then in fashion: 'Wil
tread a measure with me, sweet lady? Fain would I thread the
mazes of this saraband with thee.' But when one morning
she wanted him to read a book by her father, a Scottish
author, he turned abruptly away with the remark 'I hate
Scotch stories, and everything else Scotch.' His wife, who
was equally involved, flushed, laughed nervously, but
reassured Eleanor: 'Don't mind him; he doesn't mean it.'

Sometimes his high spirits went beyond the limits of good-
natured fun, and the actor, who was soon to appear as Quilp
in one of his novels, took control. When Eleanor was walking

with him on the little pier one night, he suddenly seized her, rushed her to the far end of it, put one arm round a tall post, held her tightly with the other, and declared that he would keep her there till 'the sad sea waves' submerged them. 'Think of the sensation we shall create!' he cried. 'Think of the road to celebrity which you are about to tread! No, not exactly to tread, but to flounder into!' She fought to free herself but his grip did not slacken. 'Let your mind dwell on the column in *The Times*', he went on, 'wherein will be vividly described the pathetic fate of the lovely E.C., drowned by Dickens in a fit of dementia! Don't struggle, poor little bird; you are powerless in the claws of such a kite as this child.'

'My dress, my best dress, my *only* silk dress will be ruined!' she shrieked, calling upon Mrs. Dickens to come to her aid, as the waves were already up to her knees.

'Charles! how can you be so silly?' was all Mrs. Dickens could say. 'You will both be carried off by the tide, and you'll spoil the poor girl's silk dress.'

'Dress!' exclaimed Charles theatrically. 'Talk not to me of *dress*! When the pall of night is enshrouding us in Cimmerian darkness, when we already stand on the brink of the great mystery, shall our thoughts be of fleshly vanities? Am I not immolating a brand-new pair of patent leathers still unpaid for? Perish such low-born thoughts! In this hour of abandonment to the voice of destiny, shall we be held back by the puerilities of silken raiment? Shall leather or prunella (whatever that may be) stop the bolt of Fate?'

At last she contrived to get away, but she was soaked through and had to change. Twice again he ran her down the promontory where the waves came breaking over, and two of her bonnets were ruined. Once they all drove over to Pegwell Bay, and he, again in Quilpish mood, sang vulgar songs on the journey. That his holiday moods were not continuously serene is shown in a letter to Forster about a man who had been responsible for one of the many piracies of his work: 'Well, if the Pickwick has been the means of putting a few shillings in the vermin-eaten pockets of so miserable a creature, and has saved him from a workhouse or a jail, let him empty out his little pot of filth and welcome. I am quite content to have been the means of relieving him.' But contentment is not the animating note of this passage.

At the end of October '37 they went to Brighton for the first time, where they put up at the Old Ship and experienced one of those seasons of rough weather which are almost as enjoyable as the sunshine in that most beautiful and exhilarating of seaside towns. 'On Wednesday it blew a perfect hurricane, breaking windows, knocking down shutters, carrying people off their legs, blowing the fires out, and causing universal consternation. The air was for some hours darkened with a shower of black hats (second-hand) which are supposed to have been blown off the heads of unwary passengers in remote parts of the town, and have been industriously picked up by the fishermen. Charles Kean was advertised for Othello . . . I have not heard whether he got to the theatre, but I am sure nobody else did.'

On his return to London he added to his labours by editing the *Memoirs of Grimaldi* for Bentley. This was hack-work, for which he wrote a preface, dictating to his father a number of additions and emendations to a mass of material which he described as 'twaddle.' It sold well, on the strength of his name, but he attached no importance to it. He did the job because he was momentarily pleased with Bentley. But as this friendly concord was soon to be converted into frenzied discord, the story of their relationship must now be unfolded. As usual with cases of strife between individuals, there is much to be said in favour of each combatant, and plenty to be said against both of them.

We have seen that Dickens agreed to edit *Bentley's Miscellany* for £20 a month in November '36. This was raised to £30 a month the following March, and Dickens expressed his satisfaction. He also agreed in August '36 to write two novels for Bentley, the sum for both being £1000. The magazine was successful; and as the serialisation of *Oliver Twist* in it had set the seal on Dickens's popularity as an author, he became conscious of the fact that the contract was one-sided and that Bentley would do too well out of it, while he would not do well enough. The thought of having to write two novels on terms which had been reasonable before his success became phenomenal irritated him, and in July '37 he wrote to ask Bentley, who had expressed an anxious desire to treat him liberally, to make a different agreement more in accord with 'my very different situation, and the increased popularity of my works.' Bentley, to gain time, suggested a conference.

Dickens, not to lose time, stated his requirements by letter: £600 for 3,000 copies of *Barnaby Rudge*, (originally called *Gabriel Vardon*), and £700 for 3,000 copies of *Oliver Twist* when published as a book. They met in August, and Bentley did the one thing most calculated to annoy Dickens, telling him that their original contract was binding, that having already bought the entire copyright of the two novels he would not consent to take a limited interest in them, but that he was willing to *present* Dickens with the additional sums he demanded. In other words, he made a favour of handing Dickens an extra £300 for the two novels, but insisted on retaining the copyrights whereby he could go on selling them in any form he liked to his own inestimable advantage. Naturally Dickens 'exhibited considerable irritability, threatening amongst other intemperate expressions that he would not write the novel at all.'[1] Arbitrators were proposed, but Dickens was in the sort of mood that can only tolerate one arbiter, and he informed Bentley that 'any direct communication between us would henceforth be most unpleasant to me and repugnant to my feelings.' Bentley consulted his friends, who advised him to stand firm. But in September, Dickens having sent in his resignation from the *Miscellany*, Bentley drew up a new contract more favourable to his editor, and also consented to pay £750 for each of the novels. Peace was restored; Dickens edited the Grimaldi memoirs; and then came a fresh commitment.

In order to recover a share in the copyright of *Pickwick*, and in return for Chapman and Hall's assistance over the Macrone business, Dickens agreed at the end of '37 to write another novel for that firm, for which the monthly numbers would bring him £3,000, the publishers to retain the copyright for five years, after which it would revert to him. This novel, *Nicholas Nickleby*, began to come out in April '38, closing its career in October '39, and appeared simultaneously with the later portions of *Oliver Twist*. Little wonder, then, that in January '39 the intense pressure of his work, coupled with the knowledge that it was earning enormous profits for Bentley and a relative pittance for himself, produced another explosion from the harassed author, driven almost crazy by the intense concentration necessary to keep two novels up to

[1] See an article on Dickens and Bentley by David A. Randall in *The Times Literary Supplement*, October 12th, 1946.

standard month after month. He resigned the editorship o
*Bentley's Miscellany*, and Harrison Ainsworth stepped into hi
place.

Incidentally, Ainsworth played a rather sinister part i
Dickens's troubles with Macrone and Bentley. He wa
friendly with all three, yet he advised Macrone 'in the stricter
confidence' to place the matter between Dickens and himsel
in the hands of his solicitors, to hold Dickens to his contract
and to take legal action against him if he tried to back out
Also there is very little doubt that Ainsworth advised Bentley
how to deal with Dickens, all the time keeping up an appear
ance of great friendship and sympathy with his fellow-author
When Dickens retired from *Bentley's Miscellany* a rumou
spread that Forster's interference had caused the breach
between publisher and editor, and apparently Ainsworth
propagated this rumour, because Dickens wrote him a very
strong letter demanding his instant contradiction of it. Bu
Dickens never knew that Ainsworth had acted shabbily
during his quarrels with publishers, and they remained or
friendly terms for many years.

Hostilities between Bentley and Dickens were temporarily
suspended when the former offered better terms for the
novels, but broke out afresh when Bentley again began to ge
on Dickens's nerves. In June '40 Chapman and Hall once
more came to the rescue with £2,250, for which Bentley sold
his rights in *Oliver Twist* and surrendered his right to *Barnaby
Rudge*, the purchase money to be repaid by the author out of
the sum he would make on *Barnaby*.

In this conflict between author and publisher people have
tended to take sides. But one can only blame Dickens for
not being Bentley, and Bentley for not being Dickens. Each
behaved according to his light, and the lights were in opposition. Bentley on legal grounds was wholly justified; Dickens
on human grounds was equally justified; but each would have
had to shift his ground in order to see the other's point of
view. On the general subject of contracts a word must be
said. According to Bernard Shaw, who had more business
sense than any publisher or author of his age, a good contract
is one that is good for both parties. When it becomes bad
for one of the parties, it should be redrafted to make it fair
for both, if for no other reason because people will not give
of their best when suffering from a sense of grievance. No

contract should be considered as permanently binding, and sensible publishers recognise this. Most authors are solely concerned with the writing of books. Few of them have the patience to read a contract, let alone understand it, their interest in it being confined to the payment of a lump sum, preferably in advance. It is however the concern of publishers to prepare and understand contracts, and they would be saints, not business men, if they considered the author's interest as much as their own.

In the early part of his life Dickens found that the publishers were amassing wealth out of his creative energy, while he was making 'little more than a genteel subsistence', and, quite rightly, refused to be bound by contracts which ensured such a state of things. The fact that he had signed them meant nothing: in those early needy years he would have signed anything that promised a reasonable advance on previous agreements. Had the publishers cared to insist on the original terms of their contracts, they could have done so; but they recognised that his popularity gave him the upper hand, and having already done extremely well out of him they succumbed, at a handsome profit to themselves. Dickens, suffering from the strain of overwork and exasperated by the knowledge 'that my books are enriching everybody connected with them but myself', assured Forster that 'morally, before God and man, I hold myself released from such hard bargains as these.' In such a frame of mind he charged Bentley with sundry other misdemeanours, all of which Bentley described as false; but whether true or false, they were merely the sort of things that people always bring up against those with whom they quarrel, and had nothing to do with the point at issue. Bentley wrote on the letter containing these charges: 'Dickens was a very clever, but he was not an honest man.' The obvious comment is that Dickens, in his relations with Bentley, was neither clever nor dishonest. Had he been clever he would have handled Bentley with care. Had he been dishonest he would have been less impulsive, less inclined to let personal antipathy influence business negotiations.

Every new contract for Dickens which Bentley drew up was not the result of a spontaneous desire on his part to be fair to the man who was making him a fortune, but the outcome of much quibbling and vexatious discussion; and it is clear that Dickens began to dislike him from the moment in July '37 when a handsome gesture on the publisher's part would have mollified the author. True, Bentley had the law on his side, but there was something niggardly and grasping about him, for Dickens was not the only person who had cause for complaint. He drove hard bargains with writers, and Charles Reade brought an action against him which revealed the unfairness of the profit-sharing contract (still used by unscrupulous publishers) and helped towards the institution of the royalty system. 'I neither require nor expect any sympathy from the class (of which I am one) whose pens are their support', wrote Dickens. 'But I am resolved at whatever sacrifice of peace or pocket to show this fellow that he cannot count on always doing as he pleases with them.'[1] It does not therefore surprise us to learn from Hans Andersen, who stayed with Bentley at Sevenoaks in 1847, that the publisher had a fine country-house and lived elegantly, even keeping silk-stockinged footmen to wait upon his guests. 'There's a bookseller!' said Hans. Silk-stockinged footmen were not a feature of Dickens's home, and it was many years before he could afford a country-house. Meanwhile, he had to fight the publishers, and it is hardly necessary to say that Chapman and Hall were next on the list.

[1] From an unpublished letter quoted by Dame Una Pope-Hennessy in *The Times Literary Supplement*, November 2nd, 1946.

# THE MOGUL

N all the negotiations just recorded Dickens was greatly
helped by his new friend Forster, to whom he wrote about
six months after their first meeting: 'It shall go hard, I hope,
ere anything but Death impairs the toughness of a bond so
firmly riveted.' But another four months went by, and a hint
appeared in a letter from Dickens to Ainsworth that a rivet
or two might get loose in the years ahead: 'Our worthy friend
the Mogul has been very unwell for some days and has worn
a dark and gloomy appearance in consequence . . . He has
been in a very blaspheming and foaming condition . . . but
he has now greatly softened down—quite reasonable in fact.'
Let us take a close look at the man whose friendship meant
more to Dickens than that of anyone else for the next twenty
years, and who became his biographer and the executor of
his will.

John Forster was born at Newcastle-on-Tyne two months
after the birth of Dickens, on April 2nd, 1812. His father was
a cattle-dealer, though people who were on bad terms with
John called him the son of a butcher. Forster described his
mother as 'a gem of a woman', but the phrase is not pictorially
helpful and merely suggests that he was a spoilt boy. An
uncle provided the money for his education, first at a private
school, then at University College, London, and he became
a law student at the Inner Temple in November '28. He was
resolved to get on in the world, and soon managed to
ingratiate himself with Leigh Hunt and Charles Lamb. At
the age of twenty he became dramatic critic to a newspaper;
a year later he was writing regularly for three more; and
before another twelve months were out he had become chief
critic of literature and drama on a leading journal, *The
Examiner*, and had moved into what must have been the
most impressive chambers ever occupied by a youthful
journalist, at 58 Lincoln's Inn Fields. In the years to come he
edited several important periodicals, including *The Examiner*,
wrote *Lives of the Statesmen of the Commonwealth* in five volumes,
as well as Lives of Goldsmith and Landor, and obtained a

government sinecure as Lunacy Commissioner at £1500 a year, his method of securing which throws some light on his character. 'I never let old Brougham go', he informed a friend. 'I came back again and again until I wore him out. I forced 'em to give me this.'

By the age of twenty-five Forster knew pretty well everyone of note in the artistic world, an extraordinary achievement which reveals a man who was not only determined to push his way to the top but to adopt any means of getting there. He was also quite prepared to jettison those who had once been of use to him but whose services he no longer required. His success in making friends with important people was due to the assiduity of his attentions, the pains he took to serve them, the ardency with which he championed them, and the value of his position as a leading critic. But his resolution soared to a higher pitch. Having so to speak bagged the world of art, Thackeray declaring that 'whenever anybody is in a scrape we all fly to him for refuge—he is omniscient and works miracles', Forster went in search of tastier game, and managed to net several prominent aristocrats and leading politicians. The success attending his pursuit of Count D'Orsay and Lady Blessington went to his head, though the acquisition of Palmerston and Gladstone called for greater strategical skill. He was perhaps seen at his best with peers of the realm. Then he purred; his voice became mellifluous; and turning to the company he would impart sinaic pronouncements: 'His lordship has been saying with much force . . .' Inattention to the needs of titled persons deeply distressed him, and once, when D'Orsay was dining with him, he was heard above the general din of conversation shouting to his servant 'Good heavens, sir! butter for the Count's flounders.'

The Forster, however, whom we are to know is the man who got drunk, pretty frequently, in bohemian circles, and whose loud voice, rhinoceros laugh and dictatorial manner, once he had become accepted as a person of distinction, made him both liked and disliked by writers, painters and actors; liked because he could be genial, sympathetic and helpful, disliked because he could be rude, sycophantic and obstructive. Physically, he was short and burly, with a square head, broad face and pugnacious jaw. The stern features, authoritative voice, and stocky frame tightly buttoned up in a short frock-coat, gave him a certain dignity, and the monocle, which he mostly played with, could produce an awesome effect when put to its proper use. The first impression he gave was that of an extremely assertive, overbearing and independent man, who would stand no nonsense from anyone and whose opinions on every subject were infallibly right. But according to Carlyle he abandoned his views as readily as he threw over friends who were no longer useful: 'If he gets hold of any opinion that he comes to believe, he makes all manner of noise and vehement clatter about it and forwards it by any means he can devise; but if it falls into disrepute, and other people desert it, he just leaves it there and seeks out some other fancy to fondle in place of it.' When he did not like what others were saying he shouted them down, using such expressions as 'In*tol*-er-able!' 'Monstrous!' 'Incredible!' 'All stuff!' 'Don't tell me!', sometimes adding less printable phrases and rounding them off with a scornful laugh which drowned opposition. Disagreement infuriated him, and he could be grossly offensive when his blustering style and stentorian voice roused people to hostility. Trifling annoyances enraged him and set him, said Dickens, 'smoking all over his head, and fuming himself like a steamboat ready to start.' Like many over-sensitive people he was often completely insensitive to the feelings of others, and quarrelled sooner or later with nearly every friend he had so tirelessly cultivated.

His jealousy in friendship was a constant source of friction. Having seized on someone he wished to know, someone important or about to become so, he managed to create an intimate relationship in about ten days which no one else could have formed in much under ten years. From the moment a friendship was cemented the friend became his property, and he went about puffing the man's poems or personality; but if anyone else showed an equal enthusiasm or the least disposition to poach on his preserves, to compete with him in the other's intimacy and esteem, there were black looks, scenes, reproaches, explosions. He chose Robert Browning as one of his soul's companions and for a while they were inseparable, Forster singing the praises of this new wonder-poet until Browning must have fancied that his real name was Shakespeare. But when he had grappled the author of *Paracelsus* to his soul with hoops of steel, interested Macready in his friend's dramas and hallooed Robert's name to the reverberate hills, other people began to be almost as vociferous, and trouble started. Dickens, for example, wrote an unqualified eulogy of Browning's *Blot on the 'Scutcheon*, the manuscript of which Forster had privately shown him. Praise from such a quarter would have meant much to the author, but Forster kept it to himself and Browning did not know of it until after Dickens's death. The hoops of steel began to bend and then to break. Having staked his claim, Forster felt that he could treat the poet as he liked, enraging him to such a degree at dinner one day that Browning seized a decanter and was only prevented by another guest from hurling it at his patron's head. At last the soul's companion grew tired of having Forster's shoes wiped on him, as he put it, and they ceased to communicate, even refusing to recognise one another when they met in Macready's dressing-room at the theatre, by which time Forster was exasperated by the knowledge that Browning knew more titled people than he did.

There can be little doubt that Forster derived pleasure from hurting his friends. When Edward Bulwer (afterwards Lord Lytton) wrote several anonymous and stinging verses on Tennyson, the latter retaliated with some pungent lines which he sent to Forster for publication and in which he described Bulwer as 'the padded man that wears the stays', half of whose 'little soul is dirt.' He regretted them almost at once and asked Forster not to have them printed. But Forster, an intimate friend of Bulwer's, assured Tennyson that justice was more dear to him than friendship, that though Bulwer had denied the authorship of the original attack he did not believe him, and that he would like to publish the reply. Tennyson gave way, and his verses appeared in *Punch*. This see-saw treatment of his friends made those of them who found him out distrustful of Forster, and in self-defence he feigned an indirect and circumlocutionary method of speech, throwing out a cloud of words to hide facts, which enabled him to sneak out of awkward situations, but which left its mark on his prose style and its effect on his honesty as a biographer. To summarise that side of his nature which has already been sketched, we cannot do better than read two entries in Macready's diary for 1840:

'August 16. Went to dine with Dickens, and was witness to a most painful scene after dinner. Forster, Maclise and myself were the guests. Forster got on to one of his headlong streams of talk (which he thinks argument) and waxed warm, and at last some sharp observations led to personal retorts between him and Dickens. He displayed his usual want of tact, and Dickens flew into so violent a passion as quite to forget himself and give Forster to understand that he was in his house, which he should be glad if he would leave. Forster behaved very foolishly. I stopped him; spoke to both of them and observed that for an angry instant they were about to destroy a friendship valuable to both. I drew from Dickens the admission that he had spoken in passion and would not have said what he said, could he have reflected; but he added he could not answer for his temper under Forster's provocations, and that he should do just the same again. Forster behaved very *weakly*; would not accept the repeated acknowledgment communicated to him that Dickens regretted the passion, etc., but stayed, skimbling-skambling a parcel of unmeaning words, and at last finding he could obtain no more, made a sort of speech, accepting what he had before declined. He was silent and not recovered—no wonder!—during the whole evening. Mrs. Dickens had gone out in tears. It was a very painful scene.

'August 20 . . . Called on Dickens . . . We talked about Forster, and he made the same remark on him that Edward (Bulwer) had done: that he assumed a supercilious tone before people to give the idea that he was the patron, or *padrone*. How little and how silly!'

On the day following the scene which occurred on August 16th, Dickens wrote to Macready: 'What can I say to you about last night! Frankly, nothing. Nothing can enhance the estimation in which I hold you, or the affectionate and sincere attachment I bear towards you, my dear friend—and not even your manly and generous interposition can make me eloquent upon a subject on which I feel so deeply and singly. I am very much grieved, and yet I am not penitent and cannot be, reason with myself as I will. With all the regard I have for Forster, and with all the close friendship between us, I cannot close my eyes to the fact that we do not quarrel with other men; and the more I think of it, the more I feel confident in the belief that there is no man, alive or dead, who tries his friends as he does. I declare to you solemnly, that when I think of his manner (far worse than his matter) I turn burning hot and am ashamed and in a manner degraded to have been the subject of it. I have found the soul of goodness in this evil thing at all events, and when I think of all you said and did, I would not recall (if I had the power) one atom of my passion and intemperance . . .'

Those were early days in their friendship, and Dickens could not predict the quarrels that Forster would have 'with other men', one of whom, Harrison Ainsworth, had already broken with his former champion. Forster had a pretty shrewd eye for what was going to be successful, and foresaw that Dickens's popularity would easily eclipse Ainsworth's. When therefore the sales of the latter's work *Jack Sheppard* soared beyond those of *Oliver Twist* he was furious, attacked Ainsworth's story as immoral, backed Dickens as the ultimate winner, and sacrificed one friendship for another more valuable. Even his single romance was governed by like considerations. He was engaged to be married to the poet and novelist (or, more accurately, versifier and fictioniser) Letitia Landon, known to her generation as L.E.L., whose chief attraction for him, being ten years his senior, was her position as a writer. When it was rumoured that she was having an affair with a married man, William Maginn, and her social reputation began to suffer, Forster seized the excuse to break off the engagement. His sensitiveness to his own feelings was so tender that when he quarrelled with people he expected his friends to cut them too, and he felt aggrieved if a friend did not write to him at regular intervals, in which respect Tennyson told him that he was morbid. All of which implies that he was not very sure of himself, and his boisterous opinionativeness certainly concealed some uneasiness. Yet his views as a critic were read and heard with deep respect. 'What does Forster say?' was constantly asked in the forties and fifties by people who ought to have known better; and so great was the value attached to his counsel that when he told his friends what they could do best in the writing line, and practically ordered them to do it, they obeyed his instructions. He had an amazing faculty for making people go his way, not theirs.

In time he achieved such a position of dictatorial eminence that when the younger generation came along he was treated with the deference once accorded to Dr. Johnson. After one of his quarrels with Browning there was a reconciliation banquet, at which Carlyle, saluted by Forster as 'my prophet', was present. Seeing that Carlyle was smoking a church-warden pipe after dinner, two young men dared to light their cigars, receiving a pompous reprimand from their host: 'I never allow smoking in this room, save on this privileged occasion when my old friend Carlyle honours me. But I do not extend that to you Robert Lytton, or to you Percy Fitz-gerald. You have taken the matter into your own hands, without asking leave or license; as that is so, and the thing is done, there is no more to be said.' In his palmy days he would often drag his distinguished visitors into his con-versation, thus: 'As Gladstone said to me in my room . . .' 'Those were the very words Palmerston used when I reminded him . . .' 'The Duke of Westminster was astonished by my assurance that . . .'

In spite of all these objectionable traits, he was fairly generally liked. He was kind-hearted to those in distress, and tireless in his efforts on behalf of his friends. True he often undertook more than he could manage, and sometimes bungled matters as a consequence, but no trouble was too great for him to take, and he never did things by halves. A man of immense and bubbling vitality, he was also highly-strung and emotional. He responded generously to appeals for his sympathy and help, forgave people as quickly and entirely as he had previously determined never to forgive them, and wept for their misfortunes as copiously as for his own. When alone with one friend he could be extremely agreeable and good-natured, quiet, natural, unassuming, affectionate, frank as to his own failings, tolerant of the short-comings of others; and he felt hurt if he was not permitted to share in the sorrows and joys of those he liked. But he seemed a different man in the company of many, when his vanity and pomposity got the better of him.

He was by choice a host, not a guest, and his dinners in Lincoln's Inn Fields were famous. He knew the tastes of his particular guests and catered for them, though wine-glasses were replenished more often than was good for their healths. Jane Carlyle complained of being 'filled half drunk with champagne as usual' at Forster's house, and once had to tell him why her husband could not be persuaded to dine there before seeing a play: 'You pour wine into unthinking men and women until they approach the point of intoxication.' His dinners for men were uproarious affairs, and many of his guests must have got back to their homes more by luck than judgment. The conversation was freer than one might suppose from reading the novels of Dickens and Thackeray. Once it turned on the lewdness apparent in the streets at night, and Emerson wanted to know whether prostitution was always as gross as it had seemed to him in Liverpool, for if so, surely no young fellow was safe. Carlyle and Dickens replied that chastity in the male sex was a thing of the past, and was so rare in England that they could name the exceptions in their own circles. Carlyle assuming that it was the same in America, Emerson answered that in the United States 'young men of good standing and education go virgin to their nuptial beds', though in fairness to American manhood it should be stated that he adduced no proofs. Upon which Dickens remarked that incontinence was so much the rule in England that if his own son were particularly chaste he would feel alarmed and infer that the lad was in poor health.

As his dinners were so good Forster was usually allowed to lead the talk. No one was less inclined to monopolise conversation than Dickens, who listened to his friend with great interest, apparently impressed, and drolly acknowledged whatever compliments the Mogul paid him. They had a real affection for one another, but Dickens could not resist the temptation to mimic Forster's grand manner, sometimes to his face. 'How much do you pay for your champagne?' asked a guest. 'Henry, how much do I pay for my champagne?' Forster regally demanded of his servant. ''Alf a guinea a bottle', said Henry gravely. Dickens was delighted and gave several performances of the scene. At another dinner boiled beef was served without carrots. Forster rang, and the maid appeared. 'Mary . . . carrots.' Mary replied that there were no carrots. Dismissing her with a kingly gesture, Forster said 'Mary, let there be carrots', in a tone of voice that would not have demeaned a similar utterance by the Creator: 'Let there be light.' That, too, became a feature in Dickens's repertory of stories.

But in course of time Forster's proprietorial behaviour, coupled with his assertions of his own rectitude and his annoyance when his advice was not followed, began to fray their friendship, and Dickens cooled towards him, never ceasing to be grateful for his services or to hold his good

qualities in high esteem, but finding it increasingly difficult
to bear his irritating manners and to note his absurdities
without ridiculing them. Between 1855 and 1865 Dickens
kept a book of memoranda in which he jotted down ideas for
future stories. Two notes he made referred to Forster, and
were the germ of Podsnap in *Our Mutual Friend*. They read
as follows:

'I stand by my friends and acquaintances—not for their
sakes, but because they are *my* friends and acquaintances. *I*
know them, *I* have licensed them, they have taken out *my*
certificate. Ergo, I champion them as myself.'

'And by denying a thing, supposes that he altogether puts
it out of existence.'

Forster did not see himself either in these notes or in
Podsnap, no doubt because he never considered that he was
swollen with self-importance, and could not have believed
Dickens capable of picturing him with a podgy body and a
snappy nature.

# 6

## WORK AND PLAY

THE year 1838 was the busiest in Dickens's life. He was writing *Oliver Twist* and *Nicholas Nickleby*, polishing off the Grimaldi memoirs, producing more *Sketches* for Chapman and Hall, doing occasional essays for *The Examiner*, editing *Bentley's Miscellany*, and supplying articles for it. In October he was working so hard that he did not open the letters he received for three weeks, and was so short of cash that he had to apologise to the doctor for not paying his bill till the end of the year. 'I no sooner get myself up, high and dry, to attack Oliver manfully', he reported, 'than up come the waves of each month's work, and drive me back again into a sea of manuscript.' There were occasional blank days when he could do nothing at all, having worked himself to a standstill, and *Oliver Twist* in particular gave him so much trouble that the intrusions of everyday life became unbearable. He took a steamer to Boulogne, put up at an inn, and worked away until the next instalments of *Oliver* and *Nicholas* were finished, returning home just in time for the monthly issues. 'You cannot conceive the store of trouble and vexations you are preparing for yourself by entering upon the trade of authorship', he warned a woman who had sought his advice. But after all it was the work of his choice and he did not repine: 'Whosoever is devoted to Art must be content to deliver himself wholly up to it and find recompense in it.'

His work, as may be guessed by any reader, was much more the outcome of agitation than deliberation. He had to lose himself in it, to live in it as an actor lives in a part, to be carried away by it. 'I never can write with effect, especially in the serious way, until I have got my steam up', he said, 'or in other words until I have become so excited with my subject that I cannot leave off.' He therefore had no notion in advance of how a character or a scene might develop, and after a long spell at his desk was almost as surprised at the turn of events as the least sophisticated of his readers would have been. While writing *Oliver Twist* he suddenly perceived that it would make a good stage play, and wrote to a manager proposing it: 'I am quite satisfied that no one can have heard what I mean to do with the different characters in the end, inasmuch as, at present, I don't quite know myself.' Fagin he declared to be 'such an out and outer that I don't know what to make of him.' Being an actor, he wanted an audience to see the effect of his work on others, so he made a point of reading his stories to friends before they appeared in print. The famous murder scene in *Oliver* had the desired effect on his wife, 'who was in an unspeakable *"state"*, from which and my own impression I augur well.'

*Oliver Twist* won a fresh public for Dickens. It was about as different from its immediate predecessor as a book by the same writer could be. Its best scenes reveal a knowledge of the seamy side of life which owes much to his experiences in the blacking warehouse. Safely emancipated from that unpleasant period of slavery, he recognised its value to him as an artist and recreated it with gusto, converting the warehouse into a thieves' kitchen and making it all as repulsively degrading as it seemed in retrospect. This is the explanation of the otherwise inexplicable fact that he bestowed the name of the only person who had been kind to him during that nightmarish six months on the chief villain. As he need never have mentioned Bob Fagin's surname in the fragment of autobiography which he left among his papers, the use he made of it obviously did not strike him as peculiar; and as the creatures of his imagination were more real to him than the characters of everyday life, he probably felt, if he thought about it at all, that he was paying his old companion a compliment. 'I took the liberty of using his (Fagin's) name long afterwards in *Oliver Twist*', was his sole reference to the subject. He lived so intensely in his writings that he was amazed when people objected to the transfer of their characteristics to figures which they considered odious; and if Bob Fagin had written to protest against the abuse of his name, Dickens would almost certainly have felt hurt, because he was not conscious of malice and knew that there was little resemblance between Bob and the rascal of his story. The horror of the blacking factory and the uncongeniality of his former associates were only too easily recalled, and a condition of creative metamorphosis was produced, wherein the one person who had shown him sympathy became the chief villain of the book, as he had been the hero of the factory, while the Artful Dodger and Charley Bates were probably portraits of the other boys, his one-time tormentors, from whom Bob Fagin in reality protected Charles and Old Fagin in fiction protects Oliver.

The Jew contains not a little of his creator's freakish humour, and is easily the most lifelike person in the novel. Bill Sikes is a grotesque caricature, while Nancy is one of those 'fallen women' who make regular appearances in the novels of Dickens and his contemporaries and who represent the sense of guilt in an over-fed and over-secure class. Just as everyone but the poor feels ashamed of poverty, so everyone is ashamed of prostitution except the prostitute; and Nancy, like her sisters in sorrow in Victorian fiction, represents the conscience not the reality of her age. She may be dismissed as a period piece. Bumble is Dickens's first laugh at officials and institutions, a laugh that became louder and more derisive as he grew older, and which should have prevented anyone from claiming him as the forerunner of socialism or the champion of any 'ism' on earth except individualism, which is not a creed but a state of mind. Another character throws light on Dickens's methods as an author. He wanted a harsh magistrate for a police court scene, and having heard that there was a very unpleasant specimen at Hatton Garden he contrived to enter the court and make a brief study of him. The authorities had already received complaints of Laing's bad temper in court, one from a clergyman who was later convicted of stealing a silver spoon at a charity dinner over which he presided, and they seized the opportunity Dickens's portrait of Mr. Fang gave them of removing him. Dickens certainly caught him in a peevish mood. Perhaps he was drunk, or, worse still, sober. Dickens leaves it an open question:

> Mr. Fang was a lean, long-backed, stiff-necked, middle-sized man, with no great quantity of hair, and what he had, growing on the back and sides of his head. His face was stern, and much flushed. If he were really not in the habit of drinking rather more than was exactly good for him, he might have brought an action against his countenance for libel, and have recovered heavy damages.

Nowadays a paragraph like that would have brought its writer into court, not sent its victim out of one; but our social fabric is more delicate and has to be treated with greater care.

In *Oliver Twist* Dickens first displayed his amazing power of capturing the atmosphere of London. Other men, such as Dr. Johnson and Charles Lamb, were great Londoners; but Dickens was London. He identified himself with the city in such a way that he became a part of its bricks and mortar. One thinks and speaks of Dickens's London as if he had created it and its real name were Dickenstown. No other man has done this for any other city, and, next to his humour, it is his most valuable and individual contribution to literature. He is the greatest place-poet in fiction. But at the time this unique feature in his work was not noticed by the critics, upon whom it took about twenty years to dawn. His more genteel readers were primarily affected by the sudden emergence of the social reformer and the portrayer of low life, and they did not approve of him in those characters. 'There is a sort of Radicalish tone about *Oliver Twist* which I don't altogether like', wrote 'Ingoldsby' Barham to a friend. 'I think it will not be long before it is remedied, for Bentley is loyal to the backbone himself.' As we have seen, it was remedied in a very radical way for Bentley. But the strangest attack came from Thackeray, who took the view that men of genius had 'no business to make these characters interesting or agreeable, to be feeding their readers' morbid fancies, or indulging their own, with such monstrous food.' This was the first note of hostility to be sounded between the two most famous Victorian novelists, though Thackeray was then a relatively unknown man, and it was doubtless remembered by both in the years to come.

In spite of his seeming radicalism and love of low life, Dickens was now welcomed in the houses of the aristocracy and the salons of the eminent. There were in those days four gifted young men whose clothes were as remarkable as themselves and whose sartorial god was Count D'Orsay, the last of the dandies. Benjamin Disraeli was the most eccentrically garbed of the four, but he was closely followed by Edward Bulwer, Harrison Ainsworth and Charles Dickens. Gore House, Kensington, the grounds of which are now covered by the Albert Hall, was the home of Lady Blessington, and as it was also the headquarters of Count D'Orsay the best society carefully avoided it and not many women risked their reputations by calling there. Lady Blessington made Dickens feel quite at ease in that garish circle, and he became very much attached to her as well as to D'Orsay. So friendly did they become that when he went to live in Italy he sent her long accounts of his adventures. One of them started: 'Appearances are against me. Don't believe them. I have written you, in intention, fifty letters, and I can claim no credit for any one of them (though they were the best letters you ever read), for they all originated in my desire to live in your memory and regard.' Another account contained this: 'I am looking forward with great delight to the pleasure of seeing you once more, and mean to come to Gore House with such a swoop as shall astonish the poodle, if, after being accustomed to his size and sense, he retain the power of being astonished at anything in the wide world.' Returning to England, he spent a happy day at Gore House, and told her that 'It would be worth going to China—it would be worth going to America—to come home again for the pleasure of such a meeting with you and Count D'Orsay.'

At Gore House he met Walter Savage Landor, whom he described as 'like forty lions concentrated into one poet.' Early in their acquaintanceship Dickens went to stay with Landor at Bath, finding him wrong-headed, 'desperately learned and frequently first-person-singularish', but not in the least boring, and 'the finest and most chivalrous old fellow in the world.' There were to be stormy moments ahead, when Landor, irritated because Dickens did not write, told him that he might go to hell, receiving a tactful reply which commenced 'I will not go there if I can help it. I have not the least confidence in the value of your introduction to the Devil.' But that each retained the other's regard is proved by Dickens's acknowledgment of a book which Landor dedicated to him in September 1853: 'I receive the dedication like a great dignity . . . The Queen could give me none in exchange that I wouldn't laughingly snap my fingers at.'

Another famous hostess who wanted to see him was Lady Holland, and Dickens went to Holland House. This was, socially, a step above Gore House, because Lady Blessington's relations with D'Orsay were ambiguous, and Lady Holland looked down upon her. But Lady Holland had her troubles too, for her relations with her present husband had once been irregular; so that, while Lady Holland could disapprove of

Lady Blessington and refuse to know her, such ladies of the aristocracy whose relations with the opposite sex had always been regular disapproved of Lady Holland as well as Lady Blessington and refused to know either of them. These nice points in social adjustment amused Dickens and did not deter him from visiting both establishments, without his wife. Everyone worth knowing was to be met at one or other of them, the most remarkable visitor at Gore House being Disraeli, the 'star' of Holland House being Sydney Smith, concerning whom Dickens had written to the publisher, William Longman: 'I wish you would tell Mr. Sydney Smith that of all the men I ever heard of and never saw, I have the greatest curiosity to see and the greatest interest to know him.' His curiosity was gratified; they liked one another; and the richest personality of that age, the most humorous of any age, would certainly have found his way into one of Dickens's novels if he had not 'beggared all description.' The little we learn from the novelist who did such striking portraits of other prominent contemporaries is that Sydney Smith 'had such a noble wit.' At Holland House Dickens also met a less noble wit, the banker-poet Samuel Rogers, whose breakfast parties in St. James's Place included all the artistic notabilities of the time. Even Dickens, who found it impossible to work in the afternoon and evening if he went out in the morning, was once prevailed upon to breakfast with Rogers, an experience he did not repeat till the end of his life, when he breakfasted with Gladstone in May 1870. But he enjoyed the entertainments provided by Rogers at more rational hours, and admired him enough to dedicate a book to him, though from a letter written by Dickens in 1852 we may infer that the admiration was not unqualified. Rogers, he wrote, 'is the same as ever. Vivacious enough and vicious enough—tells the same stories, to the same people, in the same words, twenty times a day, and has his little dinner parties of four, where he goes mad with rage if anybody talks to anyone but himself.' Another wit of the period, though not of that circle, for whom Dickens expressed both love and admiration was Douglas Jerrold, regarded by many as sour and cynical by nature but by Dickens as 'one of the gentlest and most affectionate of men', in spite of his being 'constitutionally inconsistent and unsettled.'

It was *Nicholas Nickleby* that first made Dickens popular

among the upper classes of society: everybody at Gore House and Holland House was reading it, discussing it, and prophesying the future course of the story and the ultimate destiny of the characters as if the tale were true and the people in it real. Several of the portraits were certainly taken from living people, and one of them, the schoolmaster Squeers, was drawn so near to the life that the original suffered a premature death. Dickens got to hear of the Yorkshire schools when he was 'a not very robust child, sitting in bye-places near Rochester Castle, with a head full of Partridge, Strap, Tom Pipes and Sancho Panza.' The impression he then received was 'connected with a suppurated abscess that some boy had come home with, in consequence of his Yorkshire guide, philosopher and friend, having ripped it open with an inky pen-knife.' He picked up further scraps of information concerning the schools as he grew older, and 'at last, having an audience, resolved to write about them.'

Accompanied by Hablot K. Browne, he travelled by coach to Yorkshire, carrying a letter of introduction from a solicitor of his acquaintance to an attorney, Richard Barnes, of Barnard Castle. In the letter he was described as the friend of a widowed mother who wanted to send her boys to a school in those parts. Having given him several introductions to headmasters, Barnes called one night at the inn where the travellers were staying, confessed that the matter had weighed upon his mind all day, and said that the schools were 'sad places for mothers to send their orphan boys to', and that the widow 'had better do anything with them—let them hold horses, run errands—fling them in any way upon the mercy of the world—rather than trust them there.' Dickens and Browne went to look at a number of places, eventually picking on Bowes Academy, where they had an interview with the headmaster, William Shaw, who regarded them with suspicion and refused to show them over the school. He had good reason for caution, having been brought before the courts on several occasions for ill-treating his boys and made to pay heavy damages for his inhuman behaviour. Many of them had lost their sight from neglect; they had been fed on the meat of cattle that had died a natural death; they had been insufficiently clad, uncared-for when ill, knocked about, starved and beaten. Yet he had paid the damages and gone gaily on with the lucrative trade of boy-farming without

osing any pupils on account of this public exhibition of his
callousness and brutality. Dickens's curiosity put the man on
his guard, and after a snappy five minutes conversation,
during which he provided his two visitors with hints for a
portrait of Wackford Squeers, they found themselves in the
road. The other inquiries made by Dickens in the neighbourhood seemed to justify a complete exposure of the scandalous
treatment of children in the Yorkshire schools, and he settled
down to the job with a kind of ferocious relish, though, as he
was careful to point out, 'Mr. Squeers and his school are faint
and feeble pictures of an existing reality, purposely subdued
and kept down lest they should be deemed impossible.'

Although he also said that 'Mr. Squeers is the representative of a class, and not an individual', and although he took
some trouble to confuse the local topography, Shaw and his
school were soon recognised, the master was ruined, his life
shortened, and the 'academy' closed. The good work went
on, and soon that part of Yorkshire ceased to be a centre of
education, Dickens having discredited the entire system of
leaving children to the unchecked tyranny of sadistic masters.
Apart from a natural feeling that Shaw and his like should
have been strangled at birth, it is difficult not to sympathise
with the guiltless masters and servants of more reputable
schools who were thrown out of employment, as well as the
tradesmen and innkeepers who suffered from the picture of
juvenile misery in *Nicholas Nickleby*, and it is not surprising
that the name of Dickens was given its former significance in
the region of Barnard Castle for some years to come. A few
of the boys who had been under Shaw protested against the
novelist's description of school life at Bowes Academy; but
Dickens founded his scenes on the evidence produced in
court during the hearing of the cases against Shaw and on
information obtained locally. Just as there is honour among
thieves, so is there loyalty among bullies, and the pro-Shaw
boys were no doubt his favourites, who had enjoyed an un-
restricted field for the exercise of their cruelty.

The one person in the novel who had reasonable cause for
complaint was the novelist's mother, who luckily did not
recognise herself in the character of Mrs. Nickleby. She
might have seen the resemblance if the portrait had been less
truthful in certain particulars; for it is a living caricature of
the original, the comical aspects being magnified, the more

worthy ones glossed over, so that, as her son wrote, 'Mrs. Nickleby herself, sitting bodily before me in a solid chair, once asked me whether I believed there ever was such a woman.' According to J. W. T. Ley, a zealous Dickensian, 'this lampooning of his mother was in the worst taste.' It does not seem so to a less fervent Dickensian. The portrait is on the whole a good-natured one, and there is no earthly reason why an author (who cannot originate anything or anybody, the Almighty having forestalled him) should not use characteristics even of his own mother for the purposes of his art. Nearly every good fictional portrait is a composite portrait. 'Authors invent their personages out of scraps, heeltaps, odds and ends of characters', said Thackeray, and Mrs. Nickleby is a scrap of Mrs. John Dickens, intentionally exaggerated as she developed in her creator's imagination. 'Every "living" character in a novel is drawn, frankly or furtively, from life—is filched from biography whole or in scraps, a portrait or a patch-up', said H. G. Wells, and Mrs. Nickleby, like every other lifelike figure in Dickens's novels, is a piece of someone he knew, with so many alien patches added to it that the likeness was unrecognisable by the person most nearly concerned. Fortunately, people never see the idiotic side of themselves. If they did, every first-rate novelist and playwright would have to seek another profession.

More than any other great writer, as one would expect of a born actor and mimic, Dickens was dependent on observation for the vividness of his characterisation. When he had to fall back on his own fancy he produced figures which no intelligent person could believe possible outside a fairy tale. For example, the Cheeryble brothers in this novel. Harrison Ainsworth had often spoken to Dickens of two admirable business men named Grant who were calico printers of Cannon Street, Manchester, and when Dickens visited that city Ainsworth gave him a letter of introduction to them. Many business men resemble the Cheeryble brothers over a good dinner, and no doubt Dickens saw them enhaloed by the time they had reached the port wine and dessert; but if he had done business with them it is unlikely that they would have served his purpose in *Nicholas Nickleby*. Mr. Mantalini, on the other hand, is obviously a snapshot of reality, and the funniest scenes in the book are those between him and his wife:

'My life', said Mr. Mantalini, 'what a demd devil of a time you have been!'

'I didn't even know Mr. Nickleby was here, my love', said Mrs. Mantalini.

'Then what a doubly demd infernal rascal that footman must be, my soul', remonstrated Mr. Mantalini.

'My dear', said Madame, 'that is entirely your fault.'

'My fault, my heart's joy?'

'Certainly', returned the lady; 'what can you expect, dearest, if you will not correct the man?'

'Correct the man, my soul's delight!'

'Yes; I am sure he wants speaking to, badly enough', said Madame, pouting.

'Then do not vex itself', said Mr. Mantalini; 'he shall be horse-whipped till he cries out demnebly.' With this promise Mr. Mantalini kissed Madame Mantalini, and, after that performance, Madame Mantalini pulled Mr. Mantalini playfully by the ear: which done, they descended to business.

.           .           .           .

'I am ashamed of you', said Madame Mantalini, with much indignation.

'Ashamed? Of *me*, my joy? It knows it is talking demd charming sweetness, but naughty fibs', returned Mr. Mantalini. 'It knows it is not ashamed of its own popolorum tibby.'

But the lady whom he describes as his 'essential juice of pine-apple', who 'coils her fascinations round me like a pure and angelic rattlesnake', and for whom he will drown himself and become 'a demd, damp, moist, unpleasant body', at length abandons him, and he is last seen in a Soho basement turning a mangle to the accompaniment of another lady's objurgations:

'Oh you false traitor!' cried the lady, threatening personal violence on Mr. Mantalini's face.

'False. Oh dem! Now my soul, my gentle, captivating, bewitching and most demnebly enslaving chick-a-biddy, be calm', said Mr. Mantalini, humbly.

'I won't!' screamed the woman. 'I'll tear your eyes out!'

'Oh! What a demd savage lamb!' cried Mr. Mantalini.

'You're never to be trusted', screamed the woman, 'you were out all day yesterday, and gallivanting somewhere I know. You know you were! Isn't it enough that I paid two pound fourteen for you, and took you out of prison and let you live here like a gentleman, but must you go on like this: breaking my heart besides?'

'I will never break its heart, I will be a good boy, and never do so any more; I will never be naughty again; I beg its little pardon', said Mr. Mantalini, dropping the handle of the mangle, and folding his palms together; 'it is all up with its handsome friend! He has gone to the demnition bow-wows. It will have pity? It will not scratch and claw, but pet and comfort? Oh, demmit.'

Fifty thousand copies of the first number of *Nicholas Nickleby* were sold on the day of publication, beating the highest serial sale of *Pickwick*, its greater success being due to its retaining the freshness of the earlier work, while giving a more faithful picture of life. He was never again to write with the same sustained joviality. As usual, the story and characters were promptly appropriated by an adapter and produced on the stage with success, the victimised author being generous enough to compliment both piece and players; though when he went to a performance of *Oliver Twist* he laid down on the floor of the box during the first scene and refused to get up till the show was over. Nearly every work he wrote was subjected to theatrical piracy, often while it was still being serialised and sometimes at several theatres, and all he could do was to laugh or curse and bear it. He was still anxious to write plays, and asked Macready to produce his own version of *Oliver Twist*; but Macready was not the man for Fagin, and two generations elapsed before the very Jew that Dickens drew was acted on the stage by Beerbohm Tree. After that he read a farce to Macready. 'He reads as well as an experienced actor would—he is a surprising man', noted Macready in his diary. Forster, who was present, bellowed with laughter at all the jokes, hoping to impress the manager with its great comical possibilities; but neither the farce nor Forster's appreciation of it aroused Macready's enthusiasm, and he had to decline it. Upon which Dickens sent a cheery message: 'Believe me that I have no other feeling of disappointment connected with this matter but that arising from the not having been able to be of some use to you.' Macready was touched, and confided to his diary that Dickens's behaviour was 'an honour to him. How truly delightful it is to meet with high-minded and warm-hearted men. Dickens and Bulwer have been certainly to me noble specimens of human nature.'

The Macready and Dickens families were on intimate terms

by 1839, and Macready was constantly spending 'very cheerful' evenings at his friend's house. At a supper-party to celebrate the christening of one child and the birthday of another, there were speeches, which annoyed the actor; but he was in a more compliant mood when a dinner was given in his honour by the Shakespeare Club, and Dickens proposed his health in a manner 'most earnest, eloquent and touching', closing with 'an eulogy on myself that quite overpowered me.' This Shakespeare Club had a short life, and not even Dickens was adroit enough to save it. He was in the chair one evening when Forster's boisterous assertive manner in proposing a toast irritated some of the younger members, who made noises indicative of displeasure. Forster lost his temper, and a slanging match ensued. Dickens made several attempts to restore order, but finally had to leave the chair, and the Club met no more. But as Macready and Dickens were elected to the Athenaeum Club in the spring of '38, the dissolution of the Shakespeare did not vex them unduly. They held the same views about politics and religion, and shared the same tastes, though of course the actor was not as stage-struck as the author. Their common hobbies were various: they were both great walkers, they inspected prisons with interest, they enjoyed dancing, and on at least one occasion they were to be seen playing leap-frog with Jerrold, Maclise and Forster.

Either at Elm Lodge, Petersham, or at 4 Ailsa Park Villas, Twickenham, Dickens spent many summer months between 1836 and '40, working and playing with every atom of his energy. His old friends, Thomas Beard and Thomas Mitton, his new friends, Edwin Landseer, Daniel Maclise, Harrison Ainsworth, Clarkson Stanfield, Douglas Jerrold, T. N. Talfourd, Macready, Thackeray and others, his own family and his wife's family, all spent days or weeks with him at both places, and were compelled to take part in the games, excursions and local events. Running, jumping, cricket, quoits, bagatelle, battledore, balloon-flying, dancing, and every other form of exercise his ingenuity could devise, were uproariously performed, and Dickens flung himself body and soul into all of them, the most eager and active participant in every pursuit. Early success had intoxicated him, and he communicated the excitement to others, who were carried away by his childlike love of fun and games. There were moments when some particularly nasty review of his work depressed him for, like all great writers, he suffered from what Macaulay called 'the savage envy of aspiring dunces' in the press; but after a few minutes of explosive wrath, or an hour's bitterness he was wise enough to dismiss such futilities from his mind. Now, and for many years, *The Times* attacked his novels with savage malignity, and this was one of the recurring irritations of his early and middle life; but he was always able to console himself with the reflection that, while the hateful things appeared so conspicuous, 'the good and pleasant things are mixed up with every moment of our existence so plentifully that we scarcely heed them.'

In the autumn of '38 he took a fortnight's holiday with Hablot K. Browne. Their first stop was Leamington, whence they visited Kenilworth, 'with which we were both enraptured', Dickens wrote to his wife, 'and where I really think we MUST have lodgings next summer, please God that we are in good health and all goes well. You cannot conceive how delightful it is. To read among the ruins in fine weather would be perfect luxury.' Then to Warwick Castle, and then to Stratford-on-Avon, 'where we sat down in the room where Shakespeare was born and left our autographs and read those of other people and so forth.' Though he had been careful to eat and drink very little, he was suffering from a pain in his side, which at Stratford became unendurable and forced him to take a dose of henbane: 'The effect was most delicious. I slept soundly, and without feeling the least uneasiness, and am a great deal better this morning; neither do I find that the henbane has affected my head, which, from the great effect it had on me—exhilarating me to the most extraordinary degree, and yet keeping me sleepy—I feared it would.' They passed through Birmingham and Wolverhampton on the way to Shrewsbury, 'starting at eight o'clock through a cold wet fog, and travelling, when the day had cleared up, through miles of cinder-paths and blazing furnaces, and roaring steam-engines, and such a mass of dirt, gloom, and misery as I never before witnessed.' The journey was useful, because he used the scenes they traversed as local colour in his next novel. He closed this letter from the Lion Hotel, Shrewsbury: 'God bless you, my darling. I long to be back with you again and to see the sweet Babs.' They next went to Llangollen, and on November 5th he wrote from the Adelphi Hotel, Liverpool:

'My dearest Love . . . I am rejoiced to think that I shall see you so soon.'

Broadstairs remained his favourite spot in all England for the first seven years of his married life, and so many houses in it are associated with him or his characters that its present-day inhabitants must sometimes wonder how his contemporaries managed to find accommodation. While staying there with his family he worked hard, walked hard, bathed regularly, entertained vigorously, and, when not otherwise engaged, watched the sea: 'It has been blowing great guns for the last three days', he wrote to Forster in September '39, 'and last night (I wish you could have seen it!) there was such a sea! I staggered down to the pier, and, creeping under the lee of a large boat which was high and dry, watched it breaking for nearly an hour. Of course I came back wet through.'

Meanwhile his father and brothers were getting a little out of hand. He managed to secure a clerkship in the Treasury for Frederick, who had inherited his father's libatory tastes. But the other brothers were a problem, and his father was a problem that demanded speedy solution. John Dickens was in fact selling bits of his son's handwriting to autograph-hunters and souvenir-seekers, and raising loans from publishers, who imagined that they were obliging the son whenever they eased his father's mind. There was but one way to rid himself of such troublesome relations. He must get them out of London, and the farther out the better. With his usual despatch and efficiency, he went down to Exeter in March '39, put up at the New London Inn, explored the surrounding country, found a pleasant cottage at Alpherton ('a jewel of a place', exactly one mile from Exeter on the Plymouth road, 'in the most beautiful, cheerful, delicious rural neighbourhood I was ever in'), thought that if he were older he would love to live there, decided that his parents were bound to be happy in such a spot, promptly arranged to rent the cottage for £20 a year, rushed back to Exeter to buy carpets, crockery, furniture, garden tools, coals, and all the other things necessary for comfort, got his mother down to see that everything was in order, asked a friend to make sure that his father, brothers and a dog, were on the coach from London, and then dashed home to write a monthly number of *Nicholas Nickleby*.

His parents were not as enthusiastic as himself. Very soon his father was sending him Micawberish letters, his mother Nicklebeish letters, and he was disgusted with both. However, they settled down in time, and he was relieved of their presence in London, though John Dickens managed to move about England, whether job-finding, loan-raising or sight-seeing, it is impossible to say; probably the second of the three, for within a year of his enforced rustication Charles had to publish a statement in the press that he would not be responsible for his father's debts. Yet no son could have done more for his parents than Dickens did. He supported them for the rest of their lives; and if Mr. Micawber and Mrs. Nickleby may be regarded as interest on the sum he expended, posterity has no ground for complaint, being still in receipt of the dividend.

# 7

# QUILP AND TAPPERTIT

WHILE Dickens was living in a whirl of work, social engagements, physical exercises and domestic upheavals, his wife was quietly producing children, two daughters having followed the firstborn son at intervals of about a year; and after the birth of their fourth child in 1841 her younger sister Georgina joined their establishment in order to supervise matters, since Kate was already showing signs of fatigue, her natural indolence being increased by her regular confinements. In time Georgina more or less took charge of the household, and in most practical affairs was treated by both Dickens and Forster as its mistress, Kate's placid easy-going nature rendering her amenable to such an arrangement. Following the birth of their third child in 1839 the little house in Doughty Street became congested, and Dickens again went house-hunting, eventually choosing No. 1 Devonshire Terrace, a commodious residence, with a pleasant garden surrounded by a high wall, nearly opposite York Gate, Regent's Park. For weeks he was 'in the agonies of house-letting, house-taking, title proving and disproving, premium paying, fixture valuing, and other ills too numerous to mention', including furniture buying, house painting, and removing. They were installed by the middle of December '39, and remained its tenants for twelve years, during which five sons and one daughter were added to the family. Dickens liked it much better than any other of his London homes.

So great was the success of *Nicholas Nickleby* that the publishers Chapman and Hall not only gave the author an extra £1500 but agreed to pay him £50 a week, plus half profits, for a new publication which he proposed to them. It was to be a weekly paper, rather after the style of Addison's *Spectator* or Steele's *Tatler* or Goldsmith's *Bee*, containing stories, essays, characters, travels, etc., most of which were to be written by himself, with Phiz and George Cattermole as illustrators. Called *Master Humphrey's Clock*, the first number appeared at the beginning of April 1840, and had an immediate sale of seventy thousand copies. Dickens, who had been

away from home when the first number of *Pickwick Papers*
was published, became a prey to the superstition that his
absence from London was necessary to ensure the success of
his future undertakings, and when *Master Humphrey* came out
he was at Birmingham, where Forster joined him with news
of the sensational sale.  In a state of tremendous excitement
they rushed off to see Shakespeare's house at Stratford and
Johnson's at Lichfield, spent all their money, and had to pawn
their gold watches at Birmingham in order to get home again.
But the success of the first number was not repeated until
Dickens began a serial story in the fourth number, *The Old
Curiosity Shop*, which soon ousted all the stories, characters and
essays of *Master Humphrey's Clock*, and became the substance
of the periodical, its serialisation lasting until January '41.

One of the chief characters in the new story was named
Daniel Quilp, a character into which Dickens unintentionally
put a great deal of himself; and while it was yet germinating
in his mind he gave a performance of the part in private life
which disconcerted his wife and some of his friends quite as
much as Quilp in the book disconcerts his wife and all his
acquaintances.  The marriage of Queen Victoria and Prince
Albert in February 1840 was the excuse for his outbreak, and
life must have been a little trying for the other inmates of
1 Devonshire Terrace while the fit was on him.  He pretended
so hard that he almost believed himself wildly in love with
the Queen.  'I am utterly lost in misery and can do nothing . . .'
he wrote to Forster,

> 'My heart is at Windsor,
>     My heart isn't here;
> My heart is at Windsor,
>     A following my dear . . .

'The presence of my wife aggravates me.  I loathe my parents.
I detest my house.  I begin to have thoughts of the Serpentine,
of the Regent's canal, of the razors upstairs, of the chemist's
down the street, of poisoning myself . . . of hanging myself
upon the pear-tree in the garden, of abstaining from food and
starving myself to death, of being bled for my cold and tearing
off the bandage, of falling under the feet of cab-horses in the
New Road, of murdering Chapman and Hall and becoming
great in story (SHE must hear something of me then—perhaps
sign the warrant: or is that a fable?), of turning Chartist, of

heading some bloody assault upon the palace and saving Her by my single hand—of being anything but what I have been, and doing anything but what I have done.—Your distracted friend.' Walter Savage Landor was utterly confused by a note in which Dickens expressed his passion for the Queen and his intention to kidnap a maid of honour and take her to an uninhabited island. Another correspondent was informed that 'Maclise and I are raving with love for the Queen, with a hopeless passion whose extent no tongue can tell, nor mind of man conceive. On Tuesday we sallied down to Windsor, prowled about the Castle, saw the corridor and their private rooms—nay, the very bedchamber (which we know from having been there twice), lighted up with such ruddy, homely, brilliant glow, bespeaking so much bliss and happiness, that I, your humble servant, lay down in the mud at the top of the Long Walk, and refused all comfort, to the immeasurable astonishment of a few straggling passengers who had survived the drunkenness of the previous night. After perpetrating some other extravagance, we returned home in a postchaise, and now we wear marriage medals near our hearts, and go about with pockets full of portraits, which we weep over in secret. Forster was with us at Windsor, and (for the joke's sake) counterfeits a passion too, *but he does not love her.* Don't mention this unhappy attachment. I am very wretched, and think of leaving home. My wife makes me miserable, and when I hear the voices of my infant children I burst into tears.' After stating that he would shortly do away with himself, he concluded: 'I have heard, on the Lord Chamberlain's authority, that she reads my books, and is very fond of them. I think she will be sorry when I am gone. I should wish to be embalmed, and to be kept (if practicable) on the top of a triumphal arch at Buckingham Palace when she is in town, and on the north-east turrets of the Round Tower when she is at Windsor.' Apparently his conversation on the subject was as absurd as his correspondence, and quite a few people thought he had taken leave of his senses. In fact a rumour was shortly circulated that he had become a Roman Catholic and was raving mad in an asylum; and as he got to hear of this when he was again normal and had abandoned the part of the Queen's lover, he spent several hours grinding his teeth with rage. Whether or not his friends thought all this extremely funny, we do not know. They certainly entered into the spirit of the thing, but when the spirit had evaporated they must have felt a little languid. It was the joke of a clown, kept up long after everyone else had ceased to laugh at it, and his wife could never have mustered up more than a weary grin. But the man with an actor's temperament cannot help letting off steam occasionally, because he suffers from an excess of high spirits and feels he will burst unless he yells or turns somersaults or pretends to be mad or impersonates someone else or recites or sits on his hat or trips over nothing or pulls faces or does anything else of a discomposing nature.

Having exhausted his superfluous energy, Dickens suddenly became solemn, as if unaware of the antic disposition he had just indulged, and settled down to his new serial story, writing to Forster: 'I find it will be positively necessary to go, for five days in the week at least, on a perfect regimen of diet and exercise.' Originally envisaged as a short story which would perhaps run for half a dozen numbers of the new weekly, *The Old Curiosity Shop* took possession of the author's imagination and he worked at it in a sort of fever. 'I feel the story extremely myself, which I take to be a good sign', he wrote in March, 1840, and we can trace the effect of Little Nell upon him in his letters, mostly written to Forster:

Broadstairs. 17 June: 'It's now four o'clock and I have been at work since half-past eight. I have really dried myself up into a condition which would almost justify me in pitching off the cliff, head first—but I must get richer before I indulge in a crowning luxury. Number 15, which I began today, I anticipate great things from. There is a description of getting gradually out of town, and passing through neighbourhoods of distinct and various characters, with which, if I had read it in anybody else's writing, I think I should have been very much struck. The child and the old man are on their journey of course, and the subject is a very pretty one . . .'

July: 'I intended calling on you this morning on my way back from Bevis-marks, whither I went to look at a house for Sampson Brass. But I got mingled up in a kind of social paste with the Jews of Houndsditch, and roamed about among them till I came out in Moorfields, quite unexpectedly. So I got into a cab, and came home again, very tired, by way of the City Road . . .'

Broadstairs. 9 September: 'I have opened the second

volume with Kit; and I saw this morning looking out at the sea, as if a veil had been lifted up, an affecting thing that I can do with him bye and bye. Nous verrons . . .'

Broadstairs. 4 October: 'You will recognise a description of the road we travelled between Birmingham and Wolverhampton: but I had conceived it so well in my mind that the execution doesn't please me quite as well as I expected.'

November: 'You can't imagine (gravely I write and speak) how exhausted I am today with yesterday's labours. I went to bed last night utterly dispirited and done up. All night I have been pursued by the child; and this morning I am unrefreshed and miserable. I don't know what to do with myself . . . I think the close of the story will be great . . . The difficulty has been tremendous—the anguish unspeakable . . .'

24 November: (to Chapman and Hall) 'I am inundated with imploring letters recommending poor little Nell to mercy. Six yesterday, and four today (it's not 12 o'clock yet) already!'

22 December: (to George Cattermole) 'I am breaking my heart over this story, and cannot bear to finish it.'

7 January, 1841: 'I am the wretchedest of the wretched. It casts the most horrible shadow upon me, and it is as much as I can do to keep moving at all . . . I shan't recover it for a long time. Nobody will miss her like I shall. It is such a very painful thing to me, that I really cannot express my sorrow. Old wounds bleed afresh when I only think of the way of doing it: what the actual doing it will be, God knows. I can't preach to myself the schoolmaster's consolation, though I try. Dear Mary died yesterday, when I think of this sad story . . . I have refused several invitations for this week and next, determining to go nowhere till I had done. I am afraid of disturbing the state I have been trying to get into, and having to fetch it all back again . . .'

14 January: (to George Cattermole) 'I am, for the time being, nearly dead with work and grief for the loss of my child.'

17 January: 'It makes me very melancholy to think that all these people are lost to me for ever, and I feel as if I never could become attached to any new set of characters.'

13 March: (to Thomas Latimer) 'I think I shall always like it better than anything I have done or may do.'

The effect of Little Nell on the age was almost as soul-devastating as it had been on her creator. The explanation is that sentimentality is complementary to toughness and callous-ness, and an age that had grown fat on child-slavery, negro-slavery, the pillage of India, and many similar crimes, was easily melted by the sorrows of a pure and pretty girl, doing pleasant penitence for its villainies by crying over Little Nell. No one weeps more copiously than the hardened scoundrel, as was proved when a sentimental play was performed before a Chicago audience composed chiefly of gangsters, whose eyes were seen to be red and swollen on the rare occasions when they were not hidden by handkerchiefs. Naturally the story appealed strongly to those whom we may politely describe as the knottiest among Dickens's famous contem-poraries: to Carlyle, who wept like a child over it; to Daniel O'Connell, who was rent with sobs and flung the book out of the window because he could not bear the death of the saintly child; to Walter Savage Landor, who, when capable of speech, compared the heroine with Juliet and Desdemona; and to Francis Jeffrey, once the autocratic editor and slashing critic of *The Edinburgh Review*, then a judge, who was found dissolved in tears over the death of 'Boz's little Nelly', and who declared wherever he went that she was the most perfect creation in literature since Cordelia. The further west the book travelled, its readers becoming tougher and tougher, the convulsions became louder and louder, and we hear the crowds on the quay at New York yelling 'Is Little Nell dead?' to the passengers on the ship bringing the latest number, and listen to the groans of grief issuing from cowboys on the prairie and mining-camps in California as the odd blank verse which Dickens wrote whenever his emotions got the better of him was read out to murderers, plunderers and ravishers beneath the winking stars. The man who could thus move his age was clearly a child of the age, and Dickens had a strain of ruthlessness in him which discharged itself in the senti-mentality of his dream-figures.

Although he got the idea of Little Nell while staying with Landor at Bath, and that of Quilp from a hideous dwarf he saw in the same town, he consciously idealised Mary Hogarth in the first, and unconsciously realised bits of himself in the second. 'You cannot interest your readers in any character unless you have first made them hate or like him', he informed a correspondent. He set out with the intention of making everyone adore Little Nell and detest Quilp, succeeding with his own age in carrying it out; but a modern reader is more likely to be bored by the heroine and delighted by the villain. In the long run, as Launcelot Gobbo says, truth will come to light; and we read *The Old Curiosity Shop* nowadays for its spontaneous bits of observation and revelation, not for its emotional confusion. The scenes between Sampson Brass, the cringing shady lawyer, and his gleeful dynamic employer Quilp, to whom Dickens gives a good deal of his own impishness, are among the triumphs of humorous fiction. Nothing could be funnier in a grotesque way than the mingled terror and sycophancy of the lawyer when he calls one night at Quilp's wharf, after the two ruffians have managed to get a boy into gaol by perjured evidence, and finds the dwarf alone, roaring the newspaper report of the case in a drunken frenzy:

'How do you do tonight, sir?' said Sampson, peeping in. 'Ha ha ha! How do you do, sir? Oh dear me, how very whimsical! Amazingly whimsical to be sure!'

'Come in, you fool!' returned the dwarf, 'and don't stand there shaking your head and showing your teeth. Come in, you false witness, you perjurer, you suborner of evidence, come in!'

'He has the richest humour!' cried Brass, shutting the door behind him; 'the most amazing vein of comicality! But isn't it *rather* injudicious, sir——?'

'What?' demanded Quilp. 'What, Judas?'

'Judas!' cried Brass. 'He has such extraordinary spirits! His humour is so extremely playful! Judas! Oh yes—dear me, how very good! Ha ha ha!'

.          .          .          .          .

'Come here', said Quilp, beckoning him to draw near. 'What's injudicious, hey?'

'Nothing, sir—nothing. Scarcely worth mentioning, sir; but I thought that song—admirably humorous in itself, you know— was perhaps rather——'

'Yes', said Quilp, 'rather what?'

'Just bordering, or as one may say remotely verging, upon the confines of injudiciousness perhaps sir', returned Brass, looking timidly at the dwarf's cunning eyes, which were turned towards the fire and reflected its red light.

'Why?' inquired Quilp, without looking up.

'Why, you know, sir', returned Brass, venturing to be more familiar; '—the fact is, sir, that any allusion to these little combinings together, of friends, for objects in themselves extremely laudable, but which the law terms conspiracies, are—you take me, sir?—best kept snug and among friends, you know.'

'Eh!' said Quilp, looking up with a perfectly vacant countenance. 'What do you mean?'

'Cautious, exceedingly cautious, very right and proper!' cried Brass, nodding his head. 'Mum, sir, even here—my meaning, sir, exactly.'

'*Your* meaning exactly, you brazen scarecrow,—what's your meaning?' retorted Quilp. 'Why do you talk to me of combining together? Do *I* combine? Do I know anything about your combinings?'

'No no, sir—certainly not; not by any means', returned Brass.

'If you so wink and nod at me', said the dwarf, looking about him as if for his poker, 'I'll spoil the expression of your monkey's face, I will.'

'Don't put yourself out of the way, I beg, sir', rejoined Brass, checking himself with great alacrity. 'You're quite right, sir, quite right. I shouldn't have mentioned the subject, sir. It's much better not to. You're quite right, sir. Let us change it, if you please.'

Brass is made to drink some scalding hot spirits, and when he is almost dead from nausea and the stuffiness of the room Quilp gives him heartening advice as he stumbles off across the yard in the dark:

'Be careful how you go, my dear friend. Be sure to pick your way among the timber, for all the rusty nails are upwards. There's a dog in the lane. He bit a man last night, and a woman the night before, and last Tuesday he killed a child—but that was in play. Don't go too near him.'

'Which side of the road is he, sir?' asked Brass, in great dismay.

'He lives on the right hand', said Quilp, 'but sometimes he hides on the left, ready for a spring. He's uncertain in that respect. Mind you take care of yourself. I'll never forgive you if you don't. There's the light out—never mind—you know the way—straight on!'

So impulsive and guileless was Dickens when in the throes of composition that he even gives Mrs. Quilp the semblance of his own wife, describing her as a pretty little blue-eyed woman, with a soft mild manner, obedient, timid, loving. She is completely under the dominion of the dwarf, and there is no doubt that Mrs. Dickens would have echoed Mrs. Quilp's belief that her husband 'has such a way with him when he likes, that the best-looking woman here couldn't refuse him if I was dead, and she was free, and he chose to make love to her.' Touches of his own nature appear again and again in Quilp, who is shrewdly aware of everything that is going on around him, while perpetually gratifying his taste 'for doing something fantastic and monkey-like', who laughs at his private jokes until the tears run down his cheeks, and who 'more than once, when he found himself in a by-street, vented his delight in a shrill scream, which greatly terrifying any lonely passenger, who happened to be walking on before him expecting nothing so little, increased his mirth, and made him remarkably cheerful and light-hearted.' Dickens, too, as we shall hear, was capable of letting out a howl for no apparent reason, to the discomposure of his companions; and he would certainly have enjoyed acting the part of Quilp when travelling on top of a coach with Mrs. Nubbles inside: 'from which circumstance he derived in the course of the journey much cheerfulness of spirit, inasmuch as her solitary condition enabled him to terrify her with many extraordinary annoyances; such as hanging over the side of the coach at the risk of his life, and staring in with his great goggle eyes, which seemed in hers the more horrible from his face being upside down; dodging her in this way from one window to another; getting nimbly down whenever they changed horses and thrusting his head in at the window with a dismal squint.'

There is very little suggestion of repose, solitude or meditation in the novels of Dickens; and not only was the room in which he worked crowded with the figures of his imagination, but the house in which he lived was usually overflowing with real people. He could not bear the feeling of being cut off from his friends, and whenever he left London he did his utmost to entice them after him. Though perpetually accompanied by the figure of Little Nell, he wanted every bedroom occupied in his house at Broadstairs. Two hours after his arrival there he wrote to Thomas Beard that 'the dining-parlour closet already displays a good array of bottles, duly arranged by the writer hereof—the spirits labelled "Gin", "Brandy", "Hollands" in autograph character—and the wine tasted and approved . . . The sea is rolling away, like nothing but the sea, in front of the house, and there are two pretty little spare bedrooms waiting to be occupied.' Maclise also was begged to 'come to the bower which is shaded for you in the one-pair front, where no chair or table has four legs of the same length, and where no drawers will open till you have pulled the pegs off, and then they keep open and won't shut again. COME!' Being very susceptible to boredom, he shut himself up if anyone he did not like were staying in their London house: 'Kate has a girl stopping here, for whom I have conceived a horrible aversion, and whom I *must* fly . . . She is the Ancient Mariner of young ladies She "holds me with her glittering eye" and I cannot turn away. The basilisk is now in the dining-room and I am in the study, but I *feel* her through the wall. She is of a prim and icy aspect, her breast tight and smooth like a sugar loaf, she converseth with fluency, and hath deep mental lore—her name is Martha Ball—she breakfasted in the dining-room this morning, and I took my solitary food, tight locked-up in the study. I went out last night and in desperation had my hair cut—merely to avoid her . . . She is remarkable for a lack of development everywhere and might be useful as a model of a griffin or other fabulous monster.' Incidentally the barbers must have done a brisk side-business by selling clippings of his hair, for which there was so large a demand that, in sending a ringlet to an American female admirer, he said that it was 'the first specimen of the kind I have parted with—except to a hairdresser—and will most likely be the last, for if I were to be liberal in this respect, my next portrait would certainly be that of a perfectly bald gentleman.'

He was a born companion, and was always happy and at his best when talking or walking or playing or feasting with his friends. Extracts from two letters he wrote to Leigh Hunt in the spring and summer of 1840 will show that, drunk or sober, he loved congenial society. One was written just after they had taken a ramble in the country together: 'Ah Hunt, I'm so lazy, and all along o' you. The sun is in my eyes, the hum of the fields in my ears, the dust upon my feet—and a boy redolent of the steam engine and sweltering in warm ink is slumbering in the passage, waiting for "Copy".' The other was written after a good dinner: 'I fancied there was the slightest possible peculiarity in your speech last night—just an elaborate show of distinctness—a remarkably correct delivery—an exquisite appreciation of the beauty of the language, with the faintest smack of wine running through

it. This was mere fancy, I suppose?' Dickens himself sometimes ate and drank more than was good for him in these
years, because his youth and vigour did not save him from
attacks of pain in unexpected places: 'I am suffering—and
have suffered all night, and during the greater part of yesterday—insupportable torture from some complaint in the face,
whether rheumatism, tic doloreux, or what not, Heaven
knows', he wrote to his publishers from Broadstairs in the
autumn of '40. 'I have had fomentations of various kinds,
but with little or no relief, and am desperately beaten in
consequence. I am as bad as Miss Squeers—screaming out
loud all the time I write.—Yours inflammatorily and despond-
ingly.' He must have had a highly nervous physical constitution which was quickly affected by anything unusual and
easily upset. In the same year he was a juryman at an inquest
on the body of an infant supposedly killed by its mother. He
managed to persuade the jury to take a humane view of the
occurrence, and the mother was only charged with conceal-
ment of birth; after which he had special care taken of her in
prison, arranged and paid for her defence, and she received a
lenient sentence. But the inquest upset him: 'Whether it was
the poor baby, or its poor mother, or the coffin, or my fellow-
jurymen, or what not, I can't say, but last night I had a most
violent attack of sickness and indigestion which not only
prevented me from sleeping, but even from lying down.
Accordingly Kate and I sat up through the dreary watches.'

He would have been an admirable juryman because he was
a first-rate committee man, seeing quickly what had to be
done and doing it swiftly. But when he was asked by the
whigs of Reading in 1841 to stand for parliament, he knew
that it would be waste of time, and wrote a polite letter
excusing himself on the ground that he could not afford the
expense of a contested election. Having learnt that the
expense would not be great and that the Government would
support him, he shifted ground and informed the gentlemen
of Reading: 'I cannot satisfy myself that to enter Parliament
under such circumstances would enable me to pursue that
honourable independence without which I could neither pre-
serve my own respect nor that of my constituents.' A few
weeks later he 'declined to be brought in, free gratis for
nothing and qualified to boot, for a Scotch county that's
going a begging.' This was during the excitement caused by

his presence in Edinburgh, where the freedom of the city was bestowed upon him.

At the instance of his new friend and admirer, Lord Jeffrey, he visited Scotland with his wife in June '41, and enjoyed the first of those great public receptions of which he was to experience so many throughout the remainder of his life, and the like of which has been granted to no other artist in history. Writing to Forster from the Royal Hotel on June 23rd, he expressed the hope that he had now been 'introduced to everybody in Edinburgh. The hotel is perfectly besieged, and I have been forced to take refuge in a sequestered apartment at the end of a long passage.' On the 25th a public banquet was given in his honour, with John Wilson ('Christopher North') in the chair. There were nearly three hundred diners and two hundred female onlookers. Speeches were made, toasts were proposed, and enthusiasm prevailed. Dickens distinguished himself as a speaker, and though he felt 'it was very remarkable to see such a number of grey-headed men gathered about my brown flowing locks', he retained his self-possession and was 'as cool as a cucumber.' On the 29th he received the freedom of the city, where he stayed till July 4th, lunching and dining every day with the notables of the place, receiving ovations at the theatre, visiting the house where Scott had lived for 27 years, welcoming countless callers, and assuring Forster after a week of it 'that there is no place like home, and that I thank God most heartily for having given me a quiet spirit, and a heart that won't hold many people. I sigh for Devonshire Terrace and Broadstairs, for battledore and shuttlecock; I want to dine in a blouse with you and Mac; and I feel Topping's merits more acutely than I have ever done in my life.' (Topping was his coachman.)

Twelve days of being lionised in the capital were followed by an excursion to the Highlands. They were accompanied by an eccentric Scot named Angus Fletcher, whose quaint behaviour amused Dickens so much that Angus was always a welcome guest at Devonshire Terrace, Broadstairs, and elsewhere. They went through the Trossachs in pelting rain, and arrived at Loch Earn, where they were not expected at the hotel for several hours, and no fires were lit in their rooms. Though Angus was responsible for this omission, his method of dealing with the situation pleased Dickens: 'If you had seen him . . . running in and out of the sitting-room and the two bedrooms with a great pair of bellows, with which he distractedly blew each of the fires out in turn, you would have died of laughing.' Glencoe made a deep impression on Dickens; and as they were prevented by bad weather from crossing the loch at Ballachulish (which Dickens insisted in calling Ballyhoolish) and going on to Oban, they drove through the famous Pass twice. He described it as terrible, awful, fearful, tremendous, and horrific. At Inverary he was asked to attend a public dinner at Glasgow, but replied that he had to return home on pressing business. The rain, wind and cold of Scotland had made him pine for London, and he wrote to Forster that he 'wouldn't stop now for twenty dinners of twenty thousand each.'

In the midst of all these excitements he had been working on his next novel, *Barnaby Rudge*, which had been projected five years earlier, and which had been started just before the story of Little Nell thrust it once more into the background. It followed *The Old Curiosity Shop* in the weekly publication still called after Master Humphrey, which ceased to exist with the end of *Barnaby Rudge*, a serial which ran from February till November '41. In spite of the fact that it had been in his mind for so long a period, *Barnaby* was not written with his usual ease and spontaneity. Sitting at his desk one afternoon, he noted that he had been 'looking with an appearance of extraordinary interest and study at *one leaf* of the Curiosities of Literature ever since half-past ten this morning—I haven't the heart to turn over.' The contents of each number required at least a day's intensive thinking before he went to work. 'I didn't stir out yesterday but sat and *thought* all day; not writing a line; not so much as the cross of a t or dot of an i. I imaged forth a good deal of *Barnaby* by keeping my mind steadily upon him . . . Last night I was unutterably and impossible-to-form-an-idea-of-ably miserable.' He went to Brighton for a week's concentration on it, and returning to London wandered about 'the most wretched and distressful streets . . . searching for some pictures I wanted to build upon.' Chigwell, on the borders of Epping Forest, was a favourite haunt, and here he placed many of the scenes, converting the King's Head into the Maypole inn. He and Forster dined there once, and asking the landlord to join them over a glass of port he inquired 'Perhaps, landlord, you would like to know who I am?' 'Yes, sir.' 'I am Charles

Dickens.' 'And I', said his companion with an important air, 'am John Forster.' The landlord was undismayed.

Dickens had a pet raven which appears in the book as Grip. The bird died in March '41, and he broke the news to Maclise: 'He had been ailing (as I told you t'other night) for a few days, but we anticipated no serious result, conjecturing that a portion of the white paint he swallowed last summer might be lingering about his vitals without having any serious effect upon his constitution. Yesterday afternoon he was taken so much worse that I sent an express for the medical gentleman (Mr. Herring), who promptly attended, and administered a powerful dose of castor oil. Under the influence of this medicine, he recovered so far as to be able at eight o'clock p.m. to bite Topping. His night was peaceful. This morning at daybreak he appeared better; received (agreeably to the doctor's directions) another dose of castor oil; and partook plentifully of some warm gruel, the flavour of which he appeared to relish. Towards eleven o'clock he was so much worse that it was found necessary to muffle the stable-knocker. At half-past, or thereabouts, he was heard talking to himself about the horse and Topping's family, and to add some incoherent expressions which are supposed to have been either a foreboding of his approaching dissolution, or some wishes relative to the disposal of his little property: consisting chiefly of half-pence which he had buried in different parts of the garden. On the clock striking twelve he appeared slightly agitated, but he soon recovered, walked twice or thrice along the coach-house, stopped to bark, staggered, exclaimed *Halloa old girl!* (his favourite expression), and died.' Further details were given to Angus Fletcher: 'Suspectful of a butcher, who had been heard to threaten, I had his body opened. There were no traces of poison and it appeared he had died of influenza. He has left a considerable property, chiefly in cheese and half-pence, buried in different parts of the garden. The new raven (I *have* a new one, but he is of comparatively weak intellect) ministers to his effects and turns up something every day. The last piece of bijouterie was a hammer of considerable size, supposed to have been stolen from a vindictive carpenter, who had been heard to speak darkly of vengeance down the mews . . . Good Christians say in such cases "It was all for the best perhaps." I try to think so. He had ripped the lining off the carriage and eaten the paint off the wheels.

In the course of the summer while we were at Broadstairs, I think he would have had it all bodily.'

Early in October '41 Dickens endured an extremely painful operation: 'I laboured under the complaint called Fistula, the consequence of too much sitting at my desk.' Though Macready suffered '*agonies*' merely from hearing the patient describe his experience, Dickens made a quick recovery, and at the beginning of November sent the last number of *Barnaby* to the printers.

Although a thrillingly interesting story, the new book was not as popular as Dickens's other novels, and, with the exceptions of *Hard Times* and the uncompleted *Edwin Drood*, it is less read today than any of them. We need not pause to inquire into this, our main concern being to note what is biographically revealing in each work as we come to it; and by far the most remarkable feature of *Barnaby* is the character of Simon Tappertit. Justice has never been done to Dickens as a prophet; and yet the most astonishing feat of prophecy in the history of letters is the portrayal of Gabriel Varden's apprentice. Tappertit is a comical apotheosis of the 'little man' a century before he came into his own; that is to say, a century before he had come to believe himself a great man, had created his own image in the worlds of art and action, and had idolised that image. We who have lived to see the 'little man' personified by Adolf Hitler in the real world and Charles Chaplin in the world of fancy, each resembling the other in appearance, each ridiculous and each portentous, can now recognise in the queer antics of Simon Tappertit the prototype of what has amused us in one sphere and horrified us in another, Tappertit being simply Chaplin performing the part of Hitler. Dickens had a sixth sense which enabled him to foretell not only the very sounds of their names—'Tap' for 'Chap' and 'tit' for 'Hit'—but the synthetic forms they would take, the one being built up by the film, the other by the wireless; for, like them, Tappertit is an automaton, moving with the jerky unreality of the silent picture and speaking with the metallic unreality of the radio voice. Here is a brief pen-portrait of the comic Hitler known as Simon Tappertit:

He is 'in years just twenty, in his looks much older, and in conceit at least two hundred.' Locked up in his small body is 'an ambitious and aspiring soul. As certain liquors, confined in casks too cramped in their dimensions, will ferment,

and fret, and chafe in their imprisonment, so the spiritual
essence or soul of Mr. Tappertit would sometimes fume
within that precious cask, his body, until, with great foam and
froth and splutter, it would force a vent, and carry all before
it.' His voice, naturally cracked and shrill, becomes hoarse
when necessary, and he has some 'majestic, shadowy ideas . . .
concerning the power of his eye', which looks into a man's
very soul and pierces like a gimlet. Sometimes he screws and
twists his face into 'extraordinary, hideous and unparalleled
contortions'; but when, enthroned among his fellow-
conspirators in a cellar, he lays down the law to the 'Prentice
Knights, of whom he is the captain and moving spirit, he
folds his arms, frowns with a sullen majesty, and behaves in
a very aloof, mysterious, and awe-inspiring manner. 'Light-
hearted revellers!' he mutters moodily when he hears his
followers playing skittles. The 'Prentices love the constitution, the Church, the State, and everything established, except
their masters; and their captain is heard to express his regret
that they no longer carry clubs wherewith to mace the citizens.
It is part of their duty to molest, hurt, wrong, annoy, and
quarrel with, all those against whom they have a grudge, and
their leader promises to heal the wounds of his unhappy
country. 'I have made arrangements for you in an altered
state of society', he tells the girl whose love he does not
return, 'and mean to provide for you comfortably in life—
there! will that satisfy you?' He ponders on his great destiny:
'To drag out an ignoble existence unbeknown to mankind in
general—patience! I will be famous yet. A voice within me
keeps on whispering Greatness. I shall burst out one of these
days, and when I do, what power can keep me down? I feel
my soul getting into my head at the idea. More drink there!'
When the moment for action at last arrives, he exclaims: 'My
bleeding country calls me and I go.'

Dickens had enough of Tappertit within himself to describe
with unerring insight and unflagging brilliance the main
characteristics of the 'little man' when once he gets too big
for his boots; but as Dickens was primarily a great artist, he
could objectify the figure, chaplinise it, and make it funny.
Had he lived a century later and seen his exhibit in the flesh
he would have made it more macabre and less entertaining.

'I am expecting every day to be gray and have very nearly
persuaded myself that I am gouty', said the twenty-nine year-

old author as he looked at his fourth child in February, 1841.
He was beginning to be concerned over the future of his
family, and wanted a rest from writing. With his radical
outlook on the English political scene, he felt that there was
a world elsewhere for him to conquer, a country where
equality reigned, and where money could be made more
easily than at home. Money is a token for liberty of action,
and Dickens was anxious to obtain that token without working himself to death. 'Thank God there is a Van Diemen's-
land. That's my comfort', he wrote to Forster. 'Now, I
wonder if I should make a good settler! I wonder, if I went
to a new colony with my head, hands, legs, and health, I
should force myself to the top of the social milk-pot and live
upon the cream! What do you think? Upon my word I
believe I should.' The idea of visiting America entered his
mind, and when words of praise reached him from the back-
woods of the United States he replied warmly: 'Your expressions of affectionate remembrance and approval, sounding
from the green forests on the banks of the Mississippi, sink
deeper into my heart and gratify it more than all the honorary
distinctions that all the courts in Europe could confer . . .
to be told that in each nook and corner of the world's great
mass there lives one well-wisher who holds communion with
one in the spirit, is a worthy fame indeed, and one which I
would not barter for a mine of wealth.' By the autumn of '41
the idea had become an obsession: 'I am still haunted by
visions of America, night and day. To miss this opportunity
would be a sad thing. Kate cries dismally if I mention the
subject. But, God willing, I think it *must* be managed somehow!' Washington Irving assured him that he would have a
great triumph all over the States, and this determined him:
'I have made up my mind (with God's leave) to go to America
—and to start as soon after Christmas as it will be safe to go',
he informed Forster in capital letters. But Kate wept whenever he spoke of it, and he asked Macready to write to her,
stating her husband's views as strongly as possible. Macready
not only complied but offered to take care of the children
during their absence. Kate surrendered, and it was arranged
that her maid Anne should travel with them. Their house
was let; brother Frederick remained in charge of the servants;
and Dickens wrote to an American correspondent: 'I hope
. . . in the third week of the new year, to set my foot upon

the soil I have trodden in my day-dreams many times and whose sons (and daughters) I yearn to know and be among.'

Before leaving he came to an agreement with Chapman and Hall that *Master Humphrey's Clock* should run down and not be wound up again, that he would write a volume on his travels for them, to be followed by a novel which he would begin in a year's time; and that they would pay him £150 a month during the twelve months before the novel commenced, and £200 a month while it was being serialised, plus three-quarters of the profits. This was an extremely favourable arrangement for the author, who was delighted with it and wrote to the firm: 'I should not feel at ease on leaving England if I did not tell you once more with my whole heart that your conduct to me on this and all other occasions has been honourable, manly, and generous, and that I have felt it a solemn duty, in the event of any accident happening to me while I am away, to place this testimony upon record.' In a lighter mood he gave one of the partners, Edward Chapman, who was about to get married, the benefit of his wisdom on taking so grave a step: 'Farewell! If you did but know—and would pause, even at this late period—better an action for breach than—but we buy experience. Excuse my agitation. I scarcely know what I write. To see a fellow creature—and one who has so long withstood—still if—will *nothing* warn you.—In extreme excitement. My hand fails me. P.S. Pause. Put it off. P.P.S. Emigrate. P.P.P.S.—and leave me the business—I mean the Strand one.'

At the end of September he spent a few days with Forster at Rochester, Gravesend, and Cobham, and in November, following his operation, he stayed with his wife, first at Richmond, and then at the White Hart Hotel, Windsor. For the last fortnight of their time in England he remained with the children at home. They sailed from Liverpool on the *Britannia*, a steamboat of 1154 tons, in the first week of 1842, when Dickens was in a condition which he had recently made known to an American admirer: 'I cannot describe to you the glow into which I rise, when I think of the wonders that await us . . .'

# 8

## WITH HIS LADY

MANY reasons have been given for Dickens's visit to America, among others that, having invested some money in the Cairo Company, a notorious swindle of the period, he wished to see the town of Cairo at the junction of the Ohio and Mississippi rivers. It is however improbable that he would have crossed an ocean and half a continent merely to view the grave of his savings. He visited America for the same reason that Julius Caesar visited England: he wanted to know what it was like. Curiosity and the certainty of a warm welcome were the main inducements: he wished to see in what ways a new republic could improve on an old monarchy, and he wished to enjoy the manifestations of his own popularity.

The journey commenced in a calm sea. Before dinner on the first day was half over, 'even those passengers who were most distrustful of themselves plucked up amazingly; and those who in the morning had returned to the universal question "Are you a good sailor?" a very decided negative, now either parried the inquiry with the evasive reply "Oh! I suppose I'm no worse than anybody else"; or, reckless of all moral obligations, answered boldly "Yes": and with some irritation too, as though they would add "I should like to know what you see in *me*, sir, particularly, to justify suspicion!"' Trouble started on the third morning, and Dickens took to his bunk, staying there for several days, not actually seasick but supine, indifferent to everything, and conscious only of 'having a kind of lazy joy—of fiendish delight, if anything so lethargic can be dignified with the title—in the fact of my wife being too ill to talk to me', a state of mind which recalls Quilp's pleasantries at his wife's expense: 'I'm glad you're wet. I'm glad you're cold. I'm glad you lost your way. I'm glad your eyes are red with crying. It does my heart good to see your little nose so pinched and frosty.'

When he was able to stand again, Dickens passed most of his time talking, feeding and playing whist in the ladies' cabin. They ran into very heavy weather when more than half-way across, and for several hours 'waited quietly for the worst.

I never expected to see the day again, and resigned myself to God as well as I could.' But there was no need to trouble himself with any such thoughts just then, especially as he was kept pretty busy trying to comfort the women: 'There were in the ladies' cabin . . . Kate, Anne, and a little Scotch lady, all in their night dresses, and all nearly mad with terror. It was blowing great guns; the ship was rolling from side to side with her masts in the water at every plunge; and the lightning streamed through the skylight, awfully. I could do no less, of course, than try to comfort them, and the first thing that occurred to me was brandy-and-water. Now all along this cabin was a great fixed sofa, built so as to form a part of it and running the whole length. They were all three heaped together at one end of this sofa, when I appeared with the jorum of grog in my hand. Just as I was administering it to the lady who happened to be at the top of the live bundle, the vessel rolled, and to my horror and astonishment they all went to the other end of the couch. By the time I staggered to that end, there came another roll, and they all tumbled back to the other, as if they were in an otherwise empty omnibus and two giants were tilting it by turns at either end. I dodged them, perhaps for half an hour, without catching them once, with nothing on but a pair of rough trousers and that blue jacket I used to wear at Petersham; and in all the misery of the time, I had a keen sense of the absurdity of my position . . .' Somehow the ship got through, after which, probably because the pilot was feeling a little too sure of himself, she stuck on a mud-bank near the entrance to Halifax harbour. Freed of that, she arrived at the wharf, where a breathless man was rushing about shouting the name of Dickens at the top of his voice. This turned out to be the Speaker of the House of Assembly, who took possession of the famous author, paraded him through the streets, introduced him to the Governor, and made him an honoured guest at the opening of parliament that day. In his letters home Dickens often referred to himself as 'the Inimitable', his old Chatham schoolmaster, William Giles, having once sent him a snuff-box inscribed 'To the Inimitable Boz.' So this was how he reported his reception at Halifax to Forster: 'I wish you could have seen the crowds cheering the Inimitable in the streets. I wish you could have seen judges, law-officers, bishops, and law-makers welcoming the Inimitable. I wish you could have

seen the Inimitable shown to a great elbow-chair by the
Speaker's throne, and sitting alone in the middle of the floor
of the House of Commons, the observed of all observers,
listening with exemplary gravity to the queerest speaking
possible, and breaking in spite of himself into a smile as he
thought of this commencement to the Thousand and One
stories in reserve for home and Lincoln's Inn Fields and Jack
Straw's Castle.' After their tempestuous journey, the passengers of the *Britannia*, headed by Dickens, decided to make a
presentation to the Captain. Fifty pounds was raised, and in
due course John Hewett received a piece of plate 'as a slight
acknowledgment of his great ability and skill under circumstances of much difficulty and danger.'

The boat reached Boston on January 22nd, 1842, and
Dickens stood on deck staring about him: 'though I had had
as many eyes as Argus, I should have had them all wide open,
and all employed on new objects.' Several objects of a human
kind at once claimed his attention. 'A dozen men came
leaping on board at the peril of their lives, with great bundles
of newspapers under their arms, worsted comforters (very
much the worse for wear) round their necks', and placards in
their hands. He assumed they were newsboys, but they introduced themselves as editors and shook his hand until it was
shakeless. When he could get away, he drove with his wife,
her maid Anne, and a fellow-passenger Lord Mulgrave, who
was rejoining his regiment at Montreal, to the best hotel,
Tremont House. He was in boisterous spirits, jumped out of
the carriage, flew up the steps of the hotel, and sprang into
the hall shouting 'Here we are!' His quick eye took in everything, his laughter rang out spontaneously, and he talked
away without embarrassment as if he had just arrived at his
own home. After dinner he rushed out with Mulgrave,
followed by one or two Americans whose acquaintance he
had just made. It was a stingingly cold night with a full
moon, and every object stood out clearly, gleaming in the
frost. Enveloped in a shaggy fur coat which he had bought
in Regent Street, Dickens ran over the glittering frozen snow,
reading the signs on the shops, commenting on the architecture, and punctuating a ceaseless stream of chatter with
bursts of hilarious laughter. When they arrived opposite the
Old South Church, Dickens suddenly let forth a Quilpish
yell, which startled and bewildered his companions. 'The

mystery of that shout is still a mystery to me', wrote one of
them some forty years after. But to anyone who understands
the nature of Dickens there is nothing mysterious about it.

There had never been anything at all like Dickens's reception in the United States, and no such welcome has been
accorded a writer in any country since, except when Dickens
himself revisited the States twenty-five years later. 'How can
I give you the faintest notion of my reception here?' he wrote
to Forster; 'of the crowds that pour in and out the whole day;
of the people that line the streets when I go out; of the cheering
when I went to the theatre; of the copies of verses, letters of
congratulation, welcomes of all kinds, balls, dinners, assem-
blies without end . . . But what can I tell you about any of
these things which will give you the slightest notion of the
enthusiastic greeting they give me, or the cry that runs
through the whole country! I have had deputations from the
Far West, who have come from more than two thousand
miles distance: from the lakes, the rivers, the back-woods, the
log-houses, the cities, factories, villages, and towns. Authorities from nearly all the States have written to me. I have
heard from the universities, congress, senate, and bodies,
public and private, of every sort and kind. "It is no nonsense,
and no common feeling", wrote Dr. Channing to me yesterday. "It is all heart. There never was, and never will be,
such a triumph." . . . I am sitting for a portrait and for a bust.
I have the correspondence of a secretary of state, and the
engagements of a fashionable physician. I have a secretary
whom I take on with me. He is a young man of the name of
George Putnam, was strongly recommended to me, is most
modest, obliging, silent, and willing; and does his work *well*.
He boards and lodges at my expense when we travel; and his
salary is ten dollars per month—about two pounds five of
our English money.' Before he had been a couple of days in
the place he had engaged himself for every hour of his stay;
and when the mayor, Jonathan Chapman, solicited his
company, the following colloquy took place:

'Mr. Dickens, will you dine with me?'
'I am sorry I am engaged.'
'Will you sup with me?'
'I am engaged.'
'Will you lunch with me?'
'I am engaged.'

'Will you breakfast with me?'

'I am engaged.'

'Well, will you sleep with me?'

'Thank you, with the greatest pleasure. Nothing could gratify me more than to accept an invitation to sleep.'

But although, as he said, 'there never was a king or emperor upon the earth so cheered and followed by crowds', the élite of Boston were passing unfavourable comments on his manners, his personality and his attire. He had, they declared, a dissipated-looking mouth, a face which, minus the genius in it, might have been that of any London shopkeeper; he had a rapid off-hand manner of speaking, hearty but 'far from well-bred'; undoubtedly he was clever and fascinating, but he was too breezy, too careless of what he said, too energetic, and the tones of his voice were not those of a gentleman. Nor were the colours of his waistcoats. Most Boston gentlemen wore black satin waistcoats on full dress occasions; but Dickens wore velvet waistcoats of vivid green or brilliant crimson, with double watch-chains and a fancy cravat which concealed the collar and descended in voluptuous folds. As no Bostonian who had any claim to be called a gentleman would have dreamt of speaking what he thought or behaving as he liked, two examples of low-breeding in Dickens were soon causing the elevation of refined eyebrows in Beacon and Park Streets. At one dinner the honoured guest caught sight of himself in a mirror, saw that his hair was slightly disordered, promptly produced a pocket comb, and to the astonishment of everyone calmly combed his hair while sitting at table. On another occasion he was dining at Judge Prescott's, one of the great houses of Boston, when a discussion arose as to which was the more beautiful woman, the Duchess of Sutherland or Mrs. Caroline Norton. 'Well, I don't know', said Dickens. 'Mrs. Norton is perhaps the more beautiful, but the Duchess to my mind is the more kissable person.' An earthquake would have caused less consternation; and the cultivated circles of Boston were rather relieved when he left for New York.

But before quitting the neighbourhood he did something that outraged the more vulgar portions of the community quite as much as combing his hair at table or thinking a woman kissable had shocked the élite. At public dinners in his honour both at Boston and Hartford he had the effrontery to suggest that British authors should receive a share of the huge profits on their works made by American publishers. He did not of course go so far as to hint that an author should make a quarter as much out of his brain's product as the person who sold it; such a bizarre notion never entered his head; but he did feel that when a man slaved away for months on end and gave untold delight to countless readers, he might reasonably expect some slight financial return for his travail and the pleasure he provided. In those days there was no international copyright, and as each number of Dickens's novels reached America it was seized by publishers, who printed thousands of copies as fast as they could, sold them all over the country, and pocketed the proceeds without even sending a letter of thanks to the author whose brain was making them rich. Indeed it may be said that if the royalties which ought to have been paid in the United States on the novels of Scott, Dickens, and a host of others, on the dramatic adaptations of their stories, and on the operas of Gilbert and Sullivan when first produced, were now to be handed over with compound interest, Great Britain would no longer be a debtor nation to the United States. The contra account of American authors whose royalties were not paid by English publishers over the same period would be a drop in the ocean by comparison. The spiritual value derived from reading the British masterpieces cannot be computed, and therefore cannot be commuted.

From the moment when Dickens opened his mouth on this subject, saying that British authors had made the first move towards an international agreement and hoping that America would reciprocate, he was assailed in the press with every vituperative epithet in the dictionary of journalese. For merely remarking that fame should 'blow out of her trumpet a few notes of a different kind from those with which she has hitherto contented herself', and for reminding his listeners that the burden of Scott's last days would have been considerably lightened if a tithe of what was due to him in America had reached Abbotsford, 'such an outcry began . . . as an Englishman can form no notion of. Anonymous letters; verbal dissuasions; newspaper attacks making Colt (a murderer who is attracting great attention here) an angel by comparison with me; assertions that I was no gentleman, but a mere mercenary scoundrel; coupled with the most monstrous misrepresentations relative to my design and purpose in visiting the United States; came pouring in upon me every day.' The committee that had been formed to organise a great public dinner to him in New York wrote to beg him not to mention the subject again. 'I answered that I would. That nothing should deter me . . . That the shame was theirs, not mine; and that as I would not spare them when I got home, I would not be silenced here.'

He showed great courage in thus braving public opinion in a country that was bent on paying him honour instead of royalties. The Boston dinner alone would have turned an ordinary man's head. Fulsome flattery was the order of the evening. Nearly every speech had some reference to the characters in his novels, and the dinner lasted from five o'clock on February 1st till after one the following morning. The spectacle of a number of apparently sane gentlemen guzzling and swilling in honour of their guest, and then rising unsteadily to their feet in order to address twaddle at one another, is not wholly unknown in this age; but we now limit the ceremony to about three hours, by which time Dickens's contemporaries would have felt that it had just commenced. Nowadays the English are usually bored by the prospect of post-prandial speaking, and endure it as a sort of duty; but the Americans are eager for more after the speaking is over, largely from a belief that they derive benefit from it. In those days the two nations shared the same taste, though one suspects that English diners were comfortably drunk before the speaking began.

On their way to New York Dickens and his wife stayed at Hartford, where they held formal levees every day for a couple of hours, receiving two or three hundred people at each, and where they were serenaded one night after they had gone to bed. The singers took up their positions in the corridor outside their bedroom door and sang 'in low voices to guitars, about home and absent friends and other topics which they knew would interest us; we were more moved than I can tell you. In the midst of my sentimentality though, a thought occurred to me which made me laugh so immoderately that I was obliged to cover my face with the bedclothes. "Good heavens!" I said to Kate, "what a monstrously ridiculous and commonplace appearance my boots must have, outside the door!" I never *was* so impressed with a sense of the absurdity of boots, in all my life.' They stopped at Newhaven, where they were 'forced to open another levee for the students and professors of the college (the largest in the States), and the townspeople. I suppose we shook hands, before going to bed, with considerably more than five hundred people; and I stood, as a matter of course, the whole time.' Another town en route, Wallingford, turned out to see him, for which purpose the train was stopped; Worcester and Springfield were also seen; and in the middle of February 'Mr. Dickens, with his lady', announced the daily press, reached New York, where they put up at the Carlton Hotel.

On the evening of their arrival Washington Irving paid them a visit. Owing to the affectionate references to him in Dickens's letters and the discreet public references by him to Dickens, it was assumed for nearly a century that they had got on famously together; but we now know that such was not the case. Calling at the hotel, Washington Irving sent in his card and was shown into the guest's parlour. A sound like a minor tornado preluded the whirlwind entrance of Dickens, napkin in hand, who hailed him with enthusiasm and dragged him off to the dining-table, which was covered, Irving noted, 'with a vulgar profusion of food', and the cloth of which, the visitor did not fail to observe, was stained with gravy and wine. 'Irving', cried Dickens, 'I am delighted to see you. What will you drink?—a mint julep or a gin cock-tail?' In describing this simple hearty scene Irving used to lose his temper, talk with disgust of Dickens's tavern manners, denounce him as outrageously vulgar in dress, behaviour and mind, and speak of his friendliness as selfishness. In brief, the American gentleman was shocked by the English genius.

New York was worse than Boston. Dickens was worried and mobbed wherever he went. Some Americans objected to 'this servile homage, this sickening flattery', and one of them ironically suggested that a shrewd enterprising Yankee should 'procure Boz, put him in a cage, and take him about the country for a *show*.' There was a great Boz ball at the Park Theatre on February 14th. 'The scene on our entrance was very striking. There were three thousand people present in full dress; from the roof to the floor, the theatre was decorated magnificently; and the light, glitter, glare, show, noise, and cheering, baffle my descriptive powers.' They were received by the mayor and other dignitaries, and then 'paraded all round the enormous ball-room, twice, for the gratification of the many-headed. That done, we began to dance—Heaven knows how we did it, for there was no room.' Tableaux vivants of scenes from Dickens's novels were given, and several of the newspapers recorded that the author had never been in such good society as that of Boston and New York, where he was thunderstruck, confounded, and stricken pale by the aristocracy which had gathered together to welcome him. Whether the aristocracy were also responsible for the sore throat which afflicted him after the ball, we are not told, but he had to cancel all appointments until the 18th, when a banquet was given him at the City Hall. Washington Irving was chairman and had prepared his speech carefully in the conviction that he would break down during its delivery, which, sure enough, he did. In accordance with his threat, Dickens again referred to the question of international copyright; but by this time he had shamed several prominent Americans into public approval of his sentiments, for not only did Irving assert 'It is but fair that those who have laurels for their brows should be permitted to browse on their laurels', but an editor, Cornelius Matthews, declared that American authors suffered because publishers could get English works for nothing, and honestly proclaimed 'I desire to see something of the great debt, now accumulated for ages, which we owe to the brotherhood of British writers, cancelled.' Although Dickens was still vilified in the press to an extent that made him confess 'I vow to Heaven that the scorn and indignation I have felt under this unmanly and ungenerous treatment have been to me an amount of agony such as I have never experienced since my birth', some of the better-class papers, such as the New York *Tribune*, supported him; and to clinch his case he requested Forster to get a few leading writers in England to back him up. Carlyle at once did so, and others followed suit, but the copyright question was not settled for another half-century (1892) when the debt owed by America was so great that no one cared to mention it.

Life in New York became less and less endurable for the adored and detested visitor: 'I can do nothing that I want to do, go nowhere where I want to go, and see nothing that I want to see. If I turn into the street, I am followed by a multitude. If I stay at home, the house becomes, with callers, like a fair. If I visit a public institution, with only one friend, the directors come down incontinently, waylay me in the yard, and address me in a long speech. I go to a party in the evening, and am so inclosed and hemmed about by people, stand where I will, that I am exhausted for want of air. I dine out, and have to talk about everything, to everybody. I go to church for quiet, and there is a violent rush to the neighbourhood of the pew I sit in, and the clergyman preaches *at* me. I take my seat in a railroad car, and the very conductor won't leave me alone. I get out at a station, and can't drink a glass of water without having a hundred people looking down my throat when I open my mouth to swallow. Conceive what all this is! Then by every post, letters on letters arrive, all about nothing, and all demanding an immediate answer. This man is offended because I won't live in his house; and that man is thoroughly disgusted because I won't go out more than four times in one evening. I have no rest or peace, and am in a perpetual worry.' All the same he managed to enjoy one excursion incognito, when he spent half the night with two constables, 'and went into every brothel, thieves' house, murdering hovel, sailors' dancing place, and abode of villainy, both black and white, in the town.' But the prospect of dinners and receptions at every city in the States was more than he could bear, and he declined invitations from public bodies in Philadelphia, Baltimore, Washington, and other places, determining henceforth to live his own life as far as possible. It was not very far.

Apart from his unpopular views on the copyright question, he was now getting into hot water for his privately expressed opinions of slavery, 'that most hideous blot and foul disgrace', and of the slave-owner, 'a more exacting, and a sterner, and a less responsible despot than the Caliph Haroun Alraschid in his angry robe of scarlet.' On the general question of equality in the States, he said that the attitude of republicans was 'I will not tolerate a man above me, and of those below none must approach too near'; and he assured Forster that 'the heaviest blow ever dealt at liberty will be dealt by this country, in the failure of its example to the earth.' The table manners of the natives also repelled him. Like Thackeray, he did not care to see American men and women putting food into their mouths with knives, and he never got accustomed to the men's habit of blowing their noses with their fingers.

Another national practice jarred upon him. Travelling from New York to Philadelphia, he was admiring the sunset from the train when 'my attention was attracted to a remarkable appearance issuing from the windows of the gentlemen's car immediately in front of us, which I supposed for some time was occasioned by a number of industrious persons inside, ripping open feather-beds, and giving the feathers to the wind. At length it occurred to me that they were only spitting, which was indeed the case; though how any number of passengers which it was possible for that car to contain, could have maintained such a playful and incessant shower of expectoration, I am still at a loss to understand: notwithstanding the experience in all salivatory phenomena which I afterwards acquired.' The marksmanship of the tobacco chewers was not however as good as he had been led to expect. At Washington 'several gentlemen called upon me who, in the course of conversation, frequently missed the spittoon at five paces; and one (but he was certainly short-sighted) mistook the closed sash for the open window, at three. On another occasion, when I dined out, and was sitting with two ladies and some gentlemen round a fire before dinner, one of the company fell short of the fireplace six distinct times.' The stone floors of bar-rooms and hotel passages were, he noticed, tesselated with these deposits, as if 'paved with open oysters.'

Early in March they arrived at Philadelphia, where they received a call from a prominent citizen who asked if he might introduce a few friends the following morning. Though not feeling well, Dickens raised no objection, but was horrified when he beheld a surging mass of people in Chestnut Street, outside the United States Hotel, where they were staying. He demanded the reason for this invasion, and was informed that the prominent citizen had announced in the morning's paper that Mr. Dickens would be 'gratified to shake hands with his friends between the hours of half-past ten and half-past eleven o'clock.' He flatly declined to shake hands with anyone; but when the landlord assured him that there would be a riot and the hotel would probably be wrecked if the crowd were disappointed, he consented to receive 'his friends.' For two hours he and Kate endured the process of having their hands crushed and their arms almost dislocated, while an endless stream of visitors flowed before them. Had the mob of callers been able to foresee the use to which they were

soon to be put in *Martin Chuzzlewit*, Dickens's legs would
have been exercised as severely as his right arm. Wherever
he went the women begged for locks of his hair; but as he
did not wish to finish the tour in a wig, he gave them his
autograph instead. His great coat was already piebald, many
people in the crowds about him having screwed bits of fur
out of it as mementos. Poems of welcome and puns expressive
of joy were printed in the papers: e.g. 'We are very happy to
see him among our *living* authors, although his *Nell* has been
heard of all over the country.' He thought Philadelphia 'a
handsome city, but distractingly regular. After walking about
it for an hour or two, I felt that I would have given the world
for a crooked street.' As usual he visited the public institutions, among others the Eastern Penitentiary, where he was
appalled by the system of solitary confinement: 'I believe that
very few men are capable of estimating the immense amount
of torture and agony which this dreadful punishment, prolonged for years, inflicts upon the sufferers.' No man, he felt
convinced, had the right to inflict such pain on a fellow-
creature: 'I hold this slow and daily tampering with the
mysteries of the brain to be immeasurably worse than any
torture of the body.' And he told a friend: 'I never in my life
was more affected by anything which was not strictly my own
grief.' The intensity of his feeling on the subject reveals the
gregariousness of his own nature.

For us, if not for him, the most interesting episode in his
visit to the Quaker city followed the arrival at his hotel of a
parcel containing two volumes of 'Tales' together with a
letter from their author enclosing a review of *Barnaby Rudge*.
It is a wonder that Dickens troubled to look at the 'Tales' or
to notice the letter, for he had already been pestered past
endurance by authors who had sent him manuscripts, sternly
requesting him to read them carefully, to make any alterations
or corrections he thought proper, and to arrange for their
publication in England, after which he might receive a percentage on the sales. Others had furnished brilliant ideas for
books, proposing to collaborate with him and generously
offering him half the profits. The two volumes he received
at Philadelphia were not therefore hailed by him as harbingers
of joy; but he dipped into them, and asked the author, Edgar
Allan Poe, to call. Three years later Poe made his reputation
with a poem called *The Raven*, the idea of which had been

prompted by the bird in *Barnaby Rudge*, and four years after that he made his second big success with a poem called *The Bells*, which had largely been inspired by Dickens's story *The Chimes*. But at the time of their meeting Poe was practically unknown, and Dickens said he would do his best to get the 'Tales' published in London. They had a pleasant talk, after which Poe felt a little less pessimistic than usual. But though Dickens tried to interest several firms in the 'Tales' when he returned home, he had to report that 'they could not entertain publishing a collection of short stories by an unknown writer', which has been a leading refrain in the correspondence of publishers ever since. It is obvious that Dickens was referring to Poe in one of his letters to Forster: 'I am really indebted for a good broad grin to PE, literary critic of Philadelphia, and sole proprietor of the English language in its grammatical and idiomatic purity; to PE, with the shiny straight hair and turned-down shirt collar, who taketh all of us English men of letters to task in print, roundly and uncompromisingly, but told me at the same time that I had "awakened a new era" in his mind.'

On their way to Washington, which Dickens next visited 'with his lady', they stopped at Baltimore, where he was closely inspected at the railway station by the citizenry, who clustered 'round the carriage in which I sat; let down all the windows; thrust in their heads and shoulders; hooked themselves on conveniently by their elbows; and fell to comparing notes on the subject of my personal appearance, with as much indifference as if I were a stuffed figure . . . Some gentlemen were only satisfied by exercising their sense of touch.' They stayed at Willard's (Fuller's) Hotel in Washington, where he was invited to attend the meetings of the Senate and the House of Representatives, but was not overcome by the oratory or personality of the leading politicians; and he confessed sadly that, possibly from the imperfect development of his organ of veneration, he had neither fainted away nor been moved to tears of joyful pride by the sight of any legislative body: 'I have borne the House of Commons like a man, and have yielded to no weakness, but slumber, in the House of Lords.' While freely admitting that 'farm-yard imitations have not as yet been imported from the Parliament of the United Kingdom' into the American House of Representatives, he felt compelled to state that 'Dishonest Faction in its

8

most depraved and most unblushing form, stared out from every corner of the crowded hall.'

He was received by the President of the United States, John Tyler, a mild and gentle person, who 'expressed great surprise at my being so young. I would have returned the compliment, but he looked so jaded, that it stuck in my throat like Macbeth's amen.' Many official dignitaries called at his hotel to pay their respects, and at the conclusion of one interview his secretary informed him that he had just been talking to one of the most remarkable men in the country. 'Good God! Mr. Putnam, they are all so!' he exclaimed. 'I have scarcely met a man since my arrival who wasn't one of the most remarkable men in the country.' As usual they hardly had a minute to themselves, and on Sunday they dined with a former President, John Quincy Adams, at two-thirty, and with Robert Greenhow at five-thirty, with what effect on their digestions we do not know. At the President's levee on March 15th Dickens made his appearance between nine and ten, and the two thousand people present revolved round him at the pace of a funeral march, gazing, gaping, with popping eyes and stretched necks. Wherever he moved, said an onlooker, it was like throwing corn among hungry chickens: there was a rush to get near him. When he left, he was pursued to the dressing-room, to the carriage, to the hotel, to his bedroom; where he must have been rather relieved to find no one under the bed or in the wardrobe. We are not therefore astonished to read in one of his letters that although he had found the Americans hospitable, generous, frank, warm-hearted, enthusiastic, courteous and chivalrous, he did not feel at home among them: 'I don't like the country. I would not live here on any consideration. It goes against the grain with me . . . I think it impossible, utterly impossible, for any Englishman to live here and be happy.' Quite apart from his personal feelings, 'this is not the republic I came to see; this is not the republic of my imagination. I infinitely prefer a liberal monarchy—even with its sickening accompaniments of court circulars—to such a government as this . . . Freedom of opinion! Where is it? I see a press more mean, and paltry, and silly, and disgraceful, than in any country I ever knew'; in fact the newspapers were 'so filthy and bestial that no honest man would admit one into his house for a water-closet doormat.' He also saw 'the intrusion of the most pitiful, mean, malicious, creeping, crawling, sneaking party spirit into all transactions of life.'

It is clear that he had had enough of it by the time he had seen Washington, but he intended to go through with it, and they next visited a slave district, spending a couple of days at Richmond in Virginia, where they stayed at the Exchange Hotel and were given a supper there by local notabilities, at which the chairman warned Dickens that he must not let success turn his head as it had Napoleon's, and Dickens replied that he would do his best to keep his head in its natural position. Persiflage of this nature obtained throughout the evening, culminating with the arrival of the port, when the chairman eulogised a character in *The Old Curiosity Shop* and its author retorted that the chairman himself was a living curiosity. Such pleasantries may have enabled Dickens to forget the all-pervading horror of slavery for a few hours, but in conversation with the people he met elsewhere he was not allowed to forget it. 'It's not the interest of a man to use his slaves ill. It's damned nonsense that you hear in England', he was told by one of them. To which he replied 'that it was not a man's interest to get drunk, or to steal, or to game, or to indulge in any other vice, but he *did* indulge in it for all that. That cruelty, and the abuse of irresponsible power, were two of the bad passions of human nature, with the gratification of which considerations of interest or of ruin had nothing whatever to do.' On a different occasion he informed a judge, who had pitied the prejudice and ignorance of the British people on the subject of slavery, that 'I believed we were much more competent to judge of its atrocity and horror than he who had been brought up in the midst of it', and that 'men who spoke of it as a blessing, as a matter of course, as a state of things to be desired, were out of the pale of reason; and that for them to speak of ignorance or prejudice was an absurdity too ridiculous to be combated.'

He was inexpressibly relieved to get away from 'this accursed and detested system', and to reach Baltimore, where Washington Irving dined with him at Barnum's Hotel, and left him under the impression that there was nothing but amity between them. By train and coach they got to Harrisburg, where, to escape being mobbed, they went on board the canal-boat which was to take them to Pittsburgh. A fellow-passenger was Judge Ellis Lewis, who noticed that Kate Dickens was quiet, leaving all the conversation to her husband. Lewis wanted Dickens's autograph for his daughter, and a Quaker who was present got a sheet of paper, at the top of which Dickens wrote his signature.

'Thee begins very close to the top of the sheet', said the Quaker.

'Yes', said Dickens; 'if I left a large blank over my name, somebody might write a note or a bond over it.'

'Does thee suppose that a judge of the court would do such a thing?'

'I did not intimate anything of that kind. The paper might soon pass out of the judge's possession, and be made use of by others. But I do not suppose that judges of courts in America are any better than the judges in England.'

The canal journey to Pittsburgh was not comfortable. The cabin was cramped and overcrowded, and 'You never can conceive what the hawking and spitting is, the whole night through', he reported to Forster. '*Upon my honor and word* I was obliged, this morning, to lay my fur-coat on the deck, and wipe the half dried flakes of spittle from it with my handkerchief: and the only surprise seemed to be, that I should consider it necessary to do so. When I turned in last night, I put it on a stool beside me, and there it lay, under a cross fire from five men—three opposite; one above; and one below. I make no complaints, and shew no disgust.' In fairness to the Americans, it should be said that Dickens invariably played *Home Sweet Home* on his accordion, with great feeling and some repetition, before going to bed. His habits of early rising, of washing in half-frozen water, and of keeping up with the horses for a walk of five or six miles on the towing-path before breakfast, must also have aroused their resentment. While the fact that he found the volume of Shakespeare which he carried with him 'an unspeakable source of delight' almost certainly caused offence.

They held the usual levee at Pittsburgh, where they put up at the Exchange Hotel and shook several hundred hands. As a relief from the boredom he was beginning to feel, he decided to practise mesmerism, commencing operations with his wife, who passed through a phase of hysterics into unconsciousness. The boredom became acute when they started for the west down the Ohio river on a steamer: 'I am quite serious when I say that I do not believe there are, on the whole earth besides, so many intensified bores as in these United States. No man can form an adequate idea of the real meaning of the word, without coming here.' They stayed two days at the Broadway Hotel, Cincinnati, and on arrival were just about to issue an official notification that they were not 'at home' when two judges called to ask when they would receive the townspeople. The ceremony of arm-tugging and finger-gripping was duly performed, and at an evening party he was besieged by females, one of whom begged for the rose in his buttonhole. 'That would not do', said he. 'I could give it to no one. The others would be jealous.' As a concession to the earnest looks of the others, he distributed the leaves, one to each. But that was merely the sweet of the evening; the joint was not to his relish: 'We went to a party at Judge Walker's, and were introduced to at least one hundred and fifty first-rate bores, separately and singly. I was required to sit down by the greater part of them, and talk! . . . I really think my face has acquired a fixed expression of sadness from the constant and unmitigated boring I endure.' Nevertheless he thought Cincinnati 'a very beautiful city: I think the prettiest place I have seen here, except Boston.'

He was becoming edgy, and life on the steamboat, especially at mealtime, did not soften him: 'I never in my life did see such listless, heavy dullness as brooded over these meals', he wrote some months after; 'the very recollection of it weighs me down, and makes me, for the moment, wretched . . . to empty, each creature, his Yahoo's trough as quickly as he can, and then slink sullenly away; to have these social sacraments stripped of everything but the mere greedy satisfaction of the natural cravings; goes so against the grain with me, that I seriously believe the recollection of these funeral feasts will be a waking nightmare to me all my life.' They spent a night at Louisville, where the landlord of the hotel entered their room and offered to introduce them to the best families of Kentucky. 'Sir', said Dickens, at the end of his tether, 'are you the publican who keeps this inn?' 'Yes, sir.' 'Then, when I have need for your services, I will ring for you.' The Kentucky giant, one Porter, seven feet eight inches tall, was on the boat, and apparently did not take to Dickens, leaving it on record that 'he had a double gold chain outside his waistcoat and such breast-pins that I thought he looked like one of our river gamblers.' Dickens dismissed Porter as a drunkard.

At last they came to Cairo, where the Ohio joins the Mississippi, and Dickens looked at the place which had been described as Eldorado in a joint-stock prospectus, thereby ruining a large number of English innocents who had invested in the Cairo Company, but which yielded Dickens a handsome return on any sum he may have lost in the concern when he described it as the reverse of Eldorado in *Martin Chuzzlewit*. What he saw was 'a breeding-place of fever, ague, and death . . . A dismal swamp, on which the half-built houses rot away: cleared here and there for the space of a few yards; and teeming, then, with rank unwholesome vegetation, in whose baleful shade the wretched wanderers who are tempted hither, droop, and die, and lay their bones; the hateful Mississippi circling and eddying before it, and turning off upon its southern course a slimy monster hideous to behold; a hotbed of disease, an ugly sepulchre, a grave uncheered by any gleam of promise: a place without one single quality, in earth or air or water, to commend it.'

Entering the Mississippi, which Dickens called a foul stream of liquid mud, they went north to St. Louis, from which he travelled with a male party to inspect the Prairie. He was not impressed: 'Great as the picture was, its very flatness and extent, which left nothing to the imagination, tamed it down and cramped its interest. I felt little of that sense of freedom and exhilaration which a Scottish heath inspires, or even our English downs awaken. It was lonely and wild, but oppressive in its barren monotony.' And his advice to anyone in England who panted to behold the Prairie was: 'Go to Salisbury Plain, Marlborough downs, or any of the broad, high, open lands near the sea. Many of them are fully as impressive; and Salisbury Plain is *decidedly* more so.' At the Planter's House Hotel, their residence in St. Louis, he broke his rule and accepted a public dinner. Also there was the inevitable levee, with himself and his wife as monarchs before whom the natives bowed and stared and perambulated. The return journey down the Mississippi was even more unpleasant than the journey up: 'striking against floating blocks of timber every instant; and dreading some infernal blow at every bump. The helmsman in these boats is in a little glass-house upon the roof . . . another man stands in the very head of the vessel, listening and watching intently; listening, because they can tell in dark nights by the noise when any great obstruction is at hand. This man holds the rope of a large bell which hangs close to the wheel-house, and whenever he pulls it, the engine is to stop directly, and not to stir until he rings again. Last night, this bell rang at least once in every five minutes; and at each alarm there was a concussion which nearly flung one out of bed.'

It was a relief to get back into the Ohio river, which they left at Cincinnati in order to take a coach to Columbus. The boat arrived in the dark, and in walking to the Broadway Hotel Kate's maid, Anne, tripped over the broken pavement and fell to the ground, an incident which gave Dickens an opportunity to estimate his wife's conduct as a traveller in a letter to Forster: "I say nothing of Kate's troubles—but you recollect her propensity? She falls into, or out of, every coach or boat we enter; scrapes the skin off her legs; brings great sores and swellings on her feet; chips large fragments out of her ankle-bones; and makes herself blue with bruises. She really has, however, since we got over the first trial of being among circumstances so new and so fatiguing, made a *most admirable* traveller in every respect. She has never screamed or expressed alarm under circumstances that would have fully justified her in doing so, even in my eyes; has never given way to despondency or fatigue, though we have now been travelling incessantly, through a very rough country, for more than a month, and have been at times, as you may readily suppose, most thoroughly tired; has always accommodated herself, well and cheerfully, to everything; and has pleased me very much, and proved herself perfectly game.' This is rather as an austere parent might have written of a somewhat trying child who, against the heavy odds of an unfortunate temperament, was doing her level best to win papa's approval. The Americans who spoke with Kate found her natural, good-humoured, sensible, gentle, unexacting and self-effacing. She smiled a lot and said little. In fact she seems to have been the ideal wife for a man who enjoyed being lionised. A woman with more character would have got sick of the ceaseless adulation of her husband, would have rebelled against the tedium of enforced friendliness with numbing bores, and would flatly have refused to visit outlandish places in acute discomfort merely to hear her husband being gushed over and to feel her arm being wrenched from its socket. Kate did not even complain when, in the coach to Columbus, a man sitting in the opposite seat played a fountain of tobacco spittle over her through the greater part of the night.

The next stage of their journey, from Columbus to Sandusky, in a coach hired by Dickens, though made endurable by the absence of other passengers, cannot have made the trip more attractive to Kate, whose neck was nearly broken: 'A great portion of it was what is called a "corduroy road": which is made by throwing round logs or whole trees into a swamp, and leaving them to settle there. Good Heaven! if you only felt one of the least of the jolts with which the coach falls from log to log! It is like nothing but going up a steep flight of stairs in an omnibus. Now the coach flung us in a heap on its floor, and now crushed our heads against its roof. Now one side of it was deep in the mire, and we were holding on to the other. Now it was lying on the horses' tails, and now again upon its own back. But it never, never was in any position, attitude, or kind of motion to which we are accustomed in coaches; or made the smallest approach to our experience of the proceedings of any sort of vehicle that goes on wheels. Still, the day was beautiful, the air delicious, and we were *alone*: with no tobacco spittle, or eternal prosy conversation about dollars and politics (the only two subjects they ever converse about, or can converse upon) to bore us. We really enjoyed it; made a joke of being knocked about; and were quite merry.' They finished the journey in a terrific thunderstorm, and spent the night in a rough log-house at Lower Sandusky; thence by boat on Lake Erie to Cleveland, being very sick all the way and not in a fit condition to receive the people who streamed on board at six in the morning to see the famous writer: 'A party of "gentlemen" actually planted themselves before our little cabin, and stared in at the door and windows *while I was washing, and Kate lay in bed.*' Their behaviour, coupled with a very anti-British article which he had read in the local paper, so incensed Dickens 'that when the mayor came on board to present himself to me, according to custom, I refused to see him, and bade Putnam to tell him why and wherefore. His honour took it very coolly, and retired to the top of the wharf, with a big stick and a whittling knife, with which he worked so lustily (staring at the closed door of our cabin all the time) that long before the boat left the big stick was no bigger than a cribbage peg!'

They left the boat at Buffalo and trained to Niagara, where they stayed for ten days at the Clifton House Hotel on the Canadian side. The Falls at first stunned Dickens, drove the restlessness out of him, and then gave him 'peace of mind, tranquillity, calm recollections of the dead, great thoughts of eternal rest and happiness: nothing of gloom or terror. Niagara was at once stamped upon my heart, an Image of Beauty; to remain there, changeless and indelible, until its pulses cease to beat, for ever.' This was not the effect which the Falls made on Anne, who said 'It's nothing but water, and too much of that.'

It was pleasant to be back among Englishmen in Canada, where a dull preoccupation with business had not made the people coarse, humourless and gloomy, and after visiting Toronto and Kingston they proceeded to Montreal, where Dickens abandoned himself to the excitement of producing three one-act plays for the garrison officers of the Coldstream Guards. His wife and several other women took part in the performance, and he declared that Kate played 'devilish well.' Himself was leading actor, stage manager, general director, part prompter, property man, scenery expert, and nearly everything else, 'urging impracticable ladies and impossible gentlemen on to the very confines of insanity, shouting and driving about, in my own person, to an extent which would justify any philanthropic stranger in clapping me into a strait-waistcoat without further inquiry, endeavouring to goad Putnam into some dim and faint understanding of a prompter's duties, and struggling in such a vortex of noise, dirt, bustle, confusion, and inextricable entanglement of speech and action as you would grow giddy in contemplating . . . This kind of voluntary hard labour used to be my great delight. The *furor* has come strong upon me again, and I begin to be once more of opinion that nature intended me for the lessee of a national theatre, and that pen, ink, and paper have spoiled a manager.' He enjoyed the experience more than anything else during his five months in America, more especially because he was among his own countrymen again and on the eve of returning to his own country.

Their first journey across the Atlantic had shaken their belief in the safety of steamers, which Dickens called 'a most damnable invention', and they returned on a sailing ship, leaving New York on June 7th. He had made several friends in the United States, but his general feeling with regard to the inhabitants of that country, tinged no doubt by their reception of *Martin Chuzzlewit*, was summed up in a letter he wrote to a man who had asked if he remembered someone in New York: 'I do not know the American gentleman, God forgive me for putting two such words together.'

# 9

## FRUITS OF TRAVEL

ON the evening of June 29th, 1842, Macready was resting on a sofa in his house at 5 Clarence Gate, Regent's Park, when someone entered the room abruptly. 'Who was it but dear Dickens holding me in his arms in a transport of joy. God bless him!'

During their parents' absence the children had not been happy in the home of Macready, who treated his family with a sternness and gravity which were the very opposite of Dickens's affectionate playfulness with his. When, at a later date, Macready returned home from America, he catechised his children on the progress they had made with their lessons. When Dickens arrived home, his children were got out of bed to be hugged and romped with, the excitement being so great that one of them developed convulsions. Maclise's picture of the four children had accompanied Charles and Kate on their tour of the States, being unpacked at the conclusion of every journey and put on a table, when Charles would play *Home Sweet Home* on his accordion. The joy of an Englishman on landing in his own country after spending several months in America was never felt more intensely than by Dickens. There is no emotion at all like it, and under its influence the rain is exquisite, the fogs have a delicious taste, the dull day is paradisian, the dirt and murk of London are of heaven. Dickens dashed from one friend to another, whooping with delight, and the news that his father had been borrowing money from Macready, and that brother Frederick had been mismanaging the Devonshire Terrace establishment, hardly bothered him at all. Life in England with a needy insolvent parent, an intemperate and troublesome brother, was infinitely preferable to life in the United States with a crowd of wealthy and exemplary relations. His friends celebrated his return with a dinner at Greenwich, the lively nature of which may be inferred from the fact that 'George Cruikshank came home in my phaeton, on his head—to the great delight of the loose midnight loungers in Regent Street. He was last seen taking gin with a waterman.'

For a while he could not settle down to work, spending the days in riotous games with the children or hilarious excursions with Forster and Maclise, but in a fortnight he was busy writing his impressions of America, greatly helped by the letters he had sent from that continent to Forster. In August he was at Broadstairs, bathing, walking, playing and working. Longfellow stayed with him, and was taken to see Rochester Castle, where the custodian threatened them with the law if they went beyond the rails which surrounded the ruins. They ignored the threat and inspected the Castle thoroughly, to the accompaniment of loud curses from the apparently un-tipped official. Under police protection, Dickens, Forster, Maclise and Longfellow went slumming in London, visiting 'the worst haunts of the most dangerous classes', as Forster puts it. Maclise was not equal to this sort of thing and was so sick when they entered a Southwark lodging-house that he took no further interest in the proceedings.

In September Dickens heard that a forged letter criticising American hospitality had appeared over his name in the United States press, and that he had been violently attacked for it. He took no public notice of the incident, told his American friends what he thought of it, dismissed it from his mind, and after the publication of his *American Notes* went for a tour of Cornwall at the end of October with Forster, Maclise and Clarkson Stanfield, visiting Tintagel, Mount St. Michael, the Logan Stone, whereon Forster sat while his companions rocked it, and watching the sun set from Land's End. Dickens described what must have been an uproarious holiday in a letter to his friend C. C. Felton, a Harvard professor:

'Blessed star of morning, such a trip as we had into Corn-wall, just after Longfellow went away . . . We went down into Devonshire by the railroad, and there we hired an open carriage from an innkeeper, patriotic in all Pickwick matters, and went on with post-horses. Sometimes we travelled all night, sometimes all day, sometimes both. I kept the joint-stock purse, ordered all the dinners, paid all the turnpikes, conducted facetious conversations with the post-boys, and regulated the pace at which we travelled. Stanfield (an old sailor) consulted an enormous map on all disputed points of wayfaring; and referred moreover to a pocket-compass and other scientific instruments. The luggage was in Forster's department; and Maclise, having nothing particular to do, sang songs. Heavens! If you could have seen the necks of bottles—distracting in their immense varieties of shape— peering out of the carriage pockets! If you could have witnessed the deep devotion of the post-boys, the wild attachment of the hostlers, the maniac glee of the waiters! If you could have followed us into the earthy old churches we visited, and into the strange caverns on the gloomy sea-shore, and down into the depths of mines, and up to the tops of giddy heights where the unspeakably green water was roaring, I don't know how many hundreds of feet below! If you could have seen but one gleam of the bright fires by which we sat in the big rooms of ancient inns at night, until long after the small hours had come and gone, or smelt but one steam of the hot punch (not white, dear Felton, like that amazing compound I sent you a taste of, but a rich, genial, glowing brown) which came in every evening in a huge broad china bowl! I never laughed in my life as I did on this journey. It would have done you good to hear me. I was choking and gasping and bursting the buckle off the back of my stock, all the way. And Stanfield (who is very much of your figure and temperament, but fifteen years older) got into such apoplectic entanglements that we were often obliged to beat him on the back with portmanteaus before we could recover him. Seriously, I do believe there never was such a trip. And they made such sketches, those two men, in the most romantic of our halting places, that you would have sworn we had the Spirit of Beauty with us, as well as the Spirit of Fun.'

When he returned home he found that *American Notes* was selling briskly. His name alone keeps it alive today. Had it been written by anyone else, it would not have survived its period. 'I cannot praise it, and I will not cut it up', wrote Macaulay to the editor of the *Edinburgh Review*, his reason for refusing to attack it being that 'I have eaten salt with Dickens', whom he considered 'a good man, and a man of real talent.' Emerson thought the work superficial, ignorant, 'the broadest caricature', and not many Americans cared for it, possibly because the attitude of the author was a little like that of a civilised man among barbarians, its very friendliness making it all the more annoying. But before the year was out he had started a novel which would contain a picture of life in the

United States that even his most indulgent American critics could not describe as friendly, and which changed the sneer of depreciation which greeted his travel book into a snarl of rage.

'Men have been chained to hideous walls and other strange anchors ere now', Dickens wrote to a friend, 'but few have known such suffering and bitterness at one time or other, as those who have been bound to Pens.' The inception of *Martin Chuzzlewit* was attended by much travail and anguish. He had to shut himself up in his room for many days without writing a word, and whenever he emerged was 'so horribly cross and surly that the boldest fly at my approach . . . my publishers always come two together, lest I should fall upon a single invader and do murder on his intrusive body.' And he refused all invitations because 'the lapse of every new day only gives me a stronger reason for being perseveringly uncomfortable, that out of my gloom and solitude something comical (or meant to be) may straightway grow up.' The first number appeared in January 1843, and the monthly instalments continued until July '44. Apart from the creation of Mrs. Gamp, a character drawn from a nurse he had seen at the house of Miss Coutts, the main interest of the book's readers centred on the American scenes, which contain the liveliest pages of satire in the language, though naturally the Americans regarded them as the foulest libel in any language. Dickens declared that it was '*impossible* to caricature that people. I lay down my pen in despair sometimes when I read what I have done, and find how it halts behind my own recollection.' But as the countrymen of George Washington were exposed to derision in *Chuzzlewit* as snobs, windbags, hypocrites, liars, bores, humbugs, braggarts, bullies, hogs, savages, blackguards, murderers and idiots; and as they were accused of rudeness, meanness, jealousy, filthiness, greed, inefficiency, ignorance, pretentiousness, viciousness, social bestiality and political depravity; few of them took kindly to the work, and incoming ships carrying the last number were not welcomed by enthusiastic crowds crying for the latest news of Mr. Jefferson Brick or Mrs. Hominy. What was plainly true in the scenes caused the greatest offence, together with the pungency of such observations as:

'They've such a passion for Liberty that they can't help taking liberties with her.'

'All their cares, hopes, joys, affections, virtues, and associations, seemed to be melted down into dollars.'

Concerning slavery: 'Thus the stars wink upon the bloody stripes; and Liberty pulls down her cap upon her eyes, and owns oppression in its vilest aspect for her sister.'

Of the Republic as a whole, he said that she was 'so maimed and lame, so full of sores and ulcers, foul to the eye and almost hopeless to the sense, that her best friends turn from the loathsome creature with disgust.'

But it was perhaps worth going to America in order to come back with the knowledge that 'there is a simplicity of cunning no less than a simplicity of innocence; and in all matters where a lively faith in knavery and meanness was required as the ground-work of belief, Mr. Jonas was one of the most credulous of men.'

It seems that in those days the U.S. was like a modern totalitarian state. When Mark Tapley lets fall a little kindly criticism of local conditions, Mr. Hannibal Chollop says 'You are much too cute to last' and warns him that he will be 'riddled through and through':

'What for?' asked Mark.

'We must be cracked-up, sir', retorted Chollop, in a tone of menace. 'You are not now in A despotic land. We are a model to the airth, and must be jist cracked-up, I tell you.'

'What, I speak too free, do I?' cried Mark.

'I have draw'd upon A man, and fired upon A man for less', said Chollop, frowning. 'I have know'd strong men obleeged to make themselves uncommon skase for less. I have know'd men Lynched for less, and beaten into punkin'-sarse for less, by an enlightened people. We are the intellect and virtue of the airth, the cream Of human natur', and the flower Of moral force. Our backs is easy ris. We must be cracked-up, or they rises, and we snarls. We shows our teeth, I tell you, fierce. You'd better crack us up, you had!'

But America has taken a great leap forward since Dickens's time, and its people no longer require outside assistance to crack them up.

As with the case of Quilp and Little Nell, tastes have changed since *Martin Chuzzlewit* was published. Tom Pinch was then the sympathetic character, Pecksniff the odious one. Now Tom is unendurable, but we revel in Pecksniff, one of the funniest figures ever conceived. '"Ah, human nature, human nature! Poor human nature!" said Mr. Pecksniff, shaking his head at human nature as if he didn't belong to it.' Although the type he represents is burlesqued in Pecksniff, there is so much human nature in him that, at the end, we prefer him to all the 'good' characters. Again, as with Quilp, Dickens had put much more of himself into the part than he was aware. Unconsciously he put something else into *Martin Chuzzlewit* which must have puzzled many of those readers who like to think that a man's work is unrelated to his personality. In chapter 50 Martin reproaches his friend Tom Pinch for treachery, though he gives no reason for the reproach, does not mention what action of Tom's has caused it, and makes no further reference to it. The episode is quite unnecessary to the story, and its meaning is never explained. But, though Dickens changes parts, being sometimes Martin and sometimes Tom, the scene reflects an emotional disturbance of his own which occurred at that time.

On February 26th, 1844 he took the chair at a soirée of the Mechanics' Institution in Liverpool, and in introducing a female pianist to the audience he said that he had some difficulty and tenderness in announcing her name: Miss Weller. The shout of laughter which greeted this made Miss Weller nervous, but Dickens whispered to her that he hoped she would change her name some day and be very happy. The mere sight of her had a strange effect on Dickens, who was reminded of Mary Hogarth, and his intense desire for the spiritual sympathy and companionship of a woman who would understand him and live for him, his longing for ideal love, again took possession of him. He asked her to bring her father to lunch the following day, and he introduced her to his friend T. J. Thompson, with whom he hoped to converse and correspond on the absorbing topic. From Birmingham, whither he went to preside at another meeting, he wrote to Thompson: 'I cannot joke about Miss Weller; for she is too good; and interest in her (spiritual young creature that she is, and destined to an early death, I fear) has become a sentiment with me. Good God what a madman I should seem, if the incredible feeling I have conceived for that girl could be made plain to anyone!' A day or two later he assured his sister Fanny that 'but for the recollection of Miss Weller (which has its tortures too), I don't know but I would as

CHARLES DICKENS AT DOUGHTY STREET (*c.* 1838)

*Pencil Sketch by* GEORGE CRUIKSHANK

*Victoria and Albert Museum*

DICKENS'S FOUR ELDEST CHILDREN AT DEVONSHIRE TERRACE

(1842)

CHARLEY (*centre*), MAMIE (*right*), KATIE (*left, below*),
WALLY (*left, above*), WITH THE ORIGINAL 'GRIP' THE RAVEN
*Crayon Drawing by* DANIEL MACLISE, R.A.
*By courtesy of Major Philip C. Dickens*

soon be comfortably suffocated as continue to live in this wearing, tearing, mad, unhinged, and most extraordinary world.' He sent Miss Weller the copy of Tennyson's poems which had been given him by the poet, and wrote to her father about her wonderful spiritual qualities. On March 11th, twelve days after he had introduced her to T. J. Thompson, he heard that his friend was in love with her and wished to marry her. 'I swear to you that when I opened and read your letter this morning', wrote Dickens, 'I felt the blood go from my face to I don't know where, and my very lips turn white. I never in my life was so surprised, or had the whole current of my life so stopped, for the instant, as when I felt, at a glance, what your letter said.' Having recovered from the shock, he then told Thompson how to persuade the girl's father to give his consent; and on March 29th he was able to congratulate Thompson on his engagement to Christiana Weller, to whom Dickens confessed so much sympathy with Thompson's plight that, if he had not himself been married, he would have experienced 'the greatest happiness and pleasure' in running his friend through the body 'with good sharp steel.' Having inspired the curious passage in *Martin Chuzzlewit* already alluded to, Thompson married Christiana, and the two daughters who resulted from their union became known as Lady Butler, the painter, and Mrs. Alice Meynell, the essayist. Something of the emotion aroused in Dickens by the hopelessness of his infatuation is given to Augustus Moddle towards the close of the novel:

'I wonder', said Tom, 'that in these crowded streets, the foot-passengers are not oftener run over.'

Mr. Moddle, with a dark look, replied:

'The drivers won't do it.'

'Do you mean——?' Tom began.

'That there are some men', interrupted Moddle, with a hollow laugh, 'who can't get run over. They live a charmed life. Coal waggons recoil from them, and even cabs refuse to run them down. Ah!' said Augustus, marking Tom's astonishment. 'There are such men. One of 'em is a friend of mine.'

Nothing in the history of literature has aroused such a frenzy of wrath throughout a continent as that which swept the United States when the numbers describing Martin's American adventures reached the country. In the words of

Carlyle, they caused 'all Yankee-doodledom to fizz like one universal soda-water bottle', and Dickens reported that 'Martin has made them all stark staring raving mad across the water.' He received hundreds of packets containing the written abuse of correspondents and the printed invective of newspapers, but returned all of them unopened to the post office. Such were the public denunciations and execrations that when Macready crossed the Atlantic in the autumn of '43 Dickens would not see him off at Liverpool, lest the fact should leak out and prove detrimental to the actor's interest. 'Whatever you see or hear stated of me', wrote Dickens to Macready, 'whatever is addressed to you or to anybody else in your presence, never contradict it, never take offence at it, never claim me for your friend or champion me in any way. I not only absolve you from any such office but I distinctly entreat you to consider silence upon all such topics your duty to those who are nearest and dearest to you. It is enough for me that while you are away you hold me in your heart; I have no desire to be upon your lips . . . Further, do not write to me through the post but enclose any letter to me in some other one and let it come that way, and do not be shaken out of this by your own prepossessions or by anything else.' Macready, who thought Dickens had been rather hard on the Americans, lived to think differently. 'A crust in England is better than pampering tables here', he wrote at Boston in '48, and 'Let me die in a ditch in England rather than in the Fifth Avenue of New York.'

The English were less sensitive to ridicule than the Americans, and the embodiment of their national weakness in Pecksniff amused them. But from the point of view of sales it did not amuse them enough. The early monthly numbers only sold about twenty thousand copies each, as against forty to fifty thousand of the monthly numbers of *Pickwick* and *Nickleby*, and sixty to seventy thousand of the weekly issues of *Barnaby Rudge* and *The Old Curiosity Shop*. Dickens, who felt that *Martin* was a great improvement on his earlier novels, suffered keen mortification; and when, galling the wound, Chapman and Hall enforced a clause in their contract whereby, if the sales of the work were considered insufficient to cover the monthly sums paid to the author, the latter should make good the deficit, the chagrin of Dickens changed to angry indignation. 'I am so irritated, so rubbed in the tenderest art of my eyelids with bay-salt', he wrote to Forster, 'that a wrong kind of fire is burning in my head.' He instantly wanted to change his publisher, asked Forster to open negotiations with Bradbury and Evans, declared he would pay Chapman and Hall what he owed them, and announced his intention, the moment he had settled with the firm, to let them have a piece of his mind.

The situation was aggravated by the discouraging financial result of his next publication, *A Christmas Carol*. This little story was composed in the autumn of '43 while he was in the throes of *Chuzzlewit*, and took complete hold of him. He wept and laughed and wept again' as he wrote it, and greatly excited by his theme 'walked about the black streets of London, fifteen and twenty miles many a night, when all the sober folks had gone to bed.' With the intention of checking the rapacity of Chapman and Hall he determined to publish it on commission: that is, the costs of production were to be paid by him, and a commission on sales was to be charged by the publishers. But the arrangement did not work out well. The story was a great success, gaining golden opinions from all sorts of readers, but not the thousand golden sovereigns which the author had hoped to gain. Dickens naturally assumed that the publishers had 'run the expenses up anyhow purposely to bring me back and disgust me with the charges.' The probability is that the selling price of the little book was not sufficient to cover the costs of its handsome production. Whatever the cause, Dickens was upset when he saw the accounts, saying that he was 'not only on my beam-ends, but tilted over on the other side. Nothing so unexpected and utterly disappointing has ever befallen me.' He pictured himself ruined, and decided to let his house, go abroad with his family, and live cheaply. But before doing that he had to break with Chapman and Hall. Forster was their literary adviser, so Dickens's early friend Thomas Mitton did what was necessary. A firm of printers, Bradbury and Evans, though at first somewhat nervous at the prospect of setting up as publishers, managed to calm their nerves by the further prospect of what could be made out of Charles Dickens, and took the plunge. In return for a sum of £2800 he gave them a fourth share in whatever he would write during the next eight years, but when he would write anything or what form it would take was to be left entirely to him. Chapman and

Hall's account was squared and his business relationship with them terminated, though only seven years before he had written to assure them that 'my whole endeavours at this moment are directed to perpetuating our most pleasant and friendly associations.'

Those who have harshly judged Dickens's behaviour to his publishers have lacked the imagination to perceive that without the temperament which caused his explosions, he would not have been the author we know. The nature which produced his extraordinary works also prevented him from remaining calm under what he felt to be an injustice. He was an excitable man, capable of instantaneous change of mood, at one moment melting with pity, at the next hard as nails, which helps to explain the remarkable variety and intensity of his creative output. While writing his stories he was no one man, but twenty, or twenty aspects of one man seemingly unrelated, and in real life he was subject to as many metamorphoses. After wringing the hearts of his readers as well as his own heart with the poverty of the Cratchit family in *A Christmas Carol*, and preaching a moving sermon against the love of money, he worked himself into a fever because the profits on the sale of the story did not realise his hopes. Chapman and Hall were legally justified in enforcing the clause which became operative when the sales of the early numbers of *Chuzzlewit* showed no sign of improvement; but they were stupid and ungenerous; stupid because they did not foresee the effect of such an action on a man who was putting his whole brain and soul into the work and giving of his best; ungenerous because Dickens's past labours had made them prosperous. With a large family to support, father, mother, brothers, wife and children, with a good deal of necessary hospitality to dispense, conscious of his growing powers, and aware that his writings had brought far more to his publishers than to himself, Dickens would have had to be a saint to accept such a Scrooge-like action in the spirit of Bob Cratchit. He was not a saint, and no one but a saint who is also an over-driven genius is in a position to blame him. Chapman and Hall deserved to lose him, and got what they deserved.

He tried to help other authors as well as himself, informing Thomas Hood that 'the circumstances under which you signed your agreement are of the most disgraceful kind in so far as Mr. Colburn (the publisher) is concerned. There can be no doubt that he took a money-lending, bill-broking, Jew clothes-bagging, Saturday-night pawnbroking advantage of your temporary situation.'

Many people thought they could trade on the simple magnanimous nature displayed by some of Dickens's characters, but their belief in his indiscriminate generosity was sharply corrected. They forgot that no one has a better cause to preach a sermon on charity than the man who is fighting for his livelihood against sharks and Shylocks. More daring than the play-adapters, a weekly paper printed a 'condensed' version of *A Christmas Carol*. Dickens obtained an injunction against the publishers, and claimed £1000 damages. Whereupon an emissary waited on him and appealed to his good nature on the ground that there were sentiments expressed in his books which led them to believe, etc., etc. Dickens replied that these sentiments must not be construed into a disposition to allow himself to be robbed in all directions, and that he hoped to show they were mistaken in their reading of them. The publishers promptly went bankrupt, and he had to pay about £700 in costs and expenses; which taught him that it is better to be plundered by individuals than pillaged by the law.

While writing *Martin Chuzzlewit* Dickens had been enjoying himself in his usual vigorous way. When at Broadstairs he went for walks of twenty miles or so, seldom relaxing his pace. When in London he sometimes strolled up to Hampstead on fine days and dined with Forster and Maclise at Jack Straw's Castle. Occasionally he went to a big social gathering, but he was not much attracted to that class of thing. Thackeray saw him and his wife at one of them in May '43: 'Did I write to you about Mrs. Procter's grand ball, and how splendid Mrs. Dickens was in pink satin and Mr. Dickens in geranium and ringlets?' The other guests would have been rather astonished to hear the opinion passed upon them by the gentleman in geranium and ringlets: 'I declare I never go into what is called "society" that I am aweary of it, despise it, hate it, and reject it. The more I see of its extraordinary conceit, and its stupendous ignorance of what is passing out of doors, the more certain I am that it is approaching the period when, being incapable of reforming itself, it will have to submit to be reformed by others off the face of the earth.' The pictures of 'society' which appear in his books are not sympathetic. Now and then he attended what is called a Charity Dinner, whereat people hiccup benevolence over a costly meal, but this too made no appeal to him: 'Oh Heaven, if you could have been with me at a hospital dinner last Monday! There were men there—your City aristocracy—who made such speeches and expressed such sentiments as any moderately intelligent dustman would have blushed through his cindery bloom to have thought of. Sleek, slobbering, bow-paunched, over-fed, apoplectic, snorting cattle, and the auditory leaping up in their delight! I never saw such an illustration of the power of purse, or felt so degraded and debased by its contemplation, since I have had eyes and ears.' As a rule he was too busy to attend such functions, and when he was deep in his novel nothing could induce him to dine out except 'some tremendous provocation—such as a twin brother's coming home from China and having appointed to return next morning, which does not often happen.' Not only did he have to deny himself the society of his friends while engaged on a number of his book, but absolute privacy and silence were enforced at home; and once he was almost driven from Broadstairs by a piano next door 'which has six years agony in every note it utters.'

But there was one kind of entertainment at which his own enjoyment was so infectious that his companions caught his sense of fun and well-being and were carried away in spite of themselves. Jane Carlyle reports a riotous party at which Dickens was the leading spirit and sports-master. He had bought a conjurer's entire stock-in-trade, and spent many evenings alone in his room practising how to make watches disappear in one place and appear in another, how to effect the transition of money from this pocket to that, how to burn handkerchiefs and renovate them with the touch of a magic wand, how to convert a box of bran into a live guinea-pig, how to pour flour, raw eggs and other ingredients into a gentleman's hat, boil the whole over a blazing fire, produce a steaming hot plum pudding from it, and return the hat undamaged: such were the mysteries he studied and performed. On December 21st, 1843 Macready's daughter Nina had a birthday party in Clarence Terrace. Macready himself was in America, which was fortunate, because if he had been at home the proceedings would have been less hilarious. Normally, according to Dickens, the Macready children were only allowed 'to come in at dessert and have each a biscuit and a glass of water, in which last refreshment I was always convinced that they drank, with the gloomiest malignity, "Destruction to the gormandising grown-up company!"' It is probable therefore that even a birthday party under their father's superintendence would have been tinged with monastic melancholy. But with the actor away, the company could play; and Jane Carlyle, who had been unable to sleep for a week, felt extremely ill, and was comforted by her husband before she left for the party with the words 'I never saw you look so bilious, your face is *green* and your eyes all *blood-shot*', nevertheless confesses that no medicine would have done her so much good 'as this party which I had gone to with a sacred shudder! But then it was the *very* most agreeable party that ever I was at in London.' Forster helped Dickens with the conjuring and 'they exerted themselves till the perspiration was pouring down and they seemed *drunk* with their efforts!' Dickens, she says, was the best conjurer she ever saw, his tricks being so good that he could have made a living by performing them in public. After the conjuring came the dancing:

'Dickens did all but go down on his knees to make *me*— waltz with him! But I thought I did my part well enough in talking the maddest nonsense with *him*, Forster, Thackeray and Maclise—without attempting the Impossible—however *after supper* when we were all madder than ever with the pulling of crackers, the drinking of champagne, and the making of speeches; a universal country dance was proposed —and Forster *seizing me round the waist*, whirled me into the thick of it, and *made* me dance!! like a person in the tread-mill who must move forward or be crushed to death! Once I cried out "Oh for the love of Heaven let me go! you are going to dash my brains out against the folding doors!" to which he answered—(you can fancy his tone)—"your *brains*!! who cares about their brains *here? let them go!*"

'In fact the thing was rising into something not unlike the *rape of the Sabines*! . . . when somebody looked at her watch and exclaimed "twelve o'clock!" Whereupon we all rushed to the cloak-room—and *there* and in the lobby and up to the last moment the mirth raged on—Dickens took home Thackeray and Forster with him and his wife "*to finish the night there*" and a *royal* night they would have of it I fancy!— ending perhaps with a visit to the watch-house.'

Jane concludes with the reflection that the pleasantest company consists of blackguards: 'that is, those who have just a sufficient dash of blackguardism in them to make them snap their fingers at *ceremony* and all that sort of thing.' The result for her was that she went to bed 'and slept like a top.' It was obviously the kind of medicine she needed, and she should have indulged more frequently in doses of Doctor Dickens, who repeated his performance as a conjurer at Forster's place on New Year's eve, and again for a crowd of children and grown-ups at Devonshire Terrace on January 6th, to celebrate his son Charley's birthday, when he and Forster arrayed themselves in 'demoniacal dresses.'

It was shortly after these festivities that he visited Liverpool to address the Mechanics' Institution, and Birmingham to address the Polytechnic Institution, fortifying himself for the last with a pint of champagne and a pint of sherry at dinner. He was always ready to speak on behalf of educational organisations, and the crowds which gathered to hear him because of his notoriety as a novelist were delighted to find that a great writer could also be an excellent orator. He took as much pleasure as pains in doing things that most writers would rather die than undertake; and in the period under review we find him organising dinner-parties, borrowing money to pay his father's debts, composing a poem for Lady Blessington's *The Keepsake*, visiting prisons, applying to many people for subscriptions to help the seven destitute children of an actor, advising authors about their writings, supplying an introduction to a working-man's book, taking a keen interest in the management of a Ragged School, and entering into a correspondence with the District Surveyor concerning a smoking chimney in his Devonshire Terrace house. He asked the Surveyor to come and inspect the chimney; the Surveyor denied that he had anything to do with chimneys, and suggested that Dickens should call and see *him*; to which Dickens answered 'that I should find it inconvenient to carry the chimney and that I wanted him to survey it and say if it was right or wrong.' The Surveyor insisted that chimneys were not in his department, so this one continued to smoke.

Except for a cold which made him 'deaf in the ears, hoarse in the throat, red in the nose, green in the gills, damp in the eyes, twitchy in the joints, and fractious in the temper', Dickens was in good health while writing *Chuzzlewit* and fighting publishers and pirates. But for rest and change, no less than for economy's sake, he determined to take his family abroad for a year. He let his house, engaged a valet and courier named Louis Roche, bought a huge coach for the journey, and then threw himself into the complications of a farewell dinner at 9 Osnaburgh Terrace, where he spent the last fortnight before leaving England, his own house being needed by the new tenant. The dinner went off successfully, but it was a final farewell to one of his guests, Sydney Smith, who died during his absence in Italy. After another dinner, for men only, at Greenwich, the family crossed to Boulogne, where Dickens went to collect money at a bank, and having addressed the clerk at considerable length in laborious French, was asked in perfect English 'How would you like to take it, sir?'

The capacious coach, with four horses and a postilion, rumbled and jingled its way across France, carrying Dickens, his wife, his sister-in-law, five children, three servants, a courier and a nurse.

# UNREST AND DISQUIET

THEY arrived at Albaro, the seaside suburb of Genoa, in the middle of July '44, and settled into the Villa di Bagnarello, which had been taken for them by Angus Fletcher at about four times the rent they need have paid. Fletcher was given the ground floor, and they occupied the rest. It was roomy, bare, uncomfortable, the haunt of beetles, mosquitoes, fleas, flies, scorpions, lizards, frogs, rats, and scores of cats; but the view was beautiful. Dickens had brought letters of introduction to many leading residents of Genoa, but did not use them, and before long the leading residents were calling on him, among others the British and French consuls. 'I very much resort to my old habit of bolting from callers, and leaving their reception to Kate', he said. He bathed, explored the neighbourhood, went for walks on the hills, penetrated into the odd corners of Genoa, and gained an impression, common among English travellers in Latin countries then and for another sixty years, that the place was infested by villainous-looking priests.

> There is some soul of evil in things godly
> Would men observingly distil it out,

as Shakespeare might have said, and Dickens was equally repelled by the sinister clergy of the Catholic Church and the ranting nonconformist ministers of his own country. But unlike most English travellers he took pains with the language, studying it every day, engaging an Italian to talk it with him, and at length becoming 'as bold as a lion in the streets. The audacity with which one begins to speak when there is no help for it, is quite astonishing.' Though every prospect pleased him and only man seemed vile, the climate at first did not come up to expectation. The heat was so oppressive that he felt an overpowering tendency 'to tumble down anywhere and lie there.' The sky was no bluer than the one he had seen so frequently from Hampstead Heath, but he had to admit that the Mediterranean was a great deal bluer than the North Sea, and everything else was on a more excessive scale than at home, from insects to human beings. The grasshoppers were Brobdingnagian: they chirped so loudly. Two Genoese friends 'conversing pleasantly in the street, always seem on the eve of stabbing each other forthwith.' And even the laundry was conducted on passionate principles: 'My white trousers, after six weeks washing, would make very good fishing nets.'

His invariable curiosity and activity took him to all sorts of places, and on at least two occasions made him suffer. At a dinner given by the French consul-general some verses by an Italian marquis were recited for his benefit. As they concerned the taking of Tangiers by Joinville and were written in a style of declamation popular with patriots, Dickens had great difficulty in keeping a straight face, in showing by an attentive eye that he was following the poem closely, and in expressing admiration by his rapt demeanour. His efforts must have been successful because the marquis asked him to a big reception. He went, and for a while contented himself with ices and dancing; but when it dawned on him that there would be four more hours of dancing and ices, he decided to leave before the gates of Genoa were closed at midnight. Running fast downhill in the darkness, he fell head first over a pole that had been placed across the street, got up white with dust, found his clothes torn but himself unhurt, sprinted on to the gate, reached it in the nick of time, and walked the rest of the way home; but the fall brought on an attack of the 'unspeakable and agonising pain in the side' to which he had been subject from childhood. About three weeks later he suffered another shock. His brother Frederick came to stay with them, went bathing, was caught in a strong current, and would have been drowned but for the fact that a fishing-boat was leaving the harbour at the same time. The whole family witnessed the accident, and 'it was a world of horror and anguish crowded into four or five minutes of dreadful agitation.'

In October the family moved into Genoa from Albaro, and occupied the Palazzo Peschiere (Palace of the Fishponds), one of the loveliest residences in Italy, which stood within its own grounds and commanded a superb view of the city and harbour. The palace itself, with its great hall fifty feet high and its frescoes designed by Michael Angelo, the fountains, the scents from the gardens, the terrace, entranced Dickens.

It was like 'a palace in a fairy tale', and he often stood in the
hall gazing at the view 'in a perfect dream of happiness.' The
rent was about five pounds a week, and he found that he
could live like a prince in Italy on a sum that would only
suffice to keep a poet in England. They had a box at the
opera, a pleasant circle of acquaintances, and the weather
began to improve; yet Dickens could not settle down to work
and he missed London, feeling as if he had been plucked out
of his proper soil: 'Did I tell you how many fountains we
have here? No matter. If they played nectar, they wouldn'
please me half so well as the West Middlesex water-works at
Devonshire Terrace.' The streets and crowds of London
were necessary to his inspiration: 'Put me down on Waterloo
Bridge at eight o'clock in the evening, with leave to roam
about as long as I like, and I would come home, as you know
panting to go on. I am sadly strange as it is, and can't settle.
For more than a year he had been meditating a new Christmas
book which should strike 'a great blow for the poor', but he
had not been able to write a line of it since his arrival in Italy
He knew what he wanted to say, but not the means of saying
it, and one day when he was trying to drive himself to work
the clanging and crashing of all the bells in Genoa maddened
him and frustrated his efforts. But when he had recovered
from the din a phrase of Falstaff's came into his head, and it
suggested the form and title of the book: 'We have heard the
chimes at midnight, Master Shallow.' From that moment his
story *The Chimes* gripped him; and when the Governor arrived
in the city and held a levee, Dickens asked the consul to
explain his absence.

'Where's the great poet?' said the Governor: 'I want to see
the great poet.'

'The great poet, your Excellency, is at work writing a book
and begged me to make his excuses.'

'Excuses!' exclaimed the Governor: 'I wouldn't interfere
with such an occupation for all the world. Pray tell him that
my house is open to the honour of his presence when it is
perfectly convenient for him, but not otherwise. And let no
gentleman call upon Signor Dickens till he is understood to
be disengaged.'

Which is the correct attitude of rulers to artists.

Dickens no longer minded the discord of the bells: 'Let
them clash upon me now from all the churches and convents

in Genoa; I see nothing but the old London belfry I have set them in.' He reported to Forster that he was in 'regular, ferocious excitement with the Chimes; get up at seven; have a cold bath before breakfast; and blaze away, wrathful and red-hot, until three o'clock or so; when I usually knock off (unless it rains) for the day . . . This book has made my face white in a foreign land. My cheeks, which were beginning to fill out, have sunk again; my eyes have grown immensely large; my hair is very lank; and the head inside the hair is hot and giddy. Read the scene at the end of the third part, twice. I wouldn't write it twice for something . . . I have undergone as much sorrow and agitation as if the thing were real; and have wakened up with it at night. I was obliged to lock myself in when I finished it yesterday, for my face was swollen for the time to twice its proper size, and was hugely ridiculous . . . I am going for a long walk, to clear my head. I feel that I am very shaky from work, and throw down my pen for the day.' He finished *The Chimes* on November 3rd, weeping profusely. 'All my affections and passions got twined and knotted up in it', he said; for which reason he believed that he had written 'a tremendous book, and knocked the Carol out of the field.'

He was so much excited about it that he arranged to visit London in order to pass the proofs and illustrations and to read the story in Forster's chambers to a select circle of friends. Before starting he saw something of northern Italy, visiting Parma, Bologna, and Verona, where he was 'rather shocked' to find that Romeo had only been banished twenty-five miles, the distance from there to Mantua. He also went to Venice, which impressed him more than any city he had ever seen: 'The gorgeous and wonderful reality of Venice is beyond the fancy of the wildest dreamer. Opium couldn't build such a place, and enchantment couldn't shadow it forth in a vision . . . It is a thing you would shed tears to see . . . the glory of the place was insupportable! . . . I never saw the thing before that I should be afraid to describe. But to tell what Venice is, I feel to be an impossibility.' Brush, pen and pencil could give but a faint idea of the unimaginable reality, the memory of which would be a part of him for the rest of his existence: 'The three days that I passed there, were like a Thousand and One Arabian Nights wildly exaggerated a thousand and one times.' His wife and sister-in-law joined him at Milan for a day or two, and then returned to Genoa, leaving him to cross the Simplon and make his way to London via Strasburg and Paris.

He went straight to the Piazza Coffee House in Covent Garden 'and rushed into the arms' of Maclise and Forster. Two of the engravings for his Christmas story, one by Richard Doyle, the other by John Leech, did not please him; so he invited the artists to breakfast, 'and with that winning manner which you know of', he wrote to his wife, 'got them with the highest good humour to do both afresh.' The reading took place in Forster's chambers. Carlyle, Maclise, Stanfield, Macready, Laman Blanchard, Douglas Jerrold, and several others were present; and Dickens announced his success: 'If you had seen Macready last night, undisguisedly sobbing and crying on the sofa as I read, you would have felt, as I did, what a thing it is to have power.' Indulgence in this sense of power some years hence shortened his life. Soon after the reading Macready went to Paris to act in Shakespeare, and Dickens broke his journey to Genoa in order to spend a day or two with his friend. On the night of his departure Macready wrote in his diary: 'Dickens dined with us, and left us at half-past five, taking with him the last pleasant day that I expect to pass in Paris.' It was the middle of December; the journey to Marseilles was bitterly cold; and Dickens reported that he was taken out of the coach on arrival there 'in a perfectly torpid state, and was at first supposed to be luggage. But the porters not being able to find any direction on me, led to a further examination, and what the newspapers called "the vital spark" was finally discovered . . . After that, I was so horribly ill on board a steam-boat that I should have made my will if I had had anything to leave, but I had only the basin; and I couldn't leave that for a moment.'

Back in his palace, he wanted to see more of Italy, and started for the south with his wife towards the end of January '45. It was not a very happy trip for Kate because Mrs. De La Rue and her husband joined them at Rome and remained with them for the rest of the tour. In Genoa they had made the acquaintance of a Swiss banker named De La Rue and his English wife. The rest must be told in Dickens's own words, written twenty-five years after the events described: 'I became an intimate friend of her husband's . . . and, seeing that she suffered most frightfully from tic (I knew of her having no other disorder, at the time), I confided to her husband that I had found myself to possess some rather exceptional power of animal magnetism (of which I had tested the efficacy in nervous disorders), and that I would gladly try her. She never developed any of the ordinarily-related phenomena, but after a month began to sleep at night— which she had not done for years, and to change, amazingly to her own mother, in appearance. She then disclosed to me that she was, and had long been, pursued by myriads of bloody phantoms of the most frightful aspect, and that, after becoming paler, they had all *veiled their faces*. From that time, wheresoever I travelled in Italy, she and her husband travelled with me, and every day I magnetised her; sometimes under olive trees, sometimes in vineyards, sometimes in the travelling carriage, sometimes at wayside inns during the midday halt. Her husband called me up to her, one night at Rome, when she was rolled into an apparently impossible ball, by tic in the brain, and I only knew where her head was by following her long hair to its source. Such a fit had always held her before at least 30 hours, and it was so alarming to see that I had hardly any belief in myself with reference to it. But in half an hour she was peacefully and naturally asleep, and next morning was quite well. When I left Italy that time, the spectres had departed. They returned by degrees as time went on, and have ever since been as bad as ever.'

Dickens thought Mrs. De La Rue 'a most affectionate and excellent little woman', and no doubt she was; but such is the nature of wives that they detest good qualities in women for whom their husbands display a sentimental interest, and Kate eventually had to break it to Charles that she could not stand the company of the De La Rues. It was certainly a trying period for Kate, who can hardly be censured for resenting her husband's magnetic efforts to straighten out a lady in a nightdress at three o'clock in the morning. Dickens was compelled, as he told her, 'to make that painful declaration of your state of mind to the De La Rues'; but about nine years later he visited Genoa, saw the De La Rues again, and wrote to complain of her attitude. He reminded her that one of the qualities which made him different from other men was 'the intense pursuit of any idea that takes complete possession of me.' This quality had enabled him to give her position and luxury, but it also explained his hypnotic treatment of Mrs.

De La Rue; and he intimated that, as she had enjoyed the first, she might have endured the second. The De La Rues had sent her their love, and as 'your position beside these people is not a good one, is not an amiable one, a generous one—is not worthy of you at all', she should reciprocate. He did not ask her to do so, he stressed, but left it to her own sense of what was fit and upright. She must take counsel with herself and act on her own responsibility. The statement that he did not *ask* her to do as he wished was true enough. Put in such a manner, it was a command; and she meekly obeyed. Within three months of writing this letter of admonition, he was sending her love to Mr. De La Rue and wondering whether Mrs. De La Rue had received her letter 'about the Italian dishes.'

Clearly the atmosphere of Genoa was not congenial to Kate, whose treatment of Macready's daughter Susan did not please Dickens; and for the same reason Kate's sister Georgina fell under his displeasure. Susan Macready came to stay with them in the autumn of '44. She was, it seems, a silly girl, who had certain characteristics which got on people's nerves, and both Kate and Georgina showed their annoyance. Upon which Dickens reminded his wife, in a letter from Parma, how much they owed to Macready for having looked after their children while they were in America. 'Do not let any natural dislike to her (Susan's) inanities interfere in the slightest degree with an obligation so sacred', he warned her. 'You are too easily run away with—and Georgy is too—by the irritation and displeasure of the moment in such a case . . . and I was pained to see (as I should have told Georgy before I left if I had had an opportunity) that in such a case as the messages to Forster (she will know what I mean) she does a glaringly foolish and unnecessary silliness, and places huge means of misrepresentation in very willing hands. I should never forgive myself or you, if the smallest drop of coldness or misunderstanding were created between me and Macready, by means so monstrously absurd. And mind what I say. It will be created—I see it very clearly—unless you are as careful with that girl as if you were treading on hot ploughshares; and unless you are something more tender too. I am sure her presence at the Peschiere during the past month has worried nobody more than me . . . But I do hold hospitality, even when there is no other tie upon it, to be so high a thing, that

CHARLES DICKENS (1839)

*Painting by* DANIEL MACLISE, R.A.
*National Portrait Gallery*

DANIEL MACLISE, R.A. (1857)

*Drawing by* CHARLES BAUGNIET

I spare even Fletcher, when I am tempted to "put him down".'
Dickens wound up by giving his wife further instructions on
the proper treatment of Susan, and then continued his journey
to London for the reading of *The Chimes* and for the pleasure
of seeing Forster, whom he was already beginning to see
through, judging from a sentence in the letter just quoted;
though when Forster's only brother died at about this time,
Dickens wrote that 'you have a brother left—one bound to
you by ties as strong as ever Nature forged.' His changeable
temperament was also exemplified when, a week after writing
so sternly to his wife from Parma, he asked Douglas Jerrold
to bring Mrs. Jerrold to Genoa for Christmas, adding as an
inducement: 'I will warrant my wife to be as gentle a little
woman, and as free from affectation or formality of any kind,
as ever breathed.'

On his return from London, as we have noted, Dickens
and his wife left Genoa for the south at the beginning of '45.
They went to Rome and took part in the Carnival: 'At two
o'clock each day we sally forth in an open carriage, with a
large sack of sugar-plums and at least five hundred little nose-
gays to pelt people with . . . I wish you could have seen me
catch a swell brigand on the nose with a handful of very large
confetti every time we met him. It was the best thing I have
ever done. The Chimes are nothing to it.' He was deeply
impressed by the old part of Rome, the Coliseum and the
Campagna, but thought nothing of the modern town, and
far preferred many English cathedrals to St. Peter's. At
Naples they were joined by Georgina, and the three of them
climbed Vesuvius, suffering the usual agonies and terrors
incident to such pleasure-trips. The famous bay was 'immeasurably inferior to the Bay of Genoa', the town itself was
dirty, the people repulsive, and their homes like pig-sties.
The De La Rues joined them when they returned to Rome,
and trouble began. After visiting Florence, the party reached
Genoa early in April, Dickens and his wife having been away
some ten weeks. He had put on weight during the holiday—
'I find my waistcoat-buttons flying off occasionally with great
violence'—and his face was now decorated with longish
moustaches, without which he declared 'life would be a
blank.' In June the family left Genoa for home, crossing the
St. Gothard into Switzerland, a perilous journey in those days,
and spending a pleasant week in Flanders with Forster,

10

Maclise and Jerrold, sightseeing intensively, talking continuously, and laughing prodigiously.

It did not make his home-coming less agreeable to hear that Bradbury and Evans could show a much better profit on *The Chimes* than Chapman and Hall had been able to pay him on *The Carol*. Yet he did not feel like following up his success with another novel, but promptly began to consider the ways and means of starting a new weekly periodical which should reflect his own cheerful philosophy of life and disclose 'a vein of glowing, hearty, generous, mirthful, beaming reference in everything to Home and Fireside.' He would perhaps have liked to call it *The Dickens*; but feeling uncomfortable over the connotation of such a title, he hit on *The Cricket*, telling Forster that he would 'chirp, chirp, chirp away in every number until I chirped it up to—well, you shall say how many hundred thousand!' But Forster chirped him out of the project, and very soon he was carried away by a vaster scheme, nothing less than a daily newspaper which should compete with *The Times*, advocate radical reforms, and stand for Progress. All that remained of his original notion was half the title of his next Christmas book, *The Cricket on the Hearth*, which came out in December '45 and sold twice as well as its predecessors.

The new paper, to be known as *The Daily News*, would be published and partly financed by Bradbury and Evans, and Dickens got some personal friends, the chief being Joseph Paxton (who later designed the Crystal Palace), to raise over half the capital required. Once the thing was settled Dickens rushed hither and thither on business connected with it. He approached the best critics, leader writers, reporters, etc., and offered them better pay than they were receiving elsewhere. He also offered himself £2000 a year as editor, and accepted it, though Bradbury and Evans had named £1000 as his salary. The result was that the other newspapers either lost some of their best writers or had to raise their pay in order to keep them. Needless to say the proprietors, publishers and editors of such journals were extremely angry and gravely concerned; and Dickens was the most unpopular man in the newspaper world except among the journalists who benefited from his generosity. Wherever possible he gave jobs to friends and relations, some of the appointments being more personal than profitable. His father was put in charge of the reporters, his father-in-law became the critic of music and plays, his uncle was taken on the editorial staff, Lady Blessington was induced to supply society gossip in the strictest confidence, while Forster, Jerrold, Leigh Hunt and Mark Lemon were among the personal friends engaged to supply articles. His multifarious occupations did not interfere with his prescribed exercises, and just before Christmas '45 he informed a friend that 'I walk to Harrow still—was nearly blown away yesterday on Hampstead Heath—went to Finchley the other day in the pouring rain—take a cold shower bath every morning—and oil the machinery of the Daily News till the afternoon.'

It was due either to their irritation over Dickens's salary, or to their vanity being pricked by his dictatorial methods as an editor, that Bradbury and Evans began to give him trouble when matters were well advanced. Forster, whose biographical discretion on the subject amounts to distortion, told Macready that no one could have been a worse editor than Dickens; but in view of the latter's huge success in a similar position some years afterwards, we must discount this, especially as we have the evidence of the chief leader-writer W. J. Fox, one of the foremost orators of the Anti-Corn Law League, that Forster constantly created friction in the editorial department. 'Dickens and I are regularly against him on almost everything involving a difference of opinion', said Fox. Whatever the cause, Bradbury and Evans seriously offended Dickens when the paper was a week old. The first number appeared on January 21st 1846, though at four o'clock in the morning of that day it was doubtful whether it would appear at all. According to Joseph Paxton, the printer was incompetent, and superhuman efforts had to be made by everyone concerned. 'I never passed four hours in such a state of suspense in my life', wrote Paxton, 'not even when my own dear Love was in labour.' There was a rush for the newspaper and over ten thousand copies were sold across the counter within a few hours; but the mere sight of it soothed the nerves of rival editors, for in spite of the attraction of the first instalment of Dickens's *Pictures from Italy*, it was poorly printed on inferior paper and badly 'made-up'. Much rejoicing and gratulation took place among the competing establishments that night. After many vicissitudes *The Daily News* was turned into a success; but Dickens left it in three weeks, having done journalists a good turn by forcing up their rates of pay. Forster followed him in the editorial chair, but not for long.

A letter from Dickens to Bradbury and Evans explains why he abandoned the paper. They informed him on January 28th that, in the opinion of someone they did not name, one of his sub-editors was unfit for the post. On January 30th he wrote to ask the name of the person who had given this opinion, and said: 'When I tell you distinctly that I shall leave the Paper immediately, if you do not give me this information, I think it but fair to add that it is extremely probable that I shall leave it when you have done so. For it would be natural in any man, and is especially so in one in my position, to consider this disrespectful and quite unendurable. I am thoroughly disgusted and shall act accordingly.' This is not the sort of language usually addressed by editors to the proprietors or even part-proprietors of their papers; and, lest he should change his mind, one of the partners, Bradbury, went out of his way to keep Dickens's temper at boiling-point, achieving it with so much success that, a fortnight after leaving the paper, Dickens wrote to Evans: 'I am not in that state of feeling with reference to your partner, which would render a personal negociation with him agreeable to me. I consider that his interposition between me and almost every act of mine at the newspaper office, was as disrespectful to me as injurious to the enterprise.' He then explained in detail how Bradbury had annoyed him, mainly by paying certain journalists less than Dickens had promised them: 'The position in which I was placed in these cases was so galling and offensive to me, that I am as much irritated by the recollection of them as I was by their actual occurrence.' From his general behaviour Dickens deduced that Bradbury had 'become possessed of the idea that everyone receiving a salary in return for his services, is his natural enemy, and should be suspected and mistrusted accordingly.' To these charges Dickens felt compelled to add 'with great pain, that I have not always observed Mr. Bradbury's treatment of my father (than whom there is not a more zealous, disinterested, or useful gentleman attached to the paper) to be very creditable to himself, or delicate towards me.' The probability is that Bradbury and Evans were a sort of inverted Spenlow and Jorkins, and took it in turn to bear the brunt of their joint policy. In conclusion, Dickens assured Evans that, apart from the newspaper, he maintained his high opinion of Bradbury. Since the firm was then making arrangements to publish his *Pictures from Italy*, it was perhaps as well to make this clear.

The extraordinary thing about Dickens is that all the time he was busying himself with the organisation and preparation of *The Daily News*, which was more than enough to keep a normal man fully occupied, he was equally busy producing and acting in two plays: Jonson's *Every Man in His Humour* in September and November '45, Beaumont and Fletcher's *The Elder Brother* in January '46. All his friends took parts or helped somehow, and a recent friend, Mark Lemon, first editor of *Punch*, a Falstaff of a man, was so good that Dickens made a point of getting him for all future theatrical ventures by the troupe. Macready was consulted, gave his advice, regarded the whole affair as rather childish, and was put out by the amount of notice and praise bestowed by the press on the Jonson play. As usual Dickens did pretty nearly everything single-handed: he rehearsed the company and got the best out of them, arranged the scenery and sometimes altered it, invented the costumes and wrote the playbills, advised the carpenter and directed the bandmaster, managed the front of the house and numbered the seats, in addition to being chief actor, property-master, stage-manager, call-boy and prompter. Considering his excitable temperament his patience with the actors was beyond praise. He told Cattermole that he would drag his own brother Frederick to the theatre by the hair in order to 'go at your scenes on Monday over and over again, as often as you like. You can't tire me.' The performance of *Every Man in His Humour* at the Royalty Theatre, Soho, made a sensation, and it had to be repeated two months later at the St. James's Theatre before Prince Albert and as much of the peerage as could be crowded in. For this occasion Thackeray offered to sing between the acts, but his services were declined, and he was rather hurt. The proceeds were given to a charity; but judging by a remark made by Lord Melbourne during one of the intervals it was not a very charitable audience. Speaking in a voice that could be clearly heard all over the house, he said 'I knew this play would be dull, but that it would be so damnably dull as this I didn't suppose.'

Dickens himself did not seek the company of the peerage; but he was an extremely sociable being and gave many parties in Devonshire Terrace at a time when he was producing plays, running a newspaper, writing a travel-book, and indulging in feats of pedestrianism. Just as he attended to every detail in his editorial and managerial capacities, so did he anticipate every household need; and we find him dropping a hurried line to Kate from his office in Whitefriars on Twelfth Day '46: 'The weather is so very bad, that I really think you had better send down to Edginton's in Piccadilly, and see if they can't, at a reasonable charge, put up an awning from the street-door to the curb-stone. They do such things every day. It is really too far for Ladies to go in the wet.' He could not help spending a lot of money on entertaining, and he knew that the only way to practise economy was to live abroad. His wife produced a sixth child in the autumn of '45, and he began to get panicky about the future, feeling perhaps that children with such high-sounding names required a good start in life. Except for the first two children, a boy called after himself and a girl called after his wife's sister Mary but known in the family circle as Mamie, those who survived infancy carried the christian and surnames of his friends, Macready, Landor, Jeffrey, D'Orsay, Tennyson, Bulwer Lytton and Sydney Smith, and one of them was dubbed Henry Fielding after the great novelist. The latest arrival was christened Alfred D'Orsay Tennyson, and both D'Orsay and Tennyson made the necessary vows on his behalf at the font in Marylebone Church. With all these famous names weighing on his mind, with the agitations over the newspaper impairing his health, and with a feeling that his creative power was stagnating, Dickens asked a cabinet minister if there was any chance of his getting a job as a paid magistrate in London. The reply was not encouraging; so he determined to let his house again, go abroad, write a new book, and save money. Already he had been subject to the fermentation that always preluded the act of creation. 'Vague thoughts of a new book are rife within me just now', he told Lady Blessington in March '46, 'and I go wandering about at night into the strangest places, according to my usual propensity at such a time, seeking rest, and finding none.' He had been so much bothered and upset by the newspaper business that he even fancied his chief needs were rest and quiet; but when the means to achieve both were realised, he usually became more restless and less quiet than ever.

His wife resolutely declined to re-visit Genoa with its De La Rue memories, though he did his utmost to persuade her; and as they had enjoyed their passage through Switzerland they agreed to settle on the shore of Lake Geneva for six months. The family, again accompanied by Louis Roche, left home on June 1st '46 and travelled down the Rhine, discovering at Mainz that the novels of Dickens were very popular in Germany. From Basle they proceeded in three coaches to Lausanne, the journey taking three days, and on the way there occurred the sort of incident which Dickens delighted to retail with appropriate inflections and gesticulations. One of their drivers told the landlord of an inn at which they stopped that the food was bad: 'After various defiances on both sides, the landlord said *Scélérat! Mécréant! Je vous boaxerai!* to which the voiturier replied *Aha! Comment dites-vous? Voulez-vous boaxer? Eh? Voulez-vous? Ah! Boaxez-moi donc!*—at the same time accompanying these retorts with gestures of violent significance, which explained that this new verb-active was founded on the well-known English verb to boax, or box. If they used it once, they used it at least a hundred times, and goaded each other to madness with it always.' Putting up at the Hotel Gibbon in Lausanne, Charles and Kate went house-hunting, soon finding a fascinating little villa called Rosemont, situated on a hill rising from the water, with lovely gardens and a gorgeous view of Lake and mountains, all for £10 a month. They took it and moved in.

Feeling responsible for the spiritual no less than the material future of his children, Dickens did not start his new novel at once but wrote the story of Jesus for them in simple language. He was soon the centre of a pleasant circle of friends, which included William Haldimand, a former M.P., a Swiss gentleman named de Cerjat, and Richard Watson and his wife, with whom Dickens was sometimes to stay at Rockingham Castle, Northamptonshire. The country in the immediate vicinity of Lausanne reminded the newcomers of England, and the Swiss Protestants had the virtues of the best English: they were clean, neat, industrious, dependable, cheerful, and independent. The streets of Lausanne were crammed with bookshops and blessedly free from monks and priests. But whenever Dickens visited a Catholic canton he noticed the sudden change to 'dirt, disease, ignorance, squalor, and misery', from which he concluded that 'the religion of

Ireland lies as deep at the root of all its sorrows, even as English misgovernment and Tory villainy.'

They entertained many English visitors during their stay in the country, including the Talfourds, Harrison Ainsworth and the newly wedded T. J. Thompsons. Another guest was Tennyson, for whom Dickens had a great admiration. But the admiration was not returned, for when Dickens had asked the poet to share a house with him in Switzerland during the summer months, Tennyson, on whom Dickens's sentimentality jarred, had refused, feeling certain that discord would ensue. There was wisdom in this, because Dickens, though a perfect host for a week or two, quickly tired of people and preferred a rapid succession of guests to a few stationary ones. He closely studied the French language, and was able in a short time to speak it fluently, though he never lost a strong English accent. He walked as strenuously as ever, covering fifteen miles most evenings after work. And before the summer was over he took Kate and Georgina to Chamounix and the Great St. Bernard. 'Mont Blanc, and the valley of Chamounix, and the Mer de Glace, and all the wonders of that most wonderful place, are above and beyond one's wildest expectations. I cannot imagine anything in nature more stupendous or sublime. If I were to write about it now, I should quite rave—such prodigious impressions are rampant within me.'

He began his new story, *Dombey and Son*, at the end of June, but he could not maintain his usual speed of composition, partly because he was bothered by the thought of having to produce his Christmas book while engaged on the novel, and partly owing to depression of spirits which constantly recurred while he was at Lausanne, making him feel that he was in serious danger of a mental or physical breakdown. Then, too, he missed the London streets and crowds at nighttime: 'I can't express how much I want these. It seems as if they supplied something to my brain, which it cannot bear, when busy, to lose.' On the other hand his inventive faculty was as strong as ever; he restrained himself with difficulty from 'launching into extravagances in the height of my enjoyment'; and some of his comic passages made him laugh so much that he could not see the paper on which he was writing. In September he put *Dombey* on one side in order to start the promised Christmas book, *The Battle of Life*, but having done a third of it he suddenly became despondent at the thought that he was writing against time and that *Dombey* would suffer from the energy he was putting into the other work. He made up his mind not to produce a Christmas book after all. The decision worried him and made him feel ill. He dashed off to Geneva to recuperate, and to see whether a change of place would alter his decision. It did. He felt better, and capable once more of tackling both the stories. Back at Lausanne he polished off *The Battle of Life* and a new number of *Dombey*; then he returned to the Hotel de L'Ecu at Geneva and knocked off another number, which included an early memory: 'I hope you will like Mrs. Pipchin's establishment. It is from the life, and I was there—I don't suppose I was eight years old; but I remember it all as well, and certainly understood it as well, as I do now . . . I thought of that passage in my small life, at Geneva.'

The first number of *Dombey and Son* was published in October '46, and to Dickens's joy was a huge success, beating the sale of his last novel *Chuzzlewit* by more than twelve thousand copies. The monthly numbers were continued until April '48. He thought well of the book, and after finishing it confided in his father-in-law 'I have great faith in Dombey, and a strong belief that it will be remembered and read years hence . . . All through, I have bestowed all the pains and time at my command upon it—and I feel in the strangest of states, now that it is gone from me.' Like all his novels, it is full of good things that only he could have written, and full of bad things that no one but he would have dared to write. His successes are as glorious as his failures are monstrous; and perhaps it takes a man capable of imagining a Cuttle to conceive a Carker, who is not a human being at all but an object on which Dickens can vent his feelings of hatred and repugnance. He is pictured as 'feline from sole to crown'; he sits at his work 'as if he were waiting at a mouse's hole'; he purrs; and he is ready 'for a scratch or for a velvet touch.' As he rides past his employer's house, the dog Diogenes barks and growls, and the chronicler suddenly flings off all restraint and behaves in a manner that would have disconcerted Flaubert: 'Well spoken, Di, so near your mistress!' exclaims Dickens. 'Another, and another with your head up, your eyes flashing, and your vexed mouth worrying itself, for want of him. Another, as he picks his way along! You have a good scent, Di,—cats, boy, cats!' From which we may risk the inference that Dickens was not a cat-lover. Clearly Carker is not destined to a peaceful end, but there are no half-measures with Dickens. An express train takes him unawares: he 'uttered a shriek . . . was beaten down, caught up, and whirled away upon a jagged mill, that spun him round and round, and struck him limb from limb, and licked his stream of life up with its fiery heat, and cast his mutilated fragments in the air.' Carker must have been a publisher in disguise.

Railways and engines were novelties in the decade that first read *Dombey and Son*, and so we hear a lot about iron monsters rushing through the countryside, belching flame and steam. The air was becoming laden with smoke; the spiritual atmo-sphere of the age, as if in sympathy, began to thicken; and Dickens, the master-medium of his age, was already reflecting its gloom, as in his description of a 'fallen woman', a creature of darkness whom he dismisses 'into the deepening night, and howling wind, and pelting rain.' But there are some ex-quisitely comical scenes in the book, one of the best being the indignation of Mrs. Chick over the shocking discovery of Miss Tox's intentions—'"The scales": here Mrs. Chick cast down an imaginary pair, such as are commonly used in grocers' shops: "have fallen from my sight".' And Captain Cuttle has no fellow in nautical literature. He is one of the few Dickensian characters who impart to the reader a sense of repose, perhaps because his creator was as tranquil as his nature allowed him to be when watching the sea. Even Cuttle's favourite literature is of a restful order, 'for he made it a point of duty to read none but very large books on a Sunday, as having a more staid appearance; and had bargained, years ago, for a prodigious volume at a book-stall, five lines of which utterly confounded him at any time, insomuch that he had not yet ascertained of what subject it treated.'

In the middle of November '46 Dickens removed his family to Paris, experiencing some discomfort at the frontier custom-house, where 'they weighed our plate . . . spoon by spoon, and fork by fork, and we lingered about there, in a thick fog and a hard frost, for three long hours and a half, during which the officials committed all manner of absurdities, and got into all sorts of disputes with my brave courier', largely no doubt because 'the latter insisted on volunteering the most astonish-ing and unnecessary lies about my books, for the mere pleasure of deceiving the officials.' They put up at the Hotel Brighton, and Dickens promptly commenced to walk all over the city, losing himself again and again. 'The agonies of house-hunting were frightfully severe', he wrote from No. 48 Rue de Courcelles. 'It was one paroxysm for four mortal days. I am proud to express my belief that we are lodged at last in the most preposterous house in the world. The like of it cannot, and so far as my knowledge goes does not, exist in any other part of the globe. The bedrooms are like opera-boxes. The dining-rooms, staircases, and passages, quite inexplicable. The dining-room is a sort of cavern, painted (ceiling and all) to represent a grove, with unaccountable bits of looking-glass sticking in among the branches of the trees. There is a gleam of reason in the drawing-room. But it is approached through a series of small chambers, like the joints in a telescope, which are hung with inscrutable drapery. The maddest man in Bedlam, having the materials given him, would be likely to devise such a suite, supposing his case to be hopeless and quite incurable.' At first he could not work in so strange a place, and sat for hours at his desk writing nothing. The cold at the beginning of December was intense: 'The water in the bedroom jugs freezes into solid masses from top to bottom, bursts the jugs with reports like small cannon, and rolls out on the table and washstands hard as granite.' But the crowds in the streets inspirited him, and the dead bodies in the Morgue soothed him, and soon he was working at high pressure. His illustrators were giving him anxious moments. Phiz failed entirely to realise his conception of Mrs. Pipchin, and Leech made a grave mistake in one of his pictures for *The Battle of Life*. Careful directions were henceforth sent to the former; but as it was too late to withdraw the engraving by Leech, and as Dickens did not wish to pain him needlessly, nothing was said; besides, 'What is such a monstrous enormity to me', remarked the author, 'may not so present itself to others.'

From the 15th to the 23rd of December he was in London, supervising the rehearsals of a dramatic version of his new Christmas book *The Battle of Life*. He found that very few of the company understood what it was about or what they were supposed to represent; so he gave them a reading in Forster's chambers. In spite of his occupation and anxiety, not a thing escaped his notice: 'The reading to the Lyceum people took place here. Forster provided 76 ham sandwiches (purchased in Holborn) of the largest size and newest bread; and when the shapes of the ladies were horribly deformed by the distribution of these materials within them, his despatching the 42 uneaten sandwiches to the poor of the neighbourhood, with strict injunctions to Henry to find out very poor women and institute close inquiry into their life, conduct, and behaviour, before leaving any sandwiches for them, was sublime.' The play was received with immense enthusiasm, and yells for the author of the story, who returned to Paris with the knowledge that twenty-three thousand copies of *The Battle of Life* were sold on the day of publication.

But his old enemy *The Times* was down on him again. It had described *The Cricket on the Hearth* as 'a twaddling manifestation of silliness', had advised the author to complete his neglected education by reading in tranquillity, and had accused him of setting the poor against the rich; though a closer study of his scenes dealing with home life among the labouring classes might have suggested the possibility that he was setting the rich against the poor. He did not see reviews of his work unless friends drew his attention to the pleasant ones; but he happened upon some reference to what *The Times* had said about *The Battle of Life*, and it was more than usually nasty. It not only accused him of being responsible for 'the deluge of trash', in other words Christmas stories, that annually glutted the book-market, but of having himself produced '*the very worst*' story of the lot. There was not, said the critic, 'one spark of originality, of truth, of probability, of nature, of beauty' throughout his latest production; the genius apparent in *Pickwick* made the author's 'unheard-of effrontery' inexcusable; and he was warned to 'refrain from a further repetition of his error.' Dickens called this review 'another touch of a blunt razor on B's nervous system . . . Inimitable very mouldy and dull. Hardly able to work. Dreamed of *Timeses* all night. Disposed to go to New Zealand and start a magazine.' But the mood was only momentary. Two days had not elapsed before he was deep in the number of his serial story which closed with the death of Paul Dombey, and considering the advisability of 'demanding my passport in consequence of the immense extent to which the French nation makes a water-closet of my wall.'

He killed Paul on January 14th '47 at 10 p.m., 'and as I had no hope of getting to sleep afterwards, I went out, and walked about Paris until breakfast-time next morning.' The death of little Paul shook the English reading world as much as the death of Little Nell had done, induced the Americans to regard *Martin Chuzzlewit* as a temporary aberration, and, according to Dickens, amazed Paris. Thackeray, the second number of whose *Vanity Fair* had just come out, rushed into the office of *Punch* and exclaimed 'There's no writing against this; one hasn't an atom of a chance; it's stupendous!' And Jeffrey wrote: 'Oh, my dear dear Dickens! . . . I have so cried and sobbed over it last night, and again this morning; and felt my heart purified by those tears, and blessed and loved you for making me shed them; and I never can bless and love you enough.' All of which helped Dickens to forget *The Times*.

Forster spent the last fortnight of January with his friend in Paris, seeing every person, prison, palace, picture gallery and place of entertainment they could crush into the time. They went to Versailles and St. Cloud, inspected the Louvre and the Morgue, witnessed operas, plays, variety performances, supped with Alexandre Dumas and Eugène Sue, called on Chateaubriand and Victor Hugo, met Théophile Gautier, Lamartine and Scribe, and did all the other things which are done by people who like doing that sort of thing.

Dickens's sojourn in Paris was suddenly cut short by the news that his eldest son, at King's College School, was ill with scarlet fever. He returned to London at once with his wife, followed shortly by Georgina and the other children. Their home in Devonshire Terrace being still tenanted, they took No. 1 Chester Place, Regent's Park, from the beginning of March, remaining there until they went to Broadstairs in June for the summer months. The boy recovered, and a fifth son was born in April. This was their seventh child; and as Dickens had expressed the hope that 'my missis won't do so never no more' after the birth of their fourth, he would not have relished the knowledge that she would one day present him with a tenth.

## II
## C. D. AND D. C.

ACTORS, like advertisers, create a demand, and where the
drama is concerned the demand follows the supply. Plays
were not originally written for audiences to see but for players
to act in: they founded a need, but the primary need was the
actor's. With Dickens and his troupe, all sorts of reasons
were given for their performances, except the real reason,
namely that Dickens wanted to act; and the others caught the
infection from him. The first excuse in 1847 for repeating
their exploits of the preceding years was to help Leigh Hunt.
But no sooner was their intention announced than the
government granted Hunt a pension. This inconsiderately
speedy action, so unlike the usual tardiness of governments,
forced the players to find another cause without loss of time.
Hunt again came to the rescue: he was deeply in debt. And
another author, John Poole, whose comedy *Paul Pry* had
been successful over twenty years before, obliged them: he
was in financial difficulties. So they repeated Ben Jonson's
play in Manchester and Liverpool that July, and Dickens was
again in his element. 'I have often thought that I should
certainly have been as successful on the boards as I have been
between them', he once said; but he was a born producer as
well as a born actor, and he nursed his company with a
patience that would have won the admiration of Job. When
their elocution was faulty, he gave them lessons in voice
production. When their movements were awkward, he spent
hours in showing them how to appear at ease on the stage.
When they forgot their words, he taught them how to
memorise. When they were nervous, he gave them confidence. When they were over-confident, he made them self-
critical. When they said they would be 'all right on the
night', he saw to it that they were all right at rehearsal. And
not a clumsy movement, not a false inflection, not an artificial
gesture, escaped his attention. He drilled his company for
hours on end, exhausted everybody but himself, rose fresh
as a lark next morning, and was ready for another fortitude-
testing, patience-trying, nerve-teasing session.

In 1848 Dickens got to hear that the dramatist Sheridan Knowles, whose *Virginius* and *The Hunchback* had been rapturously received earlier in the century, was in straitened circumstances. There was a movement on foot to purchase Shakespeare's birthplace at Stratford-on-Avon, and Dickens snatched at the opportunity of putting on a play and raising enough money to endow a curatorship, the post to be held by Knowles. Once again his laudable object was defeated, this time by the action of the Stratford authorities, who took charge of the house and made their own arrangements. But his enthusiasm did not cool; and most of the proceeds of the series of performances given by his company in London, Birmingham, Edinburgh, Glasgow, Manchester and Liverpool, during May, June and July, 1848, were handed over to Sheridan Knowles, who, having recently become a Baptist minister, preferred the cash to the curatorship. For these performances Shakespeare's *The Merry Wives of Windsor* was chosen, with Mark Lemon as Falstaff and Dickens as Shallow. The play was given twice at the Haymarket Theatre, London, and was witnessed by the Queen and Prince Albert. The entertainment always concluded with a farce, which was followed by a supper to the performers, when Dickens, refreshed by his labours as actor, producer and factotum, played the part of host in a way that kept everyone's spirits at delirium pitch. Such undertakings were meat and drink to him, and when they were over he bemoaned the drabness of everyday life: 'I have no energy whatever, I am very miserable', he wrote to Mrs. Cowden Clarke, who had played Mistress Quickly; 'I loathe domestic hearths. I yearn to be a vagabond . . . A real house like this is insupportable, after that canvas farm wherein I was so happy.' And again: 'I am completely blasé—literally used up. I am dying for excitement. Is it possible that nobody can suggest anything to make my heart beat violently, my hair stand on end . . . Oh, Memory, Memory!' He longed to travel all over the country and act everywhere, for 'there's nothing in the world equal to seeing the house rise at you, one sea of delighted faces, one hurrah of applause!' At the end of his life he confessed that he had always wished 'to be *the* great actor, to have the public at my feet.'

As we shall shortly learn, the years 1849–50 were fully occupied in other ways; but his appetite for vagabondage was partly satisfied between November '50 and September '52. Anxious to make sure of the suffrages of the forty-shilling freeholders in his constituency, and unable to bribe them directly with money, Bulwer Lytton conceived the idea of inviting them to Knebworth in order to see Dickens and company perform *Every Man in His Humour*. Whatever the forty-shilling freeholders may have thought, Dickens was overjoyed at the prospect, and might even have given his vote to the Tories in return for the pleasure of acting before them. Flinging himself into the business with his customary impetuosity, he was soon attending to everything and giving his well-known performance of a human dynamo. 'Once in a thing like this—once in anything, to my thinking—it must be carried out like a mighty enterprise, heart and soul', he wrote to Lytton. At an early rehearsal Kate fell through a trap-door and sprained her ankle badly; but within a few hours of the doctor's assurance that she would be unable to appear in the play, Dickens was coaching her sister Georgina in the part. 'Ah, sir', said the master carpenter at a theatre where they rehearsed, 'it's a universal observation in the profession, sir, that it was a great loss to the public when you took to writing books.' Three performances of the Jonson comedy were given at Knebworth in November '50, and in the following January Dickens stayed with the Watsons at Rockingham Castle, putting another lot of amateurs through their paces and presenting two short plays before the guests and servants.

While at Knebworth he discussed a project with Lytton which was to keep him intermittently happy and busy for the next two years. They felt that poor writers and painters should be helped by a fund; and as it was the duty of the prosperous ones to stand by their less fortunate fellows, they agreed to give the scheme, to be known as the Guild of Literature and Art, a good send-off. Lytton presented some land near Knebworth, and promised to write a comedy, which Dickens and his friends would perform wherever possible, the profits to be devoted to building houses on Lytton's land and starting the fund. They thought that, if the Queen and Prince Albert would attend the first performance, the undertaking would be successful, and Dickens wrote to ask the Duke of Devonshire to lend his London house for the occasion. 'I have projected a moveable theatre, scenery, mechanism, &c., capable of being erected and removed, in any suitable room, in a very few hours', he informed the Duke, who promptly replied 'My services, my house, and my subscription will be at your orders.' The Duke was extremely helpful in every way, and Dickens got to like him very much, even departing from his general practice so far as to stay with him at Chatsworth. The Queen and Prince Albert promised to be present; and by the middle of March '51 Dickens was rehearsing Lytton's new comedy *Not So Bad As We Seem*, and rushing from carpenters to scene-painters, from tailors to machinists, from bootmakers to musicians, from wigmakers to gasmen, in the flurry of preparation. 'My legs swell so, with standing on the stage for hours together, that my stockings won't come off', he said, '. . . I am so astonishingly familiar with everyone else's part, that I forget my own.' The play was performed at Devonshire House on May 16th '51 before an aristocratic audience which had paid five guineas a seat, whether to see Queen Victoria or Charles Dickens remains uncertain. Several representations were then given at the Hanover Square Rooms, and many towns in the provinces were visited that autumn and at intervals throughout 1852. After the first performance a farce called *Mr. Nightingale's Diary* was added to the bill. It was written by Mark Lemon, and re-written by Dickens, who acted six parts in it: a lawyer, a waiter, a pedestrian, a hypochondriac, an old woman and a deaf sexton.

We do not need to be told that this farce provided Dickens with his best chance to display his peculiar histrionic gifts. He was by temperament, as we have noted, a 'character' actor off the stage, and it was only to be expected that he would excel as a 'character' actor on it. But just as he seldom maintained for a long period a single aspect of his character in real life, going from one extreme to another with bewildering celerity, so did he enjoy playing half a dozen totally dissimilar parts on the stage in as many minutes. He was, in fact, a born quick-change artist. With a sudden turn-down of his cuffs or turn-up of his collar, he could transform himself completely and astound his friends with some eccentric impersonation, switching over at a second's notice to an entirely fresh piece of characterisation by flinging the tails of his coat over his shoulder. His minute observation of people, backed by his mental and bodily alertness, his mobile face

11

and flexible voice, enabled him to give a startling variety and vividness to his portraiture. He was good as Bobadil in Jonson's play; better as Shallow in Shakespeare's, when he gave a performance that breathed a senility refusing to be senile, the stiff limbs, tottering gait, shaky head and toothless utterance, being opposed by an effete energy of action, a would-be fire of spirit, and a feeble assumption of dignity. He was best of all in *Mr. Nightingale's Diary*, when he changed his dress, voice, face, deportment, mannerisms and personality, with such completeness and rapidity that the audience were dumbfounded to discover a few seconds before the curtain came down that most of the characters had been played by Dickens. Where he failed, as we might guess, was in a 'straight' part. Sudden assumption, not steady delineation, being his forte, Lord Wilmot in Lytton's comedy, an airy fashionable young man, became in Dickens's conception something like the captain of a Dutch privateer: he was rigid, dry, conventional, commonplace, with a quarter-deck manner. But as it was a very important part he dared not trust anyone else with it, telling Lytton 'I know from experience that we could find nobody to hold the play together in Wilmot if I didn't do it.' He wanted to act another character, which he abandoned with a pang, revealing the truth about himself in a letter to the author: 'Assumption has charms for me—I hardly know for how many wild reasons—so delightful, that I feel a loss of, oh! I can't say what exquisite foolery, when I lose a chance of being someone in voice, etc., not at all like myself.' However, he made up for the loss by fooling exquisitely in the after-piece.

His restless desire to be someone else makes it necessary for us to pause at this point and fix in our minds a picture of what he was in himself. And the first thing to observe, the most distinctive thing about him, was the intensity of his nature. Whatever he did was done without an atom of reserve or uncertainty: he flung the whole of himself into his work, his pleasure, his likes and dislikes, his loyalties, affections, interests, admirations and indignations. 'Whatever Genius does, it does well', he told a correspondent, 'and the man who is constantly beginning things and never finishing them is no true Genius, take my word for it.' His advice to someone who wished to become a writer shows us how he applied himself to his own work: 'Concentrate on this pursuit all the patience that would be required in all the other pursuits of his world put together.' The fact that he was perpetually living in extremes might suggest a certain instability or independability of character; but running through all his emotional excesses was a hard core of will-power which kept him purposeful and steady. His male friendships afford the best example of this. Most men are more interested in women than in men, and so are most women. But Dickens was a man's man, at his best in male society, and, as his novels and letters show, far more interested in his own sex than in the other, except where his sentimental interest was aroused. Though his emotional and self-willed nature put many strains on his male friendships, and there were periods when some of them appeared to have ceased, he never permanently lost a friend. He was particularly loyal to early companions like Mitton and Beard. 'I have a capacity and a strong inclination for feeling warmly towards all those whom I have known in less successful times', he once said.

But his relations with Forster are the best index to this side of his nature. Forster's overbearing and possessive behaviour must have produced many explosions from one so touchy and independent as Dickens, and Macready 'was sorry to hear of intemperate language between them' five years after the painful scene' he recorded in his diary for August 1840. By the end of '45 they were obviously having frequent disagreements, because Forster poured his grievances into Macready's ears. 'Dickens', said he, 'was so intensely fixed on his own opinions and in his admiration of his own works . . . that he, Forster, was useless to him as a counsel, or for an opinion on anything touching upon them, and that, as he refused to see criticisms on himself, this partial passion would grow upon him, till it became an incurable evil.' Two years after he had thus unburdened himself, Forster told Macready that the friendship between himself and Dickens 'was likely to terminate or very much relax.' Yet, though Forster's proprietorial attitude and pinchbeck-Johnsonian manner must have maddened Dickens again and again, they remained friends to the end, though there was a considerable cooling of their relationship after Forster's marriage and Dickens's discovery of a more congenial companion.

The statement that Dickens refused to read criticisms of his novels touches another leading aspect of his character, and qualifies the assertion that he was fixed in admiration of his own works. The more conceited a man is, the less vain he is, conceit resulting from an exalted view of oneself, vanity implying a high opinion of others. The really conceited writer can read hostile criticisms of his work with amusement, because his view of what he does is not affected by the depreciation of friends or strangers. The vain man, on the contrary, squirms under the pricks of the critic's pen and suffers sleepless nights over what he would like to think is, but cannot quite believe to be, personal malice. Dickens was vain, and coveted the good opinion of the world. 'I have a strong spice of the Devil in me', he wrote in 1843, 'and when I am assailed, as I think falsely or injustly, my red hot anger carries me through it bravely, until I have forgotten all about it. When I first began to write, too, I suffered intensely from reading reviews, and I made a solemn compact with myself that I would only know them, for the future, from such General report as might reach my ears.' He never broke that rule, and was the happier for it. As he put the whole of himself into his work, living in it so intensely that the creatures of his fancy became more real to him than the men and women he knew, he certainly did not undervalue it; but he was always conscious that it could not mean to others what it had meant to himself, and this made him modest in his claims for it and frugal in his public references to it. Considering the adulation heaped upon him from his twenties till the close of his life, he kept his head remarkably well, maintaining a balanced estimate of his achievement. If Forster had said that Dickens was fixed in his affection for his own works, he would have been right; but when he told Macready that Dickens would not listen to other people's opinions, he was lying and he knew it. Right up to his final novel Dickens attended carefully to the counsel of his friends, and spoilt the end of *Great Expectations* by following it. There are dozens of letters to prove that for as long as their intimacy lasted he asked Forster's advice while writing his stories, and very often took it. Dickens's admirations, which were expressed with the openness and emphasis of his nature, were for Carlyle and Tennyson and Browning and Washington Irving and Hans Andersen and one or two others, and he made no attempt to conceal what he felt either from themselves or from his friends. His hero-worship of certain contemporaries is one of his most engaging qualities, and his complete lack of professional jealousy is another.

The will-power that permeated his being and directed his genius made him in certain respects hard and egotistical. There was always something of the spoilt child in him, though few people can have been less spoilt as a child. 'I know that in many points I am an excitable and headstrong man', he confessed; and there is no doubt that he completely dominated his social world, imposed his wishes on it, led it, dictated to it. His home was conducted according to his whims and tastes. Dinners were given on his instructions, rooms were arranged as he wished, holidays and other removals were undertaken at his command. His autocratic behaviour was heightened by his wife's docility and lack of responsibility; and had his disposition not been a kindly one, had he not been a benevolent autocrat, their family life would have been unusually trying. As it was, there were too many things to be borne in mind for Kate and the children always to feel quite at home when they were at home. Tidiness and punctuality, for example, both of which Dickens enforced to a degree that must have made his family jump when they saw a book on the floor and palpitate when they heard the clock strike. 'I can warrant myself in all things as punctual as the clock at the Horse-Guards', he said. His appointments were kept to the minute, and the meals at his house started on the stroke of the hour. The furniture of a room had to be placed exactly as he wanted it, chairs, sofas, tables, ornaments, to the square inch. 'Keep things in their places. I can't bear to picture them otherwise': such phrases appear in his letters to Kate. And when he moved into a furnished house, or took rooms at a hotel, he promptly changed the position of nearly everything, including the wardrobes and beds. 'Everything is in the neatest order of course', he wrote in his cabin on a steamer; 'and my shaving tackle, dressing case, brushes, books, and papers, are arranged with as much precision as if we were going to remain here a month.' On the eve of his return from America to England he busied himself 'in thinking how my books look, and where the tables are, and in what positions the chairs stand relatively to the other furniture.'

In spite of his passion for order and regularity, due partly to his reaction against the disorder and irregularity of his upbringing, their family was a happy one, for he was devoted to his children, loved to see them enjoying themselves, and was himself the most high-spirited child amongst them. On summer evenings he often drove Kate, Georgina and the two girls to Hampstead, where they wandered over the Heath picking flowers while he told stories, or romped around the bushes, or played games, finishing up at Jack Straw's Castle, where they took refreshment before returning home. The love of children professed by many people is really a love of power, for it is noticeable that their love is restricted to 'good' or controllable children and is not extended to 'bad' or intractable children; but Dickens's love of children was primarily a love of his own childhood, a desire to recapture it in the company of his sons and daughters. When not insisting on their cleanliness, tidiness and punctuality, he was more a playmate than a parent; and when they were ill, he was better than any nurse, for he not only sat with them and kept them amused with stories, but he knew what to do in an emergency, was practical, cheerful, active, sensible and sympathetic.

His desire to control so many things, to master so much, coupled with his craving for a single-hearted and understanding love which he could not find, helped to produce his restlessness, which was intensified by a tirelessly creative mind acting upon a highly excitable temperament. 'That unspeakable restless something', of which he spoke, 'the vague restless craving for something undefined, which nothing could satisfy', is more characteristic of the man of action or the actor than of the reflective and creative artist. Dickens experienced it in a fuller measure perhaps than any other great writer; there were periods when he walked the streets and countryside like one possessed, when, like Nicholas Nickleby, he 'increased his rate of walking as if in the hope of leaving his thoughts behind'; and as the years went by this mental pressure increased, driving him on to exploits which killed him before his time. His internal disquietude is symbolised in his work by frequent reference to the sound of footsteps in the streets, from *The Old Curiosity Shop*: 'That constant pacing to and fro, that never-ending restlessness, that incessant tread of feet wearing the rough stones smooth and glossy', to *A Tale of Two Cities*: 'The corner echoed and re-echoed with the tread of feet; some, as it seemed, under the windows; some, as it seemed, in the room; some coming, some going, some breaking off, some stopping altogether; all in the distant streets, and not one within sight.'

Along with his energy and restlessness there went a faculty for minute and exact observation that has never been equalled. There are some men, Macaulay, Oscar Wilde, Sidney Webb, who have had the extraordinary gift of being able to read a book photographically: as they turned each page, its entire content was instantly printed on their minds, and they could recite whole passages verbatim long after they had glanced through the work. Dickens possessed this power, not of seeing pages, but of seeing and sensing people and places and episodes, every detail being photographed on his memory, so that he could recall at will the slightest expression in a face, the least intonation of a voice, the smallest detail in a room, the almost imperceptible variation of atmosphere in scene or conversation. He could have out-Boswelled Boswell, but he preferred to boswellise his impressions, to record his own view of the universe. These mental photographs were transferred to the written page, and no other scenes in literature have the sparkle and variety of his. But as in life, so in letters, he was a quick-change artist, and he could not sustain a character for any length of time without repeating the tricks and mannerisms which are amusing on the stage or in a literary sketch but become wearisome in a long novel. There is one notable exception, old Dorrit, but that was a partial portrait of his father, for whom he retained to the end his childlike affection and admiration. On the whole his comic characters have the vividness and super-ficiality of theatrical figures; they have not the depth, richness, sympathy and significance which Shakespeare and Scott gave to their humorous creations; but they are more brilliant, more grotesque; they tingle with his own electricity, and stand out in the spot-light of his observation so sharply that to this day any odd or extravagant personality is instantly called 'Dickensian'.

The uncanny exactitude of his studies in mental derange-ment proves the power and closeness of his observation. Though he had no medical training, and wrote at a time when practically nothing was known of neurosis, we learn from an expert, W. Russell Brain, that his descriptions of nervous symptoms 'are so detailed and accurate that they can justly be compared with those given by clinicians of genius.'[1] The

[1] Charles Dickens: Neuro-Psychiatrist, by W. Russell Brain, *The London Hospital Gazette*, Jan. 1942.

case of Mrs. Joe Gargery in *Great Expectations* illustrates this. Then there is Mrs. Skewton in *Dombey and Son*, who suffers from cerebral arteriosclerosis, 'and Dickens's account of her illness is remarkable not only for the accuracy of his description of individual symptoms but even more, perhaps, for the skill with which he conveys the relentless progress of the disease, with its insidious onset and catastrophic exacerbations.' After showing how unerringly Dickens describes senile dementia, hypomania, agraphia, aphasia, paranoia, narcolepsy, paraplegia, and locomotor ataxy, the very names of which would have given our author some anxious moments, Mr. Russell Brain affirms that 'Dickens is as good a psychiatrist as neurologist.' It was lucky for the criminal classes that he did not set up as a detective: he would have put every Sherlock Holmes out of business.

But he had quite enough on his hands without the addition of sleuthing to his other avocations. The summer of '47 was spent at Broadstairs, writing *Dombey* and exercising himself so vigorously that most people considered his hobbies equivalent to hard labour. At the end of the year he went to Scotland to speak at the opening of the Glasgow Athenaeum. Kate had a miscarriage in the train and could not attend the function. He had a terrific reception, was lunched and dined and lionised, visited Abbotsford, saw something of Jeffrey, and was pleased with everything except the Scott Monument in Princes Street, which 'is like the spire of a Gothic church taken off and stuck in the ground.' Early in '48 he nearly finished *Dombey* at Brighton; completed the job in Devonshire Terrace towards the close of March; dashed off to the White Hart at Salisbury; spent a day on horseback, accompanied by Forster, Leech and Lemon, when they inspected Hazlitt's 'Hut' at Winterslow, saw Stonehenge, and galloped about the Plain; went on to Marlborough; and then returned home to celebrate the completion of his novel with a dinner, an event which took place at the conclusion of every novel, and to start rehearsals of *The Merry Wives*. Again at Broadstairs that summer, where his wife, who seemed committed to miscarriages of one sort or another, was nearly killed in a runaway pony-chaise, he enjoyed a spell of what he called idleness: that is, he bathed every morning at 7.30, played with his children, entertained his friends, went for twenty-mile walks, saw plays at Margate and Ramsgate, and filled in the unemployed moments by changing his clothes, which were usually soaked through either with rain from exposure or with perspiration from exercise. In September his sister Fanny died, leaving a young husband and family. She had been ill for some time with consumption, and during the many hours that Charles had passed at her bedside they had talked of their childhood days in Chatham, Rochester, and the woods of Cobham. Her death affected him profoundly. It was the first link with his youth to snap, and it probably decided the form of his next serial story. But he dared not think of that before writing his fifth and last Christmas book, *The Haunted Man*, for which he began to 'wander about the streets full of faces at night.' He finished it at the Bedford Hotel, Brighton, in November, 'having been crying my eyes out over it—not painfully but pleasantly as I hope the readers will—these last three days.'

He was now about to commence what became his most popular novel, his own favourite, and certainly one of his three best. It was to be largely autobiographical, but as he did not wish this to be recognised he shifted the scene of his youth, changed many other circumstances, and dramatised the characters taken from life in such a way that he hoped they would be the last to recognise themselves. Fixing on the Yarmouth district for his earliest years, partly perhaps because he wished to visit the scene of a notorious murder near Norwich, he went there with Leech and Lemon in the first week of January '49. Their fellow-travellers in the train to Bishop Stortford were going to stay with a friend who had 'newly come into property and port wine, bequeathed him by an uncle. The host himself, who came down to the station to receive them, made up a picture that I never saw surpassed. It was so evident that his late uncle's gifts wouldn't last long —and that he would be imbecile with his own port in five minutes, and leave his distinguished guests to enjoy themselves in their own way, after he was carried off to bed.' Having pitched on Blundestone, near Yarmouth, as the village of his birth, because he liked the sound of the name, which he saw on a signpost on the road to Lowestoft, he then described a place which, since he never visited it, had no more resemblance to the original than Chatham had to Yarmouth. Whether or not he captured the atmosphere of Yarmouth more successfully, no modern visitor to that grotesque seaside resort is able to judge. He thought it 'the strangest place in the wide world', and he made it so, but not so strange as it has become. They put up at the Royal Hotel, and Dickens at once insisted on a twenty-two mile walk to Lowestoft and back, after which Lemon went to sleep in front of the fire, dog-tired: 'He breaks into a snore in the most wonderful manner, instantly after he has been broad awake.'

In February '49, a sixth son having just been born, he took Kate to 148 Kings Road, Brighton, and worked hard on *David Copperfield*. Leech and his wife were staying with them when, a few days after their arrival, the landlord of their lodgings suddenly went mad; the landlord's daughter followed suit; and the lodgers had a lively time of it: 'If you could have heard the cursing and crying of the two; could have seen the physician and nurse quoited out into the passage by the madman at the hazard of their lives; could have seen Leech and me flying to the doctor's rescue; could have seen our wives pulling us back; could have seen the M.D. faint with fear; could have seen three other M.D.s come to his aid; with an atmosphere of Mrs. Gamps, strait-waistcoats, struggling friends and servants, surrounding the whole; you would have said it was quite worthy of me, and quite in keeping with my usual proceedings.' They went to stay at the Bedford Hotel, and Dickens wrestled with David, though it took him some time to get the right title, carefully considering The Copperfield Disclosures, The Copperfield Records, The Copperfield Survey of the World as it Rolled, The Last Living Speech and Confession of David Copperfield Junior, The Last Will and Testament of Mr. David Copperfield, Copperfield Complete, Copperfield's Entire, and so on, at length hitting on *The Personal History of David Copperfield*. So busy was he that his daughter Mamie wanted to know whether he would be able to attend her birthday party. He reassured her: 'Even if I had an engagement of the most particular kind, I should excuse myself from keeping it, so that I might have the pleasure of celebrating at home, and among my children, the day that gave me such a dear and good daughter as you.' He spent the spring in London, dining in with a succession of guests and dining out with a succession of hosts, and working hard all the time.

The first number of *David Copperfield* appeared in May '49, the last in November '50. The success of *Dombey* had placed him in a firm financial position, and he had no more anxieties about money, but the numbers of *Copperfield* did not sell as well as those of its predecessor, and he was temporarily cast down. Also he found it more difficult to write than he had expected: 'My hand is out in the matter of Copperfield. Today and yesterday I have done nothing. Though I know what I want to do, I am lumbering on like a stage-waggon.' A nasty fall in July did not increase his rate of composition; he was cupped and blistered and went off to the Albion at Broadstairs to see what the sea air would do. It did very well, but a trifling episode upset him. Going into a shop to buy some paper, he heard a woman ask for the latest number of *David Copperfield*, which was handed to her. 'Oh, I have read this: I want the next one', she said, and was told it would be out at the end of the month. As not a word of the number she wanted had yet been written, Dickens declared that he felt frightened for the first time in his life.

He needed a quieter place than Broadstairs, and having finished the number so eagerly awaited by the woman in the shop he made a hurried tour of the Isle of Wight, soon finding 'the prettiest place I ever saw in my life, at home or abroad', at Bonchurch. It was called 'Winterbourne' and belonged to a friend of his, the Rev. James White, who lived nearby. He took it at once, arranged with a carpenter to convert a waterfall in the grounds into a perpetual shower-bath, and dashed home to fetch his family. Thackeray saw them at Ryde and reported their appearance to Mrs. Brookfield on July 24th: 'I met on the pier as I was running for the dear life, the great Dickens, with his wife, his children, his Miss Hogarth, all looking abominably coarse and vulgar and happy.' Again Leech and his wife joined them, and all went well to start with. The time was pleasantly passed with picnics, walks, climbs, swims, races, conjuring tricks, entertainments of all sorts, games of all kinds, and for him work until two every day; but after they had been there for a few weeks they began to feel lazy and sleepy. Dickens himself could scarcely walk ten miles; he felt 'a disposition to shed tears from morning to night'; his energy seemed to be leaving him; he had 'no purpose, power, or object in existence whatever'; when he brushed his hair in the morning he was so weak that he had to sit down to do it; he could not read; physically and mentally he was a wreck; and he felt that if he remained there a year he would die. Towards the end of September Leech was knocked over by a big wave while bathing and laid up with congestion of the brain. Dickens sat by his bedside for hours and perceived that he could not recover unless he went to sleep. Proposing to Mrs. Leech that he should mesmerise her husband, and she agreeing, he set to work 'and, after a very fatiguing bout of it, put him to sleep for an hour and thirty-five minutes.' Leech began to mend at once, and soon made a complete recovery. The moment he was out of danger Dickens left Bonchurch for Broadstairs, where the bracing air soon restored him to high spirits, good health, sound sleep, and long walks.

Home again, he witnessed the public execution of the Mannings in November, and was so much horrified by the levity, callousness and savagery of the crowd, the jokes, oaths and drunkenness of the hangman, and the unrelieved repulsiveness of the show, that he wrote two letters to *The Times* describing the sickening scene and strongly urging the privacy of the punishment, quoting Fielding: 'The mind of man is so much more capable of magnifying than his eye, that I question whether every object is not lessened by being looked upon.' His letters opened a general controversy on the subject and he was submerged by correspondence, but his protest had some effect and he lived to see the end of these degrading exhibitions.

Later that month he and Kate visited the Watsons at Rockingham Castle. A fellow-guest was a great admirer of his work: her name was Mary Boyle. She was also a good amateur actress, and they performed scenes from *The School for Scandal* as well as the episode of the lunatic on the wall from *Nicholas Nickleby*. He suffered the usual reaction after such excitements and described himself as 'a blight and mildew on my home'; but he soon recovered. As a result of that visit, he and Mary became lifelong friends.

All through 1850 he was busy with *David Copperfield*, together with another undertaking which would have been a whole-time job for anyone else, and of which we shall hear more in the next chapter. But none of his occupations prevented him from tearing about the universe when he felt a craving for motion, and in the middle of '50 he was at the Hotel Windsor in Paris, boring himself with 'sights I don't care for', and dragging Maclise to the Morgue, which 'made him so sick, that to my infinite disconcertment he sat down on a doorstep in the street for about ten minutes, resting his cheek . . . on his hand.' August, September and October were spent at Fort House, Broadstairs, finishing *Copperfield*, covering enormous distances on foot, keeping his guests amused, and finding his future biographer rather too much for him. One day his son Charley, Forster, two others and himself walked to Richborough Castle and back: 'Forster was in a tip-top state of amiability, but I think I never heard him *half so loud*. (!) He really, after the heat of the walk, so disordered me that by no process I could possibly try, could I get to sleep afterwards. At last I gave it up as a bad job, and walked about the house till 5—paying Georgina a visit, and getting her up for company . . . But I tumbled out again at half past 7 this morning, and tumbled into the sea.' In the evenings they sometimes played *vingt-et-un*, but Dickens never cared for cards, and he was so much preoccupied with his book that his mind would wander from the game and he would get up to straighten a picture on the wall or alter the position of a chair.

As it dealt with his early years, the story he was now writing brought back so many memories that he had great difficulty in rejecting those which were unessential to the plot. His past was always vividly present to him, often when he was asleep: 'My own dreams are usually of twenty years ago', he wrote in February '51. 'I often blend my present position with them, but very confusedly, whereas my life of twenty years ago is very distinctly represented. I have been married fourteen years and have nine children, but I do not remember that I ever, on any occasion, dreamed of myself as being invested with those responsibilities, or surrounded by those relations.' In *David Copperfield* he could re-live his past, and that was why he stated towards the end of his life: 'Of all my books, I like this the best . . . like many fond parents, I have in my heart of hearts a favourite child. And his name is David Copperfield.' It took him some time to get under way, but once properly started the story flowed from his pen. The fragment of autobiography which he had written a few years previously was easily adapted to the narrative, the progress of which we can trace in phrases from his letters:

6 June, 1849: 'I feel, thank God, quite confident in the story. I have a move in it ready for this month: another for next, and another for the next.'

17 November: 'I am wonderfully in harness, and nothing galls or frets.'

20 November: 'Copperfield done after two days' very hard work indeed; and I think a smashing number. His first dissipation I hope will be found worthy of attention, as a piece of grotesque truth.'

23 January, 1850: 'I feel a great hope that I shall be remembered by little Em'ly, a good many years to come.'

20 February: 'I begin to have my doubts of being able to join you, for Copperfield runs high, and must be done tomorrow. But I'll do it if possible, and strain every nerve. Some beautiful comic love, I hope, in the number.'

7 May: 'Still undecided about Dora, but MUST decide today.'

13 August: 'Work in a very decent state of advancement, domesticity notwithstanding. I hope I shall have a splendid number. I feel the story to its minutest point.' (The 'domesticity' concerned Kate, who gave birth to a third daughter on August 16th. She was called Dora after the heroine of *David Copperfield*, and died the following year.)

20 August: 'I have been very hard at work these three days, and have still Dora to kill. But with good luck I may do it tomorrow.'

26 August: (to his wife) 'I read the number to Stone and Georgy yesterday, and threw them (especially the former) into a dreadful state. I hope you are affected by it.' (The number describing Dora's death.)

15 September: 'I have been tremendously at work these two days; eight hours at a stretch yesterday, and six hours and a half today, with the Ham and Steerforth chapter, which has completely knocked me over—utterly defeated me!'

17 September: 'I am in that tremendous paroxysm of Copperfield—having my most powerful effect in all the Story on the Anvil—that you might as well ask me to manufacture a Cannon seventy-four pounder . . . or do anything NOW.'

24 September: 'Coming out of Copperfield into a condition of temporary and partial consciousness, I plunge into histrionic duties . . . There are some things in the next Copperfield that I think better than any that have gone before. After I have been believing such things with all my heart and soul, two results always ensue: first, I can't write plainly to the eye; secondly, I can't write sensibly to the mind.'

21 October: 'I am within three pages of the shore; and am

strangely divided, as usual in such cases, between joy and sorrow. Oh, my dear Forster, if I were to say half of what Copperfield makes me feel tonight, how strangely, even to you, I should be turned inside out! I seem to be sending some part of myself into the Shadowy World.'

23 October: 'I have just finished Copperfield and don't know whether to laugh or cry . . . I have an idea of wandering somewhere for a day or two—to Rochester, I think, where I was a small boy—to get all this fortnight's work out of my head . . .'

Although he had been working on the book at Brighton, Bonchurch and London, the greater part had been written at Broadstairs, which he preferred to any other seaside place, and where, though he placed her at Dover, Betsey Trotwood lived in his imagination. He was constantly praising it in his letters—'Broadstairs is charming. The green corn growing, and the larks singing and the sea sparkling, all in their best manner'—and he probably spent more happy days there than elsewhere. His relative tranquillity at the spot is reflected in *David Copperfield*, which is his most agreeable as well as his most personal novel, and is a great deal truer to life than most so-called autobiographies. In one respect it was much too true. A lady named Mrs. Hill saw herself in the part of Miss Mowcher; and since that character was described as mentally vicious and physically hideous, she wrote to complain. Dickens replied that his creations were composite, not individual, that bits of the character were undoubtedly taken from Mrs. Hill, bits from other people; but that as he felt he had wronged her, he would change his intention of making Miss Mowcher wicked and turn her into a model member of society. This he did in later numbers, and Mrs. Hill was apparently placated by the spiritually reformed though still bodily deformed Miss Mowcher.

There is no evidence that the novelist's father John Dickens saw his resemblance to Micawber; but that the character was based on him is proved by the scraps of his conversation which appear in his son's letters: *e.g.*

'To be deprived, to a certain extent, of the concomitant advantages, whatever they may be, resulting from his medical skill, such as it is, and his professional attendance, in so far as it may be so considered . . .'

'. . . Manifest to any person of ordinary intelligence, if the term may be considered allowable.'

'And I must express my tendency to believe that his longevity is (to say the least of it) extremely problematical.'

'The Supreme Being must be an entirely different individual from what I have every reason to believe Him to be, if He would care in the least for the society of your relations.'

This is obviously the same man who, as Micawber, says to his wife: 'My dear, your papa was very well in his way, and Heaven forbid that I should disparage him. Take him for all in all, we ne'er shall—in short, make the acquaintance, probably, of anybody else possessing, at his time of life, the same legs for gaiters, and able to read the same description of print, without spectacles.'

Mrs. Micawber has some resemblance to Mrs. John Dickens; there are several other characters, such as Steerforth and Creakle, the originals of which have been recognised; and Dickens could have found a Mrs. Gummidge complaining of her lot in nearly every household. Again we are given in Agnes the ideal girl whom he thought he had found in Mary Hogarth, the abstract perfection of womanhood which existed only in his imagination. By way of contrast, we have one more of his 'untouchables', partly drawn from contemporary melodrama, partly due to the Victorian sense of property in woman, Martha being soiled property, but chiefly an expression of the period's sense of guilt. The faiths of one age are the falsities of another, and nothing separates our own from the Victorian so completely as the importance they attached to the pre-nuptial chastity and post-nuptial fidelity of women, whatsoever the licentiousness of men, and the endless humbug arising from such an attitude. The chapters devoted to this theme in *David Copperfield* would be painful if they were not comical; but the reader who is not amused may leave them as Martha left her virtuous company: 'Making the same low, dreary, wretched moaning in her shawl, she went away.'

The first fourteen chapters of the book contain the best description of childhood and early youth we possess; but after the scene between Betsey Trotwood and the Murdstones the story flags, being reanimated with the entrance of Dora, who is Dickens's most successful female portrait, apart from his purely humorous or grotesque creations. Maria Beadnell had got into his blood; Dora is a fascinating representment of Maria; and no one has equalled Dickens in delineating every fleeting frenzy, every idiotic action, every sort of joy, torment, abasement, exaltation, suspicion and certainty, in adolescent love. Knowing his liking for personal adornment, we may accept the following as a bare statement of fact: 'Within the first week of my passion, I bought four sumptuous waistcoats . . . and took to wearing straw-coloured kid gloves in the streets, and laid the foundations of all the corns I have ever had. If the boots I wore at that period could only be produced and compared with the natural size of my feet, they would show what the state of my heart was, in a most affecting manner.'

Though David Copperfield himself is far from being a complete portrait of Charles Dickens, he is given several of his creator's main characteristics:

'I looked at nothing, that I know of, but I saw everything.'

'I never could have done what I have done, without the habits of punctuality, order, and diligence . . . which I then formed.'

'Whatever I have tried to do in life, I have tried with all my heart to do well . . . whatever I have devoted myself to, I have devoted myself to completely . . . in great aims and in small, I have always been thoroughly in earnest. I have never believed it possible that any natural or improved ability can claim immunity from the companionship of the steady, plain, hard-working qualities, and hope to gain its end.'

'Never to put one hand to anything, on which I could throw my whole self; and never to affect depreciation of my work, whatever it was; I find, now, to have been my golden rules.'

David also shares his creator's restlessness, and passes through the same experiences: the blacking factory, the Marshalsea, the love-affair, Doctors' Commons, parliamentary reporting, successful authorship; and the actor in Dickens appears in the actions of David, who, when the news of his mother's death reaches him at school, walks in the playground while the other boys are at work: 'When I saw them glancing at me out of the windows, as they went up to their classes, I felt distinguished, and looked more melancholy, and walked slower.' Finally, David's realisation that his marriage has not fulfilled its promise is the author's, and Kate must have paused upon such passages as these:

'I did feel, sometimes, for a little while, that I could have wished my wife had been my counsellor: had had more character and purpose, to sustain me, and improve me by; had been endowed with power to fill up the void which somewhere seemed to be about me . . .'

'Thus it was that I took upon myself the toils and cares of our life, and had no partner in them.'

'There can be no disparity in marriage like unsuitability of mind and purpose.'

'But, that it would have been better for me if my wife could have helped me more, and shared the many thoughts in which I had no partner; and that this might have been; I knew.'

Dickens's autonovel is the most popular masterpiece of fiction in the English language; and though it could be claimed that *Tom Jones*, *Old Mortality*, *Vanity Fair* and *Little Dorrit* are greater works, few will dispute that *David Copperfield* is among the half-dozen greatest. In June, 1850, shortly before Dickens retired to Broadstairs for the summer months, he wrote to Macready: 'Between Copperfield and Household Words I am as busy as a bee. I hope to go down to that old image of Eternity that I love so much, and finish the former to its hoarse music. May it be as good a book as I hope it will be, for your children's children's children to read.' His wish has been realised.

## 12

## EDITORIAL, ETCETERA

EVER since his abandonment of *The Daily News*, Dickens had been brooding on his original plan of a weekly newspaper which should be a conspectus of life, a reflection of the spirit of the age, critical, hortatory, discursive, devoted to 'the general improvement of our social condition', and above all readable. He again started writing to Forster about it when he was half-way through *Copperfield*, and for a while he toyed with such titles as *The Robin, Mankind, Charles Dickens, The Comrade, The Household Voice*, at length finding in Shakespeare precisely what he wanted: *Household Words*. Bradbury and Evans undertook its publication and took a quarter of the profits; Dickens received £500 a year as editor and half the profits; Forster's share was an eighth; and W. H. Wills, who had been Dickens's secretary on *The Daily News*, became assistant editor for £8 a week with the remaining eighth of the profits. The first number appeared on March 30th, 1850, and the paper was continued weekly until the end of May '59, when Dickens, for reasons which will duly appear, started a similar paper under a different name.

It might be thought that a busy novelist, producer, actor, orator, correspondent and family man, would after the first burst of enthusiasm leave the purely editorial work of the paper to his assistant. Not so Dickens, who never slackened off for a single number. Whether at home or away he kept an eye on everything, writing reams of advice to Wills, reading, rejecting, accepting and revising articles and stories submitted to his judgment, finding new writers, suggesting fresh subjects, mostly abbreviating, sometimes lengthening, often re-writing the work of others, and never failing to produce his own essays and notes. Some of his contributors were much annoyed by the appearance of their work in print after he had pruned or embellished it. Mrs. Gaskell, whose *Cranford* was serialised in *Household Words*, was extremely vexed by the activity of his blue pencil on some of her stories, and wrote to complain. He was always impenitent; but as he was also prompt and generous with his payments, the rage of hurt pride was quickly transmuted into the relief of solvency. Anonymity was a strict rule, and readers often wondered why so many of the articles were written in the style of Dickens, the reason being, partly, that not a little of the contents had been revised by the editor, who must have spent as much time in sending letters of explanation and advice to his contributors as most editors spend over their leading articles. His father and father-in-law were given jobs on the paper, and one of his early discoveries was George Augustus Sala, who made a reputation in *Household Words* and quickly became a notable figure in Fleet Street. When he was in town Dickens worked at the office in Wellington Street most mornings from 8 till 11, combining physical with mental exercise by marching about his office while dictating.

The tone of the new periodical was outspoken within the limits of decorum. Public abuses were not spared: private blushes were. 'Beware of writing things for the eyes of everybody, which you would feel the smallest delicacy in saying anywhere', he once wrote to a man who had sent him an article on Wat Tyler: 'Mrs. Scutfidge may have stripped in public—I have no doubt she did—but I should be sorry to have to tell young ladies so in the nineteenth century, for all that.' In those days it was considered religious to be exceptionally miserable on Sundays, the point being, apparently, that righteousness and wretchedness were synonymous terms. Dickens did not agree with this view, and he constantly dwelt on the evils of Sabbatarianism and the value to the poorer classes of Sunday entertainment. He liked to see people enjoying themselves, and was even glad when the less reputable members of the community gave themselves up to pleasure. Going to a theatre where the highest price for a seat was a shilling, he 'noticed some young pickpockets of our acquaintance; but as they were evidently there as private individuals, and not in their public capacity, we were little disturbed by their presence. For we consider the hours of idleness passed by this class of society as so much gain to society at large; and we do not join in a whimsical sort of lamentation that is generally made over them, when they are found to be unoccupied.' In one form of idleness however he foresaw the main danger to democracy, the idleness resulting from strikes: 'Masters right, or men right; masters wrong, or men wrong; both right, or both wrong; there is certain ruin to both in the continuance or frequent revival of this breach. And from the ever-widening circle of their decay, what drop in the social ocean shall be free!' But knowing the employers as well as the employed, he had this to say: 'It is not agreeable . . . to contemplate the English artisan as working under a curb or yoke, or even as being supposed to require one. His spirit is of the highest; his nature is of the best. He comes of a great race, and his character is famous in the world. If a false step on the part of any man should be generously forgotten, it should be forgotten in him.' Dickens derived no hope from the Houses of Parliament. The aristocracy were futile, the Commons were incompetent, red tape was omnipotent, and somebody who would do something was the vital need of the nation. 'Reserving Nobody for statues, and stars and garters, and batons, and places and pensions without duties, what if we were to try Somebody for real work?' he suggested. In his own sphere he attended to everything, showing why Peace Societies were foolish and why Disarmament was reckless, attacking all forms of oppression, deriding every sort of cant, ridiculing stupidity, exposing cruelty, hitting at this, laughing at that, and making his paper much more popular in the suburbs than in Mayfair.

He knew that the most important lesson his writers had to learn was that every article must be readable and entertaining, and he drove this lesson home again and again in his letters to Wills and the rest of them. It did not matter how clever, how profound, how true a statement was: unless it were presented attractively, it might just as well be left unstated. 'Let John Hollingshead do it', Dickens would say to Wills: 'he's the most ignorant man on the staff, but he'll cram up the facts, and won't give us an encyclopaedical article.' And one of his letters to Wills about a number of *Household Words* ends with: 'Brighten it, brighten it, brighten it!' The editor and his assistant were soon on very friendly terms, much to the annoyance of John Forster, who felt that Wills was poaching on his property. Forster, said Dickens, 'complains of Wills as not consulting him enough, and is evidently very sore in that connection.' But his soreness was really due to the familiarity between the other two; and when Forster learnt that Wills had complimented him on the way he had negotiated matters with Bradbury and Evans, he burst out: 'I am truly sorry, my dear Dickens, that I cannot reciprocate your friend's compliment, for a damnder ass I never encountered in the whole course of my life!' He did his best to sow discord between Dickens and Wills, though anyone might think from his reference to Wills in his Life of Dickens that they were the best of friends; but at last he gave it up as hopeless, and in 1856 relinquished his share in *Household Words*.

Serious though Dickens was in his management of the paper, he could not help clowning when the humour took him. At one council meeting only he and another member, John Robinson, were present. Knowing Dickens's business-like habits, and foreseeing that he would insist on going through the whole routine, Robinson felt rather alarmed. For a while they discussed the latest news; then, punctual to the minute, Dickens said 'Will you move me into the chair?' Robinson did so, nervously risking the feeble joke that he felt Dickens could be trusted to keep order in a large gathering. The minutes of the last meeting were read, and then came the resolutions to be considered at the present meeting. Dickens, with the utmost gravity, moved each resolution in the voice and manner of an absent member, carried on the discussion following each proposal in the characters of the mover, the seconder and the chairman, treated occasional interruptions by Robinson, himself, and those who were not present, with the exact dialectical method of Forster or Wills or Bradbury or Evans or whoever it might be; and after each resolution had been passed, solemnly entered it in the minutes.

*Household Words* was an instantaneous success, and after finishing *Copperfield* towards the close of '50 Dickens gave the paper a good deal of attention; but much of '51 was taken up with acting in Lytton's comedy, public speaking, and private anxieties. Following the birth of their third daughter, Kate Dickens was extremely ill, and for a while it looked as if she and her baby would die. But Dora rallied, and Kate was well enough to be moved to Malvern in March '51. She was how-ever in a precarious mental condition; she had behaved strangely when 'staying in the country houses even of intimate friends'; and her husband told a doctor that 'great caution' was necessary in treating her. They took lodgings at Knuts-ford Lodge, Great Malvern, and Dickens spent many hours of the next weeks in express trains between London and Malvern, the children being in Devonshire Terrace, Georgina with her sister. Having arranged Macready's Farewell

performance and organised a dinner in his honour, Dickens
was in the midst of rehearsals for Lytton's play and articles for
*Household Words* when his father, who had been suffering from
disease of the bladder without saying a word to anyone about
it, collapsed and was taken to a hospital. What Dickens called
'the most terrible operation known in surgery' was then performed upon him without chloroform, as the only chance of
saving his life. 'He bore it with astonishing fortitude, and I
saw him directly afterwards—his room a slaughterhouse of
blood. He was wonderfully cheerful and strong-hearted . . .
I have been about, to get what is necessary for him, and write
with such a shaking hand that I cannot write plainly . . . All
this goes to my side directly, and I feel as if I had been struck
there by a leaden bludgeon.' John Dickens died on March
31st at the age of sixty-five, and was buried in Highgate
cemetery, his son's epitaph on his tombstone bearing witness
to his 'zealous, useful, cheerful spirit.' Charles never took the
common view of his father. 'The longer I live, the better man
I think him', was his sincere tribute.

Driven by worry and work, Dickens could not rest for
several nights, and walked the streets till morning brought
more work and worry. He spent many hours at the bedside
of his five-months old daughter, and on the evening of
April 14th he went straight from nursing her to preside at the
dinner of the General Theatrical Fund. Half an hour before
he rose to make a speech, the news arrived that Dora had
suddenly died. Forster kept him in ignorance of it until he
left the chair. Mark Lemon sat up with him all that night,
and Forster went to Malvern early the next morning with a
letter to Kate from her husband, from which we gather that
she was practically incapable at that time of coherent thought,
and liable to hysteria. 'Now observe', it began. 'You must
read this letter very slowly and carefully.' He informed her
that Dora was very ill: 'Mind! I will not deceive you', he said,
though every word of the letter was, in her then condition, a
necessary deception; 'I think her *very* ill . . . I do not—why
should I say I do, to you my dear—I do not think her recovery
at all likely.' Having told her that Forster would bring her
home, he finished by saying that he could not close his letter
'without putting the strongest entreaty and injunction upon
you to come home with perfect composure—to remember
what I have often told you, that we never can expect to be

exempt, as to our many children, from the afflictions of other parents—and that if—*if*—when you come, I should even have to say to you "our little baby is dead", you are to do your duty to the rest, and to show yourself worthy of the great trust you hold in them.' Kate behaved well under the shock, her husband reporting her 'so good and amiable that I hope it may not hurt her', and Dora was buried at Highgate a fortnight after her grandfather. The two blows unnerved Dickens; he postponed the first performance of *Not So Bad As We Seem*; and the Queen, the Prince, the dukes, the duchesses, and all the other big-wigs, had to rearrange their engagements accordingly.

Although his manifold duties that spring kept him fully occupied from early morning till late at night, he managed to take Kate about 'under a variety of pretences' in order to keep her mind busy with change and movement; but her health showed no improvement, and again he rented Fort House, Broadstairs, from May till October. This was the last time they stayed at Broadstairs, for the place was becoming too noisy to work in. Five years earlier 'vagrant music' had bothered him, and 'unless it pours with rain, I cannot write half-an-hour without the most excruciating organs, fiddles, bells, or glee-singers.' Now the din was so disagreeable that he could only write journalism indoors and escape from it out-of-doors by going elsewhere. That was the summer of the great Exhibition in Hyde Park, and Dickens was glad to be out of London. He 'had an instinctive feeling against the Exhibition, of a faint, inexplicable sort', and thought that the public would come out of it with a 'feeling of boredom and lassitude.' He went twice and was bewildered by the number of exhibits: 'I have a natural horror of sights, and the fusion of so many sights in one has not decreased it . . . It is a dreadful thing to be obliged to be false, but when anyone says "Have you seen ——?" I say "Yes", because if I don't, I know he'll explain it, and I can't bear that.' As usual all his friends went down to stay with him at Fort House, among them his future biographer: 'Here has Forster been and gone, after patronising with suavity the whole population of Broadstairs, and impressing Tom Collins with a profound conviction that he (F) did the ocean a favour when he bathed.'

All through the summer Dickens was in a fever of excitement over the alterations being made to his new home. His tenancy of No. 1 Devonshire Terrace having expired, he was moving in the autumn to Tavistock House in the Square of that name; and the amount of care, forethought, energy, movement, will-power, concentration and attention to detail which he put into the business was probably more than the Prime Minister gave to running the country. With Dickens a change of address resembled an earthquake. His youngest sister's husband, Henry Austin, an expert in sanitary matters, was directing the repairs in the house, and Dickens's letters to him are those of a man to whom the dilatory methods of British workmen made no appeal: 'I am perpetually wandering (in fancy) up and down the house and tumbling over the workmen', he wrote from Broadstairs; 'when I feel that they are gone to dinner I become low; when I look forward to their total abstinence on Sundays, I am wretched. The gravy at dinner has a taste of glue in it. I smell paint in the sea. Phantom lime attends me all the day long. I dream that I am a carpenter and can't partition off the hall. I frequently dance (with a distinguished company) in the drawing-room, and fall in the kitchen for want of a pillar . . . I dream, also, of the workmen every night. They make faces at me, and won't do anything.' A month later: 'Oh! if this were to last long; the distraction of the new book, the whirling of the story through one's mind, escorted by workmen, the imbecility, the wild necessity of beginning to write, the not being able to do so, the, O! I should go——O!'

He made a ground-plan of the garden, gave detailed instructions to the gardener about the transplanting of trees and the draining of paths, demanded an estimate of the cost, and wished to know 'the utmost length of the time you would require for the work; as *punctuality and dispatch* are conditions on which I invariably rest in all transactions, and for which I always stipulate . . . I attach such paramount importance to them that I think it indispensable to impress this upon you, as the first feature of any contract I make.' He had the curious idea of adding to his library a number of books which did not exist, the backs of which were carefully made, painted in different colours, and then fixed to the walls, so as to look as much like the real books as possible. Some of the titles were: History of the Middling Ages, 6 vols; Jonah's Account of the Whale; Drowsy's Recollections of Nothing; The Books of Moses and Sons, 2 vols; King Henry the Eighth's Evidences of Christianity; Lady Godiva on the Horse; Hansard's Guide to Refreshing Sleep. Many visitors must have tried to extract one or other of these works, and much innocent laughter was no doubt caused by their failure to do so. At the end of October '51 Dickens reported to Henry Austin that progress on the house was noticeable, even though the painters were spending most of their time whistling, the carpenters most of theirs in contemplation, the Irish labourers in howling, the paper-hangers in staring, and the carpet-layers in playing tunes with the stair-rods. By the beginning of November the family had moved in, and before the year was out Dickens had completed the first number of his new novel, *Bleak House*, which was published in March '52, the remaining numbers coming out monthly until September '53, and selling half as well again as *Copperfield*.

More than the usual amount of internal commotion preceded the commencement of *Bleak House*. In August '51 he was pondering the theme at Broadstairs: 'Violent restlessness, and vague ideas of going I don't know where, I don't know why, are the present symptoms of the disorder.' And then: 'I very nearly packed up a portmanteau and went away . . . into the mountains of Switzerland, alone! Still the victim of an intolerable restlessness, I shouldn't be at all surprised if I wrote to you one of these mornings from under Mont Blanc. I sit down between whiles to think of a new story, and, as it begins to grow, such a torment of a desire to be anywhere but where I am . . . takes hold of me, that it is like being *driven away*.' There followed a period when he could not think of *Bleak House* on account of Tavistock House, but the moment he was in residence at the latter he pegged away at the former. The success of the first chapters heralded the birth of his last child, Edward Bulwer Lytton Dickens, on March 13th. He invented the oddest nicknames for his boys, and this was called Plornishghenter, or Plorn for short. Though the lad became his father's favourite son, he was not altogether welcome at first. Two months after his birth, Dickens wrote to a friend: 'My wife is quite well again, after favouring me (I think I could have dispensed with the compliment) with No. 10.' And four months later: 'I have some idea, with only one wife and nothing particular in any other direction, of interceding with the Bishop of London to have a little service in St. Paul's beseeching that I may be considered to have done enough towards my country's population.' It was a perfectly natural feeling in the hard-working father of a large family; but his wife was not entirely responsible.

The birth pangs of Mrs. Dickens were as nothing to his. The children of his brain occupied all his thoughts, and month by month he was prostrated by the throes of mental parturition: 'In a frenzied state of interest in *Bleak House*, I had got up at 5, and gone furiously to work, so that at about noon I was comparatively insensible.' The Duke of Devonshire wanted him to stay at Chatsworth, but he would not quit his book for a week-end. Alluring invitations were all declined: 'Seriously, I have long learnt the lesson that when I have a book to write I must give it the first place in my life, and my undivided mind. I have become content to set the pains and care it requires against the pleasures of society . . . and to put my fictitious companions in the upper place at feasts.' One of these fictitious companions had been a real companion at many feasts, and would have caused Dickens a great deal of annoyance if his first consideration had not been the maintenance of his place at the table. This was Leigh Hunt, of whom Dickens gave a perfectly faithful, quite delightful, and extremely damaging portrait in the character of Harold Skimpole. Of course Dickens was accused of bad taste in thus delineating a man with whom he had been fairly intimate. But every great writer has been accused of bad taste in some form or another by his contemporaries, who, irritated by his superiority, have fastened on to the one thing about him of which every fool would disapprove. Good taste is the conventional behaviour of ordinary people, and great writers are bound to offend against it because they are not ordinary people. Bad taste is one of the diagnostics of genius. We need say no more about it at this time of day, except that Leigh Hunt, having lived most of his life at the expense of others, had no right to complain when the tables were turned. Complain he did, however, when the likeness between himself and Skimpole was brought to his attention; and Dickens, who had toned down the portrait considerably on the advice of Forster, first tried to explain that Hunt and Skimpole were not identical, and afterwards frankly admitted that he had done wrong and was deeply sorry. Hunt inclined to harp on his grievance, and Dickens kept away from him for some time. Then, in 1855, Hunt begged him to call, and he promised to do so, 'but I hope you will not think it necessary to renew that painful subject with me.' After Hunt's death, he assured the readers of his periodical that the only resemblance between Hunt and Skimpole was in the charm of their manners and conversation, which, being a thundering lie, was no doubt considered good taste. The fact is that he captured Hunt's philosophy of life, or rather Hunt's attitude to himself, in so masterly a way that the portrait of a sprightly egotist and epicurean which he gives us in Skimpole is unsurpassable:

'It's only you, the generous creatures, whom I envy', said Mr. Skimpole addressing us, his new friends, in an impersonal manner. 'I envy you your power of doing what you do. It is what I should revel in, myself. I don't feel any vulgar gratitude to you. I almost feel as if *you* ought to be grateful to *me*, for giving you the opportunity of enjoying the luxury of generosity. I know you like it. For anything I can tell, I may have come into the world expressly for the purpose of increasing your stock of happiness. I may have been born to be a benefactor to you, by sometimes giving you an opportunity of assisting me in my little perplexities. Why should I regret my incapacity for details and worldly affairs, when it leads to such pleasant consequences? I don't regret it therefore.'

Skimpole naturally wishes to spread happiness and distribute his benefactions over as wide a circle as possible. Having borrowed from one old friend, he turns to two new acquaintances, saying he would 'rather develop generosity in a new soil, and in a new form of flower', and placing himself entirely in their hands: 'The butterflies are free. Mankind will surely not deny to Harold Skimpole what it concedes to the butterflies!' Occasionally he earns money, but his labours in that direction are carried out in the same airy spirit with which he borrows or spends it:

'Vholes? My dear Miss Clare, I had had that kind of acquaintance with him which I have had with several gentlemen of his profession. He had done something or other, in a very agreeable, civil manner—taken proceedings, I think, is the expression—which ended in the proceeding of his taking *me*. Somebody was so good as to step in and pay the money—something and fourpence was the amount; I forget the pounds and shillings, but I know it ended with fourpence, because it struck me at the time as being so odd that I could owe anybody fourpence—and after

that, I brought them together. Vholes asked me for the introduction, and I gave it. Now I come to think of it', he looked
inquiringly at us with his frankest smile as he made the discovery,
'Vholes bribed me, perhaps? He gave me something, and called
it commission. Was it a five-pound note? Do you know, I think
it *must* have been a five-pound note!'

Leigh Hunt was not the only famous contemporary to
appear in *Bleak House*. Boythorn is a friendly portrait of
Walter Savage Landor; at least Dickens meant it to be friendly
and thought it so. Landor himself was not enthusiastic; but
very few people see themselves as comic personalities, and
fewer still enjoy the exhibition of their absurdities in a book;
he probably considered it bad taste on the part of one he
admired so much, and thenceforth spoke of Dickens with
some acerbity, though their outward relationship remained
unchanged.

Three further points about the novel are worth mentioning.
Dickens's admiration for Carlyle is becoming apparent in his
writing, parts of the book being done in the staccato style
popularised by *The French Revolution*. His growing familiarity
with, and dislike of, upper class society is also manifested in
his scenes at the town and country houses of Sir Leicester
Dedlock. Though he never got to know the Dedlock type
well, he was clever enough to hit off many of its characteristics, and the common assumption of his time that he could
not portray a gentleman of the old landowning class must
have been made either by those members of it who did not
perceive their own oddities or by those who admired it and
wished they belonged to it; in other words, by the bulk of the
community. The description of Sir Leicester sitting in his
great chair gazing at the fire while his solicitor reads affidavits,
and appearing to have 'a stately liking for the legal repetitions
and prolixities, as ranging among the national bulwarks', is
one of many perfect strokes. As for the crowd of social
butterflies who flit from place to place in search of novelty
and gossip to overcome their boredom with themselves, they
are the same today as they were a hundred years ago, or a
thousand before that, and will be the same a thousand years
hence: 'She is discussed by her dear friends with all the
genteelest slang in vogue, with the last new word, the last
new manner, the last new drawl, and the perfection of polite
indifference.' Finally we notice the growing oppressiveness

of the London scene. The smoke from the factories and railway engines had blanketed the sky and made the atmosphere opaque with fog. Dickens was beginning to loathe the city which was a source of his inspiration. 'London is a vile place, I sincerely believe', he wrote in '51. 'I have never taken kindly to it since I lived abroad. Whenever I come back from the country now, and see that great heavy canopy lowering over the house-tops, I wonder what on earth I do there except on obligation.' The fog in *Bleak House* is almost a character in the book, and the Court of Chancery is another. Lord Denman, a former Chief Justice and an old friend of Dickens, attacked the work in a series of articles; and though many learned counsel, their livelihood endangered, expressed the opinion that it was a monstrous travesty of the facts, a reform of procedure in the Court of Chancery followed closely on its publication.

Sometimes one is tempted to define the work of Dickens as a blazing volcano of genius almost entirely surrounded by a morass of imbecility. Nowhere does he sparkle more brightly or drivel more inanely than in *Bleak House*. Harold Skimpole alone would have made the reputation of any other novelist, and there are a dozen more portraits worthy to hang in the National Gallery of masterpieces which he painted. But much of Esther Summerson's diary would as surely have blasted the reputation of any novelist but Dickens. Perhaps he thought that as he had just been so successful in writing a boy's autobiography, he might as well try his hand at a girl's diary. If so, it is a pity that he did not think again.

In July '52 he tried another seaside resort, staying with his family at 10 Camden Crescent, Dover, till October, and finding it 'too bandy (I mean musical, no reference to its legs) and infinitely too genteel. But the sea is very fine, and the walks are quite remarkable. There are two ways of going to Folkestone, both lovely and striking in the highest degree; and there are heights, and downs, and country roads, and I don't know what, everywhere.' Just before starting on a new number of a novel, he nearly always went for long solitary rambles: 'This is one of what I call my wandering days before I fall to work. I seem to be always looking at such times for something I have not found in life, but may possibly come to a few thousands of years hence, in some other part of some other system. God knows . . . I'll go and look for it on the

Canterbury road among the hop-gardens and orchards.' Three of his friends died while he was at Dover: Watson of Rockingham Castle, D'Orsay, and Mrs. Macready. Life seemed to him like a field of battle, and he wondered whether it was all a dream, and death was the awakening. Certainly life was sufficiently bizarre: 'There seems to be an attraction in me for all the mad people. They *will* take me into their confidence. One woman in Scotland has left me such an immense amount of imaginary property that I think of retiring on it.' In August and September he visited the north of England with his troupe, and collected much money for the Guild of Literature by performing Lytton's play. At Manchester they had an audience of 4000 people in the Free Trade Hall. At Newcastle the performance was given in a building that many local people considered unsafe. Dickens accepted an expert's word that there was nothing to fear, did not mention the rumour to any member of the company, but suffered agonies when the audience applauded, because of its possible effect on the building. In spite of public dinners, social engagements, and his daily managerial work at the theatre, he found time to walk from Nottingham to Derby and from Newcastle to Sunderland. In October he, Kate and Georgina spent a fortnight at the Hotel des Bains, Boulogne, in order to see whether the town would be suitable for future summer holidays. They were fascinated by it, made arrangements to stay there the following summer, and returned home.

Situated in a secluded spot just off the main Square, Tavistock House attracted dogs, whose barking prevented Dickens from working. He hired a gun, peppered them with small shot, and peace descended on the neighbourhood. But seclusion invites nuisances, and his letter to a neighbour discloses another price he had to pay for peace: 'I saw your baker's man this morning using the corner just outside our gates into the Square, for his private purposes—very objectionable under my windows, and not agreeable to any of us. I spoke to him on the subject, and told him that I knew you would sanction no such conduct. He was *very impertinent*, and I gave him the information that I should let you know it; also that I should, on all our behalfs, give him into custody under the Police Act if I saw him do it again. He was rather urgent to know what I should do "if I was him",—which involved a flight of imagination into which I didn't follow him.'

Apart from a visit to Brighton in March '53, he remained in London until June, when the family went to Boulogne, remaining at the Château des Moulineaux, Rue Beaurépaire, until October. With the exception of their palace at Genoa, he thought it the best place he had ever lived in abroad. The landlord, M. Beaucourt, was an admirable person, very proud of his 'property', as he always spoke of it, and anxious to do everything possible to make his tenants comfortable. The villa, cottage, or, as Beaucourt liked to call it, château, was beautifully situated on high ground, surrounded by gardens 'made in terraces up the hill-side', and backed by a wood, which Beaucourt referred to as a forest. The landlord was a great admirer of Napoleon and named various parts of the garden after his battles. Medallions, portraits and busts of the Emperor were sprinkled all over the place, and 'during the first month of our occupation, it was our affliction to be constantly knocking down Napoleon: if we touched a shelf in a dark corner, he toppled over with a crash, and every door we opened shook him to the soul.' Before going to Boulogne Dickens had been seriously ill with his old childhood complaint, a weak kidney; he had even spent six days in bed for the first time in his life, and had been strongly advised not to leave home; but after a day or two in France he recovered completely, and sent hilarious letters to his friends about the glories of the garden, the eccentricities of his landlord, the charm of the place, the perfect climate, and the absolute necessity that they should stay with him for their own sakes, for his sake, for every sake. 'If you have anything to do, this is the place to do it in. And if you have nothing to do, this is also the place to do it in to perfection', he wrote to Wilkie Collins, who had been introduced to him by the painter Augustus Egg early in '51, who had acted with Egg and himself in Lytton's comedy, and for whose society he soon showed a marked inclination. Collins, Leech and his wife, Forster, Beard, Mary Boyle and others, crossed the Channel to stay with him; and though finishing off *Bleak House*, dealing with *Household Words*, and dictating *A Child's History of England*, he yet contrived to go many excursions with them, to Amiens, Beauvais, and elsewhere. Four of his boys, at different times, attended a school at Boulogne kept by two Englishmen, and from a letter Dickens wrote to Landor we learn how discipline was maintained in the family: 'Walter'—

Landor's godson—'is a very good boy, and comes home from school with honourable commendation. He passed last Sunday in solitary confinement (in a bath-room) on bread and water, for terminating a dispute with the nurse by throwing a chair in her direction. It is the very first occasion of his ever having got into trouble, for he is a great favourite with the whole house, and one of the most amiable boys in the boy-world. (He comes out on birthdays in a blaze of shirt-pin.)'

Having finished two books almost simultaneously, he took a holiday away from his family, accompanied by Augustus Egg and Wilkie Collins. But first he had to attend a London dinner given in his honour by the Guild for which he had done so much. Forster was in the chair, and his irritation over the friendship which Dickens was beginning to form with Wills and Collins came to the surface. In July '51 Dickens had reported that Forster was 'wet-blanketing the proceedings' of the Guild, having left the cast of *Not So Bad As We Seem* after doing his best to make everyone feel that touring the provinces in a play was beneath the dignity of a gentleman. Now, in October '53, he was 'a very uncomfortable and restless chairman', otherwise the dinner would have been perfect, Dickens told his wife. Being what he was, the friendship that had sprung up between Dickens and Collins, who was also at the dinner, following that between Dickens and Wills, who was likewise present, and the knowledge that the more recent friends were just off for a continental tour together, must have disqualified Forster from any position demanding serenity and tact.

The travellers left early in October for Switzerland, and Dickens saw his old friends at Lausanne. Then they went on to Chamounix, where they at once ordered three hot baths at the Hotel de Londres. 'A horrible furnace was lighted, and a smoke was raised which filled the whole valley', but there seemed to be no co-operation between the elements, and they were still unwashed six hours after the preparations were put in hand. Otherwise they did all the things usually done by people who went to Chamounix. At the commencement of the journey Dickens was pleased to find that Collins 'takes things easily and is not put out by small matters—two capital requisites', also that he 'eats and drinks everything, gets on very well everywhere, and is always in good spirits'; but less pleasing aspects of his fellow-travellers became noticeable at

Chamounix: 'Egg sometimes wants trifles of accommodation —in a place like this, for instance—which could hardly be got in Paris, and Collins sometimes wants to give people too little for their trouble . . . Collins (with his short legs stretched out as far as they will go) is reading, and Egg writing in a marvellous Diary of an aggravatingly small kind and unearthly shape, concerning the materials of which he remembers nothing, but is perpetually asking Collins as I write about the names of places where we have been, signs of hotels we have put up at, and so forth—which Collins with his face all awry, blowing old snuff down one nostril and taking new snuff up the other, delivers oracularly'. Collins would have been surprised to know that his habits were so carefully chronicled, especially his morning practice of spitting and snorting rather more than was agreeable to his friend. Another reasonable cause for complaint was the pride which both Collins and Egg took in their beards and moustaches, which were begun in imitation of Dickens's more imposing excrescences, and constant association with these growths on the faces of his companions was a little intimidating: 'They are more distressing, more comic, more sparse and meagre, more straggling, wandering, wiry, stubbly, formless, more given to wandering into strange places and sprouting up noses and dribbling under chins, than anything in that nature ever produced, as I believe, since the Flood. Collins has taken to wiping his (which are like the Plornishghenter's eyebrows) at dinner; and Egg's are not near his nose, but begin at the corners of his mouth, like those of the Witches in Macbeth. I have suffered so much from the contemplation of these terrific objects from grey dawn to night in little carriages, that this morning, finding myself with a good looking-glass, and a good light, I seized my best razor, and as a great example, shaved off the whole of the Newgate fringe from under my chin! The moustache remains, and now looks enormous; but the beard I have sacrificed as a dread warning to competitors —which I am bound to add does not produce the least effect; they merely observing with complacency that "it looks much better so".'

Like many other men, Dickens was never so fond of his wife as when they were apart. Ten days after he had left home, he wrote 'I should like to see you all very much indeed', and a month of absence brought this: 'I shall be very happy to be at home again, and to embrace you—for of course I miss you *very much*.' He could not impose his will on two male friends quite so easily as he did on his wife, and several times during this trip he referred to the inability of his companions to 'understand the idea of never going to bed': having travelled all day, they objected to travelling all night, and they resolutely declined to walk the mileage covered by Dickens. All the same they got on very well together, and much enjoyed their progress in vehicles 'like swings, like boats, like Noah's Arks, like barges and enormous bedsteads.' They crossed the Simplon and reached Genoa via Milan. Of course he visited all the people he had known at Genoa, including the De la Rues, and was rather pleased when a lady did not recognise him until he made himself known by name. 'I expected to find you a ruin, we heard you had been so ill', she said; 'and I find you younger and better-looking than ever. But it's so strange to see you without a bright waistcoat. Why haven't you got a bright waistcoat on?' He picked up many scraps of gossip for his wife, among others that Lady Walpole had left her husband: 'It was officially sworn before Brown that Lord Walpole used to drag her downstairs by her long hair, and throw burning logs of wood at her as she lay at the bottom!'

They went by sea to Naples, 'one of the most odious places on the face of the earth', where warm baths were more necessary and more easily obtained than in Switzerland: 'I was frothed all over with Naples soap, rubbed all down, scrubbed with a brush, had my nails cut, my corns cut, and all manner of extraordinary operations performed. He (the attendant) was as much disappointed, apparently, as surprised, not to find me dirty, and kept frequently ejaculating under his breath "O Heaven, how clean this Englishman is!" He also remarked that the Englishman was as fair as a beautiful woman—but there, he added, the resemblance ended.' Arrived in Rome, he was perturbed at not finding a letter from Kate, but it came next day and he told her why it had been delayed: 'I am rather surprised that I got it at all, for I do assure you that the illegibility of my name on the address would endanger it at any Foreign post office. How any Frenchman or Italian could ever make out the first necessary condition—that my name begins with a D—I cannot imagine. I apprehend that it had been laid aside in positive despair.'

Needless to say, Egg and Collins had been compelled to

ascend Vesuvius, but they had their revenge: 'Collins's moustache is gradually developing', wrote Dickens. 'You remember how the corners of his mouth go down, and how he looks through his spectacles and manages his legs. I don't know how it is, but the moustache is a horrible aggravation of all this. He smooths it down over his mouth, in imitation of the present great Original, and in all kinds of carriages is continually doing it. Likewise he tells Egg he must "cut it for it gets into his mouth"—and he and Egg compliment each other on that appendage. To make the thing still more ridiculous, Edward, either incited by example or stimulated by failure, is growing a moustache too!' Edward was Dickens's travelling valet, Roche having died. After Rome they went to Florence, where Collins, who had been a painter, was again in the ascendant. 'The Fine Arts', confessed Dickens, 'afford a subject which I never approach; always appearing to fall into a profound reverie when it is discussed. Neither do I ever go into any gallery with them. To hear Collins learnedly holding forth to Egg (who has as little of that gammon as an artist *can* have) about reds, and greens, and things "coming well" with other things, and lines being wrong, and lines being right, is far beyond the bounds of all caricature. I shall never forget it. On music, too, he is very learned, and sometimes almost drives me into frenzy by humming and whistling whole Overtures—with not one movement correctly remembered from the beginning to the end. I was obliged to ask him, the day before yesterday, to leave off whistling the Overture to William Tell. "For by Heaven," said I, "there's something the matter with your ear —I think it must be the cotton—which plays the Devil with the commonest tune." He occasionally expounds a Code of Morals, taken from modern French novels, which I instantly and with becoming gravity Smash. But the best of it is, that he tells us about the enormous quantities of Monte Pulciano and what not, that he used to drink when he was last here, and what distinguished people said to him in the way of taking his opinion, and what advice he gave them and so forth—being then exactly Thirteen years of age. On this head Egg is always very good, and makes me laugh heartily. All these absurdities are innocent enough. I tell them in default of having anything else to tell. We are all the best friends, and have never had the least difference.'

From Venice Dickens wrote asking his wife to get a covering for the mantelpiece in his study, and giving her minute instructions as to the particular shade of green velvet he required; from Turin he sent her a letter, already quoted, in which he suggested that she should adopt a more becoming attitude towards Mrs. De la Rue; and by the middle of December he was back at Tavistock House.

The year 1853 closed for Dickens with bursts of popular applause, which for his biographer have an ominous ring. To raise money for the Birmingham and Midland Institute, he gave public readings in the Birmingham Town Hall of *A Christmas Carol* on December 27th, of *The Cricket on The Hearth* on the 29th, and, by his own desire, to an audience of working men and women at sixpence a head on the 30th, when he repeated the *Carol*. Nearly six thousand people attended these readings, and the enthusiasm was so great that requests to give them again came to him from philanthropic organisations all over the country. A histrionic nature such as his could not resist the temptation, and in due time he realised the ambition of his life, and killed himself in the attainment.

SULLEN SOCIALISM
# 13

## SULLEN SOCIALISM

WHILE working on *Bleak House* Dickens had also been
dictating to his sister-in-law *A Child's History of England*,
which was the only book he did not write with his own hand.
He had meditated something of the sort ten years before, his
object then being to prevent his eldest boy from becoming a
High Churchman in religion or a Tory in politics, to instil in
him a horror of war, and to warn him against the wrong kind
of heroes. In this Dickens showed a strange innocence, which
he shared with many of his contemporaries and not a few of
his successors. The man who really believes that people
benefit from reading history had better read history, which
proves that historians are the last people to benefit from it.
The record of imbecility and butchery known as history
imparts some fact and much fiction to those who care about
such things; but intelligent people know all that is needful
about the actions of men by intuition, checked by personal
observation, fortified by an understanding of Shakespeare.
Intelligence is inborn, not taught, and appears so early that
schoolboys show their possession of it by refusing to learn
what they do not wish to know. But Dickens honestly
believed that with education people would become intelligent,
which is the same as believing that when people know what
is wrong they always do right. Apart from this quaint
hallucination, he had not the temperament to narrate the
hideous drama of men's blackguardism and beastliness in a
spirit of detachment; and when history is not treated with
irony it is tiresome, because the language of vituperation is
not rich and varied enough to do it justice and to hold the
reader's attention. To know that creeds breed criminals, and
that the story of mankind is largely a chronicle of crime committed in the name of God, is satisfactory, but not sufficient
for a serial of thirty-seven chapters in *Household Words*, mostly
written in indignation.

The lesson Dickens wished to inculcate throughout *A
Child's History* was that which he had put into the mouth of
Haredale in *Barnaby Rudge*: 'Let no man turn aside, ever so

198

slightly, from the broad path of honour, on the plausible pretence that he is justified by the goodness of his end. All good ends can be worked out by good means. Those that cannot, are bad.' But his method of teaching this lesson was too emotional: 'O Conqueror', he apostrophises William I, 'of whom so many great names are proud now, of whom so many great names thought nothing then, it were better to have conquered one true heart, than England!' His summaries of character lack subtlety, e.g. of King John: 'I doubt whether the crown could possibly have been put upon the head of a meaner coward, or a more detestable villain, if England had been searched from end to end to find him out.' John is given no quarter, being dismissed from the earthly scene at Newark in these terms: 'And there, on the eighteenth of October, in the forty-ninth year of his age, and the seventeenth of his vile reign, was an end of this miserable brute.' His successor, Henry III, is not much better: 'The King was now so much distressed that we might almost pity him, if it were possible to pity a King so shabby and ridiculous.' The Order of the Garter, instituted by Edward III, is described as 'a very fine thing in its way, but hardly so important as good clothes for the nation.' On the other hand, Wat Tyler receives the historian's sympathy: 'Wat was a hard-working man, who had suffered much, and had been foully outraged; and it is probable that he was a man of a much higher nature and a much braver spirit than any of the parasites who exulted then, or have exulted since, over his defeat.' Dickens also sides with Joan of Arc against her English persecutors and her French betrayers, but speaks of her as 'a moping, fanciful girl, and, though she was a very good girl, I dare say she was a little vain, and wishful for notoriety.'

He had no illusions about the Popes of Rome: 'There were two Popes at this time', he writes, adding in parenthesis 'as if one were not enough!' And he refers to another Pope as being 'so indefatigable in getting the world into trouble.' But his attitude to them does not make him warm towards his 'favourite ruffian' Henry VIII, 'whom I shall take the liberty to call, plainly, one of the most detestable villains that ever drew breath', who is also referred to as 'a mean and selfish coward', 'a frightened cur', 'a Royal pig', 'a disgrace to human nature, and a blot of blood and grease upon the History of England.' This was not the general Victorian verdict on Henry VIII, though Dickens took a more popular line with Henry's daughter Mary: 'As bloody Queen Mary this woman has become famous, and as Bloody Queen Mary she will ever be justly remembered with horror and detestation in Great Britain . . . The stake and the fire were the fruits of this reign, and you will judge this Queen by nothing else.'

Dickens did not think the Stuarts a great improvement on the Tudors. 'But a creature like his Sowship set upon a throne is like a Plague, and everybody receives infection from him', he writes of James I, whose grandson, Charles II, is 'a merry Judas', one who 'though he had had ten merry heads instead of one . . . richly deserved to lose them by the headsman's axe', while James II is a 'besotted blunderer.' Cromwell receives favourable treatment, though the men he led were not to our historian's taste: 'The very privates, drummers, and trumpeters, had such an inconvenient habit of starting up and preaching long-winded discourses, that I would not have belonged to that army on any account.'

From such passages it will be seen that Dickens was too ardent to make a sound historian. Indeed, many of his contemporaries thought him too ardent in the cause of reform; but his nature was such that when he saw inhumanity, or injustice, or indifference, he did not bother his head with the whys and wherefores: he simply exposed and attacked it with burning zeal. Much of his character was revealed in his attitude to social questions, an attitude which, though he did not recognise it, was at variance with that of Carlyle, the one famous contemporary for whom he had an unqualified respect and admiration. We have a description of the two at dinner with a couple of friends, Dickens treating Carlyle with the deference, affection and playful good humour with which David Garrick used to treat Dr. Johnson, and Carlyle enjoying it as much as Johnson had done. But while Dickens was a much greater man than Garrick, and probably as great an actor, Carlyle was a pinchbeck Johnson and secretly envied the huge success of Dickens as a writer, at the same time pretending to despise it. In *Past and Present* he speaks of the Anglo-Saxon St. Edmund, hypothetically martyred by the Danes, and quite unnecessarily drags in this contemptuous reference to Dickens's American tour: 'Oh, if all Yankee-land follow a small good "Schnüspel the distinguished Novelist" with blazing torches, dinner-invitations, universal hep-hep-hurrah, feeling that he, though small, *is* something; how might all Angle-land once follow a hero-martyr and great true Son of Heaven!' An even more unpleasant reference to Dickens appeared in Carlyle's Life of Sterling, in which a letter from Sterling to his mother is quoted: 'I got hold of the two first numbers of the "Hoggarty Diamond"; and read them with extreme delight . . . There is more truth and nature in one of these papers than in all ——'s Novels together.' Carlyle's comment on this runs: 'Thackeray, always a close friend of the Sterling House, will observe that this is dated 1841, not 1851, and have his own reflections on the matter!' Which simply means that Carlyle sympathised with Sterling's view that Thackeray was a far better writer than Dickens long before the appearance of *Vanity Fair*. Both of these unfriendly passages must have been read by Dickens, who devoured every one of Carlyle's works, and must have hurt him considerably coming from such a source; but never a word of complaint escaped him, and the only irreverence he allowed himself at Carlyle's expense occurred in a letter to Wilkie Collins (1867) about the French actor François Régnier, when he parodied Carlyle's style: 'A deft and shifty little man, brisk and sudden, of a most ingenious carpentering faculty, and not without constructive qualities of a higher than the Beaver sort. Withal an actor, though of a somewhat hard tone. Think pleasantly of him, O ye children of men!'

Carlyle could not help expressing a liking for Dickens, but always with a note of patronage, calling him 'a good little fellow', 'one of the most cheery innocent natures I have ever encountered', 'the only man of my time whose writings have genuine cheerfulness', and so on. He laughed heartily over the humorous passages in Dickens's novels, but he considered their author an ignorant man whose theory of life was entirely wrong: 'He thinks men ought to be buttered up, and the world made soft and accommodating for them, and all sorts of fellows have turkey for their Christmas dinner. Commanding and controlling and punishing them, he would give up without any misgivings in order to *coax* and *soothe* and *delude them* into doing right. But it is not in this manner the eternal laws operate, but quite otherwise. Dickens has not written anything which will be found of much use in solving the problems of life. But he is worth something; worth a penny to read of an evening before going to bed.' We need not pause to inquire whether Carlyle was more conversant with the operation of the eternal laws than Dickens; but enough has been quoted to show the difference between them, which was, roughly, the difference between the prophet and the artist.

The prophet is a frustrated man of action. Failing to be a doer, he becomes a seer, equipping himself with much knowledge for the job. He prophesies catastrophe unless his teaching is heeded: a foreboding of calamity is his stock-in-trade; and as misfortunes are constantly occurring, he is always a popular figure. From the time of Adam who probably made dismal predictions to Eve as they left the Garden of Eden together, the prophet has been accorded the respect of his contemporaries, and mankind has perpetually lived in a state of suspense, though many modern prophets seem to think that they have a monopoly in catastrophe, forgetting in their fervour that, according to their predecessors, the world has always been going to the dogs and civilisation has always been on the verge of collapse. The prophet is often half an artist, but he affects to despise his artistic faculty, using it solely to enforce his message. Thus Carlyle showed his irritation with artists like Dickens and Thackeray by calling them rope-dancers, not reapers; and because the prophet is taken seriously, the artist is still regarded with some suspicion in England.

The artist is at the opposite pole from the prophet, though it would be truer to say that the artist is at the centre of life, the prophet outside it. 'Dickens is doing the best in him and goes on smiling in perennial good humour', patronised Carlyle. In other words Dickens enjoyed life, as all first-rate artists do, and responded to its multifarious emotions wholly and impulsively. He knew nothing about statistics, cared nothing for blue books, realised there were imperfections in civilisation without wishing to analyse them, and foresaw the modern priesthood of economics with its mystical figures and symbols that can be made to prove anything. In *Dombey and Son* he described a woman 'who had a surprising natural gift of viewing all subjects in an utterly forlorn and pitiable light, and bringing dreadful precedents to bear upon them, and deriving the greatest consolation from the exercise of that talent.' He might have been writing of Carlyle and the

majority of egotistical intellectuals who maunder about the
miserable present and the desolate future of the universe.
Unlike them, he made every day of his life as well worth
living as possible; and when wretched himself, he did not
expect everyone else to be so. 'Nothing is ever so good as it
is thought', said Lord Melbourne at a dinner-party. 'And
nothing so bad', interjected Dickens. 'It is not the province
of a Poet to harp upon his own discontents, or to teach other
people that they ought to be discontented', he admonished
one versifier. The man who feels that life is all sorrow and
suffering helps to create both, and his rage against the vices
of humanity is his rage against the vices in himself./ 'Men
who look on nature, and their fellow-men, and cry that all is
dark and gloomy, are in the right', said Dickens in *Oliver
Twist*; 'but the sombre colours are reflections from their own
jaundiced eyes and hearts. The real hues are delicate, and
need a clearer vision.' On the whole Dickens found life an
amusing and thrilling experience, and did not feel that it
would be improved by the adoption of any political creed.
He could not accept Carlyle's faith in the dictatorship of a
superman, knowing quite well that the people would then be
at the mercy of a corps of sub-supermen. He thought that
old tyrants, having no sense of oppression and resentment to
work off, were better than new tyrants; but unconvinced that
happiness would result from any known form of government, he contented himself with exposing particular evils that
came to his notice, and preaching the christian virtues of
loving-kindness and toleration, though he no more tolerated
politicians and bureaucrats than did Christ the Scribes and
Pharisees. He had no confidence in the perfectibility of the
human species, saying that unanimity among authors for their
own good 'may be expected to come to pass on the afternoon
of the last day but one.' And he had a hatred of *Isms*: 'Oh
Heaven for a world without an ism. The wickedness of us
moles to each other in our isms is enough to have brought a
comet on the head of this, a thousand years ago.' To imply,
as some unimaginative person has done, that if Dickens had
read Karl Marx he would have been a communist, is like
saying that if a sceptic were to read the New Testament he
would be a Christian, or that if an Englishman were to read
the Esquimau language he would become an Esquimau.
Human beings are not influenced by anything to which they

are not naturally disposed; and Dickens was a born individual-
ist, hating everything the state-worshippers idolise, indicting
'the system' over and over again in his books, and pillorying
the men who used it to screen their personal responsibility.
He was an instinctive rebel: that is, he rebelled against everything that did not accord with his own sense of what was
right. In short, he was a Dickensian.

His contempt for the House of Commons was profound,
and he refused many offers to enter parliament free of
electioneering expense. He distrusted all governments, Whig
or Tory, knowing that self-interest was their main motive.
'Chartist fears and rumours shake us now and then', he wrote
in '48, 'but I suspect the Government make the most of such
things for their own purpose.' And six years afterwards, the
Crimean campaign in progress, he said that 'the war will be
made an administrative excuse for all sorts of shortcomings',
which might be said after any war. He liked a few individual
M.P.s, particularly Lord John Russell, whose enormous self-
assurance and energy appealed to him. He disliked the
greatest politician of the age, Benjamin Disraeli, giving plenty
of reasons for his antipathy, but unaware that the real cause
of it was the inevitable annoyance of the 'character' actor with
the 'straight' actor who achieves success by trading exclusively
on a carefully built-up personality. We have read what he
thought of upper class Society: he did not care for aristocrats
in a mob, though he liked individual specimens, and addressed
them in the free and equal manner that was habitual with him.
Carlyle was tickled to see him give Lord Holland a 'little bob'
when introduced, as if to intimate that he did not feel especially
honoured. But why Dickens should pretend to feel especially
honoured when he had no sense of it, Carlyle does not say.

His attitude to the religious beliefs of his time was as
independent as his attitude to the political faiths. He accepted
the teachings of Christ, not the doctrines of the Christian
churches; and he would have agreed with the view that, while
the congregation is more important than any individual in it,
the meanest worshipper is more important than the church.
He formed a friendship with Edward Tagart, minister of the
Unitarian chapel in Little Portland Street, at which he and
his family attended for two or three years while they were in
Devonshire Terrace; but as time went on he became reconciled
to the Church of England, the traditions and teachings of

which made a stronger appeal to him than those of any other faith, though he was always extremely restive under the infliction of tedious or dogmatic sermons. For him the teaching of Christ was simple and sufficient, the example of Christ faultless, the life of Christ perfect. And he strove against many temperamental obstacles to be a Christian. Let us see how far he was successful.

He had a benevolent attitude to people: he wished them well, and had no desire to know the worst of them. 'The prospect of finding anybody out in anything, would have kept Miss Miggs awake under the influence of henbane', he wrote in *Barnaby Rudge*. This was not one of his own characteristics. He wanted to believe the best of everyone, but when the unpleasant side was exposed to his view his disappointment was soon transformed into humour, and the comic force of certain portraits from life in his novels is in proportion to the violence of his disillusion. He was, as we know, extremely charitable to his family; but benevolence to one's blood relations is no remarkable virtue. Rats and rabbits are kind to their families, and what places men above rats is their feeling, not for their kin, but for their kind. Giving money to one's wife or husband, to one's children, parents, brothers, sisters, and so on, is a form of egotism or family pride; the money so given reflects credit on oneself. Who are my mother, my sisters and my brothers? asked Christ, and the answer was not 'my near relations.' The assistance Dickens rendered his family does not therefore prove his benevolence: it merely proves his resemblance to the great majority of the rabbit-human species. We must look further afield for his christian virtues.

'There is not a successful man in the world', he once said, 'who attaches less importance to the possession of money, or less disparagement to the want of it, than I do.' None of his publishers would have agreed with this statement; but as Bentley, Chapman and Hall, and Bradbury and Evans, all made fortunes out of him, they had no reason to grumble, unless their successful investment in his works was the cause of their irritation. He, on the other hand, did not begin to feel financially secure until he was half-way through his career as a novelist. That he was not a money-grabber was also proved when, though it would have benefited him as controller of *Household Words* if the duty on paper had been repealed, he refused to press for it on the ground that the taxes which were hard on the poor, such as the soap duty, should be first removed. But apart from his failure to exploit his genius to the full, and to make as much as he could out of his journal, he was generous with his money, lending sums to those of his friends who were in difficulties, supplying many people who wrote to him for food, clothes, coal or cash, tipping lavishly wherever he went, and especially rendering all the help he could to artists who were in distress. Wills, his assistant editor, and another man on *Household Words* named Holdsworth, were employed by him as almoners, and when away from home he was continually sending them money for distribution; though he insisted that they should carefully inquire into the circumstances of the applicants, for he was the victim of begging-letters from all sorts of people, some of whom were found to be living in comfort on their eleemosynary earnings. One professional beggar was proceeded against by the Mendicity Society, and Dickens was asked to give evidence; but the man's wife appealed to his chief victim, and Dickens declined to appear against him. Neglected children and the wives of drunkards were sure of his help, and he either gave them money or managed to get them into institutions; while the number of poor writers and actors for whom he collected subscriptions or obtained pensions and grants, was sufficient to occupy the exclusive attention of most philanthropists.

But this was not all. He became the confidential adviser and charity-distributor of Angela Burdett Coutts, a wealthy woman who thought the world of him and always did as he suggested when making donations or founding institutions. There was a vast field for the operation of her benefactions. Mid-Victorian London was a sink and cesspool for the poor, breeding crime and disease in equal measure. Unemployment and abject poverty produced a population of half-starved, wholly brutal parents, and semi-naked, utterly neglected children, all huddled together like vermin in disgusting courts and insanitary alleys, in windowless rooms where the floorboards were rotten and the walls were mildewed, with the stench of excreta in their nostrils, living on garbage, exuding infection, promoting contagion, and carrying lice. The human degradation was so horrible, the reek of decaying matter so foul, that visitors to these plague-spots frequently fainted or vomited. Dickens told his readers that far more people were killed by bad sanitation at home than in wars abroad, that the money raised for destruction in war would save the lives of countless people in England, and that the sufferings and wrongs of the poor were obscured by the news of battles and the excitements of pumped-up patriotism. During one year of the Crimean campaign, cholera alone exterminated over twenty thousand human beings in England and Wales.

Little could be done by a single female philanthropist in such a bog of filth and evil, but Angela Burdett Coutts did what she could. At first she confined her charity to special cases, and Dickens personally inquired into them and sent her long reports, adding many names from his own list of mendicants. Then she became interested in the Ragged Schools, and Dickens advised her not to support the clergy education subscription list, as religious mysteries and difficult creeds were not the first consideration: the children should be *washed*. He also wrote at great length on the Ragged Schools to Lord John Russell. Next came a Home for Fallen Women. He arranged for the purchase of the land and buildings at Shepherds Bush, superintended the furnishing and the necessary repairs, drew up a list of rules, visited prisons, selected the more hopeful cases, and got them into the Home. He wrote pages and pages of advice on how it should be run. Orthodox religion must be kept out of it, he said, and the clergy be made to realise that the women should be *tempted* to virtue, not frightened into it. He was against the principle of sending missionaries abroad, and advised that the money should be used to christianise the English, to remove the crowd of neglected and ignorant children from the streets and to give them homes where they could be cleaned, fed, and educated. Finally they tackled the question of slum-clearance together. They went down to Bethnal Green, and picked on a spot known as Nova Scotia Gardens, which was nothing but a vast dung-heap, played upon by the dirty, ragged, barefooted children of thieves and prostitutes. The place was cleaned up, and by 1862 Columbia Square, four blocks of model flats, had been built, accommodating about a thousand people. All this was pioneer work, and Dickens spent as much time on it as if he had nothing else to do; yet apart from his manifold labours in other directions, he was a

busy correspondent, writing anything from twelve to twenty
letters a day either on business or in reply to folk who wanted
his advice.

Foul language as well as foul lodgings engaged his attention, but it is doubtful whether Christ would have approved
his efforts to check it. In his opinion bad language was a
source of corruption, and he declared that more objectionable
expressions were openly used in the streets of London, chiefly
by the young, than in all the rest of Europe. Although
parliament had passed an Act making the offence punishable,
the police took no notice of it; and Dickens decided to wake
up the police and make the Act operative. He was living in
Devonshire Terrace at the time; his children were daily taken
by their nurses into Regent's Park; and desirous to protect
them by suppressing the obscene talk which was rife in the
Park, he had a private as well as a public reason for what he
did. The occasion soon presented itself. A girl of eighteen,
surrounded by a gang of youths, passed down the street and
addressed him in an unseemly manner, her remarks being
appreciatively received by her attendants. He followed them
for a mile on the opposite side of the road, being subjected
all the way to much coarse raillery by the gang. At last a
policeman appeared; and the moment Dickens spoke to him,
the youths fled, leaving the girl behind. Having made himself
known to the constable, Dickens said: 'Take that girl into
custody, on my charge, for using bad language in the streets.'
The policeman had never heard of such a charge, but Dickens
pledged his word that the officer would not get into trouble,
and the girl was arrested. Dickens went home for a copy of
the Act and called at the police station, where the inspector,
who was also ignorant of the charge, read and re-read the
penal clause. Next morning Dickens turned up at the magistrate's court to give evidence. But the charge was likewise
unknown to the magistrate, who received Dickens in a rather
surly manner, and then conferred with his clerk: 'During
conference I was evidently regarded as a much more objectionable person than the prisoner—one giving trouble by
coming there voluntarily, which the prisoner could not be
accused of doing.' The magistrate doubted whether the
charge could be entertained, as it was unknown. Dickens
replied that he wished it were better known, and that he
would do his best to make it so. He then handed over his

copy of the Police Act with the marked clause. Another
conference between magistrate and clerk; after which the
former asked: 'Mr. Dickens, do you really wish this girl to
be sent to prison?' 'If I didn't, why should I take the trouble
to come here?' answered Dickens grimly. He was sworn,
gave his evidence, and the girl was fined ten shillings or a
few days imprisonment. 'Why, Lord bless you, sir', said the
policeman who showed Dickens out, 'if she goes to prison,
that will be nothing new to *her*. She comes from Charles
Street, Drury Lane!'

Against this enterprising episode we must set the occasions
when he went slumming and provided food and shelter for
many human derelicts, often mere girls who, after a short
season's hop-picking, came to London to look for work,
failed to find it, spent their small savings, and then took to
begging or prostitution. He recorded one such occasion,
when, trudging with a friend through the mud of Whitechapel
on a rainy night in winter, they came to a Workhouse, near
the wall of which were 'five bundles of rags' which turned out
to be human beings in a condition of exhaustion and despair,
having been refused admission to the Casual Ward on account
of its being already overcrowded. Dickens promptly obtained
entrance to the Workhouse and speech with its master:

'Do you know that there are five wretched creatures
outside?'

'I haven't seen them, but I dare say there are.'

'Do you doubt that they are there?'

'No, not at all. There might be many more.'

'Are they men, or women?'

'Women, I suppose. Very likely one or two of them were
there last night, and the night before last.'

'There all night, do you mean?'

'Very likely.'

The master of the Workhouse had given preference to
women with children, and there was not room for another
person in the Ward.

They left, and questioned the women outside, all of whom
were starving, dirty, haggard, and young. 'In every one,
interest and curiosity were as extinct as in the first. They were
all dull and languid. No one made any sort of profession or
complaint; no one cared to look at me; no one thanked me.'
He gave each of them enough for supper and a lodging, and

14

quitted the scene, wondering hopelessly what would be the end of a social system that permitted such things.

Experiences like these, taken with the complete indifference of the wealthy classes to the mass of human degradation at their doors, and the easy optimism of fashionable economists who said that the country was prospering, and the calm complacence of successful business men who knew that *they* were prospering, impelled Dickens to write his next book, *Hard Times*, which was serialised in *Household Words* from April 1st to August 12th, 1854. To get some local colour for his story he went to Preston in Lancashire during a strike, but it was all as boring as he had hoped it would be exciting. 'It is a nasty place', he wrote, 'and I am in the Bull Hotel, before which some time ago the people assembled supposing the masters to be here, and on demanding to have them out were remonstrated with by the landlady in person. I saw an account in an Italian paper, in which it was stated that "the populace then environed the Palazzo Bull, until the padrona of the Palazzo heroically appeared at one of the upper windows and addressed them!" One can hardly conceive anything less likely to be represented to an Italian mind by this description, than the old, grubby, smoky, mean, intensely formal red brick house with a narrow gateway and a dingy yard, to which it applies.' He was concerned to show that the English workingman was generally misunderstood, and expostulated with a correspondent: 'The English are, so far as I know, the hardest-worked people on whom the sun shines. Be content if, in their wretched intervals of pleasure, they read for amusement and do no worse. They are born at the oar, and they live and die at it. Good God, what would we have of them!'

From June to October '54 the family were again at Boulogne, this time at the Villa du Camp de Droite, part of the 'property' of M. Beaucourt, situated on the top of the hill behind their previous residence. 'The house is a regular triumph of French domestic architecture—being all doors and windows. Every window blows every door open, and all the lighter articles of dress and furniture fly to all points of the compass. A favourite shirt of mine went to Paris (as I judge from the course it took) this morning.' After moving every article of furniture, Dickens continued his serial story. A large camp was formed while they were there, and the countryside was overrun with soldiers, the peace destroyed by buglers. The Prince Consort visited the French Emperor, and a review took place near Wimereux. Dickens met them on one of his walks and doffed his hat, the Emperor and Prince returning the compliment. Boulogne was illuminated for the occasion; the French soldiers fraternised with the English sailors; Dickens hoisted the Union Jack on a hay-stack; and the eighteen front windows of his establishment blazed with a hundred and twenty wax candles, to the great satisfaction of his landlord.

On the 14th July he reported himself 'three parts mad, the fourth delirious, with perpetual rushing at *Hard Times*', which he finished on the 17th, and 'it being over, I feel as if nothing in the world, in the way of intense and violent rushings hither and thither, could quite restore my balance.' However, he tried a rush to London, warning Wilkie Collins that he intended passing the time 'in a career of amiable dissipation and unbounded license . . . If you will come and breakfast with me about midnight—anywhere—any day, and go to bed no more until we fly to these pastoral retreats, I shall be delighted to have so vicious an associate.' Returning to Boulogne with Collins, he took life easily for some weeks, lying on the grass in the sun, reading books, and going to sleep. He attributed his laziness to the fact that he had intended doing nothing for a year, but that the idea of *Hard Times* had 'laid hold of me by the throat in a very violent manner', and the close condensation necessary for a weekly serial had given him perpetual trouble.

*Hard Times* more than doubled the circulation of *Household Words*, but its popularity has not been maintained because it was written as propaganda. The book was dedicated to Carlyle, in the belief that he would sympathise with the feelings expressed therein. Dickens described the appalling conditions of life in factory towns; preached that the poor were entitled to the same justice, the same healthy conditions, the same freedom, as the rich; attacked every kind of public pest, especially those whose love for the public was really a love of publicity; and above all ridiculed the typical bureau-cratic mentality which substituted scientific accuracy for imaginative reality, convinced that facts and figures were all-important, while fancies were beneath contempt. Dickens would not be surprised to find that civilisation has now gone the way of his government inspector who 'had it in charge from high authority to bring about the great public-office Millennium, when Commissioners should reign upon earth', or that the modern trend in education is wholly along the lines of Mrs. Gradgrind's advice to her daughter: 'Go and be something-ological directly.' Macaulay, with unerring inaccuracy, called *Hard Times* 'sullen socialism.' If he had called it rampant anarchism, he would have been nearer the mark, if still wide of the target. But apparently the plea that the poor were entitled to a share of the world's beauty was too much for him, because in his History of England he wrote about 'the thousands of clerks and milliners who are now thrown into raptures by the sight of Loch Katrine and Loch Lomond.' Upon which Dickens commented in *Household Words*: 'No such responsible gentleman, in France or Germany, writing history—writing anything—would think it fine to sneer at any inoffensive and useful class of his fellow subjects. If the clerks and milliners . . . will only imagine their presence poisoning those waters to the majestic historian as he roves along the banks, looking for Whig members of parliament to sympathise with him in admiration of the beauties of Nature, we think they will be amply avenged in the absurdity of the picture.' But apart from the fact that the proletarian hero of *Hard Times* is anathematised by his comrades and stigmatised by his employers, the whole tendency of Dickens's mind was individualistic, humanistic, anti-bureaucratic, anti-socialistic; and an alternative title for this chapter could be Macaulay's Misnomer.

He did not however spoil social intercourse by discussing public affairs; and when he returned home from Boulogne in October '54 he found that everyone was obsessed with the Crimean War, Forster in particular talking as if he alone knew how to win it. 'Forster having to direct the whole war', wrote Dickens to Leigh Hunt, 'and being troubled in his mind with doubts as to whether the ships have been as well brought into action before Sebastopol, as he intended, is in a fearful condition on Thursdays and Fridays. Consequently if you can avoid those days for his (and the world's) sake— do.' Relief from the boredom of listening to rumours, theories and expatiations on the theme was found in more public readings for private charities; and in December he gave the *Carol* at Reading, Bradford and Sherborne, where he went for the sake of his old friend Macready, now living there in retirement. What he described as 'a little fireside party of four thousand' gathered to hear him at Bradford: 'I found arrangements made for seating 60 people in two rows behind me. These (on which the committee immensely prided themselves) I instantly overthrew: to the great terror and amazement of the bystanders, who inquired in a dismal manner "Where was the Mayor to go then?" I said the Mayor might go—anywhere—but must not come near me.'

He finished off the year by producing playlets, acted by his family, in a small theatre which he had rigged up at Tavistock House. Select audiences attended these performances, and Thackeray laughed so heartily at one of them that he fell off his seat. The programme announced the 'first appearance on any stage of Mr. Plornishmaroontigoonter (who has been kept out of bed at a vast expense)'—in other words, the baby of the family, aged two years and nine months.

# 14

## A FRESH FRIEND

JUST before leaving home for Paris, where he and Wilkie
Collins were to spend ten days together in February '55,
Dickens received a letter from Mrs. Winter, who, as Maria
Beadnell, had been the love of his life. Instantly the years
between their separation and the present moment 'vanished
like a dream, and I opened it with the touch of my young
friend David Copperfield when he was in love.' One of his
deepest feelings was a nostalgia for the past; and this unexpected resuscitation of a dead romance, at a time when his
yearning for an unattainable happiness was seeking relief in
a new male friendship and a fresh outburst of restlessness,
made him feel that Maria might still be the lodestar of his life.
In his reply he told her that he had forgotten nothing of those
early times: 'They are just as still and plain and clear as if I
had never been in a crowd since, and had never seen or heard
my own name out of my own house. What should I be worth,
or what would labour and success be worth, if it were otherwise!' He said that he was about to visit Paris, asked if he
could buy anything there for herself or her children, recalled
the old days of his blighted love, and concluded: 'The associations my memory has with you made your letter more—I want
a word—invest it with a more immediate address to me than
such a letter could have from anybody else. Mr. Winter will
not mind that . . .'

He and Collins put up at the Hotel Meurice, and as Collins
was not in good health he prowled about Paris by himself;
but they dined at different restaurants every day, visited a lot
of theatres together, got through a good deal of writing; and
Dickens heard again from Maria, who, seeing what she had
missed in the way of fame and comfort by turning him down,
and delighted by the warmth of his response, felt that all was
not lost if she could cultivate a friendship with the most
famous living author, especially if it were generally known
that she had been the object of his first and most poignant
passion. His second letter, written from Paris, was even more
emotional, more intimate and more promising than his first.

He told her that his early success had been due to her, that
'the most innocent, the most ardent, and the most disinterested days of my life had you for their sun', that 'I have
never been so good a man since, as I was when you made me
wretchedly unhappy', and that she had inspired Dora in
*David Copperfield*: 'I have a strong belief—and there is no harm
in adding hope to that—that perhaps you have once or twice
laid down that book, and thought "How dearly that boy must
have loved me, and how vividly this man remembers it!"'

His third letter, written on his return home, began 'My dear
Maria', and answered one from her which must have implied
that their youthful separation had been due to a misunderstanding: 'Ah! Though it is so late to read in the old hand
what I never read before, I have read it with great emotion,
and with the old tenderness softened to a more sorrowful
remembrance than I could easily tell you . . . if you had ever
told me then what you tell me now, I know myself well
enough to be thoroughly assured that the simple truth and
energy which were in my love would have overcome everything.' He saw no reason why there should not still exist
between them a confidence shared by no one else. He declined
to accept her description of herself as 'toothless, fat, old and
ugly', pictured her as she had lived in his memory, and said
that no worldly reputation could repay the loss of his youthful
vision: 'You ask me to treasure what you tell me, in my heart
of hearts. O see what I have cherished there, through all this
time and all these changes!' He arranged to meet her, first by
herself, and then with his wife and her husband, and closed
his letter with the words 'Remember, I accept with my whole
soul, and reciprocate all. Ever your affectionate friend.'

The precise nature of his reciprocation appeared in his next
novel, *Little Dorrit*, where Maria is portrayed as Flora
Finching; and we may feel fairly confident either that Maria
did not recognise herself in the character or that, if she did,
she considered Dora in *David Copperfield* a more striking
resemblance. Dickens must have had the shock of his life
when the dream of his youth appeared in so substantial and
so stupid a form. As he put it in *Little Dorrit*: 'Clennam's eyes
no sooner fell upon the subject of his old passion, than it
shivered and broke to pieces . . . Flora, whom he had left a
lily, had become a peony; but that was not much. Flora, who
had seemed enchanting in all she said and thought, was diffuse

and silly. That was much. Flora, who had been spoiled and
artless long ago, was determined to be spoiled and artless
now. That was a fatal blow.' But uniting within himself the
tragic hero, the clown, and half a hundred other characters,
he was able to turn the disenchantment into comedy, the
tender memory of love into a lampoon. In the sphere of action
he promptly cut his losses, and within a month of seeing the
fat and foolish Mrs. Winter he was writing to her: 'I am going
off, I don't know where or how far, to ponder about I don't
know what.' All her attempts to maintain contact with him
were unavailing, and he informed her that he was extremely
busy every day of every week and would be out of London
'for several Sundays in succession.' Her baby died, but he
was not to be drawn: 'It is better that I should not come to
see you. I feel quite sure of that, and will think of you
instead.' Georgina was given the job of holding Maria at bay,
and the two ladies became occasional correspondents.

The perturbation of spirit customary on such occasions
preluded the creation of *Little Dorrit*. As early as October '54
he 'had dreadful thoughts of getting away somewhere altogether by myself' in order to begin the new book 'in all sorts
of inaccessible places', such as the Pyrenees or 'above the
snow-line in Switzerland, and living in some astonishing
convent.' He was driven by the demon Restlessness, and in
January '55 was 'in a dishevelled state of mind—motes of new
books in the dirty air, miseries of older growth threatening to
close upon me.' By May he had reached 'the wandering-
unsettled-restless uncontrollable state of being about to begin
a new book. At such a time I am as infirm of purpose as
Macbeth, as errant as Mad Tom, and as ragged as Timon.
I sit down to work, do nothing, get up and walk a dozen
miles, come back and sit down again next day, again do
nothing and get up, go down a Railroad, find a place where
I resolve to stay for a month, come home next morning, go
strolling about for hours and hours, reject all engagements to
have my time to myself, get tired of myself and yet can't come
out of myself to be pleasant to anybody else, and go on turning
upon the same wheel round and round and over and over
again until it may begin to roll me towards my end.' In this
state he walked about his room, wandered through the house,
perambulated the streets at night, made engagements, broke
them, wanted to go a sea-voyage, wished he could ascend in

a balloon, longed for society, yearned for solitude, laughed at his thoughts, cried over his emotions, and behaved at one and the same time like a lunatic, a lover and a poet.

He was temporarily rescued from this condition by Wilkie Collins, who sent him a melodrama called *The Lighthouse*, which he instantly wanted to produce in his little theatre at Tavistock House. The new novel was completely forgotten in the excitement of preparation. His home became a scene of feverish activity. Scene-painters, carpenters, dress-designers, gasmen, musicians, actors, thronged the rooms and corridors, and the sounds of hammers and saws mingled with those of fiddles and voices, while the house echoed with the scraping and bumping of scene-setting and furniture-moving. Dickens was again in his element: the world of the theatre was his real world; and he behaved like a child with a new toy, just as he displayed the excitement of a child at a party when the exhausted actors sat down to supper after every rehearsal and watched him brew the punch. Stanfield painted the act-drop (still preserved at Kenwood House, Hampstead), Dickens played the part of the lighthouse-keeper, and his daughter Mary, Mark Lemon, Augustus Egg and Wilkie Collins took the other characters. The stage was enlarged, and there was only room for an audience of twenty-five; but the play was performed three times in the middle of June and again for a charity at Campden House early in July. Everyone wept audibly over the melodrama, everyone laughed heartily at the farce which succeeded it, and Dickens himself was chiefly responsible for both sobs and cachinnations. 'O Mr. Dickens, what a pity it is you can do anything else!' said one over-wrought female to the chief actor, who reported that 'Longman the bookseller was seen to cry dreadfully—and I don't know that anything could be said beyond that!'

The author of *The Lighthouse* had now ousted Forster from the position of Dickens's most intimate friend; so we must take a close look at him. The best sight will be rewarded with little more than a silhouette, for he covered up his traces so completely that there must have been a good deal to hide. Miss Dorothy Sayers informed the present writer that it was 'the extreme obscurity which surrounds the whole of Collins's private life which discouraged me from getting on with the biography that I had contemplated.'

Wilkie Collins, born in London on January 8th, 1824, was

almost exactly twelve years younger than Dickens. His early life was dominated by a strong-willed Scottish mother. His father was a painter, and he had enough talent in that direction himself to joke about it in the years ahead: 'Ah! you might well admire that masterpiece. It was done by that great painter Wilkie Collins, and it put him so completely at the head of landscape painters that he determined to retire from the profession in compassion for the rest.' His real profession, according to himself, was determined by the treatment he received at school, where a bully in his dormitory forced him to tell stories when he wanted to go to sleep. 'My tyrant made for himself a cat-o-nine-tails, and as often as my voice died away he leaned across the bed and gave me a cut or two with it which started me afresh . . . But I owe him a debt of gratitude, for it was this brute who first awakened in me a power of which, but for him, I might never have been aware . . . when I left school I still continued story-telling for my own pleasure.' Apparently he learnt more from the bully than from the masters, because twenty years after he had started writing for a living he confessed that 'I still make the most absurd mistakes in spelling, and my grammar is sometimes awful. I assure you the printers have to correct my grammar.'

He entered Lincoln's Inn in '46, and was called to the bar five years later. One of his earliest literary works was a Life of his father. From the beginning of manhood he decided to enjoy himself, and a discreet reference in the Dictionary of National Biography tells us enough to whet our appetite for more: 'Intimacies formed as a young man led to his being harassed, after he became famous, in a manner which proved very prejudicial to his peace of mind.' It is clear that he embarked on many amorous and alcoholic adventures, and objected to the conventions of the age. He stage-managed the runaway marriage of the painter E. M. Ward to a girl of under sixteen, and gave her away at the ceremony. Asked to be godfather of their first child, he celebrated the festivities attending the christening a little too heartily; and trying to focus his eyes on the infant as it lay in the clergyman's arms, he said 'The baby sheems moving in a very odd way, and is making funny faces. Why, 'pon my soul, the baby's drunk, the baby's drunk!'

There was nothing remarkable in his personal appearance.

He was slightly built, with small hands and feet, his height being about five feet six inches. The prominent feature of his face was a tall white bulging forehead. He wore spectacles, and in the fifties grew a beard and moustache. His solemn expression was contradicted by his humorous eyes. He was pale in complexion and delicate in constitution. There always seemed to be something wrong with his heart or his liver or his stomach or his lungs, and as he ate too much and drank not a little he was frequently confined to his house with bouts of indisposition. During one painful illness he experienced so much relief from the administration of opium that he became a drug addict, and towards the end of his life he took enough laudanum daily to kill several men unaccustomed to it.

His private life was unfashionable, and even those friends of his who kept mistresses felt that he was going too far in not keeping up appearances. He lived with one lady or another without going to the trouble of consecrating the connection in church, was invited alone to other people's houses, and only had male parties at his own. 'Cast respectability to the winds and write me a line to say you will come', he summoned a friend. His conversation was agreeable, amusing, easy, cynical, and sometimes frank to the point of vulgarity. He might be described as a genial pessimist, and when in good health he was comically voluble. Though respectable women considered him 'as bad as he could be', he was gentle, kind-hearted, idle and modest, not in the least minding when someone told him 'Your books are read in every back-kitchen.' He objected to violent effort of any kind, disliked games because of the competitive and pugnacious qualities they engendered, showed a surprising alacrity in avoiding the ball when fielding at cricket, and wrote a play which expressed his conviction that the young men of England were being brutalised by their growing passion for athletics. He had an abhorrence of cruelty, and late in life wrote an anti-vivisection novel. But on the whole he enjoyed existence, and was quite satisfied with himself.

Such, or roughly such, was the man of whom Forster was so frantically jealous for usurping his place in the affection of Dickens that he vitiated his biography by almost ignoring a relationship which largely explains the later development of its hero. It is no wonder that on reading Forster's book Harrison Ainsworth said 'I see he only tells half the story', while Collins described it as 'The Life of John Forster, with occasional anecdotes of Charles Dickens.'

Many of the habits and characteristics of Collins were so much opposed to those of Dickens that one wonders how they managed to put up with one another; and their intimacy is a proof of the intensity of Dickens's need for someone who was utterly unlike Forster. To note a few of their dissimilarities: Dickens had a mania for punctuality, Collins could never keep an eye on the clock; Dickens was extremely tidy, Collins was slovenly; Dickens was generous and reckless, Collins was mean and prudent; Dickens was incredibly energetic and enthusiastic, Collins was excessively indolent and sceptical. Dickens's idea of idleness was useless industry, and when he took a holiday he was actively idle, while Collins was passively idle. 'You make work of everything', said Collins. 'A man who can do nothing by halves appears to me to be a fearful man.' And when Dickens, returning from a walk, said that he had just been over a lunatic asylum, Collins, reclining on a sofa, cast his eyes up to the ceiling and exclaimed: 'He has been over a lunatic asylum! Not content with being as great an ass as Captain Barclay in the pedestrian way, he makes a Lunacy Commissioner of himself—for nothing!' Even on the subject of clothes they could not agree. 'What shall I do with this?' asked someone, displaying a gorgeous piece of silk-work. 'Oh, send it to Dickens', said Collins; 'he'll make a waistcoat of it.'

Why, then, did Dickens enjoy the company of Collins more than that of anyone else during the last fourteen years of his life? The answer is that he had reached a point in his life when he craved for freedom from all restraint. To a nature like his, constant change of places and persons was as necessary as the rapid changes of impersonation in himself and his work; and he was getting tired of Forster's jealousies, animosities, and egotistical unadaptableness, just as he was getting tired of his wife's placidity, fatuity, and lack of vitality. Forster stood for restriction, respectability, and pretentiousness; Collins for liberation, disreputableness, and licentiousness; and Dickens had reached a stage in his development when the world, the flesh and the devil meant more to him than the Ten Commandments, of which he had had more than enough. 'I shall be happy to start on any Haroun Alraschid expedition', he wrote to Collins at the end of '55; and again

'I think I am very likely to be on the loose that day.' By May '57 he was writing like this: 'Any mad proposal you please will find a wildly insane response in—Yours ever'; and, in the same month, 'if the mind can devise anything sufficiently in the style of sybarite Rome in the days of its culminating voluptuousness, I am your man . . . If you can think of any tremendous way of passing the night . . . do. I don't care what it is. I give (for that night only) restraint to the Winds!'

While Collins helped to free Dickens's mind for pleasure, Dickens managed to inoculate Collins with the need to work, and an early novel, *Hide and Seek*, was dedicated by the disciple to the master. 'Neither you nor Catherine did justice to Collins's book', wrote Dickens to Georgina. 'I think it far away the cleverest novel I have ever seen written by a new hand. It is much beyond Mrs. Gaskell, and is in some respects masterly.' Collins began to write for *Household Words* in the spring of '53, and in September '56 he was taken on the staff at a salary of five guineas a week, being handsomely paid for his serials as well. Dickens laboured on Collins's stories as if they had been his own, correcting, deleting, adding; and even departed from his editorial policy of anonymity by announcing Collins's name as the author of the novels which made him famous. In spite of their temperamental clashes and their differing customs, they got on together remarkably well, Dickens being equally fascinated and amused by the idiosyncrasies, the worldly-wise conversation and the free behaviour of the younger man, Collins feeling flattered by the friendship of his famous senior, by the pleasure Dickens so obviously derived from his company, and by the hospitality so freely lavished upon him.

After the performances of *The Lighthouse* they were constantly in one another's company, and when Dickens went to Folkestone with his family in July '55 Collins had to stay with them. Their 'very pleasant little house', No. 3 Albion Villas (now named 'Copperfield'), was on The Leas, and here they remained for three months while Dickens wrote the opening numbers of *Little Dorrit*. A clearer impression of the old town was given by him in a phrase than H. G. Wells managed to convey in a novel: 'I stopped in the rain, about half way down a steep, crooked street like a crippled ladder, to look at a little coachmaker's . . .' With the sea in front of him, he worked strenuously from nine till two every day, after which he dashed out for three hours of intensive exercise, clambering up the hills, sliding down them, 'swarming up the face of a gigantic and precipitous cliff', and only varying these performances when friends were with him and he had to go for 'crawls rather than walks.' Occasionally he visited 'the great oven', as he called London, on *Household Words* business; but the novel had sole possession of him, and on commencing a fresh number he suffered from 'a hideous state of mind in which I walk downstairs once in every five minutes, look out of window once in every two, and do nothing else . . . I am steeped in my story, and rise and fall by turns into enthusiasm and depression.' Even on his walks he could not get away from it: 'The new story is everywhere—heaving in the sea, flying with the clouds, blowing in the wind.' He called it *Nobody's Fault* at first, changing the title just before the first number appeared. He kept open house, and many friends stayed at what he called his 'sanitary establishment, always to be known by having all the windows open, and soap and water flying out of all the bedrooms.' Somehow, too, he managed to deal with his correspondence: 'Hundreds of letters from every conceivable kind of person of whom I have no sort of knowledge, on every possible and impossible subject with which I have nothing to do, are addressed to me every week of my life.' Requests that he should give readings for charitable purposes poured in daily. All had to be refused, though he agreed to read the *Carol* at Folkestone to a Literary Institution on condition that the members of a Working Men's Institution should be admitted at threepence a head. This took place in a long carpenter's shop.

In the middle of October he went alone to Paris in order to find lodgings before transporting his family there for a residence of six months. He got what he wanted just above the Jardin d'Hiver, at No. 49 Avenue des Champs Elysées, a dozen rooms for seven hundred francs a month. But the place wanted thoroughly cleaning, and he broke the news to the proprietors, saying that dirt drove him mad and that he would do the job himself: 'Imagine co-proprietors at first astounded —then urging that "it's not the custom"—then wavering— then affected—then confiding their utmost private sorrows to the Inimitable—offering new carpets (accepted), embraces (not accepted), and really responding like French Bricks.' He got the place in order, sent for his family, settled them in, and tore off to London, whence he wrote to Kate giving her minute instructions about a letter of credit: where she would find it, where present it, how to reach the place where it was to be presented, and so on; the tone of his letter suggesting that its recipient was a child of eight. Forster threatened to return with him to Paris, but to Dickens's great relief abandoned the project at the last moment. Collins was the companion he wanted, and he became quite peevish with Georgina early in '56 because she had not arranged Parisian quarters for Wilkie and written to tell him so.

As in Russia and Germany, so in France, Dickens's works were being widely read, and he found that he was almost as well known to the man in the street as to his eminent French contemporaries. The newspapers announced the arrival in Paris of 'L'illustre Romancier, Sir Dickens' or 'Lord Charles Boz', and when he presented his card at a shop he was greeted with such exclamations as 'Ah! C'est l'écrivain célèbre! Monsieur porte une nomme très distingué. Mais! Je suis honoré et intéressé de voir Monsieur Dick-in. Je lis un des livres de Monsieur tous les jours.' *Martin Chuzzlewit* was being serialised in the *Moniteur*; a porter confided in Georgina that Madame Tojair (Todgers) was 'drôle, et précisément comme une dame que je connais à Calais'; and the creator of Todgers arranged with Hachette's to bring out a French translation of his complete works.

He met, among others, Auber, Lamartine, Scribe, Dumas, Georges Sand ('Just the kind of woman in appearance whom you might suppose to be the Queen's monthly nurse'), and was the honoured guest at Lucullan repasts given by the press magnate Emile de Girardin. One day he received a curious invitation from Alexandre Dumas, who proposed an adventure. Dickens was to be at the corner of a certain street at a certain hour on a certain evening. There he would be accosted by an individual muffled to the eyes and wearing a mantle of Spanish cut, who would escort him to a carriage drawn by four horses, in which he would be conveyed to a certain place. But this was a little too romantic for 'L'illustre Romancier', whose notion of an Arabian Night was not Monte Cristo's, and whose adventures were less spectacular: 'On Saturday night I paid three francs . . . and went in, at 11 o'clock, to a Ball. . . . Some pretty faces, but all of two classes—wicked and coldly calculating, or haggard and wretched in their worn beauty. Among the latter was a woman of thirty or so, in an Indian shawl, who never stirred from a seat in the corner all the time I was there. Handsome, regardless, brooding, and yet with some nobler qualities in her forehead. I mean to walk about tonight and look for her. I didn't speak to her there, but I have a fancy that I should like to know more about her. Never shall, I suppose.'

One form of boredom he could not escape. Ary Scheffer painted his portrait, and 'I can scarcely express how uneasy and unsettled it makes me to have to sit, sit, sit, with *Little Dorrit* on my mind.' The fact that he could not discern the slightest resemblance between himself and the portrait made these sessions less bearable. Another nuisance was the literary mendicant: 'Every Frenchman who can write a begging letter writes one, and leaves it for this apartment. He first of all buys any literary composition printed in quarto on tea paper with a limp cover, scrawls upon it "Hommage à Charles Dickens, L'illustre Romancier"—encloses the whole in a dirty envelope, reeking with tobacco smoke—and prowls, assassin-like, for days in a big cloak and an enormous *cachenez* like a counterpane, about the scraper of the outer door.' But dining with the hosts and evading the beggars of Paris did not occupy all his spare time. Any young English journalists who wrote for *Household Words* and happened to be in the French capital enjoyed good meals at their editor's expense, and cash advances on unwritten work if hard-up. George Augustus Sala called on him for the purpose of borrowing money, and found him sitting in an armchair, holding his head between his hands, having made up his mind to get through the third and fourth volumes of Macaulay's History of England, which had just been published. Dickens noticed that there was 'a strong flavour of the wineshop and the billiard table' about Sala, but let him have £5.

Now and again the presence of the editor was required at the office of *Household Words*, and Dickens made a flying-visit to London. While there on March 11th '56 he heard 'the most prodigious, overwhelming, crushing, astounding, blinding, deafening, pulverizing, scarifying secret of which Forster is the hero, imaginable by the united efforts of the whole British population. It is a thing of that kind, that after I knew it (from himself) this morning, I lay down flat, as if an Engine and Tender had fallen upon me.' The secret which drove

Dickens to superlatives was that Forster, regarded by his friends as a confirmed bachelor, had become engaged to the widow of a well-known publisher, Henry Colburn. She was in her thirties, agreeable, fairly pretty, unfairly wealthy. But, according to Maclise, the prospect of marriage to Forster lessened her physical attractions. 'By God, sir, the depreciation that has taken place in that woman is fearful,' said Maclise to Dickens in May '56. 'She has no blood, sir, in her body— no colour—no voice—is all scrunched and squeezed together —and seems to be in deep affliction; while Forster, sir, is rampant and raging, and presenting a contrast beneath which you sink into the dust. She *may* come round again—*may* get fat—*may* get cheerful—*may* get a voice to articulate with— but by the blessed Star of Morning, sir, she is now a sight to behold!'

During one of his business jaunts to London Dickens was able to do his assistant editor Wills a good turn by arranging that he should be paid £200 a year for helping Angela Burdett Coutts with her many charitable projects. Dickens was also able to do himself a good turn by purchasing, on March 14th 1856, Gad's Hill Place, near Rochester, the one house in the world he had longed from boyhood to possess, the house of which his father had said that if he worked very hard he might some day be the owner. It had suddenly been offered for sale, and after a certain amount of haggling with the agent he paid £1790 for it. There was much to be done in the way of alterations and repairs, and he would not be able to take possession of it till '57, after which he intended to occupy it every summer and to let it for the remaining months of the year; but fate disposed otherwise.

Wilkie Collins was with him at Paris early in '56, sleeping and working in an apartment nearby, dining with the family every day, joining him on many excursions, and accompanying him to many plays. Dickens had an idea for a new melodrama to be produced at Tavistock House on the following Twelfth Night. Collins set to work on it, and it became the main theme of their conversation. But month by month Dickens was still labouring with *Little Dorrit*, the first numbers of which sold over forty thousand copies, beating even *Bleak House*. The usual mental crises preceded each instalment. At one moment he wanted to be 'among the blinding snows' of the St. Bernard monastery; at another 'it suddenly came into my head that I would get up and go to Calais. I don't know why; the moment I got there I should want to go somewhere else.' Sometimes he tried to escape from the pervasion of the story: 'My head really stings with the visions of the book, and I am going, as we French say, to disembarrass it by plunging out into some of the strange places I glide into of nights in these latitudes.' He knew what a difficult housemate he was on these occasions, but his mental disquiet was as merciless as physical pain; and so, when he settled down to a new number, he described himself as 'prowling about the rooms, sitting down, getting up, stirring the fire, looking out of window, tearing my hair, sitting down to write, writing nothing, writing something and tearing it up, going out, coming in, a Monster to my family, a dread Phenomenon to myself.' He realised now that for him there would be no peace on this side of the grave: 'However strange it is to be never at rest, and never satisfied, and ever trying after something that is never reached, and to be always laden with plot and plan and care and worry, how clear it is that it must be, and that one is driven by an irresistible might until the journey is worked out! It is much better to go on and fret, than to stop and fret. As to repose—for some men there's no such thing in this life.' He happened to be struggling with a chapter when the family moved from Paris at the beginning of May '56; so he left them to get on with the job and went by himself to the Ship Hotel, Dover, putting in three days' work there before returning to Tavistock House.

He only spent a month or so in London, where he made a speech on behalf of the Artists' Benevolent Fund, 'at the end of which all the company sat holding their napkins to their eyes with one hand, and putting the other into their pockets.' Then he and his family settled at Boulogne for three months, staying in the Villa des Moulineaux, which they had occupied on their first visit to the place. Here he gave himself up to *Little Dorrit*, the serialisation of which lasted from December '55 till June '57.

Apparently no one but the general public recognised that Dickens had put his best work into this novel. Carlyle enjoyed the satire on party government, which, with his invariable habit of nullifying his own praise, he called 'priceless after its sort', and a few distinguished soldiers who had suffered from the bungling of the Crimean War by the

Circumlocution Office saw the truth in Dickens's description of the Barnacles; but no eminent contemporary perceived that the picture of Old Dorrit, drawn with modifications and amplifications from the author's father, was the most subtly conceived character in Dickens's work, and the one leading figure in all his novels which was not only sustained with brilliance of execution but developed throughout with absolute fidelity to nature. Old Dorrit is the most satisfying full-length serious portrait in English fiction. Yet *Blackwood's Magazine* summed up the book as 'twaddle', and when Dickens accidentally came across that summary in another paper he was 'sufficiently put out by it to be angry with myself for being such a fool.' Thackeray called the book 'dead stupid' and 'damned rot', but his judgment was excusable because he must have perceived what no one else has been able to see: that the character of Henry Gowan, though not a portrait of him in the sense that Skimpole was a portrait of Hunt, contained Dickens's opinion of him. Thackeray's attitude to his art is exposed in a scene where Dickens as Clennam argues with him on the subject:

'Clennam, I don't like to dispel your generous visions, and I would give any money (if I had any) to live in such a rose-coloured mist. But what I do in my trade, I do to sell. What all we fellows do, we do to sell. If we didn't want to sell it for the most we can get for it, we shouldn't do it. Being work, it has to be done; but it's easily enough done. All the rest is hocus-pocus . . .'

And Thackeray's habit of blowing hot and cold, his way of interspersing cynical comments on life with enthusiastic appreciations of it, is also given to Gowan:

'Most men are disappointed in life, somehow or other, and influenced by their disappointment. But it's a dear good world, and I love it! . . . It's the best of old worlds! And my calling! The best of old callings, isn't it?'

All Dickens's faults and all his compensating virtues appear in the novel. The appalling archness in the descriptions of Clennam's love for Pet Meagles is more than atoned for by the delicious comedy of young Chivery's hopeless passion for Little Dorrit:

'It's the only change he takes', said Mrs. Chivery, shaking her head afresh. 'He won't go out, even in the back-yard, when there's no linen; but when there's linen to keep the neighbours' eyes off, he'll sit there, hours. Hours he will. Says he feels as if it was groves!'

Mrs. Plornish is another of those glorious creations that could only have come from the unequalled observation and teeming fancy of Dickens; and although *David Copperfield* is a more agreeable work, and *Nicholas Nickleby* has a freshness he could never repeat, *Little Dorrit* must be considered the maturest expression of his genius.

Home again in the autumn of '56, Dickens spent every minute he could snatch from *Little Dorrit* preparing for Collins's play *The Frozen Deep*, written specially for the Tavistock House theatre. At the end of October we hear of his walking twenty miles in order to learn his part, 'to the great terror of Finchley, Neasden, Willesden, and the adjacent country', the inhabitants of which naturally thought him an escaped lunatic with homicidal tendencies. For ten weeks he worked in a chaos of ladders, scaffolding, beams, canvases, paint-pots, sawdust, gas-pipes, and artificial snow. One of the acts taking place at the North Pole, many books by Polar voyagers were consulted for details; and to add to the realism of the play Dickens increased his imperial to a beard, while Collins began the bushy growth we see in his pictures. The leading female characters were played by Georgina and the producer's two daughters. Dickens took the part of an unsuccessful lover who at the moment of crisis, instead of killing his rival, saves him for the arms of his adored, and dies as a result of the hardships he has endured, with a blessing for the two on his lips. We are not surprised to learn that he got the idea for his next novel, *A Tale of Two Cities*, while appearing in *The Frozen Deep*. A squad of workmen enlarged the theatre to seat about a hundred people; several performances were given early in January '57; and the audiences were reduced to tears and roused to enthusiasm.

When the tumult and the shouting had died, and even the carpenters and scene-shifters had departed, Dickens was miserable; but in April he was able to divert his mind with a form of activity which faintly recalled the pleasures of stage-management, by staying with his wife and sister-in-law at Waite's Hotel, Gravesend, and superintending the alterations at Gad's Hill Place. In May several friends went down for a house-warming, and in June Hans Andersen arrived for a stay of five weeks. We may judge of Dickens's delight at the prospect of receiving the famous Dane from a passage in one of his letters: 'I assure you that I love and esteem you more than I could tell you on as much paper as would pave the whole road from here to Copenhagen.' And we may judge of Dickens's relief when he saw the last of his illustrious contemporary from the words he wrote on a card commemorating the visit: 'Hans Andersen slept in this room for five weeks—which seemed to the family AGES!'

Early in June Dickens heard with sorrow of the death of his old friend Douglas Jerrold. But he lost no time in turning the occasion to account. Whether they knew it or not, he decided that the Jerrold family had been left in straitened circumstances; which meant that Jerrold's friends must rally to their assistance; which meant that *The Frozen Deep* must be performed and *A Christmas Carol* read both in London and Manchester for their benefit. Jerrold's son was inconsiderate enough to protest against these high-handed if high-minded proceedings, even going so far as to state positively that his mother was in no need of charity. But nothing short of government action backed by artillery would have stopped Dickens from doing what he had determined ought to be done, and the announcement was made and rehearsals were called before the family woke up to the assumed gravity of their financial situation. By the time they perceived that they were to be the unwilling objects of public benefaction, the Queen had been asked to give her name to the cause, and it would have seemed ungracious to damp the ardour of so many eager philanthropists. Her Majesty, though sympathetic, could not allow her name to be used, because assent would have brought upon her innumerable similar requests; but as she was most anxious to see Dickens in the play, she offered a room in Buckingham Palace for a private performance. Dickens would not permit his daughters to appear before the Queen as actresses in circumstances that necessitated their presentation to her socially, and suggested instead a private performance at the Gallery of Illustration in Regent Street. The Queen agreed, and the play was performed for the royal party on July 9th. After the farce which followed the play, she sent a request that Dickens should receive her thanks personally. He asked to be excused, as he was in his farce dress. She sent again, saying that his dress 'could not be so ridiculous as that', and repeating her request that he should see her. Again he excused himself on the ground that he did not wish to be presented to her in a costume and appearance that were not his own.

*A Christmas Carol* was read by him twice in London and once in Manchester for the Jerrold fund, and *The Frozen Deep* was performed three times in London during July and twice the following month in the Free Trade Hall, Manchester. He knew that Georgina and his daughters would not be heard in such a large building, and engaged professional actresses to take their places: Mrs. Ternan, and her two daughters Ellen and Maria. The last-named was so deeply affected in the scene where Dickens as the hero dies that her tears soaked his beard and clothes. 'She sobbed as if she were breaking her heart', he wrote, 'and was quite convulsed with grief . . . By the time the Curtain fell, we were all crying together . . .' Of Dickens's acting Wilkie Collins said that he 'played the principal part and played it with a truth, vigour, and pathos never to be forgotten by those who were fortunate enough to witness it . . . At Manchester this play was twice performed, on the second evening before 3000 people . . . Dickens surpassed himself. The trite phrase is the true phrase to describe that magnificent piece of acting. He literally electrified the audience.' The financial result of his labours was satisfactory, two thousand pounds being handed over to the widow and unmarried daughter of Douglas Jerrold, whether they liked it or not; but they probably did. The effect of the Manchester performances on himself was perhaps less satisfactory than the six thousand people who paid to see him might have hoped; for he fell in love, not with Maria, but with Ellen Ternan, and the remainder of his life was influenced by that fact. A week after the final curtain had fallen on *The Frozen Deep*, he wrote to Wilkie Collins: 'We want something for *Household Words*, and I want to escape from myself. For when I *do* start up and stare myself seedily in the face, as happens to be my case at present, my blankness is inconceivable— indescribable—my misery amazing.'

*A Lazy Tour of Two Idle Apprentices*, which Collins and Dickens wrote for *Household Words*, is a description of their visit to the Lake District in September '57. They stopped at the Ship Hotel, Allonby, and climbed Carrick Fell in the company of a local innkeeper. A thick dark mist, aided by a storm of rain and the breaking of Dickens's compass, made them lose their way. Collins could not keep up with the others, and was frequently missing. The innkeeper gave in at intervals, and had to be laughed out of despair by Dickens. At last Collins fell into a stream and sprained his ankle. Dickens carried him to the foot of the mountain, where he remained propped up against a pile of stones while the innkeeper went off for a dog-cart. For a few days Dickens had to convey Collins in and out of carriages, up and down stairs, to and from wherever he had to go. As the accident prevented them from going on to Maryport, Dickens walked there and back, a distance of twenty-four miles, to fetch their letters. The landlady of their little inn had seen him at Greta Bridge when he went into Yorkshire before writing *Nicholas Nickleby*. She was now extremely fat, and her husband lamented that in those early days he could tuck his arm round her waist. 'And can't you do it now, you insensible dog!' cried Dickens. 'Look at me! Here's a picture!' He got round as much of the landlady as he could and considered his gallant action the most successful he had ever performed.

Lancaster was their next stop, and they put up at the King's Arms, 'a very remarkable old house, with genuine old rooms and an uncommonly quaint staircase. I have a state bedroom, with two enormous red four-posters in it.' Their dinner on arrival consisted of two small salmon trout, a sirloin steak, a brace of partridges, seven dishes of sweets, five dishes of dessert (including a bowl of peaches) and a huge bride-cake which the landlord said was the custom of the house: 'Collins turned pale, and estimated the dinner at half a guinea each.' While at Lancaster Dickens wrote to Georgina: 'Accustomed as you are to the homage which men delight to render to the Inimitable, you would be scarcely prepared for the proportions it assumes in this northern country. Station-masters assist him to alight from carriages, deputations await him in hotel entries, innkeepers bow down before him and put him into regal rooms, the town goes down to the platform to see him off, and Collins's ankle goes into the newspapers!!!'

They went on to Doncaster for the races, and stayed at the Angel Hotel. Dickens was unfavourably impressed by the bookies, tipsters, gamblers, and who-not, seeing nothing in them but 'cruelty, covetousness, calculation, insensibility, and low wickedness.' He did not bet himself, but he bought the card for the St. Leger and jokingly wrote down the names of three horses as winners of the three chief races, never having heard of them before. Each race was won by the horse he had picked. It was a pity he could not spot winners as easily in the human field.

## 15

# THE SPARKLER

DR. JOHNSON called David Garrick the cheerfullest man of his age, a description that would have fitted Dickens, who was not only cheerful himself but the cause of cheerfulness in others. He was a born companion, loving the society of his friends, and very gravely concerned if anything occurred to mar the harmony of their intercourse. 'Never did anybody want a companion after dinner so much as I do', he declared. There was a deep vein of affection in him, and he longed for affection as much as he lavished it on those he loved. 'Friendship is better than criticism', he once remarked, 'and I shall steadily hold my tongue.' So attached was he to his friends that he could not bear to say 'good-bye' when the time for separation came, even though they were to meet again in the near future. He would resort to almost any subterfuge to avoid saying it. 'All partings', he wrote, 'foreshadow the great final one.'

Up to the year 1858, when something happened which, people thought, altered his nature, his social relationships were never severed by himself, though two of his friends behaved in a way that produced temporary estrangements. One of them was Douglas Jerrold, who took exception to his criticism of public executions and advocacy of private hanging, and for some months would not speak to him. Then, one day, both were entertaining parties at a club, and each was sitting with his back to the other. Suddenly Jerrold swung round and said 'For God's sake, Dickens, let us be friends again. A life's not long enough for this.' They clasped hands. George Cruikshank was another who did his best to make trouble. In their early days they were constant companions, and Dickens enlivened many parties with his story of a ceremony which they had attended together. An author and publisher named William Hone had died, and Dickens drove Cruikshank five miles to the funeral, at which they were both mourners:

'It was such a day as I hope, for the credit of nature, is seldom seen in any parts but these—muddy, foggy, wet, dark,

cold, and unutterably wretched in every possible respect.
Now, Cruikshank has enormous whiskers, which straggle all
down his throat in such weather, and stick out in front of
him, like a partially unravelled bird's-nest; so that he looks
queer enough at the best; but when he is very wet, and in a
state between jollity (he is always very jolly with me) and the
deepest gravity (going to a funeral, you know), it is utterly
impossible to resist him; especially as he makes the strangest
remarks the mind of man can conceive, without any intention
of being funny, but rather meaning to be philosophical. I
really cried with an irresistible sense of his comicality all the
way; but when he was dressed out in a black coat and a very
long black hat-band by an undertaker (who, as he whispered
me with tears in his eyes—for he had known Hone many years
—was a "character, and he would like to sketch him"), I
thought I should have been obliged to go away. However,
we went into a little parlour where the funeral party was, and
God knows it was miserable enough, for the widow and
children were crying bitterly in one corner, and the other
mourners—mere people of ceremony, who cared no more for
the dead man than the hearse did—were talking quite coolly
and carelessly together in another; and the contrast was as
painful and distressing as anything I ever saw. There was an
Independent clergyman present (the Rev. Thomas Binney, a
Nonconformist), with his bands on and a bible under his arm,
who, as soon as we were seated, addressed Cruikshank thus,
in a loud emphatic voice: "Mr. Cruikshank, have you seen a
paragraph respecting our departed friend, which has gone
the round of the morning papers?" "Yes, sir", says Cruikshank, "I have", looking very hard at me the while, for he
had told me with some pride coming down that it was his
composition. "Oh!" said the clergyman. "Then you will
agree with me, Mr. Cruikshank, that it is not only an insult
to me, who am the servant of the Almighty, but an insult to
the Almighty, whose servant I am." "How is that, sir?" said
Cruikshank. "It is stated, Mr. Cruikshank, in that paragraph",
says the minister, "that when Mr. Hone failed in business as
a bookseller, he was persuaded by *me* to try the pulpit; which
is false, incorrect, unchristian, in a manner blasphemous, and
in all respects contemptible. Let us pray." With which, and
in the same breath, I give you my word, he knelt down,
as we all did, and began a very miserable jumble of an

extemporary prayer. I was really penetrated with sorrow for the family, but when Cruikshank (upon his knees, and sobbing for the loss of an old friend) whispered me "that if that wasn't a clergyman, and it wasn't a funeral, he'd have punched his head", I felt as if nothing but convulsions could possibly relieve me.'

In the eighteen-thirties and forties Cruikshank was a regular toper, but continual association with his fellow-artists drove him to temperance, and by the fifties he was a fanatical total abstainer, writing and speaking in a cause that has always appealed to gluttons. Dickens had no sympathy with that kind of nonsense, and allowed articles to appear in *Household Words* which were unfavourable to Cruikshank's form of dementia. This hurt poor George, who felt that Dickens was cooling towards himself, and wrote to ask if such were the case. Dickens replied in April '51: 'I assure you that I have never felt the slightest coolness towards you, or regarded you with any other than my old unvarying feeling of affectionate friendship . . . I shall come to see you very soon, when I hope with one shake of the hand to dispel any lingering remainder, if any there be, of your distrust.' But Cruikshank was determined to assert his particular brand of stupidity, and when dining at Dickens's house snatched a glass of wine from the hand of a female guest with the intention of throwing it on the floor. Dickens was furious. 'How dare you touch Mrs. Ward's glass? It is an unpardonable liberty. What do you mean? Because someone you know was a drunkard for forty years, surely it is not for you to object to an innocent glass of sherry!' Cruikshank was too much taken aback to reply, and left the house at the first opportunity. In later years the water he drank must have gone to his brain, because he claimed to have created the characters in *Oliver Twist* and several other books. But anything can be expected of a fanatical temperance reformer, or indeed of any other class of fanatic.

Among strangers Dickens was rather reserved, but among friends his was the invigorating spirit, his liveliness being so contagious that hosts would beg him, if he could not spare a whole evening, to drop in merely for the purpose of making gin punch or carving a goose for their guests. His punch-making was a ritualistic performance, accompanied by serious comments on the ingredients, humorous asides about the effect they would have on different drinkers, elaborate speeches on the concoction; and when the business was completed to his satisfaction, the brewage was poured out in the manner of a conjurer producing strange articles from a hat.

Though much sought as a guest, he was at his best as a host, and preferred entertaining people to being entertained. He liked to take charge of things, to arrange matters to his taste; and as he could not very well manage other people's gatherings, he was only quite happy at his own. Being a first-rate prompter, producer and actor, his receptions and dinner-parties went without a hitch and were enjoyed by everybody. No one felt overlooked or out-of-place. Everyone felt at home, with the additional pleasure of being continuously amused. Jane Carlyle thought that the hospitality in Devonshire Terrace was on too ostentatious a scale: 'The dinner was served up in the new fashion—not placed on the table at all—but handed round—only the dessert on the table and quantities of *artificial* flowers—but such an overloaded dessert! pyramids of figs raisins oranges—ach! At the Ashburton dinner served on those principles there were just *four cowslips* in china pots—four silver shells containing sweets, and a silver filigree temple in the middle! but here the very candles rose each out of an artificial rose! Good God!' But the actor in Dickens could no more help splashing colour into his social productions than he could help wearing bright waistcoats or combing his hair in public or adding a flamboyant flourish to his signature or singing comic songs or dancing with such gleeful abandon that pompous people forgot their self-importance and romped like children. He loved dancing, finding it a means of forgetting his work, his worries, his internal agitations, and he would even practice steps in the street or jump out of bed in the middle of the night to go through the necessary motions of a new dance. He put more vigour and vivacity into it than the youngest did, and appeared to be as fresh at the end of an evening as those of his own age were limp with laughter and exhaustion. But he never made the mistake of joining young men's gatherings, and when his eldest son Charles gave a coming-of-age party, which was of a riotous nature, he merely looked in on his way to bed, seemingly with the sole object of encouraging them to make as much noise as they liked for as long as they wished.

Sitting at the head of his table, he looked, and was, the ideal host. His quick eye missed nothing, and no guest was allowed to remain out of the general conversation. He was not a great talker; he was not a wit; but he was something almost as rare: a first-rate listener, and a provoker of other people's conversational faculties. No one at his table was allowed to prose for long. If anyone, like Forster, showed a tendency to do so, he would interject something to turn the talk into another channel or to make it easy for others to join in. He was often ready with a quip, as when someone was describing a huge telescope invented by a clergyman who had become an astronomer and wished to see further into heaven than . . . at which point Dickens interposed 'than his professional studies had enabled him to penetrate'; or when a morally indignant person exclaimed 'How wicked the world is!' and Dickens agreed: 'True, and what a satisfaction it is that neither you nor I belong to it!' But his real cleverness lay in his ability to bring out the best in everyone else, his own contributions to the social give-and-take being, as one would expect of an actor, humorous descriptions of scenes he had witnessed or comic imitations of people he knew or reproductions of stories he had heard; all done in a theatrically vivid manner, with suitable gestures and grimaces. We can almost see the darting eye, the mobile features, the quick assumption of character, and almost hear the sudden alteration of voice, the sigh, the chuckle, the explosive laugh, as he tells these stories, incited to each by the talk preceding it:

(*About Samuel Rogers, aged* 91): 'You know, I dare say, that for a year or so before his death he wandered, and lost himself like one of the Children in the Wood, grown up there and grown down again. He had Mrs. Procter and Mrs. Carlyle to breakfast with him one morning—only those two. Both excessively talkative, very quick and clever, and bent on entertaining him. When Mrs. Carlyle had flashed and shone before him for about three-quarters of an hour on one subject, he turned his poor old eyes on Mrs. Procter, and pointing to the brilliant discourser with his poor old finger, said (indignantly) "Who is *she*?" Upon this, Mrs. Procter, cutting in, delivered (it is her own story) a neat oration on the life and writings of Carlyle, and enlightened him in her happiest and airiest manner; all of which he heard, staring in the dreariest silence, and then said (indignantly, as before), "And who are *you?*"'

(*Dickens dreams*): '*A propos* of dreams, is it not a strange thing if writers of fiction never dream of their own creations; recollecting, I suppose, even in their dreams, that they have no real existence? *I* never dream of any of my own characters, and I feel it so impossible that I would wager Scott never did of his, real as they are. I had a good piece of absurdity in my head a night or two ago. I dreamed that somebody was dead. I don't know who, but it's not to the purpose. It was a private gentleman, and a particular friend; and I was greatly overcome when the news was broken to me (very delicately) by a gentleman in a cocked hat, top boots, and a sheet. Nothing else. "Good God", I said, "is he dead?" "He is as dead, sir", rejoined the gentleman, "as a door-nail. But we must all die, Mr. Dickens, sooner or later, my dear sir." "Ah!" I said. "Yes, to be sure. Very true. But what did he die of?" The gentleman burst into a flood of tears, and said, in a voice broken by emotion: "He christened his youngest child, sir, with a toasting-fork." I never in my life was so affected as at his having fallen a victim to this complaint. It carried a conviction to my mind that he never could have recovered. I knew that it was the most interesting and fatal malady in the world; and I wrung the gentleman's hand in a convulsion of respectful admiration, for I felt that this explanation did equal honour to his head and heart.'

(*Concerning a publisher's wife*): 'Mrs. Bradbury's account of Bradbury's setting fire to the bed on the occasion which has become historical was wonderful, and we made all sorts of ridiculous superstructures upon it. It seems that she being "hat Brihteen hat the time", he kept the secret of what had happened until she came home. Then, on composing that luxuriant and gorgeous figure of hers between the sheets, she started and said, "William, where his me bed?—*This* is not me bed—wot has append William—wot ave you dun with me bed?—I know the feelin of me bed, and *this* is not me bed." Upon which he confessed all.'

If not a notable talker himself, Dickens knew what subjects were proper to agreeable conversation, and would have sided with Dr. Johnson, who, at a time when everyone was talking of a French invasion, burst out: 'Alas! alas! how this unmeaning

stuff spoils all my comfort in my friends' conversation! Will
the people never have done with it; and shall I never hear
a sentence again without the *French* in it? . . . Among all
your lamentations, who eats the less? who sleeps the worse
for one general's ill-success or another's capitulation?' In
Dickens's time Russia, not France, provided the 'unmeaning
stuff'; in our time Germany has divided the main theme for
conversational boredom with Russia. Dickens hated argument and the heat engendered by the introduction of war,
politics, economics, religion, and such-like combustible topics.
Occasionally his indignation got the better of him, and he
would lash out angrily in writing and speech, as in the case
of the atrocities committed by the Indians in the early days of
the Mutiny: 'I wish I were Commander-in-Chief in India. The
first thing I would do to strike that Oriental race with amazement (not in the least regarding them as if they lived in the
Strand, London, or at Camden Town), should be to proclaim
to them in their language, that I considered my holding that
appointment by the leave of God to mean that I should do
my utmost to exterminate the Race upon whom the stain of
the late cruelties rested; and that I begged them to do me the
favour to observe that I was there for that purpose and no
other, and was now proceeding, with all convenient dispatch
and merciful swiftness of execution, to blot it out of mankind
and raze it off the face of the Earth.' Or his irritation with
some current humbug would produce a comical outburst, no
doubt reproduced at various tables, as in the case of the
spiritualistic craze which reduced the social world of London
in the fifties to a condition of imbecility: 'I have not the least
belief in the awful unseen world being available for evening
parties at so much per night; and, although I should be ready
to receive enlightenment from any source, I must say I have
very little hope of it from the spirits who express themselves
through mediums, as I have never yet observed them to talk
anything but nonsense, of which (as Carlyle would say) there
is probably enough in these days of ours, and in all days,
among mere mortality.' But he would not allow the general
talk to degenerate into squabbles and discord, and he seldom
travelled far from those subjects which all intelligent people
find eternally interesting and fit for civilised converse: human
nature, and its revelation either through the medium of art
and anecdote or by the exercise of a profession. Even a bore

becomes temporarily interesting when discussing his own character.

'Sadness only multiplies self. Let us do our duty and be cheerful', wrote Dr. Johnson to a friend. Dickens did his duty in society and was cheerful; but he did not have to force a gaiety that was as natural to him as it had been to Garrick. There was no limit to his interest in the human scene, and he was always at the top of his form when acting the host. He used to call himself Dick Sparkler, the National Sparkler, the Sparkler of Albion, and when he was not sparkling himself he struck the sparks out of others. His discursive glances round the table took in the least noticeable peculiarities of his guests, and such was his instinctive mimetic tendency that he sometimes copied their tricks while eating. His nearest friends did not escape this propensity, and he would imitate Forster, Bulwer Lytton, Maclise, Collins, Macready, to the life. He would even imitate himself, exaggerating his own absurdities so ludicrously that the company became hysterical. But he loved clowning, and always joined in the laughter he provoked. Once at dinner a woman addressed her husband as 'darling.' Dickens slid from his chair to the floor, lay on his back, held up one of his feet, and quivering with emotion cried 'Did she call him darling?' Back in his chair he looked extremely grave, and continued the conversation as if there had been no interlude. The changes of expression in his face were so frequent and so complete that there seemed to be countless characters in one man. He could still amaze people by the variety of his physical metamorphoses after he grew a fairly considerable beard, concerning which he said that 'much as I admired my own appearance when I was clean-shaven, I admire it much more now, and never neglect an opportunity of gazing at myself in the glass. Besides, my friends tell me that they highly approve of the change because they see much less of me.' Somehow the beard itself matched his altering expressions, looking stiff when his features were keen, silken when they were benevolent, bushy when he laughed, and flabby when he was sad. But only his closest friends saw him in sorrowful mood. In company his very presence was a challenge to melancholy. The vigorous handshake, the rich cheery voice, the eager lively countenance, the hearty manner, the lustrous eyes, the genial frank unaffected talk, above all the soaring spirit of the man, were of magnetic quality. He

JOHN FORSTER
*Photograph by*
WATKINS

ANGELA
(AFTERWARDS BARONESS)
BURDETT COUTTS
*Engraving after Painting by*
JAMES R. SWINTON

HABLOT K. BROWNE

('PHIZ')

GEORGE
CRUIKSHANK

warmed the social atmosphere, could enliven a party of dullards, and was even able to keep people in a jovial frame of mind at those dreary moments when a party was over, reaction had set in, and departure was delayed by the temporary absence of transport.

People meeting him, whether at his house or elsewhere, were never made to feel that he was an important person, and no famous writer has been less egotistical in company than he. Except when he told, or rather acted, a story prompted by the conversation, he rarely did more than interpose appreciative comments or sly remarks to keep the interest up or the fun going. We learn from several of his contemporaries that the stories which appear in his letters were, with variations, those he told at table, and we are therefore in a position to illustrate his share in the general talk. When a scene or a personal peccadillo amused him, down it went in a letter to his wife or Forster or someone else, later to be reproduced for the amusement of a party, possibly in an exaggerated form but always with telling effect, humorous or dramatic. Thus the mention of sport by one of his guests might produce the following:

'I have a novelty in the sporting way to tell you of, which happened during our trip to Italy, which was this: In the course of this trip, during which I have been to all manner of places, and slept with all manner of singular companions (chiefly mules and chickens), I became fearfully interested in certain companies I was continually falling upon in the country—Naples and Rome—companies of sportsmen, usually about six strong, got up in a most sanguinary and alarming manner—immense moustaches, prodigious beards, jet-black hair, incredible boots, fearful sombrero hats, and imitation English shooting-coats, with cuffs like gauntlets. They wore immense shot-belts, carried prodigious game-bags slung over one portly shoulder, and under the other carried heavy double-barrelled guns, and were supplied, on an average, each man with from four to five pounds of gunpowder. They were always eating great meals at little rustic public-houses, clinking their glasses tunefully together, sitting with their legs as wide apart as they could be conveniently got, and talking about the pleasures of *la caccia* (the chase).

'It was in these hostelries that I invariably saw them, and I could not conceive what their game was. I never saw any flying thing (dragons having gone out before my time) nearly large enough for their pretensions. Lions I knew there were none in Italy; wild bears of a sufficiently aspiring breed I had never heard of. It really preyed upon my mind, and whenever I came upon a knot of these hunters, ever invariably talking of *la caccia*, I looked in the yards, and behind the doors, and in the vineyards, and every place for the carcases of the slain, which I never found. One day I went to a dirty little tavern, within a dozen miles of Sontpère, and again I found these amusing men. This time they were six in number—ammunition quite stupendous in quantity—no quarter legibly inscribed on their faces, destruction in their manner, as they clinked the glasses and talked about *la caccia*. Now, when I went into this house, I had seen sitting under a grape-vine outside an extremely sleepy peasant, who had rested a long pole against the house itself. On the top of this long pole, and tied to it, was a dismal owl, laid with one cheek against the house, without the slightest regard to his being alive, whitewashing one of his large eyes in an involuntary and heartbreaking manner, and looking, on the whole, like an English judge in full costume, drunk, penitent, and drooping. As I passed this sleepy peasant and this dismal owl, I wondered what on earth they could be there for. Coming in, and sitting down among the sportsmen, it occurred to me by inspiration that they belonged to each other. I went out with a tumbler of wine—too weak to be further mentioned—gave it to the sleepy peasant, and spoke with him. Thereupon I learnt that *la caccia* was this: The party go out in great dignity, following the peasant and the owl. When the peasant comes to a place where there are numbers of small birds, he hoists up the pole and exposes the owl. The insane little fools immediately gather together from all quarters to deride the owl. The sportsmen then let off, with all possible speed, barrels right and left, and blow the idiots to pieces, occasionally shattering the owl instead. If any piece of a bird large enough to cook is left hanging together, which is not often, it is subsequently dressed and eaten. The owl catches cold, I believe, and dies early.'

Human oddity fascinated Dickens, and it would have been a very pointless and uninteresting world for him if the majority of its inhabitants had been what is commonly called normal. Fortunately he did not have to leave his house or his street in order to find sufficient material for his art, which was at its happiest when the subject was eccentric. He only had to keep his eyes open to see a world peopled with oddities; and though the story he told about two queer ladies was set in Lausanne, he could have found, and did find, curios of a quainter description in Lambeth:

'There are two old English ladies living at Lausanne . . . Originally there were four old ladies, sisters, but two of them have faded away in the course of eighteen years, and withered by the side of John Kemble in the cemetery. They are very little, and very skinny; and each of them wears a row of false curls, like little rolling-pins, so low upon her brow, that there is no forehead; nothing above the eyebrows but a deep horizontal wrinkle, and then the curls. They live upon some small annuity. For thirteen years they have wanted very much to move to Italy, as the eldest old lady says the climate of this part of Switzerland doesn't agree with her, and preys upon her spirits; but they have never been able to go, because of the difficulty of moving "the books." This tremendous library belonged once upon a time to the father of these old ladies, and comprises about fifty volumes. I have never been able to see what they are, because one of the old ladies always sits before them; but they look, outside, like very old back-gammon boards. The two deceased sisters died in the firm persuasion that this precious property could never be got over the Simplon without some gigantic effort to which the united family was unequal. The two remaining sisters live, and will die also, in the same belief. I met the eldest, evidently drooping, one day, and recommended her to try Genoa. She looked shrewdly at the snow that closed up the mountain prospect just then, and said that when the spring was quite set in, and the avalanches were down, and the passes well open, she would certainly try that place, if they could devise any plan, in the course of the winter, for moving "the books." The whole library will be sold by auction, when they are both dead, for about a napoleon; and some young woman will carry it home in two journeys with a basket.'

Such stories, embellished with dramatic dialogue, were inimitably acted, so that each character was made vivid to the listeners. But there was another kind of episode of which he was inordinately fond, and which he would retail, with grisly details, in a realistic manner that made his hearers shudder.

This again would be called forth by the occasion; but as his acquaintances knew of his predilection for the morbid and macabre, the occasion was usually forthcoming. He once expelled an unwelcome visitor from his house with the words 'Madmen! they alone amuse me.' If not amused, he was intensely interested in ghosts, dead bodies, murderers, maniacs, criminals of all sorts, executions, hangmen, torturers, and other ghoulish matters; and the stories he would relate on such themes were performed with considerable relish. But many modern writers have done this class of thing much better than Dickens, so we need not illustrate it with items from his repertoire. What was unique in him is what should interest his biographer; what was common to several millions of his fellow-creatures is part of history, and has latterly come to the surface of so-called civilisation in the form of concentration camps, totalitarianism, legalised torture, and two world wars.

The outstanding virtue of Dickens, the one thing that keeps him alive, the thing that should penetrate his biography, was his comedy; and in social life, too, his merriment was his most engaging quality, his laugh being remembered by those who had met him when everything else was forgotten. His comedy was founded upon an almost omniscient observation. He noticed everything, and was amused by nearly everything. Sometimes, at the dinner table, his blue luminous eyes lost their colour and became nondescript; his manner grew abstracted; he had a rapt faraway look; yet even in this condition nothing escaped him, and the quick change from his preoccupied air to full awareness was startling. It might be that someone was telling a funny story; upon which a knowing look appeared on his face, his eyes twinkled, an eyebrow lifted comically, a nostril twitched; then, when the point of the story was reached, his cheeks crumpled, his mouth expanded, his eyelids puckered, and a gargantuan laugh rang through the room. He seemed to laugh with his whole body. It was a laugh brimful of enjoyment, whole-hearted, tumultuous, and so infectious that the most solemn or dyspeptic guest could not resist it. The story may have dealt with someone's penuriousness; but whether it did or not, sooner or later he would be reminded of Wilkie Collins and Augustus Egg when they were with him at Venice. He would reserve the incident for a few choice friends who knew Egg and

Collins well and would enjoy his somewhat grotesque impersonations of them. Then, to heighten the effect, he would adapt what originally appeared in this form:

'It is the drollest thing in the world to see Egg and Collins burst out into economy—always on some wretched little point, and always on a point they had previously settled the other way. For example. This morning at breakfast they settled that there was no need for them to have the Servitore di Piazza today. I waited until the discussion was over, and then said "But when we met at dinner yesterday, you told me you had engaged him"—"O yes, so we did— almost—but we don't want him and it will be all the same." It is then eleven o'clock. Downstairs we all go. In the hall is the Servitore. To whom Collins—in Italian (of which Georgy will give you an adequate idea)—expounds that they don't want him. Thereupon he respectfully explains that he was told to come, has lost his day, and has been waiting an hour. Upon that, they are of course obliged to take him; and the only result of the great effort is (as it always is) that it has been a profoundly mean, and utterly fruitless, attempt at evasion. We brought some good tea with us from Genoa, and if you could have seen them, when it was first going to be used, devising how a teapot and boiling water were to be got from the Hotel for nothing, you would never have forgotten it. Of course I clinched the matter very speedily by ordering tea for one (tenpence in price) which we didn't use. Egg is always reasonable on all such points if he is spoken to, seriously. And he is a good little fellow. But there is a ridiculous contrast sometimes between their determination to have good things and their tremendous readiness to complain—and their slight reluctance in paying afterwards.'

Dickens's curiosity had no limit, and this added to his fascination as a companion, because he was eager to know as much as he could glean of the personal life of everyone who interested him. Unlike one of his characters, he never received people's confidences 'with about as much interest and surprise as an undertaker might evince if required to listen to a circumstantial account of the last illness of a person whom he was called in to wait upon professionally.' He was as good a listener with one person as he was with a tableful, and one of his favourite games, called Twenty Questions, was played for the sole purpose of finding out all he could about the tastes and nature of his guests. Since most human beings are chiefly interested in themselves, and as the majority derive their keenest enjoyment from laughing at others, Dickens was able, both in his social circle and in his books, to give more pleasure to more people than anybody else in history.

# 16

## HOME AFFAIRS

so much for the host. But what of the hostess? Did she sparkle? Did she play up to him as he played up to others? A very decided negative partly explains the unfortunate domestic situation created by their twenty years of wedlock, during which she had produced ten children and suffered several miscarriages. It is extremely doubtful whether any woman could have made a wholly satisfactory mate for Dickens, who really needed a forty-wife-power partner. But Kate was quite unequal to his requirements. She was amiable, gentle, reposeful, and rather characterless. She liked peace and quiet. Strenuous action distressed her. She was interested in her home, loved her children, was concerned over their health and troubles, liked talking about babies and needle-work and the cares of motherhood, was friendly and affection-ate, asked little of life but to be left alone with her family, and showed her disinclination for mental and physical activity by an awkwardness that resulted in dropping things or falling over them or forgetting where they were or using them for the wrong purposes.

Apart from her frequent prostration by child-birth, she had neither the temperament nor the vitality to cope with her husband's erratic demands. She had done her best in the early years, and had allowed him to drag her from her children across the Atlantic and cart her about the American continent for zoological exhibition and a course of social manhandling; for his sake she had spent days and nights travelling about the continent of Europe in extreme discomfort and constant danger; she had taken her place as hostess at his table and tried hard to talk about a hundred and one topics which did not interest her in the least; she had accompanied him to many meetings in various parts of England and Scotland, sat with him on many platforms, attended many public dinners, and been bored by many public speeches; she had listened to his readings of each number of every novel as soon as he had finished writing it and made desperate attempts to take as much interest in his creations as he did himself; she had racked her memory and her nerves by appearing in the play-productions which periodically turned her home upside down; and finally she had witnessed, without indignation or even irritation, the usurpation of her position as hostess and mistress of the house by her sister Georgina.

Continual pregnancy did not improve her, and after the birth of her tenth child she became rather infantile; but even at her best she had never been treated by her husband as an adult. They had probably been as much in love with one another when they married as the large majority of young couples usually are; that is to say, they had desired each other sufficiently to go through an ecclesiastical ceremony; but their early wedded life had been handicapped, first by his memory of Maria Beadnell, and then by his memory of Mary Hogarth. In other words Kate had been made to feel that she was a sort of deputy-wife; but being of a lazy and easily-pleased nature, she had not resented this; and when Georgina took her place and managed her home, she was rather grateful than otherwise. What made life unusually difficult for her, and forced her to suggest several times that she and Charles should live apart, was the perpetual friction that resulted from the disharmony of two utterly conflicting temperaments. This friction naturally increased with the years, as the pressure of work and the growth of responsibility aggravated the restlessness and exacerbated the turbulence of her husband's nature, and it was fairly soon after the establishment of *Household Words* that she first hinted at a separation.

For some years he rejected the idea. He told her that their first duty was to their children, for whose sake they must remain together. As far as we know, he did not tell her, what must have been uppermost in his mind, that their separation might seriously affect his position as a novelist whose popularity had largely been gained and maintained by his idealised pictures of home life, conjugal happiness, and fireside felicity. Further, as a spiritual child of his age, he did not question the proprieties of the time, and was always most careful to observe them. Once, when they were in Paris, they asked an actress to dinner at the request of Samuel Rogers. On a later visit Dickens discovered that the actress was well-known in Parisian society as the mistress of an English peer, and immediately directed his wife to call on the other ladies who had dined with them on the earlier occasion, and 'without making too much of it, just say "that her history is not quite correct, you find, and that Rogers was mistaken in presenting her, but you never mean to tell him so—though you feel you owe this explanation to them, whom you asked to meet her." *This you must do at once.*' There were, in short, many cogent reasons for keeping up appearances; and if he had not been the impulsive, excitable, histrionic, demonic creature he was, at times driven almost crazy by work, worry, and his attempts to suffer fools gladly, this chapter would be unnecessary, and his biography, to say nothing of his novels, would have been different.

The chief fools were the Hogarths: father-in-law, mother-in-law, aunt-in-law, and youngest sister-in-law. Their habits and conversation appear to have riled Dickens to an extra-ordinary degree. 'I am dead sick of the Scottish tongue in all its moods and tenses', he told Wilkie Collins in '55. Like all his other relations and connections, they got as much out of him as they could, stayed for long periods with him, some-times occupied his house when he was away, and often had their bills paid by him. In January '56 he instructed Wills that the family apothecary should 'charge his attendance, medicines, &c, for Mrs. Hogarth in her illness to my account, and just to say nothing at all about the matter to her, or her family, or anyone else.' Yet three months later he was telling Wills that he would delay his return home because 'the Hogarth family don't leave Tavistock House till next Satur-day, and I cannot in the meantime bear the contemplation of their imbecility any more. (I think my constitution is already undermined by the sight of Hogarth at breakfast.)' Georgina shared his view of her relations, who therefore took the part of his wife against Georgina and talked outside the family about the impropriety of his permitting a sister-in-law to run his home. This piece of tittle-tattle in due course reached his ears, and did not help to soothe him at a time when every pin-prick was like a sword-thrust.

There was a good deal of self-pity in Dickens, and it came out especially in his complaints that his marriage had been a failure. It takes two to make a success or a failure of matri-mony; and when Dickens said that, in low spirits, he experi-enced a crushing sense of having missed one happiness in life, of having been denied one friend and companion, he forgot that his wife could have said the same. Self-pity is a very ordinary human attribute; and, like most great creative artists, Dickens expressed every human attribute more intensely than the average man or woman. Shakespeare saw how few people are capable of feeling anything solely through the imagination, that men must endure poverty before they can sympathise with the poor, endure pain and illness before they can be sorry for those who suffer, endure hardship before they can appreciate it, and so must feel pity for themselves before they can pity others. When King Lear has experienced the exposure and neglect of his poorest subjects, and can pity his then condition, Shakespeare makes him cry:

> O, I have ta'en
> Too little care of this! Take physic, pomp,
> Expose thyself to feel what wretches feel,
> That thou mayst shake the superflux to them
> And show the heavens more just.

But if Dickens indulged in more self-pity than Shakespeare, and much more than Scott, to mention the only two writers in English who are in his creative class, it is because he was an actor by temperament; he allowed his emotions to run away with him, and too easily saw himself as the central figure in a sentimental drama. The fact that the most popular play ever written is *Hamlet*, its stage popularity being due to the ambition of nearly every actor to play the leading part, is a sure sign, not only that self-pity is the commonest of human emotions, but that it finds a perfect outlet in self-dramatisation, which is the obverse of exhibitionism, which is another term for acting. Dickens was at his happiest on the stage, and at the height of his happiness when playing the hero who sacrifices himself for love and dissolves the audience into sympathy and admiration for himself. We shall soon see how inevitably his domestic troubles brought forth his most theatrical work.

Although he stated in May '58 that he and his wife had 'lived unhappily together for many years', he had nevertheless written to her from Rome in November '53 'I shall be very happy to be at home again myself, and to embrace you—for of course I miss you *very much*.' With a nature like his, the unhappiness seemed to have been prolonged the moment it became acute; and the first sign in his letters of domestic discomfort appears in January '55, when he speaks of having

been denied one friend and companion, like his own David
Copperfield. The next reference to the subject is in April '56:
'The old days—the old days! Shall I ever, I wonder, get the
frame of mind back as it used to be then? Something of it
perhaps—but never quite as it used to be. I find that the
skeleton in my domestic closet is becoming a pretty big one.'
That was written in Paris while he was working on *Little
Dorrit*, wherein his sense of some irreparable loss comes out
in Clennam's unrequited love of Pet Meagles, in Clennam's
feeling that life has passed him by and left him too old to
marry, and in the return to a saintlike female figure: Clennam's
Little Dorrit, Dickens's Mary Hogarth.

Whether or not Dickens and his wife would have continued
to live together if Douglas Jerrold had not died just then and
professional actresses had not been engaged for the play at
Manchester, it is useless to conjecture. But on one point there
is no doubt: the future of Kate was settled from the moment
when Ellen Ternan doubled the parts of Maria Beadnell and
Mary Hogarth; because, as Dickens told Wilkie Collins in
March '58, 'I have never known a moment's peace or content
since the last night of *The Frozen Deep*. I do suppose that there
never was a man so seized and rended by one spirit.' Naturally
Forster had to be brought into a crisis of this magnitude; his
worldly advice was essential, he had known Kate for as long
as he had known Charles, and he was the only man who could
be trusted to arrange things in a prudent, business-like
manner, satisfactory to both parties. Collins was useless for
such a purpose: he was too young, too lazy, too cynical, and
inexperienced; also he was known to hold peculiar views on
the sanctity of marriage, and Kate probably distrusted his
pagan influence on her husband.

From the beginning Forster counselled reflection and
caution. Dickens answered in September '57: 'You are not
so tolerant as perhaps you might be of the wayward and
unsettled feeling which is part (I suppose) of the tenure on
which one holds an imaginative life, and which I have, as you
ought to know well, often only kept down by riding over it
like a dragoon—but let that go by. I make no maudlin complaint. I agree with you as to the very possible incidents, even
not less bearable than mine, that might and must often occur
to the married condition when it is entered into very young.
I am always deeply sensible of the wonderful exercise I have

of life and its highest sensations, and have said to myself for
years, and have honestly and truly felt, this is the drawback
to such a career, and is not to be complained of . . . But the
years have not made it easier to bear for either of us; and, for
her sake as well as mine, the wish will force itself upon me
that something might be done . . . Nor are you to suppose
that I disguise from myself what might be urged on the other
side. I claim no immunity from blame. There is plenty of
fault on my side, I dare say, in the way of a thousand un-
certainties, caprices, and difficulties of disposition.' In another
letter of the same month he unburdened himself to Forster:
'Poor Catherine and I are not made for each other, and there
is no help for it. It is not only that she makes me uneasy and
unhappy, but that I make her so too—and much more so.
She is exactly what you know, in the way of being amiable
and complying; but we are strangely ill-assorted for the bond
there is between us. God knows she would have been a
thousand times happier if she had married another kind of
man, and that her avoidance of this destiny would have been
at least equally good for us both. I am often cut to the heart
by thinking what a pity it is, for her own sake, that I ever
fell in her way; and if I were sick or disabled tomorrow, I
know how sorry she would be, and how deeply grieved
myself, to think how we had lost each other. But exactly the
same incompatibility would arise, the moment I was well
again; and nothing on earth could make her understand me,
or suit us to each other. Her temperament will not go with
mine. It mattered not so much when we had only ourselves to
consider, but reasons have been growing since which make it
all but hopeless that we should even try to struggle on. What
is now befalling me I have seen steadily coming on, ever
since the days you remember when Mary was born . . .'

The reasons that had been growing since the time when
they had only themselves to consider were no doubt manifold
in his mind when he wrote the words, but in effect they boiled
down to one: he was in love with another woman. His mental
condition was such that he could not face the prospect of
writing a novel; but as he had to occupy himself and to make
money somehow, he revived the idea that had first occurred
to him twenty-one years before: that he should give readings
from his stories, not for charity but for his own benefit.
Forster strongly opposed the idea on the ground that a

famous novelist would lose caste by becoming a public
entertainer. It was not the sort of thing a gentleman could
do, said Forster, who again advised his friend to take himself
in hand and act with moderation. But Forster's attempts to
restrain him made Dickens restive: 'Too late to say, put the
curb on, and don't rush at hills—the wrong man to say it to.
I have now no relief but in action. I am become incapable of
rest. I am quite confident I should rust, break, and die, if I
spared myself. Much better to die, doing. What I am in that
way, nature made me first, and my way of life has of late, alas!
confirmed. I must accept the drawback—since it is one—
with the powers I have; and I must hold upon the tenure
prescribed to me.'

To prove his intention of going his own way, he wrote
from Gad's Hill Place to their old servant Anne, now married
and looking after Tavistock House in the family's absence,
requesting her to convert his dressing-room into a bedroom,
which must be sealed off from his wife's bedroom, and would
henceforth be occupied by himself. This symbolical gesture
occurred in October '57, after he had returned from his trip
to the Lakes with Collins. He was making great improvements
at Gad's Hill, but in his then state of mind he felt no interest
in the place. Forster kept urging him to ease his mind by
starting a new book, but he replied 'Nothing whatever will
do me the least "good" in the way of shaking the one strong
possession of change impending over us that every day makes
stronger.' January '58 saw him back in Tavistock House,
sleeping apart from his wife, wretched, moody, and feeling
caged-up. 'What a dream it is, this work and strife, and how
little we do in the dream after all!' he wrote to Macready in
March. 'Only last night, in my sleep, I was bent upon getting
over a perspective of barriers, with my hands and feet bound.
Pretty much what we are all about, waking, I think?' And to
Wilkie Collins: 'The domestic unhappiness remains so strong
upon me that I can't write, and (waking) can't rest, one
minute.' But from a letter written in the same month it
appears that he did not wish to take the final step without
Forster's concurrence: 'Quite dismiss from your mind any
reference whatever to present circumstances at home. Nothing
can put *them* right, until we are all dead and buried and risen.
It is not, with me, a matter of will, or trial, or sufferance, or
good humour, or making the best of it, or making the worst

of it, any longer. It is all despairingly over. Have no lingering hope of, or for, me in this association. A dismal failure has to be borne, and there an end.'

Meanwhile he was steadily going ahead with his reading arrangements in spite of Forster's disapproval. The only question that bothered him was whether his appearance as a professional reader would hurt his popularity as a novelist? He told Collins that Forster was 'extraordinarily irrational' about the whole business, and suggested that 'his money must have got into his head.' In the excitement of impersonating his own creations before large audiences, he knew that he would be able to forget his internal commotion, at least temporarily, and 'I must do *something*', he said despairingly, 'or I shall wear my heart away.' In March he made up his mind, appointed a friend, Arthur Smith, as his business manager, and announced a series of readings of *A Christmas Carol*, which would commence on April 29th at St. Martin's Hall,[1] London, would continue there until the beginning of June, and would be repeated in various provincial towns in the autumn. Queen Victoria got to know of his intention and said that she was most anxious to hear him read the *Carol*, but hesitated to approach him because of his request to be excused from seeing her after she had witnessed *The Frozen Deep*. Dickens made it clear that if she wished to hear him read the *Carol* she must indulge him 'by making one of some audience or other', as he considered an audience necessary. Her indulgence did not stretch as far as that, and he heard no more of it. After giving two more charity readings, one on behalf of the Hospital for Sick Children in Great Ormond Street, the other in aid of the Edinburgh Philosophical Institution, he began to read in his own behalf, gradually adding other items, such as *The Chimes*, to the programme at St. Martin's Hall, and making such a colossal success in his new character that, had he cared to devote himself exclusively to such work henceforth, he would have earned more money by his readings than he did earn by his writings.

But before the date of his first professional appearance on the platform, his wife had left Tavistock House, accompanied by her mother and her sister Helen. Kate was, as we have seen, a simple soul, and was easily persuaded by her relations that Georgina was working against her and that Ellen Ternan

---

[1] Odham's Press in Long Acre now covers the site of St. Martin's Hall.

was her husband's mistress. Their antagonism to Dickens is quickly explained. He had made it abundantly clear that their presence irritated him by leaving Tavistock House one evening and walking all through the night to Gad's Hill, a distance of thirty miles, where he proposed to remain until they had gone away; and from several passages in his letters we can guess that his hostile feelings must have been evident for some time. Their objection to Georgina was no doubt due to the fact that she reflected Dickens's feelings and annoyed them by managing a household that should have been run by an easy-going wife whom they could control. Early in Dickens's married life, to be precise on May 8th, 1843, he had written that he could trace a strong resemblance between the mental features of his beloved Mary Hogarth and those of Georgina—'so strange a one, at times, that when she and Kate and I are sitting together, I seem to think that what has happened is a melancholy dream from which I am just awakening. The perfect like of what she was, will never be again, but so much of her spirit shines out in this sister, that the old time comes back again at some seasons, and I can hardly separate it from the present.' The passing years had emphasised the similarity, and Georgina had been enthroned in his fancy, and therefore in his establishment, as the nearest approach to the ideal woman so necessary for his peace of mind. Georgina cannot have liked being cast for a virtuous part, because there is no doubt whatever that she adored him; but she had to put up with it, and the unnatural situation embittered her against her sister Kate, who had, as she believed, the pleasures of marriage without the responsibilities of a household, which had somehow devolved upon herself.

The entrance of Ellen Ternan on the scene at first complicated and afterwards simplified matters. What Georgina felt about her we can infer from what she felt about Charles; but for the Hogarth family there was now food for the gravest gossip. Dickens was not the man to hide his feelings from his intimate friends, who must have been apprised of his infatuation for the actress inside half an hour's conversation with him; and, such being the nature of human beings, his intimate friends would have discussed it with their intimate friends, who would have mentioned it to theirs, and so on. Very soon it was the talk of clubland, because Thackeray and Browning, who were outside the immediate circle of Dickens, knew of it. Kate was first made aware of what was going on when some jewellery, which her husband had bought for Ellen, came to her in error. She was left in no doubt on the subject when, after reminding her of their early compact that if either of them should at any time fall in love with someone else the other was to be told, he requested her to call on Ellen Ternan. She was greatly upset, told her mother about it, and could not conceal it from her daughters, one of whom found her in tears. 'Your father has asked me to go and see Ellen Ternan', she complained. Her daughter told her that she must not go; but she went. Dickens was equally outspoken with Georgina, his eldest son and his two daughters; but he made it perfectly clear to everyone, in case they might think otherwise, that his affection for Ellen was of the most elevated nature, and that their relationship was perfectly 'innocent.' The Hogarths neither believed nor wished to believe this, persuaded Kate that she was a much wronged woman, and took her away from home.

Dickens returned from Gad's Hill to Tavistock House, and quickly learnt of the scandals that were flying around the social world, scandals about himself, about Georgina, about Ellen Ternan. Someone in the Garrick Club said to Thackeray that Dickens and his wife were separated 'on account of an intrigue with his sister-in-law.' 'No such thing', replied Thackeray, 'it's with an actress.' This was repeated to Dickens, who wrote to Thackeray furiously denying any and every charge against Ellen and against himself, and explaining that the separation from his wife was due to incompatibility. After careful inquiry, Dickens discovered that Mrs. Hogarth and her daughter Helen were, if not the originators, at least the disseminators of the scandal about himself and Ellen Ternan, and promptly went mad: in other words, he behaved in a way that justified his acquaintances in thinking that his reason was unhinged and his feelings were out of control. Some people said at the time that his nature seemed to alter, that he became a different man. But this was a shallow view. A man's character never changes radically from youth to old age. What happens is that circumstances bring out characteristics which had not previously been obvious to the superficial observer. Dickens's behaviour when he found that the Hogarth family, which he had supported and befriended for over twenty years, had been guilty of such ingratitude as to

WILLIAM
WILKIE COLLINS
(1850)
*Painting by*
SIR JOHN EVERETT
MILLAIS, BART., P.R.A.
*National Portrait Gallery*

WILLIAM MAKEPEACE
THACKERAY
*Painting by*
SAMUEL LAURENCE
*National Portrait
Gallery*

**DICKENS WITH HIS DAUGHTERS MAMIE (*left*) AND KATIE**
(1865)
IN THE ROSE GARDEN OF GAD'S HILL PLACE

bear false witness against him behind his back, was exactly what any intelligent person would have expected of a highly-strung emotional actor who had the driving power of a man of action. He had no self-control when thwarted in his designs; and throughout their married life his word had been law, his wife never having dared to express an opinion contrary to his. Their separation became inevitable from the moment she left home, and Forster was empowered to make all the necessary arrangements. Kate chose Mark Lemon as her representative, because Forster had always acted inimically towards her, and by the last week of May '58 the deed of separation was signed. She was to receive £600 a year for life; their eldest son went to live with her at 70 Gloucester Crescent, Regent's Park; and the other children remained with their father.

Throughout these proceedings Dickens behaved like a caged tiger, and there can have been few inducements to the children to make up merry parties at home. The moment when the agreement was ratified, the tiger broke loose and began to lash out in every direction. Those who were not with him were against him, and even an old friend like John Leech was severely reprimanded for daring to suggest that Charley had sided with his mother. 'You strike me in a tender place, and wound me deeply', said Dickens, whose sense of having been wronged was so deep, and who had suffered so much from the strain under which he had been living, that he described his heart as 'jagged and rent and out of shape.' His children were ordered to hold no further communication with their grandmother Mrs. Hogarth and their aunt Helen; and although they were not forbidden to visit their mother, he made it clear that he did not wish them to do so. Georgina was compelled to write to his former love, now Mrs. Winter, giving his version of the case and making the extraordinary assertion that 'by some constitutional misfortune and incapacity my sister always from their infancy threw her children upon other people; consequently, as they grew up, there was not the usual strong tie between them and her.' It would have been true to say that Dickens and Forster between them had determined that Kate was not a fit person to bring up her children, and that her responsibility as a mother was never abandoned because it was never assumed. There is no evidence whatever that the younger children were not fond of her; and of the three who were old enough to be taken into their father's confidence, Charley and Katie sided with their mother, while Mamie sided with him.

An unerring observer is often a devious thinker, and a clear outer vision does not imply a clear inner vision. Because a few fools who had nothing better to do than gossip in clubs and drawing-rooms were relishing the scandal about Dickens, his wife, his sister-in-law, and an actress, the man who never missed a glance or gesture or vocal tone of those about him suffered from the strange delusion that the whole world was talking about his family affairs, and the stranger delusion that a simple public statement by himself would set the minds of his admirers at rest and stop the tongue of defamation. He should have treated the rumours by closing his ears, just as he treated criticisms of his novels by shutting his eyes. But in his inmost self he knew that his behaviour had justified them; and nothing in the world could have irritated him so much as a knowledge of being innocent (as he understood it) under an accusation of guilt (as he believed it) founded on dubious conduct (as others would think it). Although his sense of humour saved him from a swollen head, his success had come too early and had been too complete to leave him without some self-significance; and he spoke of his public as if a mystical relationship existed between him and it, as if he was in a position of trust which he must not abuse. That was how he had really come to feel; and taken in conjunction with his mortification over the rumours, it goes far to explain the most extraordinary action in his astonishing career: the publication of his *Address* to the readers of *Household Words*, and its circularisation to the leading papers of the country with a request that they should print it. But his decision to write and issue this *Address* was dictated mainly by his histrionic nature; he could not resist the temptation to dramatise himself, to put his case before the world; it was, so to say, an actor's benefit performance, a theatrical puff. Having prepared the statement, he suffered a twinge of nervousness and showed it to Forster and Mark Lemon, both of whom strongly opposed its publication; but their attitude merely strengthened his own, and at last Forster advised him to seek the opinion of John Delane, the editor of *The Times*, and abide by his decision. Delane was the trusted adviser of Prime Ministers and Foreign Secretaries, and was therefore to be relied upon; what he did not know about the effect of anything on the public was supposed to be not worth knowing. Dickens showed him the *Address* and asked his advice, which was favourable to publication. Whether he disliked Dickens, whose works had always been roughly handled in *The Times*, we do not know; but we may suppose that he was sufficiently indifferent to give an affirmative opinion when he saw that Dickens was bent on doing what he wanted to do.

Before printing it Dickens sent a copy to his wife, asking whether she had any objection to the reference to herself, and letting her know how her mother, aunt and sister stood in his estimation: 'Whoever there may be among the living, whom I will never forgive alive or dead, I earnestly hope that all unkindness is over between you and me.' As usual 'Dear Catherine', as he now addressed her, had nothing to gainsay; and the statement appeared in *Household Words* on June 12th, 1858. Many papers to which it was sent ignored it, many printed it, and quite a few made editorial comments of a displeasing nature. The publication bewildered his readers, the vast majority of whom knew nothing of his domestic concerns, and embarrassed his friends, some of whom knew rather more than he had set down; and the criticisms to which he was subjected enraged him, stiffened his attitude, and made him see secret enemies among his declared friends. After reading the following paragraphs of the *Address*, his saner companions would reasonably have concluded that to discuss this subject with him in a spirit of lighthearted detachment might lead to misunderstanding:

'Some domestic trouble of mine, of long-standing, on which I will make no further remark than that it claims to be respected, as being of a sacredly private nature, has lately been brought to an arrangement, which involves no anger or ill-will of any kind, and the whole origin, progress, and surrounding circumstances of which have been throughout, within the knowledge of my children. It is amicably composed, and its details have now but to be forgotten by those concerned in it.

'By some means, arising out of wickedness, or out of folly, or out of inconceivable wild chance, or out of all three, this trouble has been made the occasion of misrepresentations, most grossly false, most monstrous and most cruel—involving, not only me, but innocent persons dear to my heart, and innocent persons of whom I have no knowledge, if, indeed, they have any existence—and so widely spread that I doubt if one reader in a thousand will peruse these lines, by whom some touch of the breath of these slanders will not have passed, like an unwholesome air.

'Those who know me and my nature, need no assurance under my hand that such calumnies are as irreconcileable with me as they are, in their frantic incoherence, with one another. But there is a great multitude who know me through my writings, and who do not know me otherwise; and I cannot bear that one of them should be left in doubt, or hazard of doubt, through my poorly shrinking from taking the unusual means to which I now resort of circulating the truth.

'I most solemnly declare, then—and this I do, both in my own name and in my wife's—that all the lately whispered rumours touching the trouble at which I have glanced are abominably false. And that whosoever repeats one of them, after this denial, will lie as wilfully and as foully as it is possible for any false witness to lie, before heaven and earth.'

But worse remained behind. In his fury he wrote at the same time another and far more explicit statement, which he gave to his readings-manager, Arthur Smith, begging him to show it to anyone who had believed the slanders and to anyone who wished to rebut them. Appended to this was a signed recantation by Mrs. Hogarth and her youngest daughter, which Dickens must have forced out of them by means of threats, since at a later date they regretted having signed it: 'It having been stated to us that, in reference to the differences which have resulted in the separation of Mr. and Mrs. Charles Dickens, certain statements have been circulated that such differences are occasioned by circumstances deeply affecting the moral character of Mr. Dickens, and compromising the reputation and good name of others, we solemnly declare that we now disbelieve such statements. We know that they are not believed by Mrs. Dickens, and we pledge ourselves, on all occasions, to contradict them, as entirely destitute of foundation.' In his desire that Dickens should be righted, Smith exceeded his commission and showed the statement and appendage to a pressman, with the result that both appeared in the New York *Tribune*, were copied by several English newspapers, and exposed Dickens to much censure. Some passages must be quoted:

'Mrs. Dickens and I lived unhappily together for many years. Hardly any one who has known us intimately can fail to have known that we are in all respects of character and temperament wonderfully unsuited to each other. I suppose that no two people, not vicious in themselves, ever were joined together who had a greater difficulty in understanding one another, or who had less in common . . .

'Nothing has, on many occasions, stood between us and a separation but Mrs. Dickens's sister, Georgina Hogarth. From the age of fifteen she has devoted herself to our house and our children. She has been their playmate, nurse, instructress, friend, protectress, adviser, and companion. In the manly consideration towards Mrs. Dickens which I owe to my wife, I will merely remark of her that the peculiarity of her character has thrown all the children on someone else. I do not know—I cannot by any stretch of fancy imagine—what would have become of them but for this aunt, who has grown up with them, to whom they are devoted, and who has sacrificed the best part of her youth and life to them. She has remonstrated, reasoned, suffered, and toiled, again and again to prevent a separation between Mrs. Dickens and me . . .

'For some years past, Mrs. Dickens has been in the habit of representing to me that it would be better for her to go away and live apart; that her always increasing estrangement made a mental disorder under which she sometimes labours —more, that she felt herself unfit for the life she had to lead as my wife, and that she would be better far away. I have uniformly replied that we must bear our misfortune, and fight the fight out to the end; that the children were the first consideration, and that I feared they must bind us together "in appearance".'

After describing the terms of the separation, and adding that 'of the pecuniary part of them I will only say that I believe they are as generous as if Mrs. Dickens were a lady of distinction and I a man of fortune', he continued:

'Two wicked persons, who should have spoken very differently of me in consideration of earned respect and gratitude, have (as I am told, and indeed to my personal knowledge) coupled with this separation the name of a young lady for whom I have great attachment and regard. I will not repeat her name—I honour it too much. Upon my soul and honour, there is not on this earth a more virtuous and spotless creature than that young lady. I know her to be innocent and pure, and as good as my own dear daughters. Further, I am quite sure that Mrs. Dickens having received this assurance from me, must now believe it, in the respect I know her to have for me, and in the perfect confidence I know her in her better moments to repose in my truthfulness . . .'

Dickens was 'exceedingly pained' when this 'private and personal communication' appeared in the English papers in the summer of '58, and instantly requested his solicitor to make it known to Kate 'that I am no consenting party to this publication; that it cannot possibly be more offensive to anyone in the world than it is to me; and that it has shocked and distressed me very much.' But here his self-pity made him utterly insensitive to the feelings of his wife; for the printed assertion that she had neglected her children must have been far more offensive to her than it was to him.

Their separation made two people wretchedly unhappy. With Dickens it became a war between his will and his conscience: he knew in his heart that he had not been fair to Kate; but he hardened his heart, and his will was victorious at the expense of much internal misery. A note he sent to Angela Burdett Coutts from Dublin in August '58 shows how desperately he was attempting to shift all the blame on to Kate's shoulders, how thoroughly he was trying to deceive himself in the process of dramatising himself. His wife had never cared for their children, he asserted, and their children had never cared for her. Throughout their married life she had never helped him in the least; but now, in conjunction with her wicked relations, whom he had loaded with benefits, she had defamed him. He wanted, he said, to forgive and forget her.

As for Kate, she carried the pain of the separation in her heart until she died, experiencing the double agony of a wife's defenceless innocence and a mother's exposed failure. 'To think of the poor matron after 22 years of marriage going away out of her house'! mourned Thackeray. 'O dear me, it's a fatal story for our trade.' That was how Henry Gowan in *Little Dorrit* demeaned his art, and it was the main cause of the uncomfortable relationship between the two greatest novelists of the age, which is now to be unfolded.

# 17

# RUCTIONS

A PORTRAIT of Dickens was painted by W. P. Frith in 1859.
'I wish he looked less eager and busy, and not so much out
of himself, or beyond himself', said Edwin Landseer when he
saw it. 'I should like to catch him asleep and quiet now and
then.' Dickens's own comment on the portrait was more to
the point: 'It is a little too much (to my thinking) as if my
next-door neighbour were my deadly foe, uninsured, and I
had just received tidings of his house being afire.' Certainly
he was not at his best for a year or two after his wife's
departure, and his daughter Katie seems to have been very
unhappy while he was busily assimilating the rôle of an
injured husband. The quarrel with Thackeray quickly
followed the separation from his wife; and though they were
always on awkward terms with one another, he would have
handled the situation more delicately, and perhaps avoided
the break, if he had been in control of himself.

From the time when Thackeray had applied for the job of
illustrating *Pickwick Papers* in 1836 until the success of *Vanity
Fair* in 1847, the two men had been on a friendly footing.
They had dined at each other's houses, met at other people's
dinners, and 'heard the chimes at midnight' in the company
of mutual friends. But their upbringings, social backgrounds,
habits, outlooks and predilections were radically dissimilar,
and in character they had scarcely a trait in common.
Thackeray was not a child of his age; spiritually he belonged
to the 18th century, and would have liked to write with the
freedom of Fielding. The smugness and respectability of the
Victorian age jarred upon him; he chafed against a convention
which prevented him from dealing frankly with sex; and
because he felt that he was writing down to the public taste,
he affected to treat his novels as of minor consequence,
sneered at his fellow-writers, patronised his readers, and let
it be understood that he thought more of being a gentleman
than a genius. Gowan-Thackeray says of his art: 'Upon my
life I can't help betraying it wherever I go, though, by
Jupiter, I love and honour the craft with all my might.'

Such an attitude irritated Dickens, who was quite at home in his age, however much he criticised it; took his work with the utmost sincerity; thought it the most important thing in the world; was proud of his profession because he was proud of himself; and had more respect for talent than pedigree. Their characters were made manifest in the limp handshake of Thackeray, the hearty grip of Dickens.

Thackeray once admitted that he had never had a purpose in life or known what he was going to do before doing it. This lack of direction, added to a lack of conviction about anything and a feeling of being unfitted to his age, made him clumsy in his social relationships, and led to frequent misunderstandings. A few examples may be given. (1) At some social function in Paris he suggested to Macaulay that each should pass himself off as the other, Macaulay posing as the author of *Vanity Fair*, himself as the historian of England. Rather to his surprise Macaulay did not embrace the idea. (2) Forster was born and Dickens was married on the same day of the year, April 2nd. 'I wish you many happy returns of your birthday, Dickens of his marriage-day, and both of you of the day previous', wrote Thackeray to his very insecure friend Forster. (3) In reviewing a book by John Leech, Thackeray said 'Fancy a number of *Punch* without Leech's pictures! What would you give for it? The learned gentlemen who write the work must feel that, without him, it were as well left alone.' As he had been a member of the *Punch* staff, his old colleagues considered this extremely offensive. (4) The author promised to send Macready a copy of his *Vanity Fair*. It duly arrived containing an inscription to the actor's wife, upon which Macready wrote in his diary: 'Displeased with Thackeray's behaviour, which may have no purpose in it, though I think it has.' (5) Thackeray was very friendly with Henry Taylor and his wife. Taylor was a wealthy man who wrote what he believed to be poetry; and as he had frequently entertained Thackeray at his table, he was not much gratified by that satirist's sketch in *Punch*, wherein one Timotheus (i.e. Taylor) was described as meeting a very pretty girl and feeling for her 'that admiration which every man of taste experiences upon beholding her, and which, if Mrs. Timotheus had not been an exceedingly sensible person, would have caused a jealousy between her and the great bard her husband. But, charming and beautiful herself, Mrs.

Timotheus can even pardon another woman for being so; nay, with perfect good sense, though possibly with a *little* factitious enthusiasm, she professes to share to its fullest extent the admiration of the illustrious Timotheus for the young beauty.' Taylor and his friends knew perfectly well who Timotheus and the pretty girl were; Mrs. Taylor, not quite so sensible as she was made out to be, stamped with rage; and Thackeray, who had meant the article to be taken in 'the most good-humoured spirit' and was amazed when he heard that the Taylors were not splitting their sides with laughter, tendered an unqualified apology, which was accepted.

The effect on his friends of Thackeray's sense of fun may be likened to the effect on a man of his hat blowing off in the street: he is as furious as he feels foolish, but tries to pretend that he is enjoying the chase as much as the grinning spectators. The literary styles of Benjamin Disraeli, Charles Lever and Bulwer Lytton were all parodied by Thackeray in *Punch*; and though these writers did their best to appear amused, not one of them ever forgave him. Thackeray could not understand their sustained enmity. It is self-righteous and self-complacent to forgive trespasses against ourselves, but Thackeray had the rarer quality of forgiving those he had trespassed against. He was going on to give Boz a chance of being magnanimous by parodying his style; but the proprietors of *Punch*, Bradbury and Evans, drew the line at that, possibly with the assistance of Boz's ruler. In fact Dickens held strong views on the subject of these parodies, and at a later date informed Thackeray, through a friend, that 'they did no honour to literature or literary men, and should be left to very inferior and miserable hands.' Yet in retrospect there is something endearing about Thackeray's lack of prudence, the bungling and artlessness of his social contacts; and indeed he was a soft-hearted, gentle, affectionate, simple fellow, who was loved by his intimate friends and adored by his two daughters. Like so many men who are careless in their treatment of others, he was extremely sensitive where his own feelings were concerned, and his touchiness under provocation would have surprised him if displayed by those whom he had provoked. But his was a grateful nature; he never ceased to be thankful for his success, which always filled him with wonder; and his innate kindliness was such that he would give money to anyone who asked for it; in which respect he was different from Dickens, who would go to endless trouble for a friend or a cause, not sparing pains or labour, but distributed his cash with discrimination; whereas Thackeray would empty his pockets for a friend in need, but would grumble and procrastinate for hours, days and weeks, when asked to write a letter of introduction or do anything else that demanded effort and energy.

Between these two men there was always an element of reserve which might one day break into hostility. Their only suitable association was as host and guest, Dickens being a born host, Thackeray a born guest. But even here there were discrepancies, as at Macready's farewell banquet, when Dickens appeared in a blue dress-coat, faced with silk and adorned with brass buttons, a black satin vest, a white satin collar, and an elaborately embroidered shirt. 'Yes', said Thackeray to a neighbour, 'the beggar is beautiful as a butterfly, especially about the shirt front.' Normally they had no common ground. Dickens was a first-rate man of business; Thackeray hated business and was quite useless at it. Dickens was as energetic as Thackeray was lazy. Dickens coveted the plaudits of the poor, Thackeray of the rich. Dickens was too proud and self-reliant to care for the aristocratic society by which Thackeray loved to be petted and lionised. The companionship of women was an absolute necessity to Thackeray who was just as much a woman's man as Dickens was a man's man. This was doubtless due to their disparate childhoods, Thackeray having been an only son who was thoroughly spoilt by his mother, Dickens having been one of a large family whose mother was too busy to lavish affection on any of them. Even as clubmen they were totally unlike each other, Thackeray being a natural lounger, taking his ease in a bar, a library or a billiard room, chatting to anyone when so disposed, sleeping in an armchair when so inclined, or hiding behind a paper when in the mood; Dickens being a brisk visitor, who went to his club with a definite purpose, usually to keep an appointment; and in the atmosphere of club or hotel Thackeray worked at his best, while Dickens required complete silence and solitude. It was observed at the Garrick that if one of them entered a room where the other was talking or reading, the newcomer would look round as if searching for something he had mislaid or someone he wanted to see, and then go out. Clearly they were not comfortable together;

and their conversational interests were not the same, Thackeray liking to discuss literature and painting, and enjoying the scandal of the hour, Dickens preferring green-room gossip, or talk about crime and criminals, or the exchange of humorous stories.

With the success of *Vanity Fair* in 1847 a fresh element entered into their relationship, for which neither was responsible. Here, at last, said the clubmen and some of the critics, was a novel written for gentlemen by a gentleman; and two camps were formed in the literary world, one by the Thacke-rayites, the other by the Dickensites. Thus the victims of this word-war found themselves in a state of artificial antagonism, each being extolled by his admirers as the greatest novelist of the age. Thackeray, quite honestly, considered Dickens his superior in genius. Dickens, as honestly, did not care for the work of Thackeray. But because of the din set up by their followers, the unpleasant comparisons and false reports that flew from camp to camp, Dickens was irritated by the presence of a serious rival in popularity, and Thackeray believed that his success had embittered his fellow-scribe. Though Dickens could console himself with the knowledge that his works sold in tens of thousands against his competitor's thousands, Thackeray could comfort himself with the reflection that the world of taste acclaimed his superiority; but since the best-seller is always envious of the highbrow's prestige, and the highbrow is always envious of the best-seller's popularity, neither Dickens nor Thackeray experienced a rush of joy or affection at the thought or sight of the other.

The fancy quickly turns mole-hills into mountains, and Thackeray confided in his mother that he had been the favourite of the literary world before the success of *Vanity Fair*, after which he was detested or distrusted by Jerrold, Ainsworth, Forster, Bulwer and Dickens. 'It makes me very sad at heart though, this envy and meanness in the great sages and teachers of the world . . . I scarcely understand any motive for any action of my own or anybody else's.' But it was not only his success that made him disliked by his brother-artists; it was partly his incalculable behaviour, and still more his sudden assumptions of gentility. It was his queer humour to be a gentleman among artists, an artist among gentlemen, making each class feel slightly apologetic. 'I do not like to think of our confrères painting their faces and grinning in farces, for the sake of their oppressed brethren': such was his attitude to the performances for the Guild of Literature which Dickens had organised. Perhaps this vaunting of superior breeding was his reaction against the unparalleled reputation of Dickens, from which he sometimes suffered in bohemian society. In the winter of '52 he was asked to a shooting-party at Watford with Dickens, Leech, Jerrold, Lemon and others. Just as they were about to start a letter arrived from Dickens addressed to their hostess, to whom it was duly handed by Thackeray. After reading it, she rushed into the hall, and was heard calling to her cook: 'Martin, don't roast the ortolans; Mr. Dickens isn't coming.' Thackeray's comment was: 'I never felt so small. There's a test of popularity for you! No ortolans for Pendennis!'

The first rift in their relationship occurred in June '47, when the early numbers of *Vanity Fair* had become the talk of Mayfair, clubland and Fleet Street. The cause of the trouble was Forster, who informed the dramatist Tom Taylor that Thackeray was 'as false as hell.' Taylor, thinking this rather funny, passed it on to Thackeray who, not thinking it funny, cut Forster dead when next they met. Forster wrote to demand an explanation of Thackeray's 'marked discourtesy', and was supplied with it. Forster could not remember having used the expression, but implied that Thackeray had given him quite as much cause for offence in the past, of which he had taken no notice. Dickens then sailed in, and told a friend of Thackeray's that these misunderstandings arose from Thackeray's 'jesting much too lightly between what was true and what was false, and what he owed to both, and not being sufficiently steady to the former.' Upon reflection Thackeray concluded that his caricatures of Forster had been responsible for the explosion to which he had objected; and as he did not wish the penitent Tom Taylor to suffer, he asked Dickens to smooth things over. The result was a reconciliation banquet at Greenwich.

The next noteworthy passage between the two famous novelists occurred in January '48, when Thackeray wrote enthusiastically about *Dombey and Son*, and Dickens replied that he had been 'cut tender as it were to the very heart by your generous letter', and that 'I think there is nothing in the world or out of it to which I am so sensitive as the least mark of such a manly and gallant regard.' But as he went on to say that he hoped to improve the position of literary men in England, and to imply that Thackeray's parodies of eminent novelists had done the opposite—though he playfully remarked that an imitation of himself should not have been omitted from the series—and, as further, he stated his intention of 'saving up the perusal of *Vanity Fair* until I shall have done *Dombey*', his communication cannot have been wholly satisfying to its recipient. Their laudable attempt to love one another received a slight check in '49, when Thackeray was asked to the Royal Academy dinner and no invitation was issued to Dickens. The following year this error was rectified, but Dickens wrote a stiff note declining the honour. In March '55 Thackeray praised Dickens warmly in a lecture, describing him as 'a person commissioned by Divine Providence to correct and instruct his fellow-men.' Dickens read a report of the lecture in *The Times*, and wrote that he was 'profoundly touched by your generous reference to me. I do not know how to tell you what a glow it spread over my heart. Out of its fulness I do entreat you to believe that I shall never forget your words of commendation. If you could wholly know at once how you have moved me, and how you have animated me, you would be the happier I am very certain.' But only six months later Dickens was writing to Wills about Thackeray's 'distorted praise' of the Charter-House Charity, and suggesting that someone should do an article on the subject in *Household Words* and 'knock that destructive bit of sentiment in connection with the poor brothers slap over as with a rifle-shot.' His advice was followed, and the article appeared in December '55.

Outwardly, however, they remained friendly until June '58, when Edmund Yates, a young journalist who was a member of the Garrick Club, wrote a sketch of Thackeray in *Town Talk*, which included these phrases: 'His bearing is cold and uninviting, his style of conversation either openly cynical, or affectedly good-natured and benevolent; his *bonhomie* is forced, his wit biting, his pride easily touched . . . No one succeeds better than Thackeray in cutting his coat according to his cloth: here he flattered the aristocracy, but when he crossed the Atlantic, George Washington became the idol of his worship . . . Our own opinion is, that his success is on the wane . . .' Nowadays the object of such criticism would be solaced with heavy damages against the writer of the article, and the editor and printer of the magazine in which it appeared. In those days the best thing to be done was to ignore it. Thackeray did the worst thing: he discovered the name of the writer, to whom he had been very kind, and sent him an angry letter describing the statements as 'not offensive and unfriendly merely, but slanderous and untrue.' He also informed Yates that the talk overheard in a club was not for publication, and begged 'as I have a right to do, that you will refrain from printing comments upon my private conversation; that you will forego discussions, however blundering, on my private affairs; and that you will henceforth please to consider any question of my personal truth and sincerity as quite out of the province of your criticism.' Yates had been of service to Dickens in his recent domestic upheaval, and at once asked his advice, showing him the draft of a reply in which all the people whom Thackeray had ridiculed in his novels and articles were mentioned. Dickens said that Yates's sketch was indefensible, that Thackeray's letter made an apology impossible, but that Yates's suggested reply was too flippant and violent. Instead he proposed a different sort of answer, in which Thackeray's accusation was turned against himself: 'If your letter to me were not both "slanderous and untrue" I should readily have discussed its subject with you, and avowed my earnest and frank desire to set right anything I may have left wrong. Your letter being what it is, I have nothing to add to my present reply.' When Thackeray received this, he sent a copy of his own letter as well as Yates's reply to the committee of the Garrick Club, asking them to decide 'whether the complaints I have against Mr. Yates are not well founded, and whether the practice of publishing such articles as that which I enclose will not be fatal to the comfort of the Club, and is not intolerable in a Society of Gentlemen.'

The committee called a meeting at which Dickens told them that they had nothing whatever to do with a private quarrel between two members. The committee did not agree, and ordered Yates either 'to make an ample apology to Mr. Thackeray or to retire from the Club.' Thereupon Dickens informed the committee that 'I cannot take upon myself the very difficult and unsatisfactory functions which you understand to attach to your Body', and resigned from it. 'The Committee seems to me to have gone perfectly mad', he

wrote to a member. 'Like Fox, I should "boil with indignation" if I had not a vent. Upon my soul, when I picture them
in that back-yard, conceiving that they shake the earth, I fall
into fits of laughter which make my daughters laugh—away
at Gad's Hill—until the tears run down their cheeks . . . It is
amazing to me that so many men can be tools to such a wonderful small inquisition. But I conceive that such notoriety
makes the whole thing and the whole club absurd . . .' It
happened that the ninth number of Thackeray's novel *The
Virginians* was published on July 1st, in which there was a
reference to Yates as 'young Grubstreet, who corresponds
with three penny papers and describes the persons and conversation of gentlemen whom he meets at his "clubs".'
On reading this, Yates wrote to the Garrick committee
refusing to resign or apologise and appealing from their
opinion to a General Meeting of the Club. At the General
Meeting on July 10th a letter was read from Yates, who said
he was willing to apologise to the Club for any unpleasantness
he had caused, but not to Thackeray. By seventy votes to
forty-six the General Meeting endorsed the authority and
action of the committee, and Yates was warned that he would
be expelled from the Club if he did not apologise to Thackeray.
He remained impervious to threats, and the committee
removed his name from the list of members, one of whom
made the remark that 'Y's conduct has been very un-Y's.'

Yates then sought legal opinion and was advised that he
had a good case against the Club secretary; but before he
proceeded with it, Dickens made an appeal to Thackeray.
The two novelists had met on the steps of the Reform Club
in August and spoken to one another 'as if nothing had
happened'; so Dickens wrote to Thackeray in November
suggesting that a 'conference be held between me, as representing Mr. Yates, and an appointed friend of yours, as
representing you, with the hope and purpose of some quiet
accommodation of this deplorable matter, which will satisfy
the feelings of all concerned.' He admitted that Yates had
asked his advice in the first instance, that he had given it, and
that he had then supported Yates at the committee-meeting.
If the conference could not take place, he concluded, 'the thing
is at least no worse than it was, and you will burn this letter
and I will burn your answer.' The letter was more creditable
to Dickens's heart than to his head. Thackeray took it as

evidence of covert hostility, and replied: 'I grieve to gather from your letter that you were Mr. Yates's adviser in the dispute between me and him. His letter was the cause of my appeal to the Garrick Club for protection from insults against which I had no remedy.' He referred Dickens to the Club committee: 'It is for them to judge if any reconcilement is possible with your friend.' He then informed the committee of Dickens's request, and added that if they could devise any peaceful means of ending the dispute no one would be better pleased than himself. But the committee were not in a mood to climb down, and there followed a certain amount of legal pother, which resulted in a victory for them and the publication of a pamphlet by Yates.

To sum up. Everyone in this affair behaved foolishly: Yates for writing as he did about a man he met frequently at the Club, Thackeray for taking any notice of it, Dickens for not advising Yates to send a conciliatory reply, Thackeray for bringing the matter before the Club, and the committee of the Garrick for treating it with pomposity. A rational explanation is that Yates was youthful and pugnacious, Thackeray was in poor health, Dickens was undergoing mental strain, and the committee was suffering from the incurable infirmity of being a committee. It should be added that, although Dickens withdrew from the committee, he did not withdraw from the Club. He had already resigned from the Garrick twice, the first time because of the election of certain members to whom his friend Macready was hostile, the second time because of the election of Albert Smith, who had parodied him in a way he could not forget; and he was to leave the Club for the third time and finally in December '65 because his nominee Wills was blackballed.

The quarrel over Yates put an end to the rather neutral friendship between Dickens and Thackeray, and we may assume that they both felt relieved. Early in 1861 they met in the stalls of Drury Lane Theatre and shook hands but did not exchange a word. 'If he read my feelings on my face, as such a clever fellow would, he knows now that I have found him out', wrote Thackeray to a friend. But Thackeray's affectionate disposition brought about a reconciliation just before his death at the close of '63. He was talking with Sir Theodore Martin in the hall of the Athenaeum Club when Dickens emerged from a room where he had been reading the papers, passed close to them without a sign of recognition, and crossed the hall to the staircase which led to the library. Thackeray left Martin abruptly, reached Dickens just as his foot was on the first stair, and said: 'It is time this foolish estrangement should cease, and that we should be to each other what we used to be. Come! Shake hands.' Dickens was momentarily taken aback, but held out his hand, and a few friendly words passed between them, Thackeray saying that he had been in bed for three days and was now the victim of cold shivers which left him weak and unable to work, but he intended to try a new remedy which he laughingly described. He then returned to Martin and declared 'I love the man, and I could not resist the impulse.' A week later he died, and the proprietors of *The Cornhill Magazine*, which he had edited, asked Dickens to write an 'In Memoriam' article. 'I have done what I would most gladly have excused myself from doing, if I felt I could', Dickens told Wilkie Collins. Allowing for his reluctance, he did it very well, though he could not help adverting to the weakness he had exposed in Henry Gowan: 'I thought that he too much feigned a want of earnestness, and that he made a pretence of undervaluing his art, which was not good for the art he held in trust.'

While the Thackeray trouble had been fermenting Dickens was engaged in a graver and more personal contest with his publishers. His intimate friend Mark Lemon, who had acted for his wife in the negotiations leading to their separation, refused to publish his statement concerning the affair in *Punch*, which refusal was backed by the owners, Bradbury and Evans. In the inflamed mental condition caused by a shaky conscience, Dickens quarrelled with Lemon, Bradbury, Evans, and indeed everyone who adopted an impartial view, which he considered a partial view, of his family dispute, and not only ordered his children to have no further connection with them but expected his loyal friends to drop their acquaintance. Evans quite frankly sympathised with Kate, and was soon made to understand that his sympathy had been misplaced. 'I have had stern occasion to impress upon my children that their father's name is their best possession', Dickens wrote to him in July '58, 'and that it would indeed be trifled with and wasted by him, if, either through himself or through them, he held any terms with those who have been false to it, in the only great need and under the only great wrong it has ever known.

You know very well why (with hard distress of mind and bitter disappointment), I have been forced to include you in this class. I have no more to say.' So incensed was Dickens that more than three years after his domestic crisis, when his son Charley married the daughter of Evans, he wrote to his old friend Thomas Beard, who was Charley's godfather, saying that he quite understood Beard's desire to attend the wedding, 'but I must add the expression of my earnest hope that it is not your intention to enter Mr. Evans's house on that occasion.'

Naturally he could no longer work with people who thought that he had treated his wife unkindly; and as Bradbury and Evans refused to sell him their shares in *Household Words*, he lost no time in destroying that magazine and creating a new one in which he would control all the shares. By the simple process of announcing his intention to dissociate himself from *Household Words* and to start another weekly paper of a similar class, he depreciated the value of the former, and the partnership terminated with the filing of a bill in Chancery, followed by the sale of the property, which Dickens bought for £3350. He had some difficulty in finding a good title for the fresh venture, and staggered Forster by suggesting a Shakespearean phrase: *Household Harmony*. When Forster pointed out that recent events in the Dickens household did not exactly harmonise with the title, he was curt: 'I could not invent a story of any sort, it is quite plain, incapable of being twisted into some such nonsensical shape.' But he saw the point, and after considering a dozen other titles, including *Charles Dickens's Own*, he hit on something else in Shakespeare ('The story of our lives from year to year') and called it *All The Year Round*, the first number of which appeared on April 30th, 1859. The office was in Wellington Street, Strand, opposite the Lyceum Theatre and only a few doors from the one he had just vacated. Wills was his co-proprietor and sub-editor, and Wilkie Collins was on the staff until '63, when he resigned on account of ill-health, his three most popular novels being serialised in the paper: *The Woman in White* (1860), *No Name* (1862), and *The Moonstone* (1868).

As usual Dickens hurled himself, mind and body, into the business, and at the end of three months could report a phenomenal success: 'So well has *All The Year Round* gone that it was yesterday able to repay me, with five per cent interest, all the money I advanced for its establishment (paper, print, etc., all paid, down to the last number), and yet to leave a good £500 balance at the banker's!' This success was a good deal due to the story by himself which began with the first number of the new journal and continued weekly until November 26th of the same year. The opening of *A Tale of Two Cities* had given him trouble, and in February '59 he confessed that he could neither settle at it nor take to it; but as he was only just emerging from his domestic débâcle, and had been reading his works to large audiences all over the country, and was in the midst of the innumerable calls upon his time and patience inseparable from the founding, organisation and future of a weekly paper, there was some excuse for the congested state of his imagination. A further impediment was the arrival of two cartloads of books dealing with the French Revolution from Carlyle, to whom he had applied for a few authorities on the period. The difficulties of condensation for short-serial publication were considerable, and an attack of illness soon after the book began to appear did not promote fluency; but as the weeks went by the subject gripped him; he expressed himself as 'greatly moved and excited' by it; he thought the story the best he had written; and he longed to act the character of Sidney Carton. Although Carlyle did not like reading the tale in what he called 'teaspoons', he pronounced it wonderful. But that word can mean almost anything; and it is quite possible that he did not depart from his habit of praising a book heartily and then letting the unfortunate author down with a crash at the end of a sentence, which must have been extremely mortifying; as for example his comment on Dr. Robert Watson's History of Philip II and Philip III of Spain: 'An interesting, clear, well-arranged, and rather feeble-minded work.' A stagey and self-important barrister of the time named Edwin James, had he been able to recognise himself in the character of Stryver, would have been more explicit than Carlyle. Wanting a type that would contrast well with Carton, and wishing to study it at first hand, Dickens called on James with Yates and spent a few minutes in his chambers. 'Stryver is a good likeness', said Yates after the entrance of that character in the book. 'Not bad, I think, especially after only one sitting', agreed Dickens.

Simply as a story Dickens was right in thinking it the best he had written. Its popularity since his time has equalled, if not surpassed, that of *David Copperfield*; but this may be due to a generation's vogue of *The Only Way*, in which John Martin Harvey made the hit of his career, and which was the most successful stage-adaptation of any first-rate novel in the language. This fact is of cardinal importance when discussing the work in relation to its author. Some critics have asserted that it is his least characteristic story. But in one sense it may be considered his most characteristic story; for what was theatrical in the man is here turned into a purely theatrical piece. It was conceived while acting in a play, written around a 'star' part for himself, and developed in the form of melodrama. If any great actor had been capable of converting his dream of a perfect part with a perfect setting into reality, *A Tale of Two Cities* would have been the result. Against a seething background of violence and villainy, with tranquil interludes of domestic bliss, the debauched and cynical hero is suddenly ennobled by love; saves the life of the husband of the woman he worships; sacrifices his own life for the sake of their happiness; and lives transfigured in the sanctuary of their remembrance, the hero of their children, the inspiration of their children's children. Could an actor ask for more? 'I have so far verified what is done and suffered in these pages, as that I have certainly done and suffered it all myself', wrote Dickens, the only great actor in history who was also a great creative artist, and who could have played Sidney Carton on the stage as well as he visualised him in the story. Nothing is allowed to interfere with the dramatic march of the narrative, in which comic relief is provided, as in *Hamlet*, by a grave-digger, or more accurately a grave-redigger, Jerry Cruncher, who is subject to 'that peculiar kind of short cough, requiring the hollow of a hand before it, which is seldom, if ever, known to be an infirmity attendant on perfect openness of character.' We are perhaps better able in these days to appreciate one aspect of revolutionary movements than anyone of that time except Dickens, who contained within himself many elements of mob-emotion; for we have lived to see in the totalitarian countries innumerable examples of self-immolatory mass hysteria:

A species of fervour or intoxication, known, without doubt, to have led some persons to brave the guillotine unnecessarily, and to die by it, was not mere boastfulness, but a wild infection of the wildly shaken public mind. In seasons of pestilence, some of us will have a secret attraction to the disease—a terrible passing inclination to die of it. And all of us have wonders hidden in our breasts, only needing circumstances to evoke them.

Innocent people condemned to die by the revolutionary tribunal cried 'Vive la Republique!' just as in modern Germany and Russia they have blessed the rulers whose judges have sentenced them to death.

This vividly conceived and thrillingly written work was the direct outcome of Dickens's emotional life at a time when he had fallen in love, believed himself to be shamefully used and wrongfully abused by people who owed everything to him, experienced the open criticism and implied disapproval of many friends, and felt the loneliness of being generally misunderstood. As a defence against this seemingly hostile outer world, and to comfort his conscience, he dramatised himself both in fact and in fiction, saw himself as a much-wronged deeply-suffering but heroic soul, and produced a work the wide popularity of which shows how many much-wronged deeply-suffering but heroic souls there must be in the world.

This consolatory process was also highly satisfactory in a financial sense, for the sales of *All The Year Round* surpassed those of *Household Words*; and except for one period, shortly to be glanced at, the weekly circulation of the paper gradually increased, reaching about three hundred thousand copies within ten years of its first number. Besides the novels of Wilkie Collins already mentioned, readers were given *Hard Cash* by Charles Reade and *A Strange Story* by Bulwer Lytton, while Dickens himself contributed one more work of fiction, a number of Christmas stories, and a series of papers eventually published in a book called *The Uncommercial Traveller*, which was probably more remunerative than the earnings of any commercial traveller on his lawful occasions. These papers dealt with all sorts of subjects, and some of them might have been entitled 'A Cure of Insomnia', for they describe his night-walks in town and country when he could not get to sleep. 'I am both a town-traveller and a country-traveller, and am always on the road', he introduced himself to the reader. 'Figuratively speaking, I travel for the great house of Human Interest Brothers, and have rather a large connection in the fancy goods way.' Theatres, workhouses, shipwrecks, tramps, churches, dockyards, boiled beef, public houses: whatever he found interesting in his journeys he tried to make interesting to his readers, and certainly succeeded, for his articles became a very popular feature of the magazine.

Most periodicals have ups and downs, but *All The Year Round* went steadily up, experiencing but one downward tendency in its founder's lifetime. This was when Charles Lever's story *A Day's Ride* appeared as a serial, from August 1860 onwards. Lever and Dickens had for years been on friendly terms, though, as in the case of Harrison Ainsworth, Dickens was the admiring ingenuous spirit, while Lever was privately saying unpleasant things about the 'fast writing and careless composition' of such works as *Dombey and Son*, the 'low verbiage and coarse pictures of unreality' which made Dickens so popular. Lever hoped that his own writings would correct the bad taste that found the works of his famous contemporary so delectable. 'I have suffered—I am suffering —from the endeavour to supply a healthier, more manly and more English sustenance', Lever told a friend; 'but it may be, before I succeed—if I do succeed at all—the hand will be cold and the heart still, and that I may only be a pioneer to clear the way for the breaching party.' There is a curious sequel to this. Soon after the serialisation of *A Day's Ride* in *All The Year Round* a small boy in Dublin named Bernard Shaw read bits of it in odd numbers; and it made such a deep impression on him that when, a generation later, he wrote plays dealing with 'the tragi-comic irony of the conflict between real life and the imagination', and the critics accused him of being influenced by Ibsen, he retorted that his viewpoint directly derived from reading Lever's novel, the hero of which, Potts, he pronounced to be 'a piece of really scientific natural history as distinguished from comic story telling. His author is not throwing a stone at a creature of another and inferior order, but making a confession, with the effect that the stone hits everybody full in the conscience and causes their self-esteem to smart very sorely.'

The self-esteem of the readers of *All The Year Round* smarted so sorely that Dickens was in an editorial quandary. Lever's novel followed Collins's *The Woman in White*, which had made a sensation, and Dickens, who had published several of Lever's articles and thought highly of his fictional work, was faced for the only time in his life with a serious decline in sales. What complicated the situation was that he had welcomed the prospect of serialising *A Day's Ride* with enthusiasm, had told its author that 'I have never had to do with a more frank, more genial, more kind and considerate friend than I have found in you', had sent the encouraging message, 'Do not be afraid to trust the audience with anything that is good: though a very large one, it is a fine one', and had even praised the opening chapters, which he thought 'full of life, vivacity, originality and humour . . . You have opened an excellent vein, as it seems to me, and have a rich working before you.' In October '60 he was forced to break the news that 'we drop, rapidly and continuously with *A Day's Ride*. Whether it is too detached and discursive in its interest for the audience and the form of publication, I cannot positively say; but it does not *take hold.*' He informed Lever that the subscribers were complaining, and the one hope of saving the situation was the early commencement of a story by himself. He begged Lever not to take it to heart, as the same thing might have happened to anyone: 'But I set such a value on your friendship, and have such a high sense of your genero-sity and delicacy, that I hate to write—dread to write—can't write—this letter!' Lever, like his hero Potts, was deeply hurt in his self-esteem, and Dickens had to write a lengthy explanation, in which he reaffirmed his high opinion of *A Day's Ride* and assured the author that its failure as a serial did not detract from its merit as a novel: 'I beg and pray you not to do yourself and me so great a wrong as to think of our connection as having been a "misfortune" to me.' As to winding up the story, he said, the author must please himself: it could run concurrently with Dickens's new novel. 'Now do take heart of grace and cheer up', was the advice of Lever's 'faithful and affectionate friend.' Few authors, after that, would have taken heart of grace and cheered up sufficiently to spin their stories out. Lever was not one of them: he pulled up, dismounted, and cut short *A Day's Ride*.

Dickens persuaded his publishers to bring it out in volume form; and thereafter for several years went out of his way to serve Lever, influencing Chapman and Hall to do his novels, arranging that they should be properly advertised, urging his claims, encouraging him, going to no end of trouble for him, and acting with far more zeal than has ever been displayed by a literary agent on a percentage basis. Articles by Lever continued to appear in *All The Year Round*, and Dickens paid for them on acceptance. Whether Lever appreciated such help at its true worth, we do not know, but in 1862 he dedicated a novel to Dickens in these terms: 'Among the thousands who read and re-read your writings, you have not one who more warmly admires your genius than myself'; and three years later he shared a friend's opinion of *Our Mutual Friend* with equal emphasis: 'It is very disagreeable reading, and the characters are more or less repugnant and repelling.' Apparently his feelings were a bit mixed.

# 18

## CLASSIC GROUND

SHAKESPEARE started life as an actor and developed into a writer. Dickens started life as a writer and developed into an actor. From this we can see why Shakespeare's characters are the deeper, Dickens's the more sparkling, of the two. We feel that Shakespeare's creations have lives of their own apart from their surroundings and the external circumstances of the dramas in which they appear, while Dickens's are only alive while exhibiting themselves in the settings he gives them. No writer in English is so brilliant as Dickens, who resembles a catherine wheel, sometimes sticking and spluttering, but mostly blazing away and throwing off showers of sparks, which vanish in isolation. He must have felt this dimly when he came to read his works in public, because he cut out the descriptions of his characters and differentiated them by his histrionic skill.

There never was and there never will be again such an amazing series of public exhibitions as these readings by Dickens. It would no doubt have been more thrilling to see Shakespeare act a leading part in one of his own dramas or to watch Beethoven conducting one of his own symphonies; but Dickens's achievement was unique, and Shakespeare would have had to act every part in his drama, Beethoven to play every instrument in his orchestra, to make a comparison possible. 'I had no conception, before hearing Dickens read, of what capacities lie in the human face and voice', said Carlyle. 'No theatre-stage could have had more players than seemed to flit about his face, and all tones were present. There was no need of any orchestra.' But Carlyle always adulterated his praise with the pretentious humbug of a prophet, and made it clear that he was superior to mummery: 'Dickens does do it capitally, such as *it* is, acts better than any Macready in the world; a whole tragic comic heroic *theatre* visible, performing under one *hat*, and keeping us laughing—in a sorry way some of us thought—the whole night.'

Dickens read his works throughout England, Scotland and

Ireland, in 1858–9, from 1861 to 1863, in 1866–7, and from 1868 to 1870. His manager, Arthur Smith, died before the second series of readings came to an end; his successor was a failure; and the third and fourth series were in the hands of George Dolby, acting for Chappell & Co., who made all the arrangements and profits. Dickens aroused as much enthusiasm by these performances as a popular politician could evoke by oratory in the days when politicians and oratory were popular; and he made as much money as a 'star' actor in the days when the theatrical firmament was not a Milky-Way. In the larger towns many thousands who came to hear him were turned away for lack of room. His appearance on the platform was greeted with thunderous applause, which he ignored, and at the end of a reading the audience often rose to its feet and went on cheering until he had changed his clothes and left the building. Crowds waited for him on the chance of touching his hand or coat, and women scrambled for any petals from the geraniums in his buttonhole which a dramatic gesture might have dislodged. Sometimes, but not often, he acknowledged the tumultuous acclamations by returning to the platform and making a short speech. To say that he enjoyed the reading as much as his hearers is an understatement. He revelled in it; he was transported into a world of his own; he was in his true element. 'It is a great sensation to have an audience in one's hand', he declared, and it was a sensation that never palled: it grew by what it fed on. He had in fact achieved the ambition of all born actors: for he was playing every part in a series of dramas devised entirely by himself, cutting what he did not want, adding what he did, producing himself, watching the effect of new methods on the audience, changing his readings of the various characters, protracting the pathos, strengthening the note of heroism, 'gagging' to his heart's content, and magnetising his hearers into any state of mind or mood that happened to suit his own. As time went on he increased his repertoire and learnt all the scenes by heart, so that he was independent of the book. He rehearsed himself continually, and after one trial reading to a few friends, including Browning, Fechter, Collins and Forster, he said: 'There! If I have gone through that already to myself once, I have gone through it *two—hundred—times!*' He strove for perfection; corrected his utterance of certain words by repeating them constantly to himself; went through each scene in his study again and again with as much pains as he gave to the public rendering; and was not satisfied until he had made himself master of every episode and had exhausted every means of reproducing the humour and pathos and oddity of his characters. 'I have never read to an audience but I have watched for an opportunity of striking out something better somewhere', he said in 1868, after he had been at it professionally for ten years.

He was the exception to the general rule that when an actor is not nervous he cannot rise to the heights of his art. Dickens was unusually self-possessed as an executant, whatever he may have been as a creator, and had complete control of his nervous organism as actor, speaker and reader. His command over himself and others was frequently put to the test. During a performance of Lytton's comedy in London the drapery on the stage caught fire, and the audience rushed towards the only means of exit. Dickens, who was acting at the time, walked straight to the footlights and said in a tone of authority, 'Sit down, every one of you!' The five hundred fashionable spectators were more scared by him than by the fire, and obeyed instantly; then he ordered others to deal with the blaze while he went on with his scene. He prevented another panic when reading at Newcastle-on-Tyne. In the middle of a quiet scene from *Nicholas Nickleby*, describing the death of Smike, a gas batten fell with a crash. There were three great galleries crammed with people; a single steep flight of stairs led up to them; and a stampede would have resulted in many deaths. A woman in the front row of the stalls screamed and ran towards Dickens, who, seeing that she was in view of the whole audience, addressed her laughingly, as if the accident were of nightly occurrence: 'There's nothing the matter, I assure you; don't be alarmed; pray sit down.' She did so, and the house rang with applause. But there was serious danger of a general conflagration; and the men who re-erected the batten were so nervous that they shook the boards on which Dickens was standing, nonchalantly looking on with his hands in his pockets. The gasman, describing the scene to his friends, said: 'There stood the master, as cool as ever I see him a-lounging at a railway-station . . . The more you want of the master, the more you'll find in him.' Again, at Birmingham, he showed the utmost unconcern when an escape of gas from the top batten 'caught the copper-wire and was within a thread of bringing down the heavy reflector into the stalls.' The audience was unaware of the danger, and Dickens calculated that he could just finish the reading in time to save the situation by turning off the gas. He did; but it was touch-and-go; and no one could have told from his manner that he was taking a terrible risk.

Whether dealing with mayoral committees or mob hostility he was never ruffled and always got his own way. At Berwick-on-Tweed he found that an immense Corn Exchange constructed of glass and iron had been reserved for him. As he made a point of testing the acoustics of every hall before reading in it, and correcting echoes by means of carpets and curtains, he soon discovered that this one was a veritable sounding-board for echoes, and flatly declined to appear in it, saying that he would not read at all unless he could do so in a pleasant room attached to the hotel which only held five hundred people. 'Terrified local agents glowered, but fell prostrate', and hundreds of people who had taken tickets were disappointed. Shortly after this he had to quell a minor revolution in Edinburgh. The local agents had made some error, and crowds of people could not get into the hall. The place was packed to suffocation within five minutes of the doors being opened, and a mob of angry ticket-holders were still trying to force their way in. Dickens appeared on the platform, and had a mixed reception. When his manner indicated that he would stand no nonsense from the noisy part of the audience, he obtained silence and then informed them that the over-issue of tickets was the fault of their own townsmen, but that he would do his best to set it right, and would either adjourn to the Music Hall, where there was room for everybody, or alter his arrangements, return later, 'and read to all Edinburgh.' There were loud cheers and many cries of 'Go on, Mr. Dickens. Everybody will be quiet now', etc. But there were counter-cries of 'We *won't* be quiet. We won't let the reading be heard. We're ill-treated', and so on. Upon which Dickens said 'There's plenty of time, and you may rely upon it that the reading is in no danger of being heard until we are agreed.' He then shut his book and smilingly surveyed the scene while the ill-treated members of the audience were being thrown out by those who wanted to hear the reading. Silence restored, he reopened his book and was about to commence when he was asked whether a

number of ladies who had been crushed in the recent proceedings would be allowed on the platform. 'Most certainly',
said he. In a minute the platform swarmed with women, and
a cry went up from the people sitting at the sides of the hall
that they could not see the reader, who at once proposed that
the ladies should sit or lie down; which they did. 'I don't
know what it looked like most—a battlefield—an impossible
tableau—a gigantic picnic', reported Dickens. 'There was
one very pretty girl in full dress lying down on her side all
night, and holding on to one leg of my table.' The evening
ended with 'a great burst of cheering.'

He took his own staff and equipment wherever he went,
but he always superintended the fitting of the screen and the
erection of the gas battens, and he personally supervised the
copper gas-tubes to make sure that they were safe. The sides
of the stage or platform on which he read were curtained off.
At his back was a screen of maroon-coloured cloth. In front
of him was a table covered with velvet of a lighter shade than
the screen. On the table was a reading-desk, and to left and
right of the table were projecting ledges, one for a water-
bottle and glass, the other for his gloves and pocket handkerchief. About twelve feet above the platform, in advance of
the table, was a row of gas-jets with a tin reflector; side-lights
and footlights, also with reflectors, made his face and figure
absolutely distinct to the audience, the light being equally
strong from every angle.

The moment he stepped on to the platform, walking rather
stiffly, right shoulder well forward as his habit was, bud in
buttonhole, gloves in hand, there was such a roar of cheering
that people wondered how he could remain unmoved by it.
Sometimes the outburst was so whole-hearted and emotional
that he was affected; but he never showed it, and always appeared to treat these demonstrations as if they were no concern of his. Then the extraordinary performance began.
With the opening words a hush fell upon the audience, which,
except for the interjectional laughter and applause, remained
throughout in a condition of rapt suspense. 'Marley was
dead, to begin with. There is no doubt whatever about that.'
The words had the effect of a trumpet blast. But, whatever
the story, the reader held his hearers with a power that can
only be called hypnotic. Occasionally the effect he produced
was too considerable to leave him untouched, and he had

great difficulty in keeping a straight face during the laughter or a steady voice during the sobs; but usually he had as strict a command over himself as over his audience.

Even from the beginning, before he had learnt all his scenes by heart, his performance could never properly be described as a reading, or himself as a reader. It was a highly theatrical representation by an actor who could impersonate any number of totally different characters and sink his own personality in each. He seemed to undergo physical transformation as he passed from one character to another, his voice, features, expression and mannerisms changing completely in a flash. He had a score of voices, male, female, old, young, middle-aged, cockney, yokel, military, naval, medical, clerical, forensic, aristocratic; and he had a score of faces, from the jolly cherubic countenance of a school-boy to the wizened avaricious features of a Scrooge. His voice was naturally rich and deep, capable of every tone and half-tone, of quiet pathos, boisterous humour, martial ardour. But in addition to his vocal variety and his mimetic genius, there was in him beyond doubt a magnetic or mesmeric quality which enabled him to hold an audience, to play on its emotions, to make it laugh, cry, cheer, applaud, at his behest. Though it is blasphemy against the holy spirit of man to mention two diseased and murderous imbeciles in the same sentence with a great artist, Napoleon and Hitler had the same sort of power over people as was possessed by Dickens, who could cure illness by its exercise.

It was noted how, by the mere action of his fingers drumming on the table, he conveyed the whole spirit and humour of the dance at the Fezziwig party; how, by simply stooping down and taking an imaginary hand in his and speaking gently, he suggested Bob Cratchit's desolation over the death of Tiny Tim; how, in the *Pickwick* trial, he contrived to keep Mr. Justice Stareleigh present throughout the proceedings by sudden snorts and convulsive starts; how Mrs. Gamp came alive in a sentence before she came on the scene, her voice being reminiscent of someone trying to sing through a comb covered with tissue-paper; how little Paul Dombey spoke in a boy's alto, and how his physical exhaustion was that of a child; how, in the scene between Fanny Squeers and Nicholas Nickleby, one side of the actor's face was Fanny, the other side Nicholas; how monstrous he looked as Squeers, how murderous as Jonas Chuzzlewit; and how his sole failure was Sam Weller. The reason why he failed as Sam was probably due to his own rise in the world; for he had created Sam as his master's master, but now saw him as his master's servant, and the contradiction disturbed the impersonation.

His own favourite reading was from *David Copperfield*. It interested him far more than the rest, and he said that he was half-ashamed to confess what a tenderness he had for it. He worked at it for weeks before satisfying himself that he had done all he could to make a coherent story, chiefly from the Steerforth part of the book, and tried it out in the provinces before risking it in London. The audiences were completely bowled over by it, laughing and weeping unrestrainedly; and after Dickens had finished reading his account of the great storm at Yarmouth, there were scenes of frantic enthusiasm. Macready went to hear it at Cheltenham, where he had re-married and retired, and his friend stayed with him. Arriving at his house after the reading, Dickens found him unable to speak, unable to do anything but roll his eyes and square his jaw all on one side. To relieve the tension Dickens said something light about the occasion, but Macready brushed it aside and began with difficulty to halt through a number of sentences, which, owing to the obstruction of parentheses, were never allowed to issue freely. 'No—er—Dickens! I swear to heaven that, as a piece of passion and playfulness—er—indescribably mixed up together, it does—er—no, really, Dickens!—amaze me as profoundly as it moves me. But as a piece of art—and you know—er—that I—no, Dickens!—By God, have seen the best art in a great time—it is incomprehensible to me. How is it got at—er—how is it done—er—how one man can—well? It lays me on my—er—back, and it is of no use talking about it!' After which Macready pulled out his pocket handkerchief and placed his hand on the breast of Dickens, who 'felt as if I were doing somebody to his Werner.' No higher tribute could have been paid to Dickens as an actor, for Macready had played with Edmund Kean, had seen Siddons and the Kembles, and held no mean opinion of his own abilities. The breath-taking performance he had just witnessed made Macready realise that he was a back-number; but Dickens was not the man to let another feel dispirited, and, 'seizing an umbrella when he had the audacity to tell me he was growing old, made at him with Macduff's defiance. Upon which he fell into the old fierce guard, with the desperation of 30 years ago.' The success of the *Copperfield* reading was repeated in London. 'It even went beyond my hopes', said Dickens, who was exhausted after the strain and semi-stupified by what can only be described as a passionate outburst of affection for the writer and admiration for the actor which rewarded the performance.

When on tour he very rarely stayed with friends or acquaintances, and hardly ever attended banquets. He felt it his duty to keep fit, to concentrate on his work, to shut himself off from society. So when the Lord Lieutenant of Ireland asked him to a grand dinner in his honour at Dublin Castle, he declined the invitation; and when the Bishop of Gloucester asked him to stay at the Palace while he was reading in the neighbourhood, he begged to be excused. His life was one perpetual rush from station to hotel, from hotel to hall, from hall to station. Many hours of the day and night were spent in railway trains, when he would pass the time chatting to his manager, and usually keeping him in fits of laughter. He lived abstemiously, his only indulgence being a dozen oysters and a glass or two of champagne in the intervals of his readings; and when Wilkie Collins accused him of having love-affairs, on account of his giving addresses which were not those of leading hotels, he replied that the mysterious addresses had been sent before his manager had discovered the names of the best hotels: 'As to that furtive and Don Giovanni purpose at which you hint, that may be all very well for *your* violent vigour, or that of the companions with whom you may have travelled continentally, or the Caliph Haroun Alraschid with whom you have unbent metropolitanly; but anchorites who read themselves red hot every night are chaste as Diana (if I suppose *she* was by the bye, but I find I don't quite believe it when I write her name).' It was well that he kept himself in good condition, for he never knew when calls might be made upon his reserve of power. Once at Birmingham, for instance, he read before 2100 people and made an absurd mistake. *Nickleby* was the concluding item on his own list, but after he had read it and the applause had died down the audience remained seated. Informed that he had been advertised to conclude the evening with the trial from *Pickwick*, he returned to the stage at ten o'clock, explained that he had done *Nickleby* by mistake, but said that if they liked he would still give them the trial. 'They *did* like, and I had another half-hour of it in that enormous place.'

All his spare time from 1860 was spent at Gad's Hill Place, which became his permanent home in the autumn of that year, when he abandoned Tavistock House and moved most of the furniture therein to Gad's Hill, leaving enough to fit up a few rooms in Wellington Street, over the office of *All The Year Round*, where he could stay when in London and where there was always a spare bedroom for one of his daughters or his sister-in-law. Although he was busy writing a new novel to save his magazine from the effect of Lever's acidity, he found time to select and allocate to each room at Gad's Hill every piece of furniture in Tavistock House, remembering the least item, even to the knick-knacks. This eye for detail made him too exigent both as parent and employer. Each of his boys had a particular peg for his coat and hat; each had a particular job assigned to him, such as collecting stumps, mallets, bats, balls, after playing games, and putting them away; all the boys were paraded from time to time and carefully inspected for the presence of stains on their clothing; and their rooms were visited every morning in case the chairs were out of place or the blinds were not straight or anything was left lying on the floor. Equally the gardens and stables and kennels were not neglected, and every morning he would see that they were in good order and condition. His tidiness in all matters was excessive; he paid the closest attention to his personal appearance; he would even go indoors to brush his hair when it had been ruffled by the wind; and mirrors were on almost every wall of every room in the house for the use of those who felt as he did. His daughters did not escape his vigilance, and he would sometimes leave written remonstrances on their pin-cushions. Punctuality, a virtue in that it expresses consideration for others, became with him almost a vice, and no excuse was accepted for lateness at meals or appointments. He disliked hearing his daughters using loose modern phrases, and checked them when they said that something was *awfully* nice or *awfully* pretty.

The elder daughter, Mamie, was his housekeeper at Gad's Hill, and he explained how she must be methodical and economical, looking closely and systematically into every sort of expenditure, and making it clear to the servants that excesses of any kind would not do. Mamie worshipped her

19

father, never saw her mother again after the separation, and declined an offer of marriage because her father did not approve of the match. She delegated certain household duties to her aunt Georgina, and certain other duties to her sister Katie, who however did not share her view of the parental dispute, thought Aunt Georgina was 'not quite straight', and even went to see her mother, an action which father regarded as a reproach to himself. In fact Katie was miserable at home and made up her mind to leave it with as little delay as possible. Charles Collins, brother of Wilkie, asked her to marry him. She did not love him, but the prospect of life with him was more pleasing than the prospect of continued life with father, and so, against her male parent's advice, she accepted him. Very nearly the entire population of the neighbouring countryside turned up for the wedding, which took place in July '60. Triumphal arches were erected; the churchyard was strewn with flowers; and a salute of guns came from the smithy. A number of friends travelled down from London by a special train, arriving just in time for the service. 'They didn't know whether they were to look melancholy, beaming, or maudlin', said Dickens; 'and their uncertainty struck me as so uncommonly droll, that I was obliged to hide my reverend parental countenance in my hand on the altar railing.' As witness to the marriage, Dickens described himself as 'literary gentleman', a curious connotation; but he was in a strange mental state that day, for at the feast which followed the ceremony his manner was heated; and when the guests had gone away Mamie found him in Katie's bedroom, his head buried in one of her gowns, on his knees, sobbing. 'But for me Katie would not have left home', he said brokenly, and went out. Katie was very fond of her father, but she sympathised with her mother; and when as an old woman she called her father a wicked man, she meant that he was a wilful man who went his way regardless of another's feelings. Shakespeare, as usual, says all that is necessary on this theme:

> But when we in our viciousness grow hard—
> O misery on't!—the wise gods seel our eyes;
> In our own filth drop our clear judgments; make us
> Adore our errors; laugh at's while we strut
> To our confusion.

A few weeks later Dickens was possessed by a desire to obliterate the past, to cut himself off from his early self, to start a fresh page in the book of life as if a new volume had just been opened and he could begin once more at a different place. This was not how he put it to himself, his own reason for the great bonfire at Gad's Hill being that he disapproved of the publication of confidential letters, which were written for one person's eyes and were of a strictly private nature. On September 3rd, 1860, he took all his private papers and correspondence into a field by his house and burnt the lot: 'As it was an exquisite day when I began, and rained very heavily when I finished, I suspect my correspondence of having overcast the face of the Heavens.' For the rest of his life he destroyed every non-business letter immediately he had dealt with it. In this way many communications from Carlyle, Thackeray, Tennyson, Browning, Wilkie Collins and other notable contemporaries disappeared in smoke, and when the last batch had been added to the flames he said: 'Would to God every letter I had ever written was on that pile!'; a sentiment his biographer is unable to echo, for his letters show, among other things, that he was a most affectionate friend and as good a father as he had been a son.

True though it is that the children of his brain meant more to him than the children of his body, it is equally true that he was as considerate to the latter as any father who could not boast of the former. His wife once said that he loved babies, liking them to be as *new* as possible; and he was certainly a child-devotee. We have a pleasant picture of him walking behind a labouring man whose small boy was slung over his shoulder, and feeding the lad with cherries surreptitiously. But when his own children reached the schoolboy stage of development, they came into conflict with the offspring of his imagination, for the birth of whom he required as much attention and seclusion as any woman labouring with child; and so we find him complaining, in the Christmas holidays of '62, that 'the house is pervaded by boys; and every boy has (as usual) an unaccountable and awful power of producing himself in every part of the house at every moment, apparently in fourteen pairs of creaking boots.' It was a little difficult to reconcile the needs of the large family that rushed about his house with the claims of the larger family that rioted in his fancy; and when the time came for the real boys to choose a profession, he discovered that he had 'brought up the largest family ever known with the smallest disposition to do anything for themselves.' Some of them wrote and printed a paper for domestic consumption which they called *The Gad's Hill Gazette*. It dealt almost exclusively with matters of interest to themselves, though announcements of the arrival home of pater-familias from a reading tour would have engaged the attention of the outside world. Dickens read the *Gazette* with interest, but did not feel that the contributors were journalists of genius; and as he knew too well the trials and vexations of an author's life, not to mention the likelihood of poverty for the majority of those who embraced literature as a profession, he usually discouraged his sons from following in his footsteps.

The eldest boy, Charley, entered the firm of Baring's, went bankrupt, was rescued by his father, and eventually took Wills's place on *All The Year Round*, inheriting the paper on the death of Dickens. The second boy, Walter, became a cadet in the East India Company's service, saw something of the Indian Mutiny, and died at Calcutta in '63. The third, Francis, wanted to be a doctor, then to be a gentleman-farmer, then again to be a doctor. Dickens gave him plenty of time to think it over; but finding that he could not reach a decision, put him into business, which he disliked, and at last took him into the office of *All The Year Round* and entered him for the Bar; but he showed no inclination for law or journalism. Eventually the boy expressed a desire to join the Bengal Mounted Police, and his father helped him into that. The fourth son, Alfred, wished to join the army and was trained for the artillery. But he changed his mind, showed an interest in business, and Dickens got him a job in the City. This did not satisfy him; he began to pine for the wide open spaces; and his father consented to his departure for Australia, leaving him free to do as he liked and to return home if Australia did not suit him. But he wrote that he was 'as happy as a King' and remained there. The fifth boy, Sydney, showed an early preference for the navy, and had such exceptional energy and purpose that Dickens wrote to his headmaster: 'If I supposed him to be quite in earnest and to have made up his small mind, I would give him his way, because I really believe he would then follow it out with spirit.' Sydney was both happy and popular in the navy. The sixth son, Henry, was perhaps the brainiest of the bunch; he did well at Cambridge, where he won two scholarships, and had a distinguished career at the Bar. A story he told reveals the curious combination of steely self-control and fluid emotionalism which was the essence of Dickens's nature. At the close of Henry's first three terms at Trinity Hall he won the best mathematical scholarship of the year, and in a state of suppressed excitement broke the news to his father, whom he met at Higham, the station for Gad's Hill. 'Capital! capital!' said Dickens, and left it at that. Henry was acutely disappointed, and they started to walk home in silence. But half-way up the road to Gad's Hill his father suddenly turned to Henry with tears in his eyes, gave his hand a grip which the youth felt for some time, and said 'God bless you, my boy, God bless you!' The seventh and youngest boy, Edward (always known as Plorn), was not comfortable at his first school; so Dickens went to much trouble to find him another more agreeable to his temperament. He was a shy boy of an amiable disposition, but though a general favourite he was not spoiled, 'for we are too fond of children here to make them disagreeable', remarked his father. He suffered from a 'want of application and continuity of purpose' and was quite incapable of doing anything if left to himself. When he asked if he might leave his second school and try another, Dickens said that he was at liberty to do so but advised him against it. He showed no aptitude for any career, but 'as he is fond of animals, and of being on horseback, and of moving rapidly through the air, I hope he may take better to the Bush than to Books', said his father, who felt he would be happier with his brother in Australia than trying to do something uncongenial at home for which he was totally unfitted; so after a brief period at the Agricultural College, Cirencester, he left for the Antipodes. But it was a painful wrench for Dickens, who broke down and wept unashamedly when seeing Plorn off at Paddington Station.

From the time that Dickens made Gad's Hill Place his real home he took a greater interest in it than in any of his London houses. He was always conscious of the fact that it stood on classic ground, and the first thing he did was to frame and place a plaque on a wall indoors, bearing the words: 'This house, Gad's Hill Place, stands on the summit of Shakespeare's Gadshill, ever memorable for its association with Sir John Falstaff in his noble fancy. *But, my lads, my lads, tomorrow morning, by four o'clock, early at Gadshill! there are pilgrims going to Canterbury with rich offerings, and traders riding to London with*

*fat purses: I have vizards for you all: you have horses for yourselves.'*
It thrilled him to think that 'Falstaff ran away from the
identical spot of ground now covered by the room in which
I write', and he mentioned the fact in several of his letters,
calling Falstaff the merriest and wittiest creature that never
lived. But he was anxious to associate himself with the district
where his happiest days had been spent, to increase the area
of classic ground, and in September '60 he announced that he
was 'on the restless eve of beginning a new big book.' At
first he intended to publish it in the usual twenty monthly
numbers, but the failure of Lever's novel made him alter his
plans, and he decided to restore the circulation of *All The
Year Round* by serialising his story in that journal, which
meant that it would have to be curtailed and set forth in
shorter chapters. As it was to be written in the first person,
he re-read *David Copperfield* to guard against repeating himself
unconsciously. The first instalment of *Great Expectations*
appeared in *All The Year Round* on December 1st, 1860, the
last on August 3rd, 1861; and before it had been running a
month the sales of the paper shot up to the pre-Lever level,
surpassed that in the months ahead, and thenceforth never
seriously declined while Dickens was alive to keep them
steady. 'This journal is doing gloriously, and *Great Expectations* is a great success', he reported in February '61, when for
the sake of his daughters he took No. 3 Hanover Terrace,
Regent's Park, for three months, continuing his novel there
until May, after which, to recover from an attack of neuralgia,
he went alone to the Lord Warden Hotel, Dover, where he
worked and walked and enjoyed the solitude. One May day
he went over the cliffs to Folkestone and back, the weather
being 'so exquisitely beautiful that, though I was alone, I
could not keep silence on the subject.' That he was in good
spirits at Dover is shown by a parody of Dr. Johnson's talk
which he inserted in a letter and which included a pregnant
observation on himself:

Johnson: Again, sir, there is Dickens, with a facile way with
him—like Davy, sir, like Davy—yet I am told that
the man is lying at a hedge ale-house by the seashore
in Kent, as long as they will trust him.

Boswell: But there are no hedges by the sea in Kent, sir.

Johnson: And why not, sir?

Boswell:   (*at a loss*) I don't know, sir, unless——
Johnson:   (*thundering*) Let us have no unlesses, sir. If your father had never said 'unless', he would never have begotten you, sir.
Boswell:   (*yielding*) Sir, that is very true.

*Great Expectations* has been overpraised in relation to Dickens's other novels, perhaps because it is shorter than most, possibly because it is less complicated than most. But the strange thing is that the more natural Dickens tries to be as a story-teller, the less natural, in a Dickensian sense, are his characters. When he recreates his own world, we surrender to his genius, accept his characters as lifelike and even believe in his weird backgrounds. But when he attempts to write a plain unvarnished tale, and to trace the psychological development of a human being, we begin to criticise the result just as we would a story by any naturalistic writer without his genius. We recognise Pumblechook at once as a living figure from the great Dickens dreamland; but we reject Magwitch, the convict turned philanthropist, and Pip, the blacksmith turned gentleman, because they are neither Dickensian nor true to nature. To picture his imaginative universe Dickens had to have enough room in which to spread himself, to perform the magic of his distillation. When his fictions were carefully abbreviated, some of the peculiarly Dickensian essence evaporated. This is true of *Hard Times* and *A Tale of Two Cities* as well as *Great Expectations*, all of which were condensed for serialisation and written with the object of keeping up the interest of a romance for the readers of a weekly magazine. Though the early scenes in *Great Expectations* are marvellously done, Pip's London life and the later Magwitch episodes prove that when Dickens attempted the realistic, naturalistic, psychological method then coming into fashion, he substituted his talent as a writer for his genius as a creator, and in abandoning his own world failed to make both story and characters convincing.

So little at ease was he in his effort to be simple and straightforward that on another man's advice he re-wrote the concluding passages of the book, giving it a commonplace and utterly unnatural ending. For a personal reason which will appear in the next chapter, and because the whole relationship between Pip and Estella is against such a consummation, he had intended that they should not marry. But Bulwer Lytton urged him to bring them together, and Dickens allowed himself to be persuaded by the vulgar opinion of a tawdry novelist.

When the tale was published in volume form everyone was surprised to find it illustrated by Marcus Stone. What had happened to Phiz, the ideal illustrator, who had been associated with Dickens ever since *Pickwick*? We know very little about Hablot K. Browne, because he was an unsociable man who dreaded company, distrusted strangers, and would suddenly disappear into corners or behind curtains when circumstances compelled him to attend social functions. A pliable fellow, he always did exactly what Dickens asked him to do; but he was so closely connected with a past which Dickens wanted to banish that when he expressed no opinion, favourable or otherwise, of the domestic imbroglio at Tavistock House, it is more than probable that Dickens viewed him with grave suspicion. What undoubtedly determined the future of Browne was his decision to join the staff of *Once a Week*, a paper commenced by Bradbury and Evans in opposition to *All The Year Round*. In Dickens's eyes this was an act of flagrant disloyalty; and if Phiz had been Raphael, Titian and Michael Angelo rolled into one, he would not have been engaged to illustrate Dickens's next work, though it were a hagiography.

While writing the story which gave additional classic lustre to his corner of Kent, for the early Pip episodes are only excelled in his work by those of the early Copperfield, Dickens was re-living his youth in the scenes of its happiest years; and the exploratory walks he enjoyed at this time became his favourites in the last decade of his life. The Cooling marshes, which he described so eerily in *Great Expectations*, were visited again and again. He never got tired of wandering about Rochester, where Pumblechook, Miss Havisham and Trabb's boy had lived in his fancy more vividly than the actual inhabitants in his memory. The village of Cobham, its Leather Bottle inn, church, almshouses, and especially the park, were shown to all his guests, and he hardly spent a week at Gad's Hill without a ramble in that neighbourhood. In the summer he would sometimes sit in the churchyard of Shorne, or pause to meditate before the monk over the porch of the church at Chalk. But he was not a regular churchgoer, and once gave up attending divine service for some time because of the long-winded and self-righteous sermons preached by a curate at Higham. 'I cannot sit under a clergyman who addresses his congregation as though he had taken a return ticket to heaven and back', he said. The road to Gravesend pleased him, and he discovered that the seven-miles stretch between Rochester and Maidstone was one of the loveliest walks in England. Usually accompanied by his dogs, he was to be seen every afternoon when at home striding along the roads and across the fields and through the woods, whatever the weather, keeping up a steady pace and seldom covering less than twelve miles. Though entirely obedient to him, the dogs were a terror to the tramps, in those days numerous, and their appearance intimidated the more reputable pedestrians, being of the mastiff, bloodhound, Newfoundland or St. Bernard variety. One of them was 'so accursedly fierce towards other dogs, that I am obliged to take him out muzzled. Also he has an invincible repugnance to soldiers, which, in a military country, is inconvenient.' After charging a company of soldiers on the march, flying at two policemen whose lives Dickens saved with difficulty, and nearly murdering a little girl, it had to be shot, much to the distress of its master, between whom and the animal there was a perfect understanding, 'but it was so very confidential that it went no further.'

He was constantly making improvements in the house on Gad's Hill, and eventually bought a meadow at the back which was used for cricket and other sports. There was a cricket club at Higham, and Dickens allowed them to play their matches in his meadow, taking a great interest in their activities, but insisting that they should run their own affairs independently, and not be patronised either by the local gentry who took part in the games or by his own sons. He always expressed his abhorrence of the way in which the poorer classes were patronised by their wealthy fellow-countrymen. The cricket arrangements were so successful that he got up races and other sports, even allowing the land-lord of the Falstaff inn nearly opposite his house to erect a drinking-booth on the ground. He gave money-prizes, and one year two thousand people turned up for the event. But in spite of the fact that many navvies, soldiers and sailors were among the crowd, complete order was maintained, no damage was done, and no one got drunk. 'The road between this and

Chatham was like a fair all day', he noted with justifiable pride, 'and surely it is a fine thing to get such perfect behaviour out of a reckless seaport town.'

He was as sociable as ever, and Gad's Hill was not often free of guests, who were fetched in a carriage from Higham station, and who, from the moment of their arrival, did what they liked and liked what they did. Sometimes there were so many that sleeping accommodation had to be provided at the Falstaff. Each bedroom in his house was fitted up with a small library of books; each had a fire in the cold weather; and there were cups, saucers, a copper kettle, a tea-caddy, a tea-pot, sugar and milk in each. In the mornings his guests enjoyed themselves while he worked. If they wished to visit Rochester or any other place in the vicinity, there was transport in the form of horse-carriage or pony-trap or Irish jaunting-car. Dickens appeared at lunch-time; and though he rarely took more than bread and cheese and a glass of ale, he seemed to enjoy watching the rest of the company tucking in. The menu for dinner would be on the sideboard, and he would discuss the items with his guests in this fashion: 'Cock-a-leekie? Good! Decidedly good. Fried soles with shrimp sauce? Good again. Croquettes of chicken? Weak. Very weak. Decided want of imagination here . . .' and so on. After lunch he would almost certainly suggest a walk. This was very pleasant for those who really enjoyed walking; but such guests as had not experienced a walk with him, and were by nature strollers, would only fall in with the suggestion once; after which they would discover that they had a lot of correspondence to clear off whenever the proposal was resumed. Occasionally a carriage had to be sent for those who succumbed on the way to blisters or breath-shortage. 'Well done! Twelve miles in three hours', was how he rewarded his more strenuous companions. Following such excursions, great relief was felt by nearly everyone in the party when it was proposed that they should all drive to some beauty-spot for a picnic, or drive to the Medway for a trip on the river; but even on such occasions exhaustion overtook them the moment their host wanted to know whether anybody would like to walk back with him, only the younger people being equal to it, and not all of those. He suffered a good deal from lumbago, which however did not lessen his stride or mileage. Though they had been idle while he had put in four hours writing and another four walking, he was more animated than any of them at dinner, paying attention to everyone at table and keeping up with all the conversation even when several subjects were being discussed at once. After dinner he nearly always had letters to write, but the moment he had finished them he would take part in games or songs or cards. At midnight he retired to bed, but did not expect his male guests to follow his example, often leaving them to their whiskies and billiards, which might occupy them till two or three in the morning.

Life at Gad's Hill was sometimes exciting. Once there was a ghost scare. People had heard strange sounds and seen strange sights at Larkin's monument nearby. The rumours spread; panic seized the cottage-dwellers; Dickens's servants were getting jumpy and giving signs of flight. He acted promptly. Loading his double-barrelled gun and arming two of his boys with sticks, he informed the servants that he would blow the head off anyone who was playing tricks, and set off by moonlight. Arrived at the gate of the field that sur-rounded the monument, he addressed anyone whom it might concern: 'Now look out! If the ghost is here and I see him, so help me God I'll fire at him!' As they entered the field they heard a ghastly, inhuman, long-drawn, dismally derisive sound, suggestive of diabolical agencies. They advanced towards it. A white object left the shadow of the monument and lumbered towards them. It was an asthmatic sheep; and the ghost was laid. Another incident was less creepy but more realistic. While dressing in his bedroom one morning he saw two natives of Savoy arrive at the Falstaff leading two bears. They were shortly joined by some English roughs, who insisted on removing the muzzles of the bears as a preliminary to dancing with them. Dickens immediately perceived that trouble would ensue and went straight to the inn, calling to his gardener on the way. While the gardener was careful to keep the fence between himself and the bears, Dickens ordered the Savoyards to a safe distance and told the roughs that if they did not instantly remuzzle the bears he would send for the police. One of the bears had already attacked one of the roughs, and in helping them to get the muzzles on Dickens was covered with blood and dust. The job done, he ordered the bears to be taken into his stable-yard, where his dogs promptly flew at them. Having separated the dogs from the bears, he went in to breakfast.

Everything at Gad's Hill had to be just right, and Dickens saw that it was so. When a clock went wrong, he wrote to tell the horologer: 'Since my hall clock was sent to your establishment to be cleaned it has . . . struck the hours with great reluctance, and after enduring internal agonies of a most distressing nature, it has now ceased striking altogether. Though a happy release for the clock, this is not convenient to the household. If you can send down any confidential person with whom the clock can confer, I think it may have something on its works that it would be glad to make a clean breast of.' Smoking chimneys, well-sinking, gardening, hay-making, re-flooring, re-papering, re-building, everything received his attention, and to the end of his life there was always some improvement being made to the house, each improvement being invariably, as he declared, 'the last', though it never was until he died. One addition to the place gave him enormous satisfaction. Returning home from a provincial reading, his coachman met him at the station, and as they drove up the hill broke the news:

'The fifty-eight boxes have come, sir.'

'What?'

'The fifty-eight boxes have come, sir.'

'I know nothing of fifty-eight boxes.'

'Well, sir, they are all piled up outside the gate, and we shall soon see.'

They were a present from the famous French actor, Charles Fechter, with whom he had formed a close friendship, and contained the various parts of a Swiss chalet, wherein he could work in the plantation which belonged to him on the opposite side of the road. Except for the brick foundation which had to be built, the chalet was complete and consisted of four rooms. Thereafter, whenever he was at home, Dickens put as much energy into superintending the erection and fitting up of the chalet as he did into everything else, taking great delight in furnishing and decorating it, in hanging pictures, adding a small conservatory, and watching the boring and building of an underground tunnel from his front garden to the plantation, whereby he could reach the chalet without crossing the road. The spring of '65 saw it completed, and he experienced a boyish pleasure in working high up among the trees, with a quantity of mirrors which reflected the river, the cornfields, orchards and hop-gardens of the surrounding country, any of which he could see whenever he lifted his eyes from his desk.

None of his friends could understand why he was so fond of Fechter, but none of his friends understood his essentially histrionic temperament. He first saw Fechter act in the fifties, and was so much struck by the performance that he made the actor's acquaintance. Fechter came to England and played Hamlet in a manner that was new to the stage. The soliloquies were rendered pensively, not spouted in the usual manner, and Dickens thought his conception 'by far the most coherent, consistent, and intelligible Hamlet I ever saw.' He played it in English, a language he spoke well with an agreeable foreign accent. Dickens backed him financially, advised him about plays and players, sometimes rehearsed his company, praised him in the press, started him off in America with a laudatory article in the *Atlantic Monthly*, and helped him in every possible way. The only person who did not hear Dickens sing the Frenchman's praise was Macready, who would not have appreciated it. Dickens's friends thought Fechter a cad: Dickens thought him a genius: but the terms are not incompatible.

# 19
## LAST LOVE

NEARLY everyone is lucky enough to have one comical parent. As a novelist Dickens was exceptionally fortunate: he had two. His brother Alfred died in August, 1860, leaving a widow and five children in poverty. Of course Dickens had to support the lot, and another load of care and trouble descended upon him. In the midst of his exertions on their behalf he went to see how Mrs. Nickleby was bearing up: 'My mother, who was also left to me when my father died (I never had anything left to me but relations), is in the strangest state of mind from senile decay; and the impossibility of getting her to understand what is the matter, combined with her desire to be got up in sables like a female Hamlet, illumine the dreary scene with a ghastly absurdity that is the chief relief I can find in it.' Three months after that he called at a moment when her head was being poulticed, and 'the instant she saw me, she plucked up a spirit and asked me for "a pound".' She died in 1863. It was a decade of death for Dickens, who also lost his brother Frederick, his brother-in-law Henry Austin, and his old friends John Leech and Clarkson Stanfield. He was greatly upset by the loss of Leech and Stanfield, though he regained one friend by the departure of 'dear old Stanny', who, dying, begged him to relent towards Mark Lemon; and the two men shook hands over Stanfield's open grave.

He kept his other friendships in good repair, still applying to Forster for advice, which he never followed, occasionally dining with him, and staying with him at Brighton in October '60: 'I walked six hours and a half on the downs yesterday, and never stopped or sat.' But he chose Wilkie Collins when he felt like 'an escapade to town for a night'; they went on a trip to Cornwall together at the close of '60; and when Wilkie fell ill in the autumn of '62, Dickens offered to return from Paris and write several chapters of that author's serial *No Name* which was appearing in *All The Year Round*: 'Absurdly unnecessary to say that it would be a makeshift! But I could do it at a pinch, so like you that no one should find out the difference.' He remained in Paris for two months, staying at

27 Rue du Faubourg St. Honoré with Georgina, who had been ill, and Mamie. Napoleon III was busy knocking the place about and building new boulevards, and Dickens frequently lost his way. The Second Empire was in its meridian, and he was constantly being assured that peace had come to stay because men would not go to war against their interests, to which he opposed: 'As if the vices and passions of men had not been running counter to their interests since the Creation of the World!' He discovered a strange ignorance among the French concerning his own country and people. In a railway carriage one day he was informed by a priest that there were no antiquities in heretical England. 'None at all?' queried Dickens. 'You have some ships, however.' 'Yes, a few.' 'Are they strong?' 'Well, your trade is spiritual, father: ask the ghost of Nelson.' A French army captain in their carriage was surprised and delighted by this riposte, and confessed that 'he had been so limited as to suppose an Englishman incapable of that bonhomie!' Early in '63 Dickens gave three readings for charity at the British Embassy in Paris: 'Such audiences and such enthusiasm I have never seen, but the thing culminated on Friday night in a two-hours' storm of excitement and pleasure. They actually recommenced and applauded right away into their carriages and down the street.'

He was often in London on business connected with his paper; and except when he brought his family to town for the spring, he stayed in the Wellington Street chambers, where his presence was quickly known to the theatrical profession: 'The poor actors waylay me in Bow Street to represent their necessities; and I often see one cut down a court when he beholds me coming, cut round Drury Lane to face me, and come up towards me near this door in the freshest and most accidental way, as if I was the last person he expected to see on the surface of this globe.' For the sake of his daughter Mamie, he rented a furnished house for several months in the season, and dined out far more than he liked.[1] 'I have had this spring the most severe dinner-eating I have ever known in London', he complained in June '64. 'Every week I had sworn to go out no more, and every week I have perjured myself seven times.' But apart from frequent trips to Paris,

[1] 3 Hanover Terrace, Regent's Park, in '61; 16 Hyde Park Gate South ('the nastiest little house in London') in '62; 57 Gloucester Place, Hyde Park, in '64; 16 Somers Place, Hyde Park, in '65; and 6 Southwick Place, Hyde Park, in '66.

most of the time he could spare from his paper and the readings was spent at Gad's Hill, where he could forget many public nuisances, though the nation-wide lamentations which followed the death of the Prince Consort also followed him to his country retreat: 'If you should meet with an inaccessible cave . . . to which a hermit could retire from the memory of Prince Albert and testimonials to the same, pray let me know of it', he appealed to a friend. 'We have nothing solitary and deep enough in this part of England.' Pensions, knighthoods and baronies were bestowed by a sorrowing monarch on all those who had recognised the Prince's transcendent merits, and 'there is no public service like having walked in the ways of the Late Lamented', declared Dickens, who, when a 'Prince Albert Pudding' appeared on his bill of fare at home, erased the words and substituted 'Flunkey Pudding'; but feeling that this might distress some of his guests, he permitted it henceforth to be styled 'The Great and Good Pudding.'

There were more than enough events of a public kind to claim his personal attention, and one of them was the Guild of Literature, to which, from its inception, he had intermittently given so much time and energy. In the summer of '65 there was a big to-do at Knebworth over this. After an interval of seven years three houses had been built on Bulwer Lytton's estate near Stevenage for the accommodation of artists who were considered worthy of assistance by the Guild. Lytton invited his genteel neighbours to a garden-party and luncheon to celebrate the event, and asked Dickens to invite a number of artists, all of whom turned up at King's Cross and travelled down by train with Dickens and his daughters. At Stevenage station they were met by Forster, who had been deputed by Lytton to receive them and arrange their transport to Knebworth. But Dickens was in holiday mood and insisted that, as it was a hot day, the party should stop at an ale-house on the way, in case their host had not allowed for their thirst. They filled the taproom and sat on the benches and horse-trough outside and drank what some of them called 'belly-vengeance' and enjoyed themselves in a boisterous manner. They then went on to inspect the three almshouses, and finally arrived at Knebworth in a brotherly condition highly displeasing to the 'county' people they had been asked to meet. The gentlemen thought the artists an odd lot, and the artists thought the gentlemen a cold crew, and neither class mingled with the other. Dickens presented his bohemian friends to Lytton, who received them in a distant manner befitting his future ennoblement, which did not accord with his 'keen Jewish look.' Forster bustled about with egregious self-importance, confining himself largely to the aristocracy, stopping here and there to confer a word on a deserving subject, aloof, wrapped in authority, constantly striding away as if on some awful mission from himself to himself, and cutting his old journalistic friends dead. One of them afterwards complained of his behaviour to Dickens, who cheerily answered: 'Lord bless you! Why, he didn't see *me*! He wouldn't, I should say. He was in the clouds, like Malvolio.' Dickens made a speech at the luncheon, in which he said that 'the ladies and gentlemen whom we shall invite to occupy the houses we have built will never be placed under any social disadvantage. They will be invited to occupy them as artists . . . and they will always claim, on equal terms, the hospitality of their generous neighbour.' Happily for the impoverished artists, the social equality with the 'county' and the hospitality of Lytton claimed for them by Dickens were never put to the test. The almshouses were not endowed; and as a season-ticket to London would have cost as much as the rental value of a single dwelling, and a premature burial at Stevenage did not appeal to artists, no one could be induced to live in them. Not caring about the future of these undesirable residences, nor about anything else except the necessity of leaving Kneb-worth and the chilling effect of gentility as soon as possible, the bohemian guests disappeared in twos and threes during the afternoon and made for the ale-house at which they had previously imbibed. When, later on, Dickens passed them in his carriage en route for the station, they rose to a man and gave him a hearty, if beery, salutation. Eventually, what was left of the Guild's funds, after several committees had helped to dissipate them, was handed over to other charities for artists.

Dickens was unwillingly involved in another public event that same summer. After a short holiday in France with Ellen Ternan,[1] he was returning on June 9th from Folkestone to London when, at Staplehurst, the train ran into a gap where the line was being repaired, and eight coaches crashed over a

---

[1] I have come across but one reference to Ellen Ternan's presence on this occasion, no authority being given; but that she was a fellow-passenger may be inferred from the solicitude shown for her by Dickens soon after the accident, at a time when he was more than usually solicitous for himself.

20

bridge into the river below. The coach in which he was travelling 'hung, inexplicably, suspended in the air over the side of the broken bridge.' His fellow-passengers were an old lady and Ellen Ternan, and during a period of violent jolting, while Ellen screamed and the old lady ejaculated, Dickens caught hold of them, saying 'We can't help ourselves, but we can be quiet and composed. Pray don't cry out.' Then they found themselves heaped up in the corner of the carriage, upon which Dickens said 'You may be sure nothing worse can happen. Our danger *must* be over. Will you remain here without stirring, while I get out of the window?' They both said they would; and he climbed through the window, stood upon the step, and saw that, with the bridge gone, there was nothing beneath him but the railway line, with a swampy field some fifteen feet below. The people in the other compartments of their coach were in a panic; so Dickens called to two guards who were running up and down on the safer side: 'Look at me. Do stop an instant and look at me, and tell me whether you don't know me.' One of them replied 'We know you very well, Mr. Dickens.' 'Then, my good fellow, for God's sake give me your key, and send one of those labourers here, and I'll empty this carriage.' With the help of two planks, they got the people out of danger; then, taking his brandy flask, Dickens climbed down the brickwork, filled his hat with water, and went to the aid of the victims. For several hours he worked among the injured and dying; and although the shock of the accident had left him calm, the terrible sights and sufferings affected him so much that for some days the effort of writing a few words turned him sick and faint. He never completely recovered from the experience. He became nervous of driving his own horses; he drank brandy to steady himself on railway journeys; he took to travelling by slow trains, but the delay and monotony were less endurable than the shaking of an express, and after a time he reverted to the speedier method; sometimes, when a train jolted in crossing the points of a line, he clutched the arms of his seat, his face grew pale, and drops of perspiration appeared on his forehead; occasionally the memory of what he had seen became too strong for him, and he left the train at the next stop; and once he and Dolby, on their way north, passed the time by calculating the number of shocks sustained by the nerves in an express train from London to Edinburgh,

Dickens estimating it at thirty thousand. Yet his nature was such that he could not refrain from giving a pantomimic reproduction of the accident, stretching and contracting himself under the table to show realistically how the people had been extricated from the wreckage. By one of those coincidences that would seem strange if life were not full of them, he died five years later on the same June day that he had miraculously escaped from death.

In addition to Ellen Ternan and the old lady, four children of his fancy were with him when the train went over the bridge at Staplehurst, for he had written the chapter of a new novel in which Mr. and Mrs. Boffin were entertaining Mr. and Mrs. Lammle at breakfast, and he had to clamber back into the suspended coach to retrieve them. The two ladies were much more concerned over their bonnet-boxes than over the Boffins, but he would scarcely have risked shaking the carriage from its perilous ledge for anything less precious than his manuscript. The main themes of this novel, which against much criticism he persisted in calling *Our Mutual Friend*, were set forth by him in a letter of the year '61; but he was so busy with his magazine and his readings, above all so distracted by a private matter shortly to be mentioned, that he did not start to write the book till the autumn of '63, when, having much on his mind, he found the labour of composition harder than usual. 'It is a combination of drollery with romance which requires a great deal of pains and a perfect throwing away of points that might be amplified; but I hope it is *very good*. I confess, in short, that I think it is.' As usual, he scorned delights and lived laborious days: 'I have never divided a book of my writing with anything else, but have always wrought at it to the exclusion of everything else.' When hard at work he refused to dine out more than once a week. In declining an invitation he wrote 'I have always given my work the first place in my life', and he devoted to it 'all the pains possible to be bestowed on a labour of love.' That he was 'a terror to the household' during such periods may be guessed from a little scene described by his daughter Mamie, who was once lying on a sofa in his study recovering from an illness when he jumped up from his desk, rushed to a mirror and made a series of extraordinary facial contortions at himself; after which he hurried back to his desk, wrote furiously for a minute or two, again dashed to the mirror, made more faces, turned round, and, apparently unaware of Mamie's presence, talked rapidly to himself in a low voice. Then he walked calmly to his desk, where he remained silently working until lunch-time. Certainly he was 'possessed' when writing, and on at least one occasion a character got completely out of hand 'and made me do exactly the contrary to what I had originally intended.'

The people in *Our Mutual Friend* were, as in his other books, a combination of fancy and observation. He saw Mr. Venus, the articulator of human bones, in St. Giles's, Charley Hexam and his father at Chatham, the Veneerings everywhere in society. The Jew, Mr. Riah, was the result of a correspondence between himself and Mrs. Eliza Davies, who had followed him as tenant of Tavistock House and who felt that Fagin was a libel on her race. Without admitting that Fagin was a libel on part of her race, Dickens made amends to the better part and produced a character that would have won Fagin's approval. Many of the scenes and individuals in the book were the outcome of Dickens's nocturnal visits to the docks and wharves of the East End, and the Thames is as much a 'character' as the fog had been in *Bleak House*. Accompanied by several police officers, he visited the haunts of criminals, opium dens, thieves' kitchens, public houses of an unsavoury sort, and derived much pleasure from these excursions. He had a partiality for the company and conversation of police constables and inspectors, and enjoyed seeing how calmly they behaved in dangerous places where the inhabitants would have murdered them with pleasure but for reprisals. One receiver of stolen goods, whom Dickens calls Bark, would certainly have cut their throats if his criminal lodgers had had a fraction of his courage:

> I won't, says Bark, have no adjective police and adjective strangers in my adjective premises! I won't, by adjective and substantive! Give me my trousers, and I'll send the whole adjective police to adjective and substantive! Give me, says Bark, my adjective trousers! I'll put an adjective knife in the whole bileing of 'em. I'll punch their adjective heads. I'll rip up their adjective substantives. . . . If the adjective coves in the kitchen was men, they'd come up now and do for you! . . . They'd come up and do for you! cries Bark again, and waits. Not a sound in the kitchen! We are shut up, half a dozen of us, in Bark's house in the innermost recesses of the worst part of London, in the

dead of night—the house is crammed with notorious robbers and ruffians—and not a man stirs. No, Bark. They know the weight of the law, and they know Inspector Field and Co. too well.

From such material did Dickens obtain the waterside figures and atmosphere of *Our Mutual Friend*, which appeared in monthly numbers, from May '64 to November '65, under the imprint of his early publishers Chapman and Hall, though there is evidence in his letters that the revival of their business connection did not imply a renewal of their friendly relations; for in January '60 he called Frederick Chapman 'a Monstrous Humbug', who was 'making holiday one half of his life, and making mistakes the other half, and making money (I suppose) in spite of himself, always'; and in July '65 he told a correspondent that she was wrong in thinking that a word from him would ensure the favourable attention of his publishers: 'I have no influence with them bespeaking the most ordinary civility in behalf of another, and I have proved it very lately.'

In *Our Mutual Friend* Dickens returned to his own world of comedy and bizarrerie, which he had last peopled in *Little Dorrit*. Silas Wegg is a masterpiece in the old style, done with all the old power; but the book is packed full of genius and contains his best social satire in the Veneering circle, which cuts with greater effect now than it did at the time, since the newly rich have vastly increased their orbit in the last eighty years. Mrs. Wilfer, who 'sat silently giving them to understand that every breath she drew required to be drawn with a self-denial rarely paralleled in history', is clearly Mrs. John Dickens in her most snobbish and least amiable mood; Betty Higden is an emblem of Dickens's lifelong detestation of institutions, first manifested in *Oliver Twist*; while Podsnap is a portrait of John Forster, sufficiently exaggerated in certain aspects to prevent Forster from recognising himself, though, after all, if the original of Podsnap had been able to see himself as Dickens saw him, he would not have been Podsnap. The pomposity, respectability, arrogance and iron-cased self-sufficiency of Forster are here; also his particular type of possessiveness:

It was a trait in Mr. Podsnap's character . . . that he could not endure a hint of disparagement of any friend or acquaintance of his. 'How dare you?' he would seem to say, in such a case. 'What do you mean? I have licensed this person. This person

has taken out *my* certificate. Through this person you strike at
me, Podsnap the Great. And it is not that I particularly care
for the person's dignity, but that I do most particularly care for
Podsnap's.'

Forster's way of brushing aside everything he did not like is
exhibited, together with his insularity, as in the scene where
he cross-examines the Frenchman:

'How do you like London?' Mr. Podsnap now inquired from
his station of host, as if he were administering something in the
nature of a powder or potion to the deaf child; 'London, Londres,
London?'

.        .        .        .        .

'I was inquiring', said Mr. Podsnap, resuming the thread of
his discourse, 'Whether You Have Observed in our Streets as
We should say, Upon our Pavvy as You would say, any
Tokens——'
The foreign gentleman with patient courtesy entreated pardon:
'But what was tokenz?'
'Marks', said Mr. Podsnap; 'Signs, you know, Appearances—
Traces.'
'Ah! Of a Orse?' inquired the foreign gentleman.
'We call it Horse', said Mr. Podsnap, with forbearance. 'In
England, Angleterre, England, We Aspirate the "H", and We
Say "Horse". Only the Lower Classes Say "Orse!"'
'Pardon', said the foreign gentleman; 'I am alwiz wrong!'
'Our Language', said Mr. Podsnap, with a gracious conscious-
ness of always being right, 'is Difficult. Ours is a Copious
Language, and Trying to Strangers. I will not Pursue my
Question.'

Forster must have been more blindly self-complacent even
than Dickens's representment of him if he did not spot the
likeness of himself which Marcus Stone caught in the dinner-
party scene (Book 2, Chapter 3), where Podsnap is sitting on
the right hand of Veneering. But there was something
monumental about Forster, who was always to be seen in the
daytime in a tightly-fitting wholly buttoned-up frock-coat,
and to be heard talking in the heavy stage-style of Macready.
Hence Dickens in *Little Dorrit*:

All buttoned-up men are weighty. All buttoned-up men are
believed in. Whether or no the reserved and never-exercised
power of unbuttoning, fascinates mankind; whether or no

wisdom is supposed to condense and augment when buttoned up, and to evaporate when unbuttoned; it is certain that the man to whom importance is accorded is the buttoned-up man.

To the biographer the most interesting portrait in *Our Mutual Friend* is that of Bella Wilfer, which is probably the nearest resemblance to Ellen Ternan in Dickens's work. In identifying Ellen with any of his female characters we are substituting inference for evidence, though we know enough about her to feel confident on several points. But what exactly do we know about her beyond reasonable doubt? She was the daughter of an actor and actress who belonged to Charles Kean's company at the Princess's Theatre in Oxford Street. She was born on March 3rd, 1839, and her father died insane when she was seven years old. She had two sisters, Fanny and Maria, the first of whom married Tom Trollope, brother of Anthony. Dickens had seen them all as child-actresses and knew their mother long before they took part in Collins's play at Manchester. Indeed he had once, in the Green Room of a theatre, sympathised with Ellen's distress, which was caused by the necessity of her appearing before an audience in scanty attire, the alternative being the loss of her job. She was weeping bitterly, but he reassured her, and she managed to overcome the shock to her modesty. When he fell in love with her at Manchester, she was eighteen years old and he was forty-five; and as we know, from an unsympathetic source, that she was small in stature, fair-haired and rather pretty, we may guess that his description of Lucie Manette in *A Tale of Two Cities* is a memory of how she appeared to him at the age of eighteen: 'A short, slight, pretty figure, a quantity of golden hair, a pair of blue eyes that met his own with an inquiring look, and a forehead with a singular capacity (remembering how young and smooth it was), of lifting and knitting itself into an expression that was not quite one of perplexity, or wonder, or alarm, or merely of a bright fixed attention, though it included all the four expressions . . .' When, later, we are reminded of Lucie's 'old look of earnestness', of her 'old and intent expression', and when, later still, we learn that Estella in *Great Expectations* has a very intent look, we may safely infer that Dickens's early notice of her evoked a similar expression on the face of Ellen.

But there is nothing else of Ellen in Lucie Manette, and it

is not till we come to *Great Expectations* that anyone could perceive, though otherwise ignorant of the fact, that another woman had entered the author's life, one who would influence his work as Maria Beadnell and Mary Hogarth had done in the past. Estella is not a portrait so much as a presence; and, even if we had no other evidence, we could deduce from the novel in which she appears that Dickens's love for Ellen was still in the hopeless stage. Estella is 'proud and wilful' and has an 'air of inaccessibility.' It amuses her to attract her lover and make him wretched: 'I never had one hour's happiness in her society, and yet my mind all round the four-and-twenty hours was harping on the happiness of having her with me unto death.' At last, distracted, he speaks of his love, and she replies: 'When you say you love me, I know what you mean, as a form of words; but nothing more. You address nothing in my breast, you touch nothing there. I don't care for what you say at all.' On which he bursts out: 'You are part of my existence, part of myself. You have been in every line I have ever read, since I first came here . . . You have been in every prospect I have ever seen since—on the river, on the sails of the ships, on the marshes, in the clouds, in the light, in the darkness, in the wind, in the woods, in the sea, in the streets . . . to the last hour of my life, you cannot choose but remain part of my character . . .' When she tells him that she is going to marry someone else, he walks all the way from Rochester to London, just as Dickens had done when his future seemed unbearable: 'I could do nothing half so good for myself as tire myself out.' As it happens, we know that Ellen was not in love with Dickens, that the thought of intimacy with him repelled her; and from two of his letters in the autumn of '62 it is obvious that she was still keeping him at bay. To Wilkie Collins he wrote: 'I have some rather miserable anxieties which I must impart one of these days when I come to you or you come to me. I shall fight out of them, I dare say, being not easily beaten—but they have gathered and gathered.' To Forster: 'I can force myself to do at that reading-desk what I have done a hundred times; but whether, with all this unsettled fluctuating distress in my mind, I could force an original book out of it, is another question.' We can now see why the inevitable ending of *Great Expectations* was an unhappy one, because more than a year after its completion Dickens had not been able to overcome Ellen's resistance.

Like many actors, Dickens had a deal of the spoilt child in his make-up. Whenever he wanted a thing badly, he wanted it instantly, and was liable to howl if he did not get it. By sheer persistence and desperation he at length compelled Ellen to yield, but it was a barren victory. Whatever may be true of the purely spiritual world, it is certainly true of this world that whoever does not ask receives, whoever does not seek finds, and the door is opened to him who does not knock; for everything that is really worth having in life comes without any direct effort to achieve it, and that which is obtained by the exercise of the will is ultimately unprofitable and un- satisfying. Such at least is the lifetime's experience and observation of one human being; and nowhere is this truth illustrated more strikingly than in the career of Dickens, who won the object of his will repeatedly, but derived no lasting benefit from his victories. The combination of his fame and his cash must have prevailed with Ellen. Hers was a poor family, dependent for a livelihood on occasional jobs, for none of them was likely to set the Thames on fire as an actress. Dickens published sister Fanny's stories in his paper, wrote to Benjamin Webster in '61 asking him to take sister Maria into his company, let Fechter know in '62 that it would be to his advantage if he gave Maria a job, and probably paid the rent of No. 2 Houghton Place, Ampthill Square, where the Ternan family lived. Apparently Ellen placed comfort before chastity. This is evident from the fact of her surrender, apart from the natures of Estella in *Great Expectations* and Bella Wilfer in *Our Mutual Friend*. 'I love money, and want money—want it dreadfully', says Bella. 'I hate to be poor, and we are degradingly poor, offensively poor, miserably poor, beastly poor.' She harps on the theme: 'I have money always in my thoughts and my desires; and the whole life I place before myself is money, money, money, and what money can make of life!' Like Estella, she is proud and wilful, and 'convinced I have no heart as people call it, and . . . think that sort of thing is nonsense.' Like Estella, too, her lover thinks her insolent, trivial, capricious, mercenary, careless, hard to touch, hard to turn. But some time before Dickens began to write *Our Mutual Friend*, almost certainly in 1863, Ellen Ternan became his mistress, and so Bella's character changes in the course of the book: 'The wayward, playful, affectionate nature, giddy for want of the weight of some sustaining purpose, and capricious because it was always fluttering among little things, was yet a captivating one.' Which reminds us of Ellen's concern over the bonnet-boxes in the Staplehurst tragedy; and as we know that she was 'histrionic in manner' we can safely link her throughout with Bella, who is the most lifelike heroine in Dickens's work except Dora.

Lust lives on the fancy, love on the reality, but the fanciful, fervent, exhibitory nature of Dickens easily confused the two where his own emotions were involved. Ellen could no doubt, especially when she was having a good time, play up to him so well that he was able to persuade himself of her love. On one such occasion his emotions outran his reason, and at the conclusion of the chapter describing Bella's wedding he forgot that he was a chronicler and spoke *in propria persona:* 'And O there are days in this life, worth life and worth death. And O what a bright old song it is, that O 'tis love, 'tis love, 'tis love, that makes the world go round!' He was as thoughtful in his attentions to her as he was careful of her reputation. Shortly after the Staplehurst accident he wrote a note to his servant telling him to take her various delicacies on different days; and a year later he informed a female friend that it would be inexpressibly painful to Ellen, whom he called Nelly, if she knew that her intimacy with himself was known to others: 'She would not believe that you could see her with my eyes, or know her with my mind . . . she could not have the pride and self-reliance which (mingled with the gentlest nature) has borne her, alone, through so much.' And he advised his friend to be very strictly on her guard, if she met Tom Trollope or his wife (Fanny Ternan), 'to make no reference to me which either can piece into anything', because Fanny was 'infinitely sharper than the serpent's Tooth.' But far more people knew about the liaison than he wished to believe, among others his own children, one of whom, it seems, talked about it in Australia; with the result that a dramatist named John Garraway wrote a one-act play which was reviewed by a Melbourne magazine, *The Imperial,* in 1895. The scene takes place in Manchester Town Hall, where Collins's play is being performed, and Dickens falls in love with Ellen Ternan, who, presumably because the author wished to have his play produced, disillusions Dickens, and the incident becomes 'an innocent love episode.' The age was not ripe for the truth; and even as late as 1893 George Augustus Sala said that 'the secret' of Dickens's later years could not be disclosed for at least another half-century.

Ellen expected to be kept in a luxury to which she was not accustomed, and from the beginning of '67, possibly because she was expecting a child by him, Dickens took a house for her: Windsor Lodge, 16 Linden Grove, Nunhead, Camberwell,[1] where he spent part of every week, and where some of his last book *Edwin Drood* was written. Whether he wished to give his connection with her the odour of respectability, or she wished it, or Georgina was curious, we shall never know; but in the summer of '69 his Nelly stayed at Gad's Hill and took part in the family cricket matches. Yet he was fully aware that she did not love him, that she suffered from remorse, that she lived in a permanent condition of self-reproach; and this final failure in love, coming at a time when he was losing his old resilience, made him more wretched than he had ever been. As Thomas Wright puts it: 'He imagined that he had entered into a new life and that it would be roses, roses all the way. He forgot that roses have thorns. He thought he was in front of the supremest felicity ever enjoyed by mortal man. He wasn't.'

For the second time in his life, but far more keenly than before, he experienced the commingled rage, despair and torment of jealousy. This is no conjecture. It is as clear as day to anyone but a Dickolater, to anyone who does not separate life from literature, a man from his work. The anguish of unrequited love has never been so painfully described as in the character of Bradley Headstone, and outside Shakespeare the passion of jealousy has not been rendered so poignantly. We do not know whether Dickens had cause for jealousy beyond his certainty that Ellen did not love him; but that alone was quite sufficient to create a universe of rivals. Everyone to whom she was pleasant, almost everyone to whom she spoke, would have been in his eyes a potential lover. He could not rid himself of this suspicion to the last, and John Jasper in *Edwin Drood* is another victim to the passion, the overmastering nature of which is expressed in its most devastating form in Bradley Headstone, who makes love in the accents of Pip in *Great Expectations*, though with a more burning intensity: 'I have no resources in myself, I have no confidence in myself, I have no government of myself when you are near me or in

---

[1] Now 'Holmdene', 31 Linden Grove.

my thoughts. And you are always in my thoughts now. I have never been quit of you since I first saw you. Oh, that was a wretched day for me! That was a wretched, miserable day! . . . You draw me to you. If I were shut up in a strong prison, you would draw me out. I should break through the wall to come to you. If I were lying on a sick bed, you would draw me up—to stagger to your feet and fall there . . . No man knows till the time comes, what depths are within him. To some men it never comes; let them rest and be thankful . . . I love you. What other men may mean when they use that expression, I cannot tell; what *I* mean is, that I am under the influence of some tremendous attraction which I have resisted in vain, and which overmasters me . . . This and the confusion of my thoughts, so that I am fit for nothing, is what I mean by your being the ruin of me.' And then, though Headstone is only the master of a school for poor boys, he suddenly talks like a famous author: 'My circumstances are quite easy, and you would want for nothing. My reputation stands quite high, and would be a shield for yours. If you saw me at my work, able to do it well and respected in it, you might even come to take a sort of pride in me . . .' Dickens, too, we may be sure, could see himself 'with the exhaustion of deferred hope' passing through the dark streets of London 'like a haggard head suspended in the air: so completely did the force of his expression cancel his figure.' We must not carry the parallel too far, because Dickens was quite capable of adding from his fancy what was lacking from his feeling; but no man could have created Bradley Headstone without passing through the central experience which brings him to life, and we happen to know what that experience was. Beyond the influence of Ellen Ternan on his characterisation of Estella and Bella, and the portrayal of Bradley Headstone, it is worth noting that his association with her had a further effect on his writings, from which the Fallen Woman theme disappeared.

Unfortunately the first signs of a break-up in his health synchronised with the enormous success of *Our Mutual Friend*. Early in '65 he contracted a frost-bitten foot, which he attributed to much walking in the snow. He loathed physical incapacitation, forced a boot on his swollen foot, and sat down to write in that condition, continuing to tramp in the snow and to thrust his left foot into a boot until he lamed himself and was compelled to lie up, suffering much pain. With the same refusal to recognise his limitations, he would not wear glasses, though near-sighted, and looked hard at distant objects until he could distinguish their outlines. The foot got better, and he started daily walks of ten or twelve miles, but he had to sit shoeless in the evenings. This went on till the end of the year. Early in '66 his heart began to give trouble. Tonics brought an improvement, and he commenced a reading tour. But both ailments were to recur, and his habits were not those of a patient. At Portsmouth, for example, he and his manager Dolby, on one of their walks, passed through an elongated square of residences open at each end, which reminded them of a pantomime set. No one being in sight, Dickens went up the steps of a house, gave three loud raps on the door, and was about to lie down across the entrance, like a clown in a pantomime, when the door was suddenly flung open by a stout woman. He did not stop to explain his intention or its humorous associations, but tore down the street followed by Dolby, eventually taking refuge in a public house. Another experience, when he was reading at Newcastle-on-Tyne, cannot have improved his health. They went on the pier at Tynemouth and watched a fleet of merchantmen tossing on a stormy sea: 'Suddenly there came a golden horizon, and a most glorious rainbow burst out, arching one large ship, as if she were sailing direct for heaven. I was so enchanted by the scene, that I became oblivious of a few thousand tons of water coming on in an enormous roller, and was knocked down and beaten by its spray when it broke, and so completely wetted through and through, that the very pockets in my pocket-book were full of sea.'

Where his health was concerned Dickens would not look facts in the face. He dismissed gout as a cold in the foot; he described heart-disease as a nervous complaint; when he fainted after a reading he said it was due to insomnia; and when something went wrong with his eyesight he thought it was caused by the medicine he had been taking. In the summer of '67 he was again laid up with a gouty foot: 'I cannot bear to have the fomentations taken off for a moment.' Rumours began to float about that his health was breaking down, as indeed it was, though he steadfastly declined to recognise the fact. He was in 'a critical state of health', said one paper, and this he declared to be a misprint for 'a cricketing state of health.' Charles Reade, who loved him and thought him the greatest genius of the century, went to stay at Gad's Hill and found him at the top of his form. Collins was there too, and Dickens's health became a theme for light entertainment. Reade and Collins gravely felt his pulse at meal-times, and sent heartening messages across to the chalet while he was working. But when his correspondence increased on account of the reports, he asked a friendly editor to publish a denial:

> This is to certify that the undersigned innocent victim of a periodical paragraph disease which usually breaks out once in every seven years (proceeding from England by the Overland route to India, and per Cunard line to America where it strikes the base of the Rocky Mountains and rebounding to Europe, perishes on the steppes of Russia), is NOT in *a critical state of health*, and has NOT consulted *eminent surgeons*, and never was better in his life, and is NOT recommended to proceed to the United States for *cessation from literary labour*, and has not had so much as a head ache for twenty years.

He was certainly not going to America for the sake of health, but he had practically decided to go there for the sake of wealth. Ever since 1859 tempting offers to give readings in that country had reached him. Then, when the Civil War broke out, he had been asked to visit Australia on a guarantee of ten thousand pounds. Incidentally, he had no illusions about the American Civil War, and if the northern states had heard that he did not believe in this 'love of the black man', nor in their 'horror of slavery having anything to do with the beginning of the war, save as a pretence', they might have indulged in another auto-da-fé of *Martin Chuzzlewit*. After the war the offers were renewed. Guarantees of sums beyond the dreams of novelists came pouring in from committees, agents, speculators and personal friends. He hated the prospect but was lured by the profit. 'I know perfectly well beforehand how unspeakably wretched I should be', he said, and again, 'If I were to go it would be a penance and a misery, and I dread the thought more than I can possibly express', but 'the prize looks so large.' American publishers and editors were now treating him well. Harper's had bought the advance sheets of each number of *A Tale of Two Cities, Great Expectations* and *Our Mutual Friend*, and issued them simultaneously with the English publication. He had received £1000 for a short story, *Hunted Down*, from one American editor, and he was to receive £1000 apiece for two more short stories just completed, *A Holiday Romance* and *George Silverman's Explanation*. These tales, like his Christmas Books and stories, one of which, *Doctor Marigold's Prescriptions*, became a popular reading item, prove conclusively that his genius did not operate when limited to a short story, though perhaps the reviewer in *The Times* was over-harsh in describing *The Cricket on the Hearth* as 'the babblings of genius in its premature dotage.' Of the lot *A Christmas Carol* alone has merit on account of Scrooge. Most of them display everything that is worst and weakest in him, everything that levels him with the herd of mankind and is therefore least worthy of remark: his maudlin sentimentality, his morbid interest in crime, and his maddening juvenility which comes out in a playful archness that is more than a little depressing. Had these been his main products, he would not have been remembered. The virtue and vice in a man's work are the virtue and vice in himself, and the preponderating virtue in Dickens's work is the predominant virtue in Dickens: his inexhaustible comedy and vivacity.

Wills and Forster did their utmost to dissuade him from the American tour, but in August '67 he sent Dolby over there to report on the prospects. When it became known in the States that he was seriously considering the visit, many people wrote to advise him against it, hinting at danger, at anti-Dickens feeling, at anti-English feeling, at New York rowdyism, and so forth. He kept all this to himself, never breathed a word about it to a soul, and ignored the pronouncement in the *New York Herald* that 'Dickens must apologise first.' Dolby returned, full of America and 'golden joys', and Dickens was impressed by the possibilities. He would not admit even to himself that his real hunger was for new sensations, for fresh histrionic conquests, for an unprecedented theatrical triumph; yet he knew, and even wrote, that he could make as much money by remaining at home and reading to British audiences.

Forster had to be consulted as a matter of form; and though Dickens was in no doubt that he would advise against the trip, Dolby was sent to see him. It happened that he was staying at Dolby's home town, Ross-on-Wye, and thither the manager repaired. It was an unpleasant interview. Forster rampaged. Podsnap took the floor and eliminated what he did not approve. He was right to oppose the enterprise, but his reasons were ridiculous and his manner was not mollifying. He disliked America because that country had treated his friend Macready badly. There was no money in America, he asserted; and even if there were, Dickens would not get it; and even if he did, he would be robbed of it in the hotel; and even if he managed to bank it, the bank would fail on purpose. As for Dolby's calculation that Dickens would make a profit of fifteen thousand pounds, that was all nonsense; the halls were not big enough; and even if they were, the population of America was not large enough to produce such a result; and even if it was, only a small proportion would attend the readings. In any case Dickens's desire to increase his property so quickly and in such a way was unworthy of him or any man of genius; the business of reading in public was a degrading one. The Yankees had taken Dickens's books without paying author's fees; why should they not do the same with the readings? There was no object in prolonging the interview, as he had fully determined that his friend should never again go to America. 'I shall write to Dickens by tonight's post and tell him how fully I am opposed to the idea, and that he must give it up.' Dolby was then shown the door. Forster's attitude compelled Dickens to visit Ross in the vague hope of partly reconciling him to the project; but Forster was intractable; and as Dickens was immovable, a wire was sent from Ross to Boston on September 30th, 1867: 'Yes. Go ahead.'

In collaboration with Collins he was writing a Christmas story for *All The Year Round* called *No Thoroughfare*. Fechter read it in proof and thought it would make a good play; so just before he left for America Dickens roughed out a scenario with Fechter and left Collins to write the drama, which was successfully produced by Fechter during Dickens's absence. On November 2nd a Farewell Banquet, presided over by Lord Lytton, was given him in the Freemasons' Hall, and on the 9th he left Liverpool for Boston, this time without 'his lady', to whom he had just written for the last time.

My dear Catherine,
    I am glad to receive your letter, and to accept and reciprocate your good wishes. Severely hard work lies before me; but that is not a new thing in my life, and I am content to go my way and do it.
                                        Affectionately yours,
                                        Charles Dickens.

Besides wishing him well on his American tour, she had sent a word of sympathy on his Staplehurst experience, to which he had formally rejoined 'I thank you for your letter' and told her of the shock he had sustained. About a year later she had applied for his advice concerning her house, and he had asked Georgina to answer 'that I never will go to her house, and that it is my fixed purpose (without any abatement of kindness otherwise), to hold as little communication with her as I possibly can.' The mother of his ten children bore it with quiet dignity, consoling herself with the belief that his letters proved he was still in love with her after the birth of their youngest boy.

# WITHOUT HIS LADY

WHENEVER one wishes to do a thing, or not to do it, there are always plenty of reasons for doing it, or not doing it. Dickens found a score of excuses for his American reading tour, in all of which cash played a conspicuous part, but never included in the number his real object, which was to retrieve his personal popularity, so gravely impaired by *Martin Chuzzlewit*, by a dazzling display of histrionic virtuosity. He wanted to astonish the Americans, to make them pay for the experience, and to convert their depreciation into admiration, their anger into affection. His success was phenomenal, the cost to himself incalculable.

The *Cuba* ran into a heavy gale half-way across the Atlantic, and one of those incidents occurred which Dickens loved to retail; indeed, as we have seen, they were the staple of his conversation. It was a Sunday, and about seventy passengers assembled in the saloon for divine service. Suddenly the double doors burst open and two stewards were seen supporting the clergyman, 'exactly as if he were coming up to the scratch in a prize-fight' or as if he were drunk, incapable, and under conveyance to a police station. The rolling and pitching of the ship did not prevent Dickens from enjoying what followed:

Stewards watch their opportunity, and balance themselves, but cannot balance minister; who, struggling with a drooping head and a backward tendency, seems determined to return below, while they are as determined that he shall be got to the reading-desk in mid-saloon. Desk portable, sliding away down a long table, and aiming itself at the breasts of various members of the congregation. Here the double doors, which have been carefully closed by other stewards, fly open again, and worldly passenger tumbles in, seemingly with pale-ale designs: who, seeking friend, says 'Joe!' Perceiving incongruity, says 'Hullo! Beg yer pardon!' and tumbles out again. All this time the congregation have been breaking up into sects—as the manner of congregations often is —each sect sliding away by itself, and all pounding the weakest sect which slid first into the corner. Utmost point of dissent

soon attained in every corner, and violent rolling. Stewards at
length make a dash; conduct minister to the mast in the centre
of the saloon, which he embraces with both arms; skate out; and
leave him in that condition to arrange affairs with flock.

'The scene was so extraordinarily ridiculous', concluded
Dickens, 'and was made so much more so by the exemplary
gravity of all concerned in it, that I was obliged to leave
before the service began.' The captain of the boat appears
to have been of a reserved and phlegmatic disposition, but
Dickens displayed his invariable genius for bringing out the
social qualities in people, and after the last dinner on board
the captain made speeches, sang duets, and staggered the other
officers by many strange solo performances of which they did
not think him cognisant or capable. 'I think I have acquired
a higher reputation from drawing out the captain . . . than
from anything previously known of me on these shores',
reported Dickens. 'I hope the effect of these achievements
may not dim the lustre of the readings.'

On arrival at Boston he found that his rooms at Parker
House had been decorated with flowers and furnished with
books by Mrs. Fields, who with her husband, the publisher,
J. T. Fields, made his visit to America as agreeable as circumstances permitted. Though loaded with invitations, he refused
to stay with people or dine out; but he made an exception in
the case of Fields, with whom he stayed during one series of
Boston readings and at whose house he met Longfellow,
Emerson and Oliver Wendell Holmes. Mrs. Fields kept a
diary, and her husband wrote a book, from both of which we
get a few interesting glimpses of their guest. At first he refused wine at meals and cigars afterwards, saying that he
neither drank nor smoked from the time his readings 'set in',
as if talking of a rainy season. When Wendell Holmes remarked that country audiences were not appreciative, and
that at one of his lectures the only face which relaxed its
grimness was his landlady's, Dickens interposed 'Probably
because she saw money enough in the house to cover your
expenses.' It was a good 'exit' line, and in the laugh which
greeted it he jumped up and said good-night to his hostess.
Emerson went to a reading, and, though naturally stoical, was
doubled up with mirth. Afterwards he said to Mrs. Fields that
Dickens 'has too much talent for his genius; it is a dreadful

locomotive to which he is bound, and can never be free from it nor set at rest. You see him quite wrong, evidently, and would persuade me that he is a genial creature, full of sweetness and amenities and superior to his talents, but I fear he is harnessed to them. He is too consummate an artist to have a thread of nature left. He daunts me! I have not the key.' Mrs. Fields thought she had the key, for she noted in her diary: 'We played a game of cards which was most curious —indeed, something more—so much more that I have forgotten to be afraid of him.'

Occasionally the subject of literature was raised, and Dickens mentioned his favourite authors and works: Cobbett, De Quincey, Carlyle's *French Revolution* and Sydney Smith's Lectures on Moral Philosophy; he preferred Smollett to Fielding, *Peregrine Pickle* to *Tom Jones*. Of Thomas Gray he said: 'No man ever walked down to posterity with so small a book under his arm.' His knowledge of Shakespeare was proved by the aptness with which he misquoted him. 'The hour has almost come when I to sulphurous and tormenting gas must render up myself', said he before leaving for one of his readings. Sometimes he spoke of spiritualism, the humbug of which excited his deepest ire; but he seldom referred to himself or his own works, and when Fields announced one day that he felt like erecting a statue to Dickens because of the heroic way in which, though extremely ill, he never failed to fulfil his reading engagements, he said 'No, don't, take down one of the old ones instead.' Now and then he made a passing reference to his own creations when out walking with Fields: 'Let us avoid Mr. Pumblechook who is crossing the street to meet us'; or 'Mr. Micawber is coming—let us turn down here to get out of his way.' But mostly, his talk was of humorous episodes, oddities of human nature, and criminals. 'How restricted one's conversation would become with a man who was to be hanged in half-an-hour', he once remarked. 'You could not say, if it rains, "We shall have fine weather to-morrow", for what would that be to him? For my part I think I should confine my remarks to the times of Julius Caesar and King Alfred!' Though he suffered severely from an inflamed foot and chronic catarrh in the later stages of his tour, his good humour never deserted him, and Mrs. Fields only saw him once in an impatient mood, when Dolby said that two gentlemen wished to see him and asked if he would allow them to come in. 'No, I'll be damned if I will!' he exclaimed, starting up from his chair. Mrs. Fields thought it odd that so many people were prejudiced against him: 'I seldom make a call where his name is introduced that I do not feel the injustice done to him personally, as if mankind resented the fact that he had excited more love than most men.' But it was not so odd as she thought, envy being the commonest, as it is the most ignoble, of human attributes.

Chiefly in the large cities, but to a less extent everywhere, the sale of tickets presented a serious problem. On the night before the sale began people arrived and stationed themselves at the door of admission. Purchasers who did not wish to wait all night sent their clerks and servants to shiver in their stead. By the early hours of the morning the street looked like the scene of a colossal picnic. Men, women and boys sat on chairs, reclined on mattresses, lay in blankets on the ground, all provided with drinks and food. To keep up their spirits they sang popular songs, such as 'John Brown's Body' and 'We won't Go Home Till Morning.' At New York the crowd shouted, shrieked and bawled ditties throughout the night in the bitter cold, reminding an onlooker of the mob that used to howl from sundown to sunrise outside the Old Bailey before a public execution. When the door opened and the booking commenced, there was a rush; the line was broken; some of those at the rear of the queue got places in front, and a bloody scrimmage took place. The police, warned for the emergency, were soon on the spot, freely using their clubs; and sometimes, when order was restored, the street resembled a battle-ground after a cavalry charge. Such happenings were almost in the order of things; but what perplexed Dolby was the trade in tickets. Not more than six seats were sold to a single applicant, and at first the speculators offered as much as twenty-six dollars for a two-dollar ticket; but when it became clear that there would be an enormous demand, they engaged people to take places in the queue, and in this way the more daring of them were able to secure three hundred seats at cost price and sell them at a fabulous profit. The moment they discovered where and when readings were to be given, they descended upon the place, opened offices, and commenced a brisk business. Such members of the public as could not afford to pay fifty dollars for a five-dollar seat assumed that Dickens's manager was responsible for the high prices and the gambling in tickets, and Dolby became 'the most unpopular and best-abused man in America.' Late in the tour Dolby discovered that one of their own staff, whom they had brought with them from England, had not only gambled himself but had been corrupted by outside speculators, and he was sacked. But the real trouble was caused by the willingness of rich people to pay almost any sum demanded by their smart fellow-countrymen for the privilege of hearing Dickens read.

George Dolby was a vulgar, jovial, boisterous, energetic, honest, cynical fellow, whom Mark Twain called 'a gladsome gorilla.' For many years he acted as agent for concerts, plays, lectures, and every conceivable kind of show, celebrity and attraction. Of all the famous people with whom he was associated, he maintained the highest opinion of Dickens, the most considerate, cheerful, practical, good-humoured man he ever met. However miserable the town, however wretched the hotel, Dickens did not complain or become self-important, but treated it as a joke and always made the best of everything. He never gave Dolby an order, but would say 'Don't you think we had better do so-and-so?' and when consulted about some detail would usually reply 'Do as you like and don't bother me.' He became much attached to Dolby, who guarded him from all sorts of people and mothered him when ill. Dolby's loud, careless, unrefined talk amused him. 'Where on earth did you get that word?' he asked when the manager had said that someone had 'bested' him. Dolby did not go out of his way to please people. The editor of a Boston newspaper applied for advertisements of the readings and said that he would publish any news paragraph the manager cared to send. The application and the offer were ignored, with the result that a news paragraph appeared from a different source: 'This chap calling himself Dolby got drunk down town last night, and was taken to the police station for fighting an Irishman.' A New York paper advised: 'Surely it is time that the pudding-headed Dolby retired into the native gloom from which he has emerged.' Dickens described how his manager was once received by a queue of ticket-speculators: 'It being severely cold at Brooklyn, they made an immense bonfire in the street—a narrow street of wooden houses—which the police turned out to extinguish. A general fight then took place; from which the people farthest off in the line rushed bleeding when they saw any chance of ousting others nearer the door, put their mattresses in the spots so gained, and held on by the iron rails. At 8 in the morning Dolby appeared with the tickets in a portmanteau. He was immediately saluted with a roar of Halloa! Dolby! So Charley has let you have the carriage, has he, Dolby? How is he, Dolby? Don't drop the tickets, Dolby! Look alive, Dolby! &c, &c, &c., in the midst of which he proceeded to business, and concluded (as usual) by giving universal dissatisfaction.'

The success of the first reading at Boston on December 2nd was 'beyond description or exaggeration. The whole town is quite frantic about it . . . The people will hear of nothing else and talk of nothing else. Nothing that was ever done here, they all agree, evoked any approach to such enthusiasm.' A few days later Dickens could boast of drawing £500 at a reading, and in those days there were seven dollars to the pound. He went on to New York, where he had a suite at the Westminster Hotel, Irving Place, which remained his headquarters throughout his sojourn in the States. 'New York has grown out of my knowledge, and is enormous. Everything in it looks as if the order of nature were reversed, and everything grew newer every day, instead of older.' The queues there reached fantastic proportions, over five thousand people waiting to book seats at 9 in the morning, when many parties were served with breakfast by waiters from neighbouring restaurants. The New Yorkers were disturbed at first to find that the characters they knew so well spoke with an English accent; but their spirits were not easily crushed, and if Dickens had been a combination of Burbage, Betterton, Garrick and Kean, he could not have made a more resounding success. He noted that 'Great social improvements in respect of manners and forbearance have come to pass since I was here before, but in public life I see as yet but little change.' Fires broke out in the hotel several times during his residence, 'but fires in this country are quite matters of course.' On the first occasion Dolby went up to his room to break the news and found him getting into bed.

'What do you want?' asked Dickens.

'The hotel's on fire.'

'I know it.'

'How do you know it?'

'I can smell it. What are you going to do about it?'

'I don't know.'

'Where is the fire?'

'Nobody knows, but they guess it's somewhere at the other end of the building.'

'When do you suppose it will get here?'

'Well, at the pace it has been going for the last five or six hours, I should say some time before breakfast in the morning.'

Dickens dressed, got his valet Scott to pack the books and clothes for the readings, pocketed his jewels and papers, and accompanied Dolby to the bar, where the other residents, in a quaint variety of costumes, had already gathered. The fire was eventually located, and the entertainment concluded with drinks in Dickens's rooms at about 2 in the morning.

The winter was unusually severe and Dickens became a victim to catarrh, which never left him until he left the country. For four months he laboured on, constantly incapacitated by a cough, a cold, a buzzing in the head, a difficulty in breathing, insomnia, and fainting fits; yet all his ailments left him the moment he mounted the platform and started to read. Sometimes it seemed impossible that he could appear in the evening, so ill was he during the day; but miraculously he came up to scratch whenever he gave a public performance; his voice lost its hoarseness, his head cleared, his temperature subsided, and not once did he disappoint the crowds which came to hear him. He never inflicted his inconveniences on anyone, behaved in company as if in a normal state of health, and when told by a doctor that he was too weak to bear the additional strain of a reading, said 'No man has a right to break an engagement with the public if he is able to be out of bed.' He did, however, decide not to visit Canada and the west; and on being informed that if he failed to read in Chicago the people there would go into fits, he answered 'I would rather they went into fits than I did.' When his decision was made known, some Chicago newspapers reported that his brother Augustus, who died there in '66, had left a wife in poverty, and hinted that Dickens should relieve her distress even though he did not wish to see her. This compelled him to issue a statement that he already supported the official widow of Augustus, who was living in England. He might have added that he also allowed Bertram, the son of Augustus, £50 a year.

For some weeks he divided his readings between Boston and New York, and the journeys to and from each place were not of a kind to forward recuperation. The heated carriages and closed windows added to his sufferings, and he thought the railway lines worse than they had been twenty-five years before: 'Two rivers have to be crossed, and each time the whole train is banged aboard a big steamer. The steamer rises and falls with the river, which the railroad don't do; and the train is either banged up hill or banged down hill. In coming off the steamer at one of these crossings yesterday, we were banged up such a height that the rope broke, and one carriage rushed back with a run down-hill into the boat again. I whisked out in a moment, and two or three others after me; but nobody else seemed to care about it. The treatment of the luggage is perfectly outrageous. Nearly every case I have is already broken. When we started from Boston yesterday, I beheld, to my unspeakable amazement, Scott, my dresser, leaning a flushed countenance against the wall of the car, and *weeping bitterly*. It was over my smashed writing-desk. Yet the arrangements for luggage were excellent, if the porters would not be beyond description reckless.'

The theatres took advantage of his presence in the country, and staged many versions of his stories in all the big cities, but he was doing too well in a financial sense to complain: 'The manager is always going about with an immense bundle that looks like a sofa-cushion, but is in reality paper-money, and it had risen to the proportions of a sofa on the morning he left for Philadelphia.' By the middle of January '68 he was at the Quaker City, where the journalists were impressed by his 'extraordinary composure.' This amused him: 'They seem to take it ill that I don't stagger on to the platform overpowered by the spectacle before me, and the national greatness. They are all so accustomed to do public things with a flourish of trumpets, that the notion of my coming in to read without somebody first flying up and delivering an 'Oration' about me, and flying down again and leading me in, is so very unaccountable to them, that sometimes they have no idea until I open my lips that it can possibly be Charles Dickens.' As his portrait was in almost every shop window, people quickly recognised him in the street; and though they would sometimes turn back and re-pass him for a closer inspection, they did not accost him, as they would have done in '42.

Having returned to New York for four readings in Brooklyn, which were given in Ward Beecher's church, he went on to Baltimore, and then to Washington, where he broke his rule and dined with his old friend Charles Sumner, the only other guest being the Secretary of War, Edwin M. Stanton, a great admirer of his books, who told him what had happened at President Lincoln's last cabinet council. Dickens celebrated his birthday at Washington, and his room was filled with baskets and bouquets of flowers from all sorts of people. The President, Andrew Johnson, had twice requested him to call at his own convenience, and he went on the morning of his birthday: 'Each of us looked at the other very hard, and each of us managed the interview (I think) to the satisfaction of the other.' That afternoon his catarrh was so bad that Sumner, finding him voiceless and poulticed with mustard, said 'Surely, Mr. Dolby, it is impossible that he can read tonight?' To which Dolby returned 'Sir, I have told the dear Chief so four times today, and I have been very anxious. But you have no idea how he will change when he gets to the little table.' As usual the change occurred, and after the reading the entire audience, President's family, Secretaries of State, Judges of Supreme Court, Ambassadors, and what-not, rose to their feet and remained cheering until he returned, when the women threw their bouquets on to the platform, the men their buttonholes, and he made a short speech.

At the end of February it became known that President Johnson would be impeached for removing Stanton from office without the consent of the Senate, and the country instantly became insane: in other words, people talked of nothing but politics and went to nothing but political meetings; so Dickens cancelled a few readings, waited for the return of relative common sense, supervised a walking-match of thirteen miles between Dolby and James Osgood (of Ticknor and Fields, the publishers), which was won by the American, and celebrated the occasion with a dinner. During this delay he read at Providence, where he was met at the station by a large part of the population, which followed him the whole way to the hotel; and as he went up the steps between the serried ranks of people, he remarked to Dolby: 'This is very like going into the police van in Bow Street, isn't it?'

Just before he began a tour of westerly towns the country was swept by storms, and reports came of inundations; but he hoped it would 'prove a wind-up' and started for Syracuse and Rochester early in March. After reading at Buffalo he treated his staff to a holiday of two days at Niagara Falls, a scene which affected him as it had done on his previous visit: 'The majestic valley below the Falls, so seen through the vast cloud of spray, was made of rainbow . . . I seemed to be lifted from the earth and to be looking into Heaven . . . The "muddy vesture of our clay" falls from us as we look . . .' He walked for hours in the snow; his left foot again became swollen and painful; and lameness was thenceforth added to his other maladies. They were held up at Utica by the floods. The only hotel was crowded, but somehow a room was found for Dickens, who invited his staff to take their meals with him. The floods subsided slightly during the night: 'And so we started, through the water, at four or five miles an hour; seeing nothing but drowned farms, barns adrift like Noah's arks, deserted villages, broken bridges, and all manner of ruin. I was to read at Albany that night, and all the tickets were sold. A very active superintendent of works assured me that if I could be "got along", he was the man to get me along: and that if I couldn't be got along, I might conclude that it couldn't possibly be fixed. He then turned on a hundred men in seven-league boots, who went ahead of the train, each armed with a long pole and pushing the blocks of ice away. Following this cavalcade, we got to land at last, and arrived in time for me to read the Carol and Trial triumphantly . . . You may imagine what the flood was when I tell you that we took the passengers out of two trains that had had their fires put out by the water, four-and-twenty hours before; and that we released a number of sheep and horned cattle from trucks that had been in the water—I don't know how long, but so long that the sheep had begun to eat each other . . .' He then read at Springfield, Worcester, Newhaven, Hartford, New Bedford and Portland; and rounded the tour off with a series of farewell readings at Boston and New York. He visited the Boston Blind Asylum, and afterwards paid the cost of having *The Old Curiosity Shop* printed in raised letters for the use of the blind in each asylum throughout the Union.

By the time he reached the east coast at the end of March he was on the verge of a collapse, though no one except himself recognised it. 'I am nearly used up', he wrote to Forster. 'Climate, distances, catarrh, travelling, and hard work, have begun . . . to tell heavily upon me. Sleeplessness besets me; and if I had engaged to go on into May, I think I must have broken down. . . . It is impossible to make the people about one understand . . . that the power of coming up to the mark every night, with spirits and spirit, may coexist with the nearest approach to sinking under it.' His appetite had forsaken him, and his regimen now consisted of a tumbler of new cream with two tablespoonfuls of rum at seven in the morning, a sherry cobbler with a biscuit at twelve, a pint of champagne at three, an egg beaten up with a glass of sherry just before the reading, some strong hot beef tea between the parts of the reading, and soup with anything he felt like drinking after ten at night. 'I do not eat more than half a pound of solid food in the whole four-and-twenty hours, if so much.' He was coughing every morning from two or three till five or six o'clock, and on March 29th he wrote from Portland: 'Last night here I took some laudanum, and it is the only thing that has done me good, though it made me sick this morning.' There is no further reference to drugs in his letters, but he would have been foolish to neglect such an obvious remedy for insomnia. Towards the end he was lame in both feet, and Dolby had to help him to and from his desk for the final readings at Boston: 'Dolby is as tender as a woman, and as watchful as a doctor. He never leaves me during the reading now, but sits at the side of the platform, and keeps his eye upon me all the time. Ditto George the gasman, steadfast and most reliable man I ever employed.' After each reading he was completely prostrated and lay flat on the couch in his dressing-room, with his head flung back until the colour returned to his face, slowly recovering. 'You can't think what resolution it requires to dress again after it is over', he told a friend.

He finished up at New York, where he was nearly finished off; and when, the day before the last reading, Dolby was trying to cheer him with a review of their success and the immediate prospect of their return home, he remarked: 'I am too far gone and too worn out to realise anything but my own exhaustion. Believe me, if I had to read but twice more, instead of once, I couldn't do it.' Dolby was

**DICKENS IN AMERICA (1868)**

*Photograph by* BEN GURNEY

GAD'S HILL PLACE
HIGHAM BY ROCHESTER, KENT

astonished: it was the first time his Chief had ever hinted at defeat.

On April 18th the New York Press gave him a public dinner at Delmonico's, with Horace Greeley in the chair. He was an hour late, which for a man of his fanatical punctuality gave some indication of the agony he was enduring and the effort he was making to be present. He had to be assisted up the stairs of the restaurant, and as he hobbled in, leaning heavily on Greeley's arm, it was noticed that his right foot was bandaged and that he could not conceal his sufferings. In his speech he said that he had everywhere 'been received with unsurpassable politeness, delicacy, sweet temper, hospitality, consideration, and with unsurpassable respect for the privacy daily enforced upon me by the nature of my avocation here, and the state of my health. This testimony, so long as I live, and so long as my descendants have any legal right in my books, I shall cause to be republished as an appendix to every copy of those two books of mine in which I have referred to America.' He spoke of the great improvements that had taken place in the country during the last quarter of a century, proclaimed that 'the English heart is stirred by the fluttering of those Stars and Stripes, as it is stirred by no other flag that flies except its own', and closed with a sentiment which shows that he had a keener prevision of the future than any of his contemporaries: 'It would be better for this globe to be riven by an earthquake, fired by a comet, overrun by an iceberg, and abandoned to the Arctic fox and bear, than that it should present the spectacle of these two great nations, each of which has, in its own way and hour, striven so hard and so successfully for freedom, ever again being arrayed the one against the other.' His condition necessitated an early retirement from the festivities; and a week later he was bound for Liverpool on board the *Russia*, a name that would not have reminded him of the freedom-fighting countries. Such were his recuperative powers that within three days of the sea-voyage his lameness vanished with his catarrh and his appetite returned with his sleep; though when the passengers asked if he would read to them, he replied that, rather than do so, he would 'assault the captain and be put in irons.' He looked so well on his return home that 'My doctor was quite broken down in spirits when he saw me. "Good Lord!" he said, recoiling, "seven years younger!" '

Apart from nearly killing him, the result of the American tour was satisfactory. He gave seventy-six readings in twenty weeks; his expenses were about £13,600; and he made a net profit of close on £20,000. The reputation he had won and the money he had earned would have been sufficient for another man; but Dickens could rest neither on his laurels nor on his dollars.

# 21

# FELO DE SE

HIS home-coming resembled that of a monarch's. Every house from Gravesend to Gad's Hill was hung with flags, and all the farmers in the district were on the main road to give him welcome. Not a brick of his own house could be seen for bunting, and on the Sunday immediately following his return the Higham bell-ringers rang him home from church. There is nothing on earth so beautiful as the month of May in England, except perhaps the months of April, June, September and October in England, and after his visit to America home was for Dickens another name for heaven. He sat writing in his chalet, the birds singing all round him, the butterflies flitting in and out of the windows, the branches rustling gently, and the light clouds making patterns on the cornfields.

But he could not remain in heaven for long. The hellish side of life, from which he was by no means averse, claimed his attention. An accident in the hunting-field had given Wills concussion of the brain and made him a permanent invalid, and Wilkie Collins, who had been helping him during Dickens's absence and whose novel *The Moonstone* was being serialised in *All The Year Round*, was not anxious to go on doing office-work. The consequence was that Dickens had to deal with the entire business management of the paper, in addition to his editorial work, and he had to learn it all from A to Z. Next, there was the play *No Thoroughfare* for which he and Collins had been responsible. He went to see it several times, and although it was enjoying a successful run at the Adelphi Theatre he felt that it dragged in places, Fechter and Collins having missed 'many pieces of stage-effect.' This meant a journey to Paris in order to supervise the French production of the play and get the effects which were omitted from the London performances. Then there was another job to be done. An old friend, the Rev. Chauncy Hare Townshend, to whom he had dedicated *Great Expectations*, had died while he was in the States, leaving him £1000, appointing him literary executor, and desiring him to 'publish without alteration' a quantity of religious opinions which the reverend gentleman had jotted down over a long life for the benefit of mankind. As these opinions were chaotically distributed throughout a mass of notebooks and slips of paper, and would have produced an utterly incoherent effect if printed without alteration, Dickens, who would gladly have made a bonfire of them, felt compelled to get them into some sort of shape; and the result, with a preface by himself, was entitled *Religious Opinions*, though the first title that occurred to the distressed executor was Religious Hiccups.

In spite of these distractions he found time that summer to entertain Longfellow at Gad's Hill, showing him the neighbouring country, the ancient buildings, the cathedral and the castle of Rochester, and turning out 'a couple of postilions in the old red jacket of the old red royal Dover road, for our ride', so that the American poet was reminded of a holiday drive in England half a century earlier. Before the Staplehurst accident Dickens himself would have held the reins, but now he suffered 'vague rushes of terror, even when riding in a hansom cab.' Longfellow was gravely concerned over his host's terrible sadness, and spoke of it to Fechter, who agreed 'Yes, yes, all his fame goes for nothing.' Though still capable of spasmodic high spirits, he had lost the joy of life that had once been habitual with him. He was not one of those unfortunate and pitiable creatures who, because they have never been happy, disbelieve in happiness, and who, because they are incapable of love, deny its existence. Such are for clinical treatment, not critical judgment; and they could never understand the tragedy of Dickens, whose wretchedness was due to the contrast between his present lot and the intensity with which he had once experienced both happiness and love; but the first, which is the prize of indolence, had been driven away by his restlessness, and the second, which is the reward of contentment, had been alienated by his insistence.

In the autumn of '68 he started another reading tour, beginning at the St. James's Hall, London, and the firm of Chappell, which had paid him £50 a night for the first series under their auspices, and £60 a night for the second, were now paying him £80 for each appearance, plus all expenses. They did very well out of it, but he always spoke gratefully of their handsome behaviour, very unlike the treatment he had been accorded by certain publishers. In October he was at Liverpool, and not feeling well enough to dine with some friends he told Dolby to go without him, but to call at a shop on the way and ask them to send him a book. What sort of book? Dolby wanted to know. 'Oh, *you* know! Anything you like.' Pressed on the point, he said that something of Scott's or his own would do. So Dolby bought *The Old Curiosity Shop*, which pleased the author, who had not read it for years. Back from the party, Dolby found him roaring with laughter over the novel; but he explained that he was not laughing at his creations so much as his recollection of the circumstances under which certain passages were written. It may have been the revival of these pleasant memories that determined him to commit suicide, or at least to be killed by the thing he loved. Horrified though he would have been by the baldness of that statement, and monstrous though he would have thought the man who made it, there is very little doubt that when he decided to add the Murder of Nancy from *Oliver Twist* to his farewell readings he condemned himself to an early death. Whether consciously, semi-consciously or unconsciously, alone he did it; and as he was not only unhappy but aware of the danger involved, we must assume that he was at any rate partly conscious of his responsibility. There is plenty of evidence to prove it, apart from the definite assertion by his friend Edmund Yates.

He first thought of adding this unpleasant scene to his repertory as far back as May '63: 'I have been trying, alone by myself, the Oliver Twist murder, but have got something so horrible out of it that I am afraid to try it in public.' This almost suggests that his love-affair was still unresolved at that date. Over five years pass by before we hear of it again, by which time he had abandoned all hope of that happiness which he could now only attain by harmonious relationship with a woman. In October '68 he wrote to Forster: 'I have made a short reading of the murder in Oliver Twist. I cannot make up my mind, however, whether to do it or not. I have no doubt that I could perfectly petrify an audience by carrying out the notion I have of the way of rendering it. But whether the impression would not be so horrible as to keep them away another time, is what I cannot satisfy myself upon.' He asked Chappell's for their advice, and they suggested a trial reading before a few friends the following month. Just before it came off his son Charley was staying at Gad's Hill when he heard the most appalling noises coming from the back of the house.

22

Going into the garden he found his father in the act of 'murdering Nancy', a performance which drove all the breath out of his body. The trial reading took place on November 14th in the St. James's Hall before an audience of personal friends and selected critics; and though they were certainly petrified, many of them thought it a perilous experiment. Forster was violently opposed to it, Dolby less so; some of the ladies thought it too horrible; one man said he felt an almost irresistible desire to scream; a physician prophesied hysterical scenes; Chappell's were in favour of it; and a famous actress said 'Why, of course do it! Having got at such an effect as that, it must be done. But the public have been looking out for a sensation these last fifty years or so, and by Heaven they have got it!' Having canvassed the opinions of his guests, Dickens treated them to a supper of oysters and champagne, which had been prepared with floral decorations behind the screen which formed the background to the Murder of Nancy. Needless to say, Dickens ignored the advice of his more temperate friends, and the first public reading was given at the St. James's Hall on January 5th, 1869

The reading began with the scene where Fagin tells Noah Claypole to watch Nancy. Then came the meeting on London Bridge where Nancy gives Fagin away; by which time, such was the skill of Dickens, all the characters were alive in the listener's imagination. After that Noah recounts what he has heard to Sikes; the killing of Nancy followed, and the performance ended with the flight of the criminal. From a quiet beginning, Dickens imparted to the murder scene such a sense of horror that the audience were semi-paralysed, and sat with blanched faces in frozen silence. The shrieks of Nancy rang through the hall in a frightening falsetto, and at the conclusion of the episode no one stirred, no one seemed to breathe. The haunted murderer's 'thick-coming fancies' were a fitting finale, and the reading closed on a note of doom. It was a searching experience; no one who heard it ever forgot it, and none but the hardiest went a second time. Dickens threw the whole of his genius as an actor into the scenes, never referred to the book at all, did not even trouble to turn the pages, and completely metamorphosed his personality as each character spoke, giving uncannily vivid sketches of the comic cunning oleaginous Jew, the lying dull-witted Noah, the bestial cruel Sikes, the well-meaning terrified

Nancy. There was an almost stupified silence of half a minute as Dickens walked off the platform, and he was prostrate, faint and breathless on his dressing-room couch before the applause had gathered into a storm of cheering.

The public had got its sensation at last, as the actress foretold, and when he went to Dublin a strong body of police was necessary to control the crowds which fought to get in. For the sake of Macready he did the reading at Cheltenham, and after it was over the once-famous Macbeth, now very infirm, went to his dressing-room and glared speechlessly at him. Dickens helped the old actor to a sofa, gave him a glass of champagne, and did his best to laugh the thing off; but Macready had to unburden himself: 'No, Dickens—er—er—I will NOT—er—have it—er—put aside. In my—er—best times—er—you remember them, my dear boy—er—gone, gone!—no—it comes to this—er—TWO MACBETHS!' The personality of Dickens always had a bracing effect on Macready who in the course of the evening became young again. At Clifton the murder scene was not what the doctors had ordered for their patients in that spa: 'We had a contagion of fainting ... I should think we had from a dozen to twenty ladies borne out, stiff and rigid, at various times. It became quite ridiculous.' This did not matter so much at Bath, where the inhabitants were already stiff and rigid. 'I have a new idea about this mouldy old roosting-place', said Dickens to Dolby. 'Depend upon it this place was built by a cemetery-full of people, who, making a successful rise against death, have carried the place by assault, and, bringing their gravestones with them, have contrived to build the city, in which they are trying to look alive. But it's a miserable failure.' He thoroughly enjoyed the novel experience of shocking people and pretending to be a murderer. 'I have a vague sensation of being "wanted" as I walk about the streets', he said, and 'There was a fixed expression of horror of me, all over the theatre, which could not have been surpassed if I had been going to be hanged ... It is quite a new sensation to be execrated with that unanimity; and I hope it will remain so!' But he liked to be loved as well, and 'one of the pleasantest things I have experienced here this time', he wrote from Liverpool, 'is the manner in which I am stopped in the streets by working men, who want to shake hands with me, and tell me they know my books. I never go out but this happens.'

As he was 'cooked' in the glare of his footlights, headlights and sidelights whenever he read, he was careful to avoid gas and crowds at all other times and would neither stay nor feed with friends; but he could not very well excuse himself from a dinner at St. George's Hall, Liverpool, which was given him by the municipal authorities on April 10th '69. Lord Dufferin proposed his health, and Lord Houghton made a speech in which he implied that Dickens should have taken some part in public affairs. But Dickens, who once said that he could not imagine 'how any man of worth can endure the personal contemplation of the House of Commons', and who had within the last year emphatically declined offers from Birmingham and Edinburgh to stand for parliament, now affirmed that his life had been dedicated to literature from the start, and that nothing on earth would induce him to turn his energies in another direction. It is well that he should have placed it on record that he felt no temptation to quit the real world of art for the unreal world of politics. 'Power (unless it be the power of intellect or virtue) has ever the greatest attraction for the lowest natures', he wrote in *Our Mutual Friend*, and he did not feel drawn to a form of activity in which, according to the prophets, the country and the Church were always going to be ruined, and had 'become so used to being ruined that they will go on perfectly well.' But it would have been better for him if he had confined himself to creative fiction, and left acting alone. By February '69 the renewed strain had become apparent, and the effect of murdering Nancy with such gusto showed itself in his foot. Rest was prescribed by his doctor, and several readings had to be postponed. But Dickens could hypnotise himself back to health, and in a few days, against the advice of his friends, he was travelling to Edinburgh on a sofa: 'The railway authorities had done all sorts of things, and I was more comfortable than on the sofa at the hotel.' He left off drinking champagne and only took a little weak iced brandy and water during the readings; but what he wanted was a little strong cold common sense, and after the Murder reading at Edinburgh his manager tried to administer it. Dolby had noticed how the shock to his system given by this particular reading produced strange after-effects, when he gave way to bursts of hilarity, or tried to return to the platform, or displayed a craving to do it all over again; so when at supper Dickens handed his manager a list of future readings, which included the Murder scene at nearly every place to be visited, Dolby said:

'Look carefully through the towns you have given me, and see if you note anything peculiar about them.'

'No. What is it?'

'Well, out of four readings a week you have put down three Murders.'

'What of that?'

Dolby then warned him that the performance of the Murder was hurtful to him; that his pulse, which after most readings was at anything between 80 and 100, shot up to something like 120 following the *Oliver Twist* scenes; that he was killing himself; that as people came to hear him whatever he read, he should reserve the Murder for the larger towns; that . . .

'Have you finished?' angrily demanded Dickens.

'I have said all I feel on that matter.'

'Dolby! your infernal caution will be your ruin one of these days!' shouted Dickens, bounding from his chair in a fury and flinging his knife and fork on to his plate, which was smashed to pieces. It was the only time Dolby ever heard him speak an angry word to anyone.

'Perhaps so, sir. In this case, though, I hope you will do me the justice to say it is exercised in your interest.'

Dolby left the table to put the tour-list in his writing-case. Turning round he saw that his Chief was crying.

'Forgive me, Dolby', said Dickens, going towards him with outstretched arms, embracing him affectionately, and speaking between sobs. 'I really didn't mean it; and I know you are right. We will talk the matter over calmly in the morning.'

A few of the Murders were cut out of the tour next morning, but not enough; and in April he began to suffer from sleeplessness, giddiness, a feeling of deadness on the left side of his body, a difficulty in taking hold of any object with the left hand, and a terrible weariness. Edmund Yates found him at Queen's Hotel, Leeds, on April 12th, lying on a sofa with a bandaged foot and looking desperately tired and depressed. He seemed to have aged quite suddenly, the lines in his cheeks and round his eyes having become deep furrows. And indeed he was on the edge of collapse. At Blackburn he was so ill that he went for a day's rest to the Imperial Hotel, Blackpool. Thence he had to make a dash for Preston, where it was necessary to send for his doctor, who instantly ordered him to cancel the remainder of the tour. Money was returned to those who had booked seats at Preston and Warrington, and Dickens settled down in his London chambers, where he placed his body at the disposal of the doctors and his mind at the service of *All The Year Round*. As usual he appeared to recover almost at once, and in a week could describe himself as 'in a brilliant condition.' But a leading physician, Sir Thomas Watson, noted in his case-book the 'first threatenings of brain mischief' in Dickens, who had been on the brink of apoplexy and paralysis, due to the hurry, overwork and excitement caused by his readings.

One of the first things he did in May '69 was to make a 'last Will and Testament', which started off with a bequest of £1000, free of legacy duty, to Miss Ellen Lawless Ternan, a piece of publicity with which she could perhaps have dispensed. Georgina Hogarth was to receive £8000 free of legacy duty, and the income of a similar sum was left to his wife, after whose death it was to benefit his children. His daughter Mamie was to get £1000 in addition to £300 a year for life if she remained single; but if she married her income would be divided equally among all his children, who also inherited the remainder of his property in equal shares, held in trust for them by his executors Georgina Hogarth and John Forster. His servants were to be given nineteen guineas apiece; special bequests of books, pictures, jewellery and furniture were made to his son Charley and his sister-in-law Georgina; and he left his watch, chains, seals, etc., together with many manuscripts of his published works, to John Forster. Having set all this down with the prolixity so necessary to the upkeep and priestcraft of the legal profession, he became natural:

And lastly . . . I solemnly enjoin my dear children always to remember how much they owe to the said Georgina Hogarth, and never to be wanting in a grateful and affectionate attachment to her, for they know well that she has been, through all the stages of their growth and progress, their ever useful self-denying and devoted friend. And I desire here simply to record the fact that my wife, since our separation by consent, has been in the receipt from me of an annual income of £600, while all the great charges of a numerous and expensive family have devolved wholly upon myself. I emphatically direct that I be buried in an inexpensive, unostentatious, and strictly private manner; that no public announcement be made of the time or place of my burial; that at the utmost not more than three plain mourning coaches be employed; and that those who attend my funeral wear no scarf, cloak, black bow, long hat-band, or other such revolting absurdity. I direct that my name be inscribed in plain English letters on my tomb, without the addition of 'Mr.' or 'Esquire'. I conjure my friends on no account to make me the subject of any monument, memorial, or testimonial whatever. I rest my claims to the remembrance of my country upon my published works, and to the remembrance of my friends upon their experience of me in addition thereto. I commit my soul to the mercy of God through our Lord and Saviour Jesus Christ, and I exhort my dear children humbly to try to guide themselves by the teaching of the New Testament in its broad spirit, and to put no faith in any man's narrow construction of its letter here or there.

His privately expressed wish that he should be buried either in the churchyard under the castle wall of Rochester, opposite the west door of the cathedral, or in the churchyards of Cobham or Shorne, was taken to mean that he would not object to being buried quietly in Westminster Abbey, where he was duly laid; and as no power on earth could prevent people from putting up memorials of some sort or another, his instructions were carried out as far as humanly possible. Of the chief persons named in his will, it may here be said that his wife survived him seven years, that Georgina died in 1917 raving about him in her delirium, that Ellen Ternan, who in '76 married the Rev. George Wharton Robinson, afterwards Principal of the High School, Margate, lived until 1914, and that Forster, the first volume of whose heavy and half-told *Life of Charles Dickens* came out in '72, the second in '73, and the third in '74, died in '76. In his last years Forster was tormented by gout on the chest and a perpetual cough. He spent nights of horror and days of exhaustion, and life must have been very trying in the grandiose Palace Gate House which he built and lived in from '62 till his death. When anything went wrong at one of his dinners he fell into a fit of rage, and if his wife tried to smooth things over she drew his wrath upon herself. His egotism and arrogance grew with the years. Dickens supplied an instance. Some time in the early sixties the behaviour of Macready's daughter Katie annoyed Forster, and when Dickens said a few words in her favour Podsnap dismissed her in his most majestic vein: 'A very offensive and improper young person, and I wish to hear no more about her.' In April '69 Katie Macready died, and Forster wrote to Dickens: 'You may imagine the shock and blow it was to me.' Upon which Dickens exclaimed: 'Me! Me! Me! as if there were no poor old broken friend in the case', meaning her father. 'I hate myself for harping on such strings', continued Dickens, 'and yet I should hate myself much more as a monstrous humbug, if I didn't.' Nevertheless this was the only dependable man of business with whom he was on intimate terms; and knowing that Forster had every intention of writing his biography, he maintained their relationship as best he could and dared not nominate anyone else as his executor, even if there had been anyone else equally trustworthy, equally capable, equally authoritative, equally well informed.

Wilkie Collins, had he been willing to act in that capacity, was not the man for the job; and apart from the absence of his name from the will, there is evidence that Dickens was cooling towards him in the last years. They were seldom together; their correspondence almost ceased; and though Dickens, having two domestic establishments to keep up, was forced to limit the time he spent with his friends, it is probable that Collins's enormous success as a writer of 'thrillers' had turned his head and made him indifferent to his early patron's advice and assistance. This view is supported by what Dickens wrote of *The Moonstone* when it was coming out weekly in *All The Year Round*: 'The construction is wearisome beyond endurance, and there is a vein of obstinate conceit in it that makes enemies of readers.' The younger man's poor health was an additional hindrance to companionship, and a note from Dickens when Wilkie had a bout of illness in January '70 proves that their old intimacy was waning: 'I don't come to see you because I don't want to bother you. Perhaps you may be glad to see me by-and-bye. Who knows?' Despite his large, continuous and increasing doses of opium, Collins almost managed to reach the age of 66, dying in 1889. He had no successor in the confidence of Dickens, whose young disciples included Percy Fitzgerald, Edmund Yates and Charles Kent, all of whom were devoted to him but none of whom could have filled the place of Forster or Collins.

The last sentence of Dickens's will calls for brief comment on his religion. He believed that Jesus Christ, by some mysterious process unavailable to other mortals, was the Son of God. He did not bore his children with religious teaching, but wrote a Life of Christ to show them the perfect exemplar. He said his prayers every morning and every night of his life, and urged his children to do the same. Too egotistic to accept the annihilation of self, and too materialistic to face the extinction of everything he had loved on earth, he fervently believed in a life beyond this world; but he was too individualistic to approve the dogmas of any known Faith, and he was more often annoyed than pleased by the clergymen of the Church of England, an institution which he preferred to all the others because it was part of the history of the people, the beauty of the country, and the literature of the race. As he wrote and spoke so often in sympathy with the oppressed members of the community, many of the clergy regarded him as a sort of literary Wat Tyler, and once he was an unwilling witness to their aversion. Two ladies and a clergyman were in the same railway carriage as himself, and the ladies were reading his novels, on discovering which the clergyman said that they should not read the works of such a man, explaining why they were subversive and showing how the writer was irreligious. Dickens sat this out as long as possible, but at length he lost control, revealed himself, and gave his traducer a severe dressing-down. The cleric's face paled; his jaw dropped; he had the punctured look of a righteous man who has been found out; and when the indignant author left the train he was followed down the platform by a parson stammering abject apologies. But Dickens had endured so many tedious and hypocritical sermons in his life that he made the most of his present opportunity, delivered a discourse on Christian charity, exhorted the man of God to think the truth, speak the truth, and act the truth, and left him incapable of thought, speech and action.

There are certain diseased minds that get a perverted pleasure from infecting healthy ones with their own misery and pessimism. Dickens did not pass on his internal gloom: his unhappiness was in his eyes, not on his tongue. In May '69 his Boston friends, J. T. Fields and his wife, came to England, and he gave them a rapturous welcome. He showed them whatever they wanted to see in London, the Temple, the Inns of Court, the churches, the theatres; he introduced them to whomsoever they wished to meet; accompanied by police

inspectors he explored the East End with Fields, and penetrated to an opium den which he was soon to describe in
*Edwin Drood*; they visited Windsor Castle, went to Richmond
where they dined at the Star and Garter, and saw Hampstead
Heath, Jack Straw's Castle and the Spaniards inn. In June
they stayed with him at Gad's Hill and had the joy of seeing
in his company all the places mentioned in his books: Rochester, Chatham, Cooling, Cobham, Canterbury. It was the last
time he was ever to see Canterbury, and he did it in an old-
fashioned style. Two post carriages were engaged, with
postilions in the red jackets, buckskin breeches and top-hats
that had been familiar on the Dover road in his boyhood. The
party consisted of J. T. Fields and his wife, two Philadelphia
friends G. W. Childs and his wife, Dolby, and several other
guests. They went via Rochester, Chatham, Sittingbourne
and Faversham, a flat and uninteresting road, though Dickens
somehow made it seem romantic. When they pulled up at
Rochester a man in the street pointed at Fields and cried
'That's Dickens!' The passers-by stopped, and Dickens, who
had alighted for a parcel, handed it up to Fields with the
words 'Here you are, Dickens, take charge of this for me.'
They lunched in a wood just short of Canterbury. The horses
and carriages were put up at the Fountain Hotel, and they
went to the cathedral, where Dickens was disgusted by the
slack and meaningless way in which the afternoon service
was gabbled and gargled. Having got rid of a tedious verger,
he took them all over the building. It was then too late to
perambulate the city, and when Fields wanted to see Dr.
Strong's house, where David Copperfield went to school,
Dickens said with a laugh 'There are several that will do.'
After tea at the hotel they started for home at 6, and did the
return journey of 29 miles in less than three hours. During
his stay in England Fields developed a passion for old furniture; so Dickens bought an ancient chair and gave it to him
with the words 'It is very old and wormy, and it is related,
without proof, that on one occasion George Washington
declined to sit down on it.'

He spent the summer mostly at Gad's Hill, though not
quite so idly as a passer-by believed. He was standing in his
garden one day when a tramp looked over the wall and said
to his companion: 'Ugly lazy devil! He never did a day's
work in his life!' Intimations of a new novel came to him in

July; by the beginning of August he had the plot in his head; and he was writing it in October. The first number of *The Mystery of Edwin Drood* was published in April '70 and met with enormous success, but only six numbers were to appear. He received the unprecedented advance of £7500 for it, but the sales were so large that if he had demanded double that sum it would not have been excessive. His insistence that a clause should be inserted in the contract stating that if he failed to complete the work fair compensation should be paid to Chapman and Hall for their loss, shows his personal apprehension and proves that his dealings with publishers, when they were not exploiting him, were punctiliously honourable. Each number was read to Forster before it was sent to the printer, which suggests that, owing to the coolness between himself and Collins, he was trying to get back to the old footing with his friend of the past, his biographer of the future. More clearly than *Great Expectations* the story shows that he had decided to abandon the picaresque type of work in which he excelled and to depend in future upon plot-interest and psychology. The working up of the story required 'a great deal of art and self-denial', he said; which simply meant that the unique portrayer of comical eccentrics had become a commonplace novelist, though his descriptive power, inventiveness and unremitting care would doubtless have enabled him to beat his contemporaries at their own fictional game. His quick eye had already taken stock of the sporting Anglican parson then becoming fashionable and he gives a sympathetic portrait of him as Crisparkle; but the only rich 'Dickensian' character in the book is Sapsea:

> Then Mr. Datchery admired the Cathedral, and Mr. Sapsea pointed it out as if he himself had invented and built it: there were a few details indeed of which he did not approve, but those he glossed over, as if the workmen had made mistakes in his absence.

From some notes which were found after his death it seems that he intended to develop Sapsea, who may be regarded as the last chip of the old Pickwickian block. It is not surprising that towards the close of his life Dickens never spoke of *Pickwick Papers* and did not care to hear it mentioned. But it might have surprised him to read a passage from a letter which he had addressed to Chapman and Hall in November, 1836:

'If I were to live a hundred years, and write three novels in each, I should never be so proud of any of them, as I am of Pickwick.'

The Christmas of '69 was spent at Gad's Hill with a houseful of children and guests. He was unable to leave his room all day owing to a painful foot, but he went downstairs with some difficulty to join the party for dinner and games. He did not like to be called 'Grandpa' by the children of his son Charley, and compromised over 'Venerable', by which he was always known to them. They had the run of the house, but his study was sacrosanct; and a guest, inspecting his library, received alarming intelligence from a grandchild who peeped in: 'Oh, Miss Boyle, you take care! If Venerable sees you at his books, you'll catch it!' Mamie wanted to spend the coming season in London, so Dickens took a house opposite Marble Arch, No. 5 Hyde Park Place, for five months, and here they arrived at the beginning of January, 1870.

His physician Sir Thomas Watson had consented to his giving twelve farewell readings on condition that there would be no more travelling. No doubt Watson was pestered before he gave way, for he was well aware of the danger; but apart from Dickens's craving for the eternal agitation and the external appreciation, he wished to compensate Chappell's for his failure to complete the last tour. The readings took place in the St. James's Hall during January, February and March. Four of them consisted of the *Oliver Twist* scenes, his pulse bounding from 72 to 112 on the first occasion, to 118 on the second, to 124 on the last, the effort leaving him practically insensible for a considerable period. One of these performances was given before an audience of actors and actresses, who had asked for it. 'I set myself to carrying out of themselves and their observation those who were bent on watching how the effects were got—and I believe I succeeded.' He always felt at home with actors, and no theatre-manager has been so quick to spot exceptional talent. Just as he was the first person to perceive that 'George Eliot' was a woman, so did he instantly recognise the genius of Marie Wilton (afterwards Lady Bancroft), whom he called 'the cleverest girl I have ever seen on the stage'; of Kate Terry, whom he saw at a rehearsal display 'the very best piece of womanly tenderness I have ever seen on the stage'; of J. L. Toole, whose 'power of passion very unusual indeed in a comic actor' was apparent to this critic long before others were aware of it; and of Henry Irving, whose unimportant rôle in a comedy called *A Lancashire Lass* by H. J. Byron drew this from Dickens: 'If that young man does not one day come out as a great actor, I know nothing of art.' About three years after this prophecy, in November '71, Irving startled London as Mathias in *The Bells*.

With his organising ability, his skill and patience at rehearsals, Dickens would certainly have had a brilliant success in theatre-management, and nothing would have given him greater pleasure. He once contemplated leasing the old Strand Theatre, being restrained by a solemn warning from his lawyer that he would be making himself responsible for untold obligations; and within a month of his death he said to his youthful disciple Charles Kent: 'What do you think would be the realisation of one of my most cherished daydreams?' Without waiting for an answer he went on: 'To settle down now for the remainder of my life within easy distance of a great theatre, in the direction of which I should hold supreme authority. It should be a house, of course, having a skilled and noble company, and one in every way magnificently appointed. The pieces acted should be dealt with according to my pleasure, and touched up here and there in obedience to my own judgment; the players as well as the plays being absolutely under my command. There', he added laughingly, '*that's* my daydream.' When he made this confession he had fulfilled his ambition as an actor and had taken his leave of the public. As he stepped on to the platform to do the Murder scene for the last time, he said to Charles Kent 'I shall tear myself to pieces'; and he carried out his threat, for he had to be supported back to the dressing-room and could not speak a comprehensible sentence for at least a quarter of an hour. At the final reading on March 15th the vast fashionable audience rose at his entrance and frenziedly cheered him for several minutes. He gave *A Christmas Carol* and the Trial from *Pickwick*, and it was noticed that some of his word-pronunciations were faulty. He made a short farewell speech, and left the stage with tears streaming down his cheeks.

Altogether, between April '58 and March '70, he had given 423 professional readings, in addition to those given for charity, and he had made a net profit of about £45,000, nearly half his total estate, which was valued at £93,000 after his death. But the achievement cost more than it was worth, for it probably took ten years off his life. A fortnight after his final engagement the strain on his nervous system was again apparent: 'My weariness and hemorrhage, after having quite left me, as I supposed, has come back with an aggravated irritability that it has not yet displayed. You have no idea what a state I am in today from a sudden violent rush of it.' He yearned for the country, was bored by the dinners he had to give and attend for his daughter's sake, and found writing irksome; but nothing could stop him from over-working, over-walking, over-exciting himself, and over-expending his energy in every way. What had once been an imp within him had now become a demon, which drove him on, giving him no rest, compelling him to rush from one thing to another in a ceaseless attempt to forget himself in his repertory of parts. Someone in the office of *All The Year Round* noticed how battered and haggard he looked as he stooped over the table and peered through his gold-rimmed glasses at the manuscript before him, how prematurely old, weighted with care, and set in sorrow.

Before his illness took a more serious turn, he sustained an interview with Queen Victoria, who had always wanted to meet the most famous Victorian. She had tried to do so several times after seeing him act, had offered him a room in the Palace for a private reading of the *Carol*, and had asked Dean Stanley's wife to invite him, Browning, Carlyle, and one or two others, to meet her privately; but Dickens alone had failed to keep the appointment. Now she was determined to meet him, and asked his friend Arthur Helps, clerk to the Privy Council, to arrange an interview. As his daughter wished to be presented at Court he agreed, and went to Buckingham Palace one March evening in 1870. Owing to some childish nonsense euphemistically termed 'court etiquette' the interview, which lasted for half an hour, was conducted vertically. The Queen described Dickens as 'very agreeable with a pleasant voice and manner', and since Arthur Helps found their conversation most interesting and amusing it is a pity that he did not record a few specimens of their humorous exchanges. But the conversation of monarchs would make a Boswell put away his notebook, and probably the one 'amusing' part of their discussion was when the Queen expressed her deep regret at not having heard one of his readings, and he replied firmly that a mixed audience was absolutely essential for their success and that he had finally done with them. They talked of the servant problem, of the cost of living, of the behaviour of Americans, of the division between the classes, which Dickens trusted would lessen in time; but none of these were themes for scintillation. Having asked him for a complete set of his works, which he promised to send her, she handed him an autographed copy of her Journal in the Highlands, saying that she felt considerable hesitation in presenting so humble a literary effort to one of the foremost writers of the age, and that she hoped he would overlook its faults. Whether he replied that he could not overlook its virtues, we are not told; but at that point the interview terminated.

In his letter conveying the Queen's wish for a meeting, Arthur Helps had apparently hinted that a baronetcy might be offered to the famous author. Dickens pretended to take this seriously, and replied: 'We will have "Of Gad's Hill Place" attached to the title of the Baronetcy, please—on account of the divine William and Falstaff.' The clerk to the Privy Council may have been putting out a feeler, or he may have been indulging his sense of humour. In any case Dickens treated the thing as a joke, and referred to himself thereafter as Helps's 'godson.' Someone must have seen or heard of their correspondence and taken this very simple fun seriously, because rumours were spread that Dickens intended to oblige Queen Victoria by accepting a handle to his name (though that was not their precise phrasing), and they grew at such an alarming rate that he had to contradict them. 'You will probably have read before now that I am going to be everything the Queen can make me', he told a correspondent. 'If my authority be worth anything, believe on it that I am going to be nothing but what I am.' It is satisfactory to know that he had no intention of honouring all the titled nonentities in the land by seeking to hide his identity in a title. Sir Charles Dickens Bart., or Baron Dickens of Gad's Hill, would have meant nothing compared with the simple dignity of DICKENS. Like Bernard Shaw over half a century later, he had already conferred upon himself every distinction it was possible for him to possess. Nor was he in the least interested in his own pedigree and its heraldic accretions. 'I have never used any other armorial bearings than my father's crest', he informed someone in '69, '. . . I have never adopted any motto, being quite indifferent to such ceremonies.' The unexciting results of his interview with Queen Victoria were that he accepted her invitation to the next levee, and his daughter Mamie was presented at the next drawing-room. He also sent the Queen the first number of *Edwin Drood,* and said that if she would care 'to know a little more of it in advance of her subjects', he would let her into the secret.

He was writing *Drood* with difficulty: the compulsion that had gripped him in his previous novels seemed to have deserted him; but he did not impart this discouraging fact to his illustrator, in whose work he showed great interest. At the suggestion of John Millais he had engaged Luke Fildes for the job. Back in 1850 Dickens had ridiculed the Pre-Raphaelites in *Household Words* and had picked out for special condemnation the picture of Christ in the Carpenter's Shop by Millais, of which he said that 'Wherever it is possible to express ugliness of feature, limb, or attitude, you have it expressed. Such men as the carpenters might be undressed in any hospital where dirty drunkards in a high state of varicose veins are received.' Much of life's irritation is due to lack of understanding, and neither Millais nor Dickens understood what the other was driving at. But in time they met; a mutual liking resulted in a mutual admiration; and the reputation of Luke Fildes was founded on their good opinion of one another. At least two members of the Pre-Raphaelite Brotherhood had reason to bless their critic, who advised Holman Hunt exactly how much to ask for his picture of The Finding of Christ in the Temple, a sum he duly obtained. As we know, Dickens was a very shrewd man of business, and one of the last things he did was to correct a contract for the actress Miss Glyn, his alterations protecting her interests most effectively.

The death of a very old friend, Daniel Maclise, in April '70, caused him much distress, though he steeled himself to speak of the loss at the Royal Academy banquet a few days later. Mark Lemon followed Maclise 'from sunshine to the sunless land' in May, and Dickens tried to hearten himself and his friends: 'We must close up our ranks and march on.' He had not far to go. Early in May he breakfasted with the Prime Minister, Gladstone, but on the 10th his foot was again inflamed; hot fomentations were continually applied, day and night; he suffered 'horrible pain', could not sleep, and resorted to laudanum. Most of his engagements were cancelled, including one to the Queen's ball, though he managed to dine with Lord Houghton in order to meet the Prince of Wales and the King of the Belgians, both of whom were anxious to know him. His foot was so bad that he could not go upstairs for the reception, but waited in the dining-room and was introduced to the Prince at the table. It worried him to hear that his son Plorn was not doing well in Australia: 'He seems to have been born without a groove. It cannot be helped. If he cannot or will not find one, I must try again, and die trying.' He talked of going to Australia to see his sons and gather material for a new book, but his last journey was only to be as far as Gad's Hill, which he reached at the end of May, 1870. Just before his final departure from London he superintended rehearsals for some pieces in which his daughters appeared at Cromwell House. After the performance he could not be found, but was eventually discovered seated in a corner behind the scenes in a dreamy abstracted state. 'I thought I was at home', he said.

The poet Edward Fitzgerald considered Dickens 'a very noble fellow as well as a very wonderful one', and confessed 'I for one worship Dickens in spite of Carlyle and the critics, and wish to see his Gad's Hill as I wished to see Shakespeare's Stratford and Scott's Abbotsford.' Though primarily associated with London, the city which he had created in words, it is at Gad's Hill that one likes to picture him, either standing as a boy outside the house and being told by his father that he might one day live there, or as the vivifying spirit of uproarious parties, or writing in his chalet among the tree-branches across the road, or striding about the neighbourhood, to Chalk, to Cobham, to Shorne, to Cooling, to Rochester, every house, alley, coign and cranny of which he knew. And it was to Gad's Hill that he went when some instinct told him that his time was short. Almost the first thing he did when he got there was to add a codicil to his will leaving his magazine *All The Year Round* to his eldest son, who had been his assistant editor ever since his return from America. His foot was better, and as the countryside was at its best he again found pleasure in walking. The garden beds were full of his favourite flowers, geraniums, and the country around him was rich with his favourite colour, green. He was delighted with the new conservatory he had built, into which he could see from both dining-room and drawing-room; and nothing was wanting to his enjoyment of life but a tranquil mind.

His daughter Katie wished to go on the stage, and visited Gad's Hill on June 2nd to obtain his permission. He dissuaded her: 'You are pretty and no doubt would do well, but you are too sensitive a nature to bear the brunt of much you would encounter. Although there are nice people on the stage, there are some who would make your hair stand on end. You are clever enough to do something else.' He closed the subject with 'I will make it up to you.' In the course of their talk, which lasted until 3 in the morning, he said that he wished he had been a better father and a better man. He might have argued that all human beings have the seeds of corruption in them, the 'good' ones usually being those who have not been provoked to evil by chance or circumstance; but though he was enough of an actor to convince himself of his rectitude as a husband and parent, he was not in the mood to make excuses. Next day she went to kiss him good-bye in the chalet, where he was working on *Edwin Drood*. On her way back to the house through the tunnel she had an impulse to return, dashed back, and again tapped at his door. He turned as she entered, held out his arms, embraced her once more, and kissed her very affectionately. After his morning's work he would arrive at the house for lunch, eat a little mechanically, and sit silently, tired out. The talking of the others did not disturb him, but any sudden sound like the dropping of a spoon or the clinking of a glass would send a spasm of pain across his face. In the evenings he would pace up and down the drawing-room while Mamie sang, or he would read and smoke. He was fond of sentimental songs and did not care for what was called classical music.

On the afternoon of Monday June 6th, accompanied by his dogs, he walked in to Rochester with his letters. He strolled through The Vines and was seen by someone, with his hands on the railings, gazing at Restoration House, which as Satis House is the home of Miss Havisham in *Great Expectations*. Nearly all tragedy arises from a major emotional frustration, and there was a tragic significance in the figure which peered through the railings at the house where Pip had fallen in love with Estella, knowing in his heart that his love would never be returned.

Mamie left Gad's Hill on the 7th to visit Katie, and that

afternoon Dickens drove with Georgina to Cobham wood, sent the carriage back, walked round the park, and so home. In the evening he put up a number of Chinese lanterns in the conservatory, and after dinner sat with Georgina in the dining-room enjoying the effect. He was glad, he said, that he had determined to live there instead of London, for he wished his name to be associated with the place, and when he died he would like to be buried in the little graveyard belonging to the cathedral, under the castle wall at Rochester. On June 8th he worked as usual in the morning; but some intuition of the coming darkness made him break his almost invariable rule, and he returned to work in the chalet after lunch, writing his farewell to Rochester:

A brilliant morning shines on the old city. Its antiquities and ruins are surpassingly beautiful, with a lusty ivy gleaming in the sun, and the rich trees waving in the balmy air. Changes of glorious light from moving boughs, songs of birds, scents from gardens, woods, and fields—or, rather, from the one great garden of the whole cultivated island in its yielding time—penetrate into the Cathedral, subdue its earthy odour, and preach the Resurrection and the Life. The cold stone tombs of centuries ago grow warm; and flecks of brightness dart into the sternest marble corners of the building, fluttering there like wings.

Dinner was ordered for 6 o'clock, so that he might have his daily walk when it was over; and before sitting down to it he went into his study to write two or three letters, in one of which he humorously reproved Charles Kent with a line from Shakespeare, 'These violent delights have violent ends', in another he seriously regretted that a reader should have mis-understood a passage in a book of his: 'I have always striven in my writings to express veneration for the life and lessons of Our Saviour; because I feel it; and because I re-wrote that history for my children—every one of whom knew it from having it repeated to them—long before they could read, and almost as soon as they could speak.'
Dinner had just begun when Georgina noticed that he was in pain. He told her that he had been very ill for an hour, but insisted that they should continue their meal. He then muttered a few disconnected phrases, followed by the remark that he must leave for London at once; upon which he rose from the table and would have fallen if Georgina had not

supported him. She tried to get him to the sofa; but the stroke had deprived him of power, and with the words 'On the ground' he sank to the floor. A telegram was sent to his daughters, who came that evening, his sons Charley and Henry arriving next day. Throughout the night of June 8th he lay motionless, breathing heavily, showing no sign of consciousness. This continued until ten minutes past 6 in the evening of the 9th, when a shudder passed over him, and he sighed; a large tear crept down his face; and the weary body was still for ever, the harassed soul at rest.

# SELECTED SOURCES

(These are only the more important works to which I am indebted. The titles of innumerable books and journals that have provided me with material of a lesser kind are omitted.)

*The Nonesuch Dickens*, 23 vols., 1938. (Includes three volumes of Letters and three volumes of Collected Papers and Reprinted Pieces.)

*The Life of Charles Dickens*, by John Forster, edited and annotated by J. W. T. Ley, 1928.

*Mr. and Mrs. Charles Dickens*, with notes by Walter Dexter, 1935. (Also MS of same in the British Museum.)

*The Life of Charles Dickens*, by Percy Fitzgerald, 2 vols., 1905.

*Memories of Charles Dickens*, by Percy Fitzgerald, 1913.

*My Father as I Recall Him*, by Mamie Dickens, 1897.

*Introductions to the Novels*, by Charles Dickens the Younger, 1892.

*Dickens and Daughter*, by Gladys Storey, 1939.

*Charles Dickens as I Knew Him*, by George Dolby, 1885.

'Four Months with Charles Dickens', by his Secretary (in 1842): *Atlantic Monthly*, 1870.

'Some Memories of Charles Dickens', by J. T. Fields: *Atlantic Monthly*, 1870.

*The Recollections of Sir Henry Dickens, K.C.*, 1934.

*Memories of a Hostess*, drawn chiefly from the *Diaries of Mrs. James T. Fields*, by M. A. DeWolfe Howe, 1923.

*Yesterdays with Authors*, by James T. Fields, 1881.

*The Diaries of William Charles Macready*, edited by William Toynbee, 2 vols., 1912.

*The Letters and Private Papers of William Makepeace Thackeray*, collected and edited by Gordon N. Ray, 4 vols., 1945–6.

*The Dictionary of National Biography*.

The Correspondence of Carlyle, Tennyson, Browning, Macaulay, W. S. Landor, H. C. Andersen, J. L. Motley, etc.

*Anecdote Biographies of Thackeray and Dickens*, edited by R. H. Stoddard, New York, 1874.

*Charles Dickens as a Reader*, by Charles Kent, 1872.

*The Childhood and Youth of Charles Dickens*, by Robert Langton, 1883.

*Dickens and the Drama*, by S. J. Adair Fitzgerald, 1910.

*Dickens v. Barabbas*, by C. J. S. and F. J. H. D., 1930.

*Charles Dickens in America*, compiled and edited by William Glyde Wilkins, 1911.

*The Dickens Circle*, by J. W. T. Ley, 1918.

*Dickens and the Stage*, by T. Edgar Pemberton, 1888.
*Pen Photos of Charles Dickens's Readings*, by Kate Field, 1868.
*Charles Dickens and His Friends*, by W. Teignmouth Shore, 1909.
*John Forster*, by one of his Friends (Percy Fitzgerald), 1903.
*Thomas Wright of Olney*, 1936.
*Dickens Days in Boston*, by Edward F. Payne, 1927.
*My Recollections and Experiences*, by Edmund Yates, 1884.
*Charles Dickens as Shorthand Writer*, by W. J. Carlton, 1926.
*With Dickens in Yorkshire*, by T. C. Cooper, 1923.
*Charles Dickens and the Yorkshire Schools*, by Cumberland Clark, 1918.
'Letters and Journals of C. C. Norton', *Scribners Magazine*, 1913.
*My Literary Life*, by Mrs. Lynn Lynton, 1899.
*Charles Dickens and Maria Beadnell*, edited by G. P. Baker, The
    Bibliophile Society, Boston, 1908.
*Paxton and the Bachelor Duke*, by Violet Markham, 1935.
*Mary Boyle: Her Book*, 1901.
*Things I Have Seen and People I Have Known*, by G. A. Sala, 2 vols.,
    1894.
*Life and Adventures of G. A. Sala*, 1895.
*My Lifetime*, by John Hollingshead, 1895.
*Recollections of Writers*, by Charles and Mary Cowden Clark, 1878.
*Letters of W. D. Howells*, 1928.
*Memories of a Publisher*, by G. H. Putnam, 1915.
*My Autobiography*, by W. P. Frith, 1889.
*The Life of Washington Irving*, by S. Williams, 1935.
*The Life and Letters of G. C. Lever*, by E. Downey.
*The Life, Letters and Friendships of Richard Monckton Milnes, 1st Lord
    Houghton*, by T. Wemyss Reid, 2 vols., 1890.
*Life of H. W. Longfellow*, by S. Longfellow.
*Life, Letters and Diaries of Shirley Brooks*, 1907.
*Life and Letters of the Rev. R. H. Barham*, by his Son, 1870.
*Fifty Years of an Actor's Life*, by John Coleman, 1904.
*W. H. Ainsworth and His Friends*, by S. M. Ellis, 1911.
*Wilkie Collins, Le Fanu and Others*, by S. M. Ellis, 1931.
*Victorian Wallflowers*, by Malcolm Elwin, 1934.
*Memories of Half a Century*, edited by R. C. Lehmann, 1908.
*The Life and Letters of Alfred Ainger*, by Edith Sichel.
*Literary Recollections*, by Francis Espinasse, 1893.
*Sketches from the Diaries of Lady Graves Saule.*
*Reminiscences of Sir Henry Hawkins (Lord Brampton)*, edited by
    Richard Harris, 1904.
*C. A. Fechter*, by K. Field, 1882.
*Memories of the Past*, by James Griffin, 1883.
*What I Remember*, by T. A. Trollope, 1887-9.
*Emerson's Journal*, 1911.
*Reminiscences, Impressions and Anecdotes*, by Francesco Berger.

*Passages of a Working Life*, by Charles Knight.
*Lucie Duff Gordon*, by W. Waterfield, 1937.
*Retrospect of a Long Life*, by S. C. Hall, 1883.
*An Old Man's Diary*, by John Payne Collier, 1872.
*Diary of Philip Hone*, edited by B. Tuckerman, 1889.
*Gossip of the Century*, by Mrs. W. P. Byrne, 1892.
*Reminiscences*, by Julia Ward Howe, 1900.
*Masters of English Journalism*, by T. H. S. Escott, 1911.
*My Confidences*, by F. Locker Lampson, 1896.
*Recollections of Sir Algernon West*, 1899.
*Glances Back Through Seventy Years*, by Henry Vizetelly, 1893.
*Recollections of a Busy Life*, by Horace Greeley, 1869.
*Glances at Europe*, by Horace Greeley, 1851.
*Correspondence of Sir A. Helps*, edited by his son E. Helps, 1917.
*Macready as I Knew Him*, by Lady Pollock, 1884.
*A New Spirit of the Age*, by R. H. Horne, 1901.
*Recollections of Charles Dickens, His Family and Friends*, by Eleanor
    E. Christian, Temple Bar, April 1888.
*Some Literary Recollections of James Payn*, 1884.
*Carlyle*, by D. A. Wilson.
*The Dickensian* (various numbers).
*Gentleman's Magazine*, February, 1871.
*The Times* (contemporary issues).
*Daily Express*, April 3rd, 1934.
Various Periodicals.

Passages of a Working Life, by Charles Knight.
Lewis Duff Cooper, by W. Wakefield, 1913.
Remarks of a Long Life, by S. C. Hall, 1881.
An Old Man's Diary, by John Payne Collier, 1872.
Diary of Philip Hone, edited by B. Tuckerman, 1889.
Gossip of the Century, by Mrs. W. P. Byrne, 1892.
Reminiscences, by Julia Ward Howe, 1900.
Masters of English Journalism, by T. H. S. Escott, 1911.
My Confidences, by F. Locker Lampson, 1896.
Recollections of Sir Algernon West, 1899.
Charles Dickens Through Seventy Years, by Henry Vizetelly, 1893.
Recollections of a Busy Life, by Horace Greeley, 1869.
Glances at Europe, by Horace Greeley, 1851.
Correspondence of M. A. Ryba, edited by his son B. Helps, 1917.
Marriage in High Life, by Lady Pollock, 1884.
A New Spirit of the Age, by R. H. Horne, 1907.
Recollections of Charles Dickens, His Family and Friends, by Eleanor
    E. Christian, Temple Bar, April 1888.
Some Literary Recollections of James Payn, 1884.
Carlyle, by D. A. Wilson.
The Dickensian (various numbers).
Gentleman's Magazine, February, 1871.
The Times (contemporary issues).
Daily Express, April 3rd, 1914.
Various Periodicals.

# INDEX

PRINTED BY
JARROLD AND SONS LTD.
NORWICH